Religion, Diaspora,
and Cultural Identity

SAN CIPRIANO
Life in a Puerto Rican Community
Anthony L. LaRuffa

THE TRAIL OF THE HARE
Environment and Stress in a Sub-Arctic Community
Second Edition
Joel S. Savishinsky

LANGUAGE IN AFRICA
An Introductory Survey
Edgar A. Gregersen

OUTCASTE
Jewish life in Southern Iran
Laurence D. Loeb

DISCOVERING PAST BEHAVIOR
Experiments in the Archaeology of the American Southwest
Paul Grebinger

REVOLT AGAINST THE DEAD
The Modernization of a Mayan Community
in the Highlands of Guatemala
Douglas E. Brintnall

FIELDWORK
The Human Experience
*Edited by Robert Lawless, Vinson H. Sutlive, Jr.,
and Mario D. Zamora*

DONEGAL'S CHANGING TRADITIONS
An Ethnographic Study
Eugenia Shanklin

MONTE CARMELO
An Italian-American Community in the Bronx
Anthony L. LaRuffa

MASTERS OF ANIMALS
Oral Traditions of the Tolupan Indians, Honduras
Anne Chapman

CRISIS AND COMMITMENT
The Life History of a French Social Movement
Alexander Alland, Jr., with Sonia Alland

See the back of this book for other titles in the Library of Anthropology.

Religion, Diaspora, and Cultural Identity

A Reader in the Anglophone Caribbean

Edited by

John W. Pulis

Adelphi University
Garden City, New York, USA

Foreword by John F. Szwed

Afterword by Richard Price

Gordon and Breach Publishers

Australia Canada China France Germany India
Japan Luxembourg Malaysia The Netherlands
Russia Singapore Switzerland

Amsteldijk 166
1st Floor
1079 LH Amsterdam
The Netherlands

The poem "Discourse on the Logic of Language" excerpted in the
Afterword, copyright © M. Nourbese Philip, originally appeared in
She Tries Her Tongue, Her Silence Softly Breaks, Ragweed Press, Prince
Edward Island, Canada, 1989. It is reprinted with permission.

British Library Cataloguing in Publication Data

Religion, diaspora, and cultural identity : a reader in the
   Anglophone Caribbean. – (The library of anthropology.
   Anthropology and religion ; v. 14 – ISSN 0141-1012)
   1.Religion and culture – Caribbean Area 2.Group identity –
   Religious aspects 3.Caribbean Area – Religion
   I.Pulis, John W.
   200.9'729

ISBN 90-5700-545-X

Contents

Introduction to the Series vii

Foreword ix

Acknowledgments xiii

List of Contributors xv

1 Religion, Diaspora, and Cultural Identity:
An Introduction
John W. Pulis 1

2 Religion in the Anglophone Caribbean:
Historical Overview
Robert J. Stewart 13

I ABROAD
Introduction to Part I by Kenneth Bilby 37

3 West Indian American Day: Becoming a Tile in
the "Gorgeous Mosaic"
Philip W. Scher 45

4 Cultural Encounters in the Diaspora: Suriname
Creole Religion in the Netherlands
Ineke van Wetering 67

5 Movements of Jah People: From Soundscapes
to Mediascape
John P. Homiak 87

6 Spiritual Baptists in New York City: A View from
the Vincentian Converted
Wallace W. Zane 125

7 Only Visitors Here: Representing Rastafari into the
21st Century
Carole D. Yawney 153

II HOME

Introduction to Part II by Carole D. Yawney 183

8 Blasphemy, Sacrilege, and Moral Degradation in the
   Trinidad Carnival: The Hallelujah Controversy of 1995
   Garth L. Green 189

9 Pentecostal Community and Jamaican Hierarchy
   Diane J. Austin-Broos 215

10 On the "Right Path": Interpolating Religion in Trinidad
   Aisha Khan 247

11 The Noise of Astonishment: Spiritual Baptist Music
   in Context
   Stephen D. Glazier 277

12 Chaos, Compromise, and Transformation in the Orisha
   Religion in Trinidad
   James Houk 295

13 Neither Here Nor There: The Place of "Community" in
   the Jamaican Religious Imagination
   Kenneth Bilby 311

14 Between the Living and the Dead: The Apotheosis of
   Rastafari Heroes
   Barry Chevannes 337

15 "Citing[Sighting]-Up": Words, Sounds, and Reading
   Scripture in Jamaica
   John W. Pulis 357

Afterword / Echoes 403

Index 413

Introduction to the Series

The Library of Anthropology now encompasses both a classical orientation and current directions in the field. It seeks to promote an awareness of new developments and changing orientations, while continuing to stress its long-term interest in traditional anthropological fields.

The section Physical Anthropology and Archaeology continues to address the substantive and theoretical issues of biological and cultural evolution. Ethnographic Studies and Theory remains a major focus. The range of interest is global in terms of contemporary cultures and ethnic populations, and ethnohistorical in terms of past cultures and societies. Three new sections augment the more traditional four-fields approach to anthropology.

Volumes in the section Anthropology and Language address issues in linguistic anthropology broadly conceived: studies of the communicative means people use to accomplish social ends — from political oratory to storytelling, from joking to sermonizing, and from gossiping to testifying. Anthropological studies that explore the interrelation of language and political economy are especially encouraged.

Works in Anthropology and Literature examine and attempt to define the areas in which these two disciplines come together and blend the personal, poetic and scientific. Cultural or ethnic studies, literature as ethnography, literary theory in anthropological studies, and anthropological theory in cultural (ethnic) studies are topics for consideration.

Volumes in Anthropology and Religion explore the practice of religion and attendant notions of ritual, identity and world view from a variety of theoretical and methodological perspectives in a number of settings and contexts.

Anthony L. LaRuffa

Joel S. Savishinsky

Foreword

Anyone paging through the richness of the papers contained in this volume will surely appreciate how much they contribute to our knowledge of the West Indies; at the same time, so much fine work leads us to reflect on how recently Caribbean studies in the United States have come of age. Thirty-five or forty years ago the West Indies was barely a subject of concern for anthropology. Graduate students were often warned off the Caribbean, and told it was "too close," "too acculturated," "too Western" to provide the necessary conditions for acceptable anthropological training; it offered no challenge. Senior professors of anthropology, sounding like Rasta elders, told students in effect they should "go cross water" if they wanted to study real peoples. Persistent students at, say, Harvard could find themselves being shunted off to Social Relations.

Work on the Caribbean that did get done almost inevitably had an economic or political tilt, whether as part of a concern with comparative plantation societies, kinship, plural societies, or poverty; meanwhile, questions of religion, magic, art, music, language, ritual, and symbolism were largely ignored. Just as the complexities and challenges of creole languages were being overlooked by linguists until well into the second half of the century, their promise for altering the way we look at all languages being delayed, anthropologists were carefully limiting their subject. In those years much intellectual energy was spent among the few Caribbeanists who existed on discrediting the work of Melville and Francis Herskovits and their students on the culture of the Caribbean, and more specifically their work on continuities between Africa and the Americas: The way was being cleared for a newer, post-war model anthropology. The results were too often a portrait of a dour, insular Caribbean, or a collection of social problems; and if there was a culture there, it was (as Ralph Ellison put it in another context) nothing more than the sum of a peoples' brutalization. Reading those studies one might well have believed V. S. Naipaul when he said that nothing had ever been created in the Caribbean and nothing would ever be created there.

How could there have been so little curiosity about the culture-building that was obviously at work? How could this have happened at the very time when emigration from the West Indies was accelerating (especially among Cubans); transplanted religions were taking hold in places like New York City, Miami and Cambridge, Massachusetts; writers such as Césaire, Brathwaite, and Walcott were rising to the top of the literary world; Lydia Cabrera (first in Havana, later in Coral Gables) was turning out volume after volume of accounts of Afro-Cuban religions, lists of African words found in Cuba, and *El Monte*, the central text of Santeria; all of this, just after the mambo had been jointly created between Havana and New York City?

But why look back? Forces were in motion that would change anthropology forever: Emigration continued to accelerate; new languages began to be heard in American schools; civil rights activities spawned Black Studies students with a curiosity about the ties between Africa and the Americas; reggae and its stars penetrated the United States carrying with them deeply coded messages about cosmology; films and television shows were opening up fresh connections to our neighbors to the south. A new breed of anthropology student knew that whatever their older colleagues' misgivings, history would absolve them.

In one of his last public lectures, distinguished African-Americanist St. Clair Drake called for a new kind of Caribbean scholar, one who could follow, if nothing else, the music trail from the Caribbean to Toronto, New York, Paris, and London to understand the linkages to what he called those other capitals of the West Indies. Judging by the fascinating and provocative papers in this remarkably inclusive book, it is obvious that there are those who understood this call, or were already on their way.

What we have come to see is that many of the issues now concerning anthropologists in the United States — transnationalism, the role of identity in community and nation, the nature of hybrid or creole cultures, variability of languages — have long existed in the Caribbean, and often in better light than here.

G. K. Chesterton, quibbling with Yeats and others over Ireland, once said that far from it being weird and wild, an exception among nations, Ireland was in many respects a model nation, one with the capacity to demonstrate it was the other countries of Europe that were weird and wild. He might well have been speaking about the Caribbean. In fact, Derek Walcott's answer to Naipaul did say something of the sort: Rather than assert that nothing had ever been created in the Caribbean, one should say that nothing will always be created in the Caribbean, because what will come out of there is like nothing one has ever seen. This collection of essays makes this point and others, and takes us more than halfway there.

John F. Szwed
Yale University

Acknowledgments

A number of people have graciously provided advice and assistance as this project unfolded over the course of the last two years. I would like first to thank both the Society for Latin American Anthropology and the Selection Committee of the American Anthropological Association for accepting our original panel.

I would also like to thank editor Carol Hollander for her patience, as reading drafts were transformed into chapters. We have benefitted immensely from the constructive comments of Carol and the outside readers in their balanced and informative reader-reports.

Special thanks to John Szwed and Richard Price, who took precious time from their own writing and research for reading and commenting on the original panel papers and for the expanded versions printed in this collection.

I owe a debt of gratitude to Ken Bilby and Carole Yawney; in addition to their own chapters, they provided overviews for Parts I and II.

Finally I would like to thank our contributors for their enthusiasm, support and dedication as this project progressed. It could not have been done without you all, and I "give thanks."

Contributors

Diane J. Austin-Broos is Radcliffe-Brown Professor of Anthropology at the University of Sydney, New South Wales, Australia. She has published widely on religion in Jamaica, including *Urban Life in Kingston* (1978) and most recently *Jamaica Genesis* (1997).

Kenneth Bilby is affiliated with the Office of Folklife Programs at the Smithsonian Institution in Washington, DC. He has published review essays on the Caribbean (1982, 1984, 1997), has contributed chapters in edited collections on Maroons (1996), and has produced several ethnographic films about life in the Caribbean.

Barry Chevannes is professor of anthropology at the University of the West Indies, Mona, Jamaica. He has published *Rastafari: Roots and Ideology* (1994) and edited a collection of essays entitled *Rastafari and other Afro-Caribbean Worldviews* (1995).

Stephen D. Glazier is professor of anthropology at the University of Nebraska, Kearny. He has published widely on the topic of pentecostalism in the Caribbean and Latin America (1982) and has recently published an edited collection entitled *The Anthropology of Religion: A Handbook* (1996).

Garth L. Green is a PhD candidate at the New School for Social Research in New York City. He has conducted fieldwork on commodification and the role of the media in Trinidad.

John P. Homiak is director of the National Anthropological Archives at the Smithsonian Institution. He has contributed chapters to edited collections (1994, 1995) and has produced documentaries about Rastafari in Jamaica and in the Washington, DC area.

James Houk is affiliated with Tulane University in New Orleans. He has published a number of articles (1994) and a monograph *Spirits, Blood, and Drums* (1995) on religion in Trinidad.

Aisha Khan is assistant professor in Africana Studies at the State University of New York at Stony Brook. She has published a number of articles (1994) on issues concerning gender and Indo-Trinidadian life and culture.

Richard Price is professor of anthropology at the College of William and Mary. He has published an edited collection on Maroons (1972), *First Time* (1982) and *Alabi's World* (1992).

John W. Pulis is assistant professor of anthropology in the Center for African-American Studies at Adelphi University in Garden City, New York. He has published a number of articles on the topic of Rastafari, has contributed entries to the *Historical Encyclopedia of Slavery* (1997) on Afro-Christianity and the role of missions in Jamaica, West Indies, and has edited a volume of historical essays entitled *Moving On: Black Loyalists in the Afro-Atlantic World* (1998). His monograph "Gates to Zion: Texts, Voices, and the Narrative World of Rastafari" is scheduled for release later next year.

Philip W. Scher is a PhD candidate at the University of Pennsylvania. He has conducted fieldwork in Trinidad and published chapters in edited collections (1996) on religion and social change.

Robert J. Stewart is a historian who teaches at the Trinity School in New York. He has published a number of articles and most recently *Religion and Society in Post-Emancipation Jamaica* (1992)

John F. Szwed is John M. Musser Professor of Anthropology, African-American Studies, and American Studies at Yale University. He is co-editor with Norman Whitten of *Afro-American Anthropology* (1976) and has published widely on issues concerning music and literacy. His most recent publication, *Space Is The Place* (1997), recounts the life and times of Sun Ra, the legendary jazz performer who died in 1993.

Ineke van Wetering is professor of anthropology at the University of Amsterdam. She has conducted research in The Netherlands on Caribbean migrants.

Carole D. Yawney is professor of anthropology at York University in Canada. She is an activist-ethnographer who has published widely on Rastafari at home in Jamaica and abroad in Europe, America and most recently in South Africa.

Wallace W. Zane is a PhD candidate in anthropology at UCLA. He has conducted field research on Spiritual Baptists in St. Vincent and in New York and has published articles on the topic (1995).

1 : RELIGION, DIASPORA, AND CULTURAL IDENTITY: AN INTRODUCTION

John W. Pulis

Issues concerning displacement and a host of ideologies that have linked displacement, enforced and voluntary, to narratives concerning diaspora loom large in the hearts and minds of Caribbean people. In the opening stanzas of what is regarded as a classic convergence of lyrics and music, Bob Marley expresses the importance of displacement to local history and culture:

> Exodus,
> oh yea,
> the movement of Jah people.
>
> Open your eyes and let me tell you this;
> Men an people will fight you down (Tell me why?)
> when you see Jah light.
>
> So we gonna walk, alright,
> through the roads of creation.
> We're the generation,
> trod thru great tribulation.
>
> Open your eyes and look within.
> We know where were going,
> we know where were from.
> We're leaving Babylon,
> an we're goin to our father's land.
>
> Exodus, oh yea,
> the movement of Jah people.[1]

The power of Marley's lyrics, keyed to a vernacular known as call and response, evokes memories of a black diaspora, the infamous

African slave trade, and a more recent displacement that has taken Caribbean people to Europe and North America as well as Africa. Although Marley set these themes to reggae and transported them around the world, they have been a part of local history for quite some time. Documents and testimonies printed in the 18th century attest to the fact that such themes have been worked and reworked as each generation has made its own history.[2]

Marley's reinterpretation provides an appropriate introduction to a collection of readings that explore the relationship between religion, diaspora, and attendant notions of cultural identity. Once considered the hallmark of Caribbean ethnology, concern for religion and world-view have taken a back seat to more secular interests and agendas. The issues and questions raised by an earlier generation of scholars and activitists have, for the most part, been eclipsed by economic histories of plantations, quantitative analyses of public opinion, and statistical accounts concerning modernization, development, and the allocation of scarce resources.[3]

Recognizing that religion and worldview are not mirrors but activities that constitute what Kamau Brathwaite has referred to as the "nommo" of Caribbean societies, anthropologists such as Mintz and Price, literary historians such as Alleyne and Cooper, and poets such as Derek Walcott have widened the purview of economic and political studies to include cultural practices and expressive forms such as language, music, and folk religion.[4] Similar to the importance of geopolitical shifts to modernization theory, the turn to culture was not intended to displace economics or politics but to explore the relationship between expressive form, everyday life, and global shifts. The explosive popularity of musical forms such as calypso and reggae in settings such as New York and London, Cape Town and Nairobi, and Los Angeles and Toronto attested both to shifts in older patterns of displacement as well as the importance of such shifts and the influence of media and related technologies on the evolution of cultural practice at home and abroad. At the forefront of this turn was a related and concomitant concern with agency, with culture as a site where hegemonic forms were contested, where older and traditional forms were renegotiated, and where new or emergent forms were invented.[5]

The chapters in this collection address a number of issues concerning the ongoing and open-ended relation between religion, cultural expression, and everyday life. Eleven of the fifteen chapters are revised and expanded versions of reading drafts presented at panel convened at the Annual Meeting of the American Anthropological Association in 1995. The remaining four were added when it became apparent that the panel papers were well on their way to becoming the core of a reader devoted to the topic. All, with the exception of one, are focused on the Anglophone Caribbean, the English-speaking islands that once constituted the British West Indies and to resident communities in Europe and America.[6]

Some disclaimers are called for. Like all cultural artifacts, scholarship is built upon tradition and breaking old and in many ways hegemonic patterns is sometimes easier said than done. No attempt has been made to include readings from either the Hispanic or Francophone islands. Since there are several such collections in print we have confined our attention to the Anglophone Caribbean. While focused on the Anglophone Caribbean, this collection is disproportionately weighted to the islands of Trinidad and Jamaica and is by no means representative of this larger and equally diverse grouping of island and mainland societies. This disclaimer has more to do with the chapters in Part Two than with those in Part One and we hope to include readings from islands other than Trinidad and Jamaica in an expanded and revised edition.[7]

Bringing a sense of order to a collection whose authors were asked to roam as far and wide as possible has been proven to be a challenge. In keeping with framework of the original panel, I have divided this collection in half and I have placed chapters into sub-sections labelled "Abroad" and "At Home" that correspond to their respective sites, landscapes, and sense of place. This division should not by any means conjure up images of isolated or disparate communities. In this postmodern age of fax machines and the Internet the relation between the two can best be characterized as a dialectical rather than a unilineal flow of ideas and people. Since this volume was conceived less as a set of theoretical essays and more as a reader devoted to ethnography or cultural description, I have asked Robert Stewart to provide an historical overview and Ken Bilby and Carole Yawney to provide brief summations of Parts One and Two for our audience.

Our choice of a reader should not in any way suggest that these chapters are devoid of theory. In addition to providing descriptions of local and global practices, this collection raises some provocative questions and address a number of fundamental issues concerning religion and cultural change. Contrary to accepted convention, religion occupies a primary domain in the lives of Caribbean folk and issues concerning ethics, morals, and what constitutes the sacred and the profane are intertwined with a concern for unemployment and exchange rates as topics in everyday discourse. This issue, that of authority, profanity, and moral discourse, is discussed by Garth Green in "Blasphemy, Sacrilege, and Moral Degradation in the Trinidad Carnival" and by Barry Chevannes in "Between the Living and the Dead: The Apotheosis of Rastafari." The politics of names and naming practices are a major concern in Caribbean societies and Green discusses the polemics that arose concerning an entry in a recent Carnival called "hallelujah." This appellation provoked an immediate reaction by a consortium of local clergy who associated such naming practices with profanity, the appropriation by a secular and civic festivity of a word and meaning that more properly belonged to the domain of institutionalized religion. Barry Chevannes discusses the dynamics of a somewhat similar national debate that has unfolded in Jamaica. He tells us how a number of Rastafarians, members of the now legendary Bob Marley and the Wailers, have undergone a deification of sorts and have joined national heroes such as Sam Sharpe, Paul Bogle, and Alexander Bustamante in a kind of postcolonial pantheon, the Jamaican equivalent of the American founding fathers. This is a truly remarkable transition when we consider that just thirty years ago members of this religious group were branded as outcasts, the lunatic fringe of a colonial society who had little to offer in terms of a national or postcolonial identity. It is virtually impossible to think of Jamaica without thinking of Bob Marley, so enmeshed have the two become.

A second and related group of issues explored in this collection focuses around cultural production and a number of chapters look at the way cultural elements have, to paraphrase a keyword from an earlier generation, undergone a process of syncretization in the molding and shaping of a distinctly Caribbean aesthetic. When we think of syncretization we tend to think in terms of the past, as historical process, Caribbean culture as the product of an African-European encounter that led to formation of creole societies and what we know today as the modern Caribbean. Several chapters have expanded upon this idea and discuss the way various elements and forms have been co-opted and subjected to what might best be described as a process of postcolonial creolization. Such is the case with "Pentecostal Community and Jamaican Hierarchy" in which Diane Austin-Broos discusses how penetecostalism, first introduced in the 19th century, is now considered a "native" or indigenous religion bearing little or no resemblance in the hearts and minds of local practitioners with North America. Are such processes confined to the Caribbean or has creolization undergone dispersal as well? In "Spiritual Baptists in New York City," Wally Zane raises some interesting questions as he tells us how in the pan-Caribbean world of contemporary Brooklyn beliefs and practices once confined to island-societies have undergone a linguistic or semantic broadening to include similar forms and elements from American, Anglophone, and other Caribbean societies as well.[8]

If an earlier generation saw the dynamics of interaction in terms of Africans and Europeans, then several chapters have drawn upon recent trends in cultural studies to move beyond polar dichotomies and have approached interaction in less formulaic terms as hybridity and multiplicity. A sense of hybridity and multiplicity is no where more evident than in James Houk's chapter on Trinidad. Entitled "Chaos, Compromise, and Transformation in Trinidad," Houk discusses how elements of Catholicism, Hinduism, Judaism, and Islam have been combined and reworked among the practitioners of Orisha, an African-derived religion, in new and novel ways. Whereas an earlier generation worked within fixed and timeless categories, a sense of agency and indeterminacy pervades this collection as they describe the ways older forms, elements, and meanings have been redefined in a variety of new contexts and situations. In "Noises of Astonishment: Spiritual Baptist Music in Context," Steve Glazier details how agency and innovation are brought to bear within the musical structure of Baptist hymns as performers move between and incorporate the secular with the sacred. Similar issues lay at the core of John Homiak's chapter as well. Entitled "Movements of Jah People: From Soundscapes to Mediascapes," Homiak describes how a primarily spoken means of communication has undergone substantial re-visioning as it incorporates electronic and visual media such as video and the Internet into a preexisting form and practice. Who could possible have foreseen during the interwar decades how

Rastafari would deploy such technologies as a necessary complement to face-to-face communication.

Our focus on agency is all-important and points to issues raised by Carole Yawney, Ken Bilby, Ineke Van Wetering, and to a lesser extent that of Phil Sher. If Houk, Homiak, and Glazier tell us about indeterminacy in cultural production, then Yawney, Bilby, and Van Wetering describe the ways and means through which local identities have undergone transformation in diaspora: how Africanisms invented in the Caribbean have been transported and reinvented in Europe and North America. As I mentioned earlier, the idea of diaspora looms large in the hearts and minds of Caribbean people. Unlike other areas in the colonial world, there was little in the way of a residual or indigenous formation extant in the region from which elements or traits deemed traditional could be invested with new meaning. Expanding upon James Clifford's ideas about traveling cultures and Benedict Anderson's notion of imagined communities, Yawney and Bilby look at the relation between community, identity, and migration. In "Only Visitors Here: Representing Rastafari into the 21st Century," Yawney details how subaltern history is made. In addition to calling for a multi-site ethnography, Yawney describes history in the making, and tells us how a locally produced narrative about a black diaspora, a major theme among Rastafari since the thirties, has been circulated around the world and is seen by practitioners in the nineties as prophecy come to pass, the link that connects distant but not disparate enclaves in Africa, Europe, North America and Jamaica into a global community. In a chapter entitled "Neither Here Nor There: The Place of Community in the Jamaican Religious Imagination," Bilby tells us how practitioners of a folk religion known as "Convince" see themselves not as isolated or confined to a local district but as constituent members of a larger if not global community of religious practitioners. Convince is a local religion that incorporates aspects of Christianity and African ancestor worship and Bilby takes us into the world of a Bongo-man (not to be confused with the use of Bongo as an appellation by Rastafarians) and the community he has created.[9]

Whereas Yawney and Bilby discuss the importance of diaspora to the imagined and invented, Van Wetering and Sher open windows on the dynamics of encounter and intervention. In a chapter entitled

"Cultural Encounters in the Diaspora," Van Wetering adds to our understanding of displacement by discussing the politics of identity between Creole and Maroon identity formations in Europe. Maroons are descendants of escaped slaves who organized semi-autonomous communities in island and mainland-societies such as Surinam and Jamaica in the 17th and 18th centuries. They have been associated with rebellion and resistance and have co-existed in an uneasy and often hostile relation within larger Creole societies. Van Wetering tells how identities such as Maroon and Creole are by no means fixed and have undergone reinterpretation as African "arrivants" to the New World became Caribbean "migrants" to the Old World some four hundred years later.

The politics of ethnicity and the tension between Caribbean and non-Caribbean communities constitutes the topic of Phil Sher's chapter. Entitled "West Indian American Day: Becoming a Tile in the Gorgeous Mosaic," Sher discusses the sequence of events that led to rupture and conflict between the Hasidic and the Caribbean or West Indian communities in Brooklyn during the Summer of 1991. Like the festivities associated with the Columbus and St. Patrick's Day parades, West Indian American Day is both a marker and a celebration of West Indian identity in New York, that most ethnic of American cities. As Sher tell us, tensions between the Hasidic and West Indian communities concerning ethnic holidays, public venues, and the perception of preferential treatment accorded to the Hasidic community were exacerbated by the accidental death of West Indian youth. In addition to sparking a two-week period of conflict, this event called into question ideas concerning ethnicity, politics, and the merits of the "gorgeous mosaic" in New York.

There are few abstract "others" in this collection and several chapters interrogate such notions as they call into question the meaning and definition associated with categories such as religion and worldview. In "On the Right Path: Interpolating Religion in Trinidad," Aisha Khan discusses the meaning of religion to Indo-Trinidadians. As Khan tell us, religion became a site of resistance for Indo-Trinidadian people soon after their arrival in the 19th century. Expanding upon Talal Asad's call for a critique of religion as a category, what Khan describes is not a bounded or unified ideology transported intact from Asia, but a shifting and fluid system of beliefs and practices that includes elements deemed magic or extra-natural as well as those deemed political or ideological in Trinidad. Known to practitioners as the "right path," this worldview combines Islam and Hinduism with Christianity (African and European) and is made to work both as a discourse prescribing and delimiting transgression and a marker setting boundaries and drawing distinctions between Indo-Trinidadian and Afro-Trinidadian identity formations in postcolonial Trinidad.[10]

Although postcolonial theory has subverted a retrenchant colonial discourse, it has been far less receptive to subject positions that lay outside its boundaries and definitions. In a chapter entitled "Citing[sighting]-up: Word, Sounds, and Reading Scripture in Jamaica," John Pulis discusses the way literacy and literacy practices have become implicated in change. Like Austin-Broos, Pulis describes a process wherein local practitioners of Rastafari deconstruct long accepted meanings and interpretations of Scripture, in this case the Revelation of John, and in so doing not only appropriate or lay claim to the Bible as a black text but transform it into an oral narrative or "living testament" as well. Similar to the "right path," the practice of citing-up raises questions concerning the ahistorical nature of literacy and literacy events and challenges polar dichotomies and terms of analysis such as literate/preliterate and oral/scribal. Rather than postcolonial theory and its tendency to flatten, silence, and homogenize, Pulis has drawn upon recent work in cultural studies and the ethnography of literacy concerning aurality, oral/scribal mixes, and reading as a subversive activity.[11]

Suffice it to say as I bring this introduction to a close, that the worldviews of Caribbean people have not been superseded by secular ideologies, nor can the linking of what would appear as oppositional and antagonistic forms, traits, and elements be dismissed as archaic, false, or utopian. Whether practiced at home in the Caribbean or abroad in Europe and North America, religious activities have always been sometimes subtle, sometimes volatile endeavors that have led to new forms of cultural expression. Along with providing cultural descriptions, these chapters open windows on the ongoing and open-ended relation between local and global and historic and contemporary change and point the way to new sites of struggle and intervention in the culture history of Caribbean people.

Endnotes

1. See *Songs of Freedom: From 'Judge Not' to 'Redemption Song'* (Birmingham, UK: Island Records, 1992) for lyrics and music.

2. See *The Speech of Mr. John Talbot Campo-Bello, A Free Christian-Negro to J. Roberts*, 1736, and see also a petition lodged on 18 May 1745 on behalf of the "The Sons of Chus" in *The Journal of the House of Assembly of Jamaica* for earlier and somewhat similar reinterpretations of Exodus in the 18th century; and see Tejumola Olaniyan, *Scars of Conquest/Masks of Resistance: The Invention of Cultural Identities in African, African-American, and Caribbean Drama* (New York: Oxford University Press, 1995) for the importance of diaspora, exile, and return to the contemporary Caribbean. See Geneva Smitherman, *Talkin and Testifyin: The Language of Black America* (Detroit: Wayne State University Press, 1986), for black vernacular and call and response.

3. For earlier and in many ways still relevant accounts of Caribbean religion see Melville J. Herskovits, *Life in a Haitian Valley* (New York: Alfred A. Knopf, 1937), *Trinidad Village* (New York: Knopf, 1947), and *The Myth of the Negro Past* (New York: Harper Brothers, 1941); and see George Eaton Simpson, *Black Religions in the New World* (New York: Columbia University Press, 1978) for an overview. For economic histories and quantitative analyses see Barry Higman, *Slave Populations of the British Caribbean, 1807–1834* (Baltimore: Johns Hopkins, 1984), Roderick A. McDonald, *The Economy and Material Culture of Slaves* (Baton Rouge, LA: LSU Press, 1993); for public opinion and political culture see the publications of the late Carl Stone especially *Class, State, and Democracy in Jamaica* (Kingston, JA: Blackett Publishers, 1985) and his earlier *Race, Class, and Political Behavior* (Kingston, JA: ISER, 1973). Individual citations to current political and economic debate are far too numerous list. See Evelyn Huber Stephens & John D. Stephens, *Democratic Socialism in Jamaica* (Princeton: Princeton University Press, 1986) and the later Prime Minister Michael Manley, *The Politics of Change* (Washington, DC: Howard U. Press, 1975) and *Jamaica: Struggle in the Periphery* (London: Writers and Readers Cooperative Society, 1982) for excellent overviews and discussions of the polemics.

4. For definitions of "nommo" and what remains one of the most eloquent essays on the importance of religion to Caribbean societies see Edward Kamau Brathwaite, "The African Presence in Caribbean Literature," originally published in *Daedalus* and reprinted in Sidney

Mintz (ed.). *Slavery, Colonialism, and Racism* (New York: Norton, 1974); see also Rex Nettleford, *Caribbean Cultural Identity* (Los Angeles: CAAS, 1979), Sidney Mintz & Richard Price, *The Birth of Afro-American Culture* (Boston: Beacon, 1992), Mervyn Alleyne, *The Roots of Jamaican Culture* (London: Pluto Press, 1988), Carolyn Cooper, *Noises in the Blood* (Durham, NC: Duke U. Press, 1995), and Derek Walcott's, "The Muse of History," in Orde Coombs, *Is Massa Day Dead?* (Garden City, NY: Doubleday, 1974) for language, music, folk culture, and programmatic statements concerning Caribbean culture.

5. Like the importance of nommo as an analytical or working construct, my understanding and application of terms and concepts such as agency, praxis, hegemony, and traditional and residual culture has been informed by Raymond Williams, *Marxism and Literature* (New York: Oxford U. Press, 1977) Paul Gilroy, *The Black Atlantic* (Cambridge, MA: Harvard University Press, 1993), and Tejumola Olaniyan, *Scars of Conquest/Masks of Resistance: The Invention of Cultural Identities in African, African-American, and Caribbean Drama* (New York: Oxford University Press, 1995).

6. Definitions and demarcations of the Caribbean according to social, cultural, and linguistic affiliation are by no means fixed and have varied over time. While I have referred to these societies in linguistic terms as Anglophone, Creole-English and varieties of English and Dutch Creole mixes are mutually intelligible and are spoken throughout the former English, Danish, and Dutch islands. See John Holm, *Pidgins and Creoles, Volume II, Reference Survey* (New York: Cambridge University Press, 1989) for Creole English in the Caribbean.

7. See Margarite F. Olmos & Lizabeth Paravisini-Gebert (ed.), *Sacred Possessions* (Newark, NJ: Rutgers University Press, 1997) for the Hispanic and Francophone Caribbean.

8. See the selections in Dell Hymes (ed.), *Pidginization and Creolization of Languages* (Cambridge: Cambridge University Press, 1985 [1971]), for an overview of creolization as both a linguistic and cultural process; see Roger Bastide, *The Religions of Brazil: Toward a Sociology of the Interpretation of Civilizations* (Baltimore: Johns Hopkins Press, 1978 [1960]), for syncretism, Africanisms, and retentions as applied to Afro-Brazilian religions; and see Kamau Brathwaite, "Caliban, Ariel, and Unprospero in the Conflict of Creolization: A Study of the Slave Revolt in Jamaica in 1831–32," in Vera Rubin & Arthur Tuden (ed.), *Comparative Perspectives on Slavery in New World Plantation*

Societies (New York: New York Academy of Science, 1993 [1976]) for the application of creolization to a historical event. For a dated but critical overview of acculturation, culture-contact, and syncretism as social theory see David Bidney, *Theoretical Anthropology* (New York: Columbia University Press, 1967); and see Mervyn Alleyne's "Introduction," *The Roots of Jamaican Culture* (London: Pluto Press, 1988) and Sidney Mintz & Richard Price's "Preface" in *The Birth of Afro-American Culture* (Boston: Beacon, 1992) for the state of current debate between two related approaches to the process of cultural formation in the Caribbean.

9. Cultural Studies is an eclectic enterprise in which scholars from anthropology, history, literary studies, and communications explore what Raymond Williams called "our common life together." See Patrick Brantlinger, *Crusoe's Footprints* (New York: Routledge, 1988), L. Grossberg, Cary Nelson, & Paula Treichler (ed.), *Cultural Studies* (New York: Routledge, 1992), Simon During (ed.), *The Cultural Studies Reader* (New York: Rout ledger, 1993), and especially Dennis Dworkin, *British Cultural Studies* (Durham, NC: Duke university Press, 1997) for histories and overviews of the field. See also Anna Lowenburg Tsing, "From the Margins," *Cultural Anthropology* Vol. 9 (1994), 279–97 for the relation of anthropology and cultural studies. See Raymond Williams, *Keywords* (New York: Oxford, 1983 [1976]) and *Marxism and Literature* (New York: Oxford, 1977) for a listing of terms and definitions.

10. See James Clifford, "Traveling Cultures," in L. Grossberg, Cary Nelson, & Paula Treichler (ed.), *Cultural Studies* (New York: Routledge, 1992), *The Predicament of Culture* (Cambridge, MA: Harvard University Press, 1988), and especially "Diasporas," *Cultural Anthropology* Vol. 9 (1994), 302–38; see Benedict Anderson, *Imagined Communities* (London: Verso, 1983) and Eric Hobsbawm and Terence Ranger, *The Invention of Tradition* (Cambridge: Cambridge University Press, 1983) for understandings and definitions of diaspora, imagined, and invented culture.

11. See Talal Asad, *Genealogies of Religion* (Baltimore: Johns Hopkins, 1993); see William Roseberry & Nicole Polier, "Tristes Tropes: Postmodern Anthropologists Encounter the Other and Discover Themselves," *Economy and Society* Vol. 18 (1989); Frederic Jameson, "Regarding Postmodernism," *Social Text* Vol. 17,(1987); and John Beverley, *Against Literature* (Minneapolis: U. of Minnesota Press, 1993) for overviews and critiques of postmodernism.

12. See Bill Ashcroft, Gareth Griffiths, and Helen Tiffen, *The Empire Writes Back: Theory and Practice in Postcolonial literature* (London: Routledge, 1989; Patrick Williams & Laura Chrisman, *Colonial Discourse and Postcolonial Theory; A Reader* (New York: Columbia University Press, 1994) and K. Anthony Appiah, "Is the post in postmodernism the post in postcolonial," *Critical Inquiry* 17 (1991), 336–57; and Alison Donnell & Sarah Lawson Welsh, *The Routledge Reader in Caribbean Literature* (London: Routledge, 1996) for overviews of postcolonial theory. As the above have commented, the single most important shortcoming to postcolonial theory has been the reification of prescriptive notions of ethnicity as a dominant ideology. This is perhaps most acute in recent attempts to legitimize orality in ahistorical and essentialized terms as African language[s] transposed intact to the New World.

2: RELIGION IN THE ANGLOPHONE CARIBBEAN: HISTORICAL OVERVIEW

Robert J. Stewart

Introduction

The Anglophone Caribbean consists of those islands that were formerly known as the British West Indies, and includes also the mainland nations of Guyana and Belize. The term Anglophone implies a linguistic identification, indicating those Caribbean countries where English is considered the official language, although the native speakers may have inherited "nation languages" (Brathwaite, 1984) that are either Afro-French or Afro-English Creoles. In theory, all the citizens of Anglophone Caribbean nations can at least hear and understand standard English, if not speak it.

The entire area was claimed by Spain following the voyages of Christopher Columbus. British acquisition began with effective colonization in St. Kitts, Barbados, Nevis, and Barbuda in the 1620s, and Britain seized Jamaica from Spain in 1655. Several islands that had been previously settled by France, such as Dominica, St. Vincent, and Grenada, were acquired by Britain in 1763 as a result of what is known as the Seven Years War. Trinidad was ceded to Britain by Spain in 1797 and St. Lucia, after changing hands several times between France and Britain, was officially acquired by Britain in 1814. The South American Dutch colonies of Berbice, Demerara and Essequibo became British Guiana in 1815, and finally, Belize was acquired in 1840 as the colony of British Honduras.

British West Indian colonial society came to consist of a minority of European planters and plantation personnel, colonial administrators, and clergy of the Church of England. There was also a community of Sephardic Jews, especially in Jamaica and Barbados, from the earliest years of colonization. After sugar cane became the primary plantation crop in the middle of the seventeenth century, a steady importation of African slaves brought about a black majority in the population. There was a gradually increasing number of "coloreds," as they were called — offspring of whites and blacks. British slave trading was officially terminated in 1808 and emancipation ended slavery in 1834. The demographic pattern was shifted in the nineteenth century with the migration of indentured laborers from India, China, and Africa. The aboriginal people of the islands were Caribs and Arawak-speaking Tainos. Only small remnants of these Native-Americans remain, although many people of mixed ethnicity, especially in the Hispanophone Caribbean, are of Native-American ancestry.

The history of religion in the Caribbean is similar in many respects to the history of religions in all colonial systems in that it is a story of the imposition of, the resistance to, and the competing claims of power. The experience and expression of religion are formed within particular historical contexts. The Anglophone Caribbean context provides a unique configuration of events, personalities, and cultures that makes the history of religion and religious practice in the region as dramatic as in any other time and place of religious creativity.

Carib and Taino Religion

European colonizers found Caribs inhabiting mainly the Lesser Antilles, the smaller islands of the eastern and southern Caribbean, and Tainos in the Greater Antilles, consisting today of Jamaica, Cuba, Hispaniola, and Puerto Rico. Caribs and Tainos had their own religious systems, mythologies, and cosmologies that were as real to them as the island coasts, hills, sea, and hurricanes that defined the cycles of their lives.

Nature and ancestors were important elements of Amerindian religion. In Taino belief, the major deities, creator parents of the land, were remote from the concerns of daily life. But there were many lesser deities and ancestral spirits, represented in *zemis*. Zemis could be wood, shell, or bone carvings, or baskets and cotton bags holding the bones of important ancestors. Spirits who dwelled in trees, rocks, and rivers could cause harm, and Tainos would take certain medicines, decorate their bodies, and wear special jewelry for protection against these spirits. Tobacco was a sacred herb that priests would smoke to induce a state of communication with the spirits. Tainos did not dread death. There were magical islands to the south, they believed, where all the departed souls lived happily together.

Carib religion was similar in many ways to that of the Tainos, but in certain features reflected the warlike or aggressive character of the Caribs and their animosity toward the Tainos. Caribs believed that the spirits of their dead enemies could inhabit their bodies. This belief led to a form of ritual cannibalism in which the Caribs acquired, through consumption, the courage of war captives. For the Caribs, the afterlife was either a place where they were served by Tainos or a kind of hell where Tainos were their masters. Perhaps because as inhabitants of small islands the Caribs were more at the mercy of the capricious sea and winds than were the Tainos on larger islands, Carib deities were more dangerous and needed more attention to be assuaged.

Did Taino and Carib religion disappear after Europeans claimed the Caribbean and began importing African slaves? Striking similarities between African and Amerindian cosmologies have led scholars to conclude that rather than disappear after the arrival of Europeans and African slaves, both could have merged in ways that scholars continue to study. Amerindian religion could also have been preserved in "syncretized" forms with both African religion and folk Catholicism in the Spanish and French Caribbean.[1] In the Anglophone Caribbean, English speaking settlers and their slaves had less contact with the aboriginal peoples, but the preservation of elements of Amerindian culture remains a possibility worthy of research.

European Churches and Missions

The Church of England, or the Anglican church, as it was also called, became the established church in the British West Indies. Anglican clergy ministered mainly to the plantocracy and showed little interest or were outrightly opposed to working among African slaves. The Society for the Propagation of the Faith in Foreign Parts was started as a missionary venture of the Anglican church in 1701. Perhaps the most noteworthy enterprise of the SPG in the West Indies began in 1710 when the planter Christopher Codrington bequeathed his estate in Barbados to the Society. The idea was that the SPG would manage a Christian plantation and thereby demonstrate to planters the compatibility of slavery and Christianity. The venture eventually failed when the commercial demands of sugar production took priority over humanitarian and religious motives.[2]

A number of other Christian churches, known as "sectarians" or "nonconformist" because they refused to conform to the established doctrine, ritual, and authority, have had a far more profound influence on religion in the West Indies than the Anglicans. The nonconformist presence began in the 1660s when Quakers arrived in Barbados, Jamaica, and Nevis. They were not an organized missionary society, as such, and had been transported or removed from England for noncompliance with ecclesiastical laws. "Transportation" was enforced exile or banishment, a common punishment during the colonial period and the means through which many Europeans arrived in America and the Caribbean. Although they were not formally missionaries, Quakers did attempt to convert slaves and legislation enacted by the Assembly of Barbados in 1676 banned black slaves from attending Quaker meetings and forbade Quakers from instructing slaves in Christianity on the grounds that such instruction would lead to notions of equality (Caldecott, 1898, p. 66). Quakers also refused militia duty, the taking of oaths, and the payment of taxes to support the established Anglican clergy, thereby continuing their passive resistance to the dominant political and ecclesiastical authority that had caused their transportation in the first place. This was the pattern of conflict — sometimes uneasy compromise, sometimes violent hostility — that would follow when other "sectarians" began to arrive in the West Indies in the following century.

Moravian missionaries from Germany first arrived in St. Thomas in the Danish Virgin Islands in 1732, and in Jamaica, Antigua, Barbados, St. Kitts and Tobago in the years between 1754 and 1790. Plans for a Wesleyan Methodist Missionary Society were first formulated in England in 1784, and a few years later the Methodists initiated activity to the West Indies. The Baptist Missionary Society, the London Missionary Society, the Scottish Missionary Society, and the evangelical Anglican Church Missionary Society were formed in the 1790s and they began working in the West Indies in the years between the abolition of the slave trade in 1808 and British slave emancipation in 1834.

Traditional African Religion

Until the British terminated the African slave trade in 1808, black slaves were acquired over time mainly from shifting West and West Central African coastal and hinterland sources between what is now Senegal in the north and Angola in the south. There was tremendous cultural and linguistic diversity in that area, and there is always the risk of oversimplification when generalizing about African culture. In the Caribbean, the already complex cultures of Africa were fragmented, dispersed, and modified. Anthropologists and historians have, nevertheless, discerned a common thread of social and cosmological presumptions in the African diaspora that are characteristic of a broad cultural area in western Africa (Mintz & Price, 1976, pp. 5 and 6; Brathwaite, 1974, pp. 34, 40, and 41; Thornton, 1992, pp. 186–87).

In traditional African religion, which has many variations in different parts of Africa, body and movement are key elements. The body is both the place and the manifestation of one's meeting with the deities and lesser spirits in the pantheon. There is generally a belief in a supreme god, a creator and source of all power. But this high god is imagined as distant and as virtually inactive in human affairs. Involvement in human fortune and misfortune is the role of lesser deities and spirits (Sawyerr, 1970, pp. 5–6).

Ultimate reality in traditional African religion is distinctly worldly and temporal. This does not mean that it is secular in the Western conception of the term. Rather it derives from the presumption of a primal unity of the material and the spiritual (Taylor, 1963, pp. 11–12, 79, and 197). This is shown in attachment to and veneration of the land. The land ties together the living and the dead, uniting past and present generations of family, clan and nation. And the land of the departed is conceived as virtually the same as the land of the living (Mbiti, 1970, pp. 34–35, 208, and 210; Parrinder, 1969, p. 54).

The spirits of the departed, the ancestors, and the minor deities are important in the maintenance of order, stability, proper human relations, and material fortune or misfortune. To be without religion — that is, to deny or ignore the world of the spirits — is tantamount to denying one's social and, therefore, individual identity. Communication with departed family members and ancestors — through the means of libation, meal sharing, dancing, and drumming — is of utmost importance in the maintenance of social well-being. This communication is real, active, and powerful, especially with the spirits of those who have most recently passed on (Mbiti, 1970, pp. 106, 107–10, 211–12, and 213).

Among African peoples, the sense of corporate life, in which the communities of the living and the dead are linked, is profound. It is in this context that distinctions between morally good and bad behavior have meaning. A person is "good" or "bad" according to social conduct. Actions are "good" when they conform to community custom and maintain the equilibrium of the community, "bad" when they do not. The effects of conduct on relationships determines its moral quality. The spirits of the departed are essentially part of the community, and proper communication with them is necessary for material and social beneficence, as they are the guides and guardians of conduct and moral order (Mbiti, 1970, pp. 278–79; Idowu, 1962, pp. 144–68).

African natural science, a function of religion, is based upon observation and control of the world, of its powers, possibilities, and effects on human life. Africans do not perceive cosmic powers as impersonal but as radically personalized through deities, ancestors, and the spirits of the departed. The maintenance of constant communication with them appears to be the primary purpose of African religious practice. Specialists in spirit communication seek augmentation of positive force by recognizing and invoking the powers of the spirits and by letting them manifest themselves through the psychological and physical functions of the human body. These specialists are trained in the harnessing of spiritual power to maintain social and individual health and to counter misfortune, suffering and disease (Parrinder, 1969, pp. 26–28; Mbiti, 1970, p. 84; Schuler, 1980, p. 33).[3]

Conflicting Worldviews

Cosmologies from Europe, Africa and pre-Columbian America intersected, competed, and, in certain ways, were synthesized through the historical experiences of colonialism, slavery, the plantation, rebellion, nationalism, and, eventually, independence, and we can see in the region the classic contradiction between religion as the sanctification of authority and social control and religion as a source of resistance and social change. Caribbean historians have used the word "creolization" to identify the process.

European Christianity and Slave Society

Continuities and changes in African beliefs, as well as the presence of the European churches in the Caribbean, can be defined largely in relation to slavery. The five hundred year history of the Caribbean from the beginning of Spanish settlement in the region has largely been the history of slave society.

The Anglican church in the Caribbean offered no systematic critique of slavery, although individual Anglican priests distinguished themselves by their prophetic outspokenness against slave society.[4] "Sectarian" missionaries did not preach a consistent anti-slavery ethic, but by their actions and their preaching, they would initiate fissures in slave society that would contribute to its demise, and, in the end, these missionaries could be said to have helped to bring about emancipation.[5]

The Baptist missionaries in Jamaica provide examples. One of the most outspoken among them, William Knibb, who arrived on the island in 1825, put it this way: "To proclaim liberty to the captive and the opening of the prisons to them that are bound, is a delightful employment, and here would I dwell that I may be thus employed." Another Baptist in Jamaica, Richard Merrick, challenged religious and secular distinctions when he explained that his purpose in running for election to local government (the parish vestry) in 1843 was to "show the poor people that I loved their bodies as well as their souls" (Stewart, 1992, pp. 16 and 17).

For evangelicals like Knibb and Merrick, a heightened sense of the nearness of God's kingdom provided a special urgency: Christian converts, whether slave or free, had social and physical needs which no Christian could ignore in conscience. This way of thinking was controversial because it undermined the current economic doctrine that society and economy are subject to their own laws with which religion should not interfere. Humanitarian evangelicalism did not turn missionaries into revolutionaries, for they retained the belief in the overwhelming priority of the life to come and the relative unimportance of the inequalities and hardships of this life. But missionary involvement with the West Indies occurred simultaneously with the organized movement in Britain for the abolition of the slave trade and slavery. Missionary response to the issue of abolition would determine their relationships with both the plantocracy and with the slaves. To steer a middle course between the two was most difficult. To demonstrate to the planters that they wished to maintain social control and to preach humanity and fraternity to the slaves proved to be irreconcilable as West Indian society responded to slave resistance and rebellion and to the pressures for abolition coming from Britain.

Evangelicals were not prepared to articulate rationales for emancipation and free society. The evangelical critique of slave society had force not as a systematic philosophy so much as the conviction of the heart, a here and now response to God's word and grace, a reflex of conscience, after it became patently obvious that slavery could not be Christianized. In their mission to the enslaved, missionaries were able to cut through the rationalizations for slavery and racial stratification but had little else to offer beyond personal redemption and self-help.

The situation that prevailed was a struggle to reconcile the realities of slavery with a traditional view of the benign Christian family, a view that accommodated slavery within a paternal relationship of unequals (Davis, 1966, p. 200). The institution of slavery was not condemned until 1823 when the Anti-Slavery Society began its campaign for emancipation. Prior to that, the main hope of Christian critics had been for the gradual Christianization of slavery and its eventual demise but not immediate abolition (see endnote 4).

Why did Christianity, whether defined as church, denomination, doctrine, or moral system, accommodate for so long a system of slave labor? How did Christian churches figure at all in the final abolition of slavery? These are complicated questions, and economic determinists, historians of ideas, and theologians of salvation history would all offer varying answers. It can be argued that abolitionism as a moral imperative in the Anglophone Caribbean can be ascribed to a changing social conscience in late eighteenth century and early nineteenth century Britain that resulted from the convergence of new methods of production, concomitantly new labor relations, philosophical humanitarianism, and the idea of democracy. All these circumstances provided a soil in which a Christian ethic of freedom could flower.[6] The problem of slavery could have remained locked within philosophical debate, and the conceptual contradictions could have stalemated action, had not certain practical realities led to commitment and action: Christian missionaries coming face to face with slavery not as an abstraction but as a bitter and daily reality, and the constant and varying manifestations of resistance and rebellion against slavery by the slaves themselves.

In the early eighteenth century English Baptists affirmed that slavery was authorized by Scripture and was part of the governing structure of the world (Davis, 1966, p. 335). It was a long way from that position to that of William Knibb, who not long after his arrival in Jamaica condemned slavery without qualification. The more common viewpoint of missionaries was qualified, however, and was represented by the view on slavery of the Scottish missionary Hope Waddell (1863), who arrived in Jamaica in 1829. "The more he has seen of the system [of slavery]," wrote Waddell in the third person of his own opinion, "the more does he condemn it, as unworthy of being maintained anywhere; bearable only when required to escape anarchy, and which it would be criminal to introduce into any country whence it can be excluded" (pp. iv–v). While this view tends toward the abolitionist one, it nevertheless reveals an ambivalence based on a fear of anarchy should slavery not be replaced by strong social controls. Such ambivalence was behind a style of missionary gradualism on slavery and other social issues, a style that would not satisfy black Christians in the West Indies.

The social role of the European missionaries was as significant as their views on slavery. Personal ambition and religious laxness were characteristic of the Anglican clergy throughout the slave period. Their church came to be regarded as little more than an ornamental adjunct of the state, the survival of a harmless home institution which would cease to be tolerated outside its own particular groove. The sympathies of the clergy were with the colonial government in each island. Those governments were basically negrophobic plantocracies. Not only were the Anglican clergy, in effect, the house chaplains for the West Indian ruling class, they were often accused by the plantocrats themselves of corruption, cynicism, and ineptitude (Ellis, 1913, p. 53; Patterson, 1967, p. 208).

Evangelical missionaries, both "sectarians" and those within the Anglican church itself, challenged the colonial clergy to attend more carefully to the Christianization of the slaves. The response, such as it was, was not enthusiastic. To the extent that Anglican clergymen began to preach, instruct, and baptize slaves it was more out of concern to counter competition from nonconformist missionaries and from the Church of England's own Church Missionary Society, which began working in the West Indies in the 1820s.

The challenge that nonconformist missionaries and Anglican evangelicals brought to plantation society was not so much a systematic critique of the system of slavery, but rather derived from the style of their presence, from their way of relating to slaves, and by the witness they gave as whites whose values and manner of living contrasted with the way of life of the plantocracy. The first missionaries in the West Indies, the Moravians, immediately established this contrast by doing manual labor, shunned by most whites, and by using Creole dialects to preach and teach the Bible (Goveia, 1965, p. 278). While they did not refuse to minister to the whites, their priority, and the priority of every missionary group that came after them, was to establish congregations among the black people.

In general, the approach of the missionaries to the slaves was one of familiarity and sympathy. Moreover, they offered a moral alternative to the corruptions of planter life. Elsa Goveia observed that converted slaves became better in terms of Christian morality than the Europeans of the established church (p. 302). Her observation was a restatement of those made by some missionaries in the nineteenth century. In a letter from Kingston dated March 1825, William Knibb exclaimed, "The poor, oppressed, benighted, and despised sons of Africa form a pleasing contrast to the debauched white population" (Clarke, 1869, p. 17).

The missionary presence brought with it a basic ambiguity, an ambiguity which was not resolved after emancipation. On the one hand, the missionaries assumed or taught that the blacks were not inherently inferior in the sight of God. The congregationalism of the nonconformist churches, including their employment of black leaders and deacons, was based on an ideal of fellowship that contradicted the class and racial distinctions that defined plantation society. And missionaries in general avoided fraternization within the dominant white society. On the other hand, this avoidance did not mean that they became acculturated to Afro-Creole folk culture. British mores and manners epitomized Christian civilization for them, and thus they expected black members to adopt them and to drop "negroism" (Olwig, 1990, p. 107). They accepted the blacks abstractly as equal while rejecting the cultural expressions which defined black life. And they preached obedience, resignation, and acceptance of social hierarchies.

This description of missionary ambiguity can be modified in the case of individual missionaries and certain missionary societies. The Methodist built for themselves a reputation for respectability and a dedication to the political and social status quo. The Baptists were more willing than the Methodists to take their religious ideals of brotherhood into the political arena, bringing upon themselves persecution by plantocratic vigilantes. Planters eventually became astute in assessing the diverse approaches to social issues among the nonconformist missions and devised strategies for co-opting missionaries in the interests of social control (Stewart, 1992, pp. 32–36 and 38–42).

Black Christianity

White missionaries were not the only preachers from overseas to arrive in the West Indies during slavery. A black Baptist presence was established in Jamaica even before the two major missionary groups, the British Methodists and Baptists, began their work there. In 1783, George Liele (or Lisle), a freedman who had been a slave to a Baptist planter in Georgia, arrived in Jamaica and began preaching in Kingston. Moses Baker, who had been a member of the free community of color in New York City and had migrated to Jamaica, was baptized by Liele and became an itinerant preacher in the island. Liele and Baker were joined by other nonwhite preachers and this core group held the seed that would grow into the "Native Baptists," as they came to be called. In 1806 they began to correspond with the English Baptists and, overwhelmed with the sizes of the congregations that were forming in response to their preaching, appealed for assistance. It was as a result of this invitation that the Baptist Missionary Society began to send their preachers and teachers to Jamaica in 1814.[7]

Native Baptists nevertheless continued to grow independently. Their black leaders, in protest against slavery and later against the slow pace of social and economic reform after emancipation, were instrumental in two major rebellions in nineteenth century Jamaica. The first was the slave rebellion of 1831–32, known as the Baptist War, led by Sam Sharpe. Sharpe and his captains were "daddies," the title of respect given them by their Native Baptist followers. Sharpe was also a deacon in the white-led Baptist missionary congregation in Montego Bay. The other incident was the 1865 Morant Bay Rebellion led by Paul Bogle. Today, Sharpe and Bogle are official National Heroes in Jamaica.

Native Baptist spirituality and practices incorporated elements of African religion that had been creolized, or reformed, in the experience of slavery and resistance in the Caribbean. Planters tended to be indifferent to African religion and its creolized versions, except when manifestations of that religion seemed directly related to resistance and rebellion. Many slave codes forbade drumming, for example, or any rhythmic and percussive use of instruments that could substitute for the drum. The drum was a sacred instrument that summoned deities and spirits into communion with the living. But what concerned the planters was not so much this "superstitious" function, as they saw it, but the fact that the drum was a means of communication among slaves and its use signaled gatherings of slaves that were always considered potentially dangerous. Planters' suspicions extended to other manifestations of Afro-Creole religion whenever they appeared to imply a power that colonial officials could not control or that was used in resistance to their control. Obeah, the private manipulation of spirit power for personal gain or harm, and Myal, which sought to counter social evil and witchcraft, were prohibited in slave codes in Jamaica, but were never eradicated.

Myal in Jamaica, and similar forms of Afro-Creole religion in the other islands of the British West Indies, continued to grow vigorously in the years after emancipation in 1834, and incorporated elements of apocalyptic Christianity. Post-emancipation Myalists, for example, preached the return of Christ to earth, and sought to purify the earth, to dig up all Obeahs, in preparation for his return. In 1860–61, the years of a Great Revival in Jamaica, Myal and evangelical Christianity were synthesized by black people into forms of Revival that became deeply rooted in rural Jamaican consciousness (Stewart, 1992, pp. 142 and 146–47). There were similar movements with different names in the other islands after emancipation. The Noahites in Nevis in the Leeward Islands appropriated and transformed Methodism in ways in which Revivalists in Jamaica transformed evangelical Christianity. Drawing its name from Noah, a former slave who in 1839 proclaimed himself "Prophet" and "Comforter," the movement attracted large congregations. Readings from the Bible and the singing of John Wesley's hymns in Noahite services were combined with dreams, prophecies, and ecstatic dancing which culminated in spirit possession (Olwig, 1990, p. 108). In the southern Caribbean, to the great chagrin of colonial officials, movements similar to the Noahites developed in the nineteenth century. Perhaps the best known of these were the Shakers in St. Vincent and the Spiritual Baptists in Trinidad and Tobago (Cox, 1994, and Glazier, 1983).

After Emancipation

After emancipation, the already varied religious traditions in the West Indies were further diversified by the immigration of indentured laborers from Asia and Africa. African immigration into the British West Indies was not on the scale of African arrivals in nineteenth century Cuba, which continued to be a slave society for most of the century, and where the symbiosis of Catholicism and African religions produced Santeria (Brandon, 1993). Nevertheless, comparable religious forms were either started or revivified in the Anglophone Caribbean with the Africans that arrived as emancipated slaves or indentured migrants. Kele in St. Lucia, Shango in Trinidad, Big Drum in Carriacou, and Kumina in Jamaica are religions which relate to the spirit world in traditional African ways, although they may include in their pantheons certain spirits that originated in other cosmologies, such as Hinduism, Native-American belief, or the Catholic tradition of the saints.

Although Chinese immigrants were among the Asians who were indentured to provide steady labor after slave emancipation, they had little impact in the history of religion in the Caribbean. They were readily assimilated by the mainstream Christian churches. In Jamaica, for example, the descendants of Chinese immigrants became a distinguishing feature of Roman Catholic congregations in the twentieth century. Immigrants from the Indian subcontinent, however, introduced major variations in the Caribbean religious scene. Where they now make up the majority of the population, such as in Trinidad and Guyana, forms of Hinduism have become defining features of the Creole religious landscape. While in India Hinduism is diversified in myriad forms of local and family religious practices, in the Caribbean it has become a more standardized and routinized pan-Indian experience. Although many East Indians converted in response to missionary activity, initiated by Canadian Presbyterians in the 1860s, Hinduism remains a more important factor than Christianity of East Indian cultural identity in Guyana and in Trinidad's fairly cosmopolitan society.

Immigrants from India also brought Islam with them. They were not the first Muslims in the Caribbean, however. There was a Mandingo Muslim community of ex-slaves in Port of Spain, Trinidad from the early nineteenth century. Over several generations, under a succession of patriarchs, and augmented by new members from among post-emancipation African immigrants, this community maintained an African identity. They kept Arabic names and made repatriation to Africa an ideal, although only a few individuals from among them managed to get back to Africa (Brereton, 1981, pp. 67–68). While there can be no doubt that many Muslim Africans were brought to other parts of the Caribbean during the years of the slave trade, their inability as slaves to reproduce an Islamic community meant that their beliefs and practices either withered or became so diffused in Creole society that it is difficult to document a Muslim tradition in the West Indies as a whole before the beginning of Indian immigration in the 1840s. East Indian Hinduism and Islam had little cultural influence in societies like Jamaica where the overwhelming majority of the population continued to be of African ancestry, and where the most viable religious forms had been derived from Afro-Christian syntheses. But in Trinidad, where manifestations of African traditions are just as strong, and with its history of Mandingo Muslims, many people of African ancestry have adopted Islam to the extent that it has defined their community values as well as their politics. In the summer of 1990, an Islamic coup attempted against the elected government of that republic showed the extent of the black Muslim challenge to the secular state.

Jews and Syrians are economically strong ethnic minorities in some West Indian nations. While there are black Jews in the Caribbean, most are of obvious European descent. In colonies like Jamaica that had a restricted elective franchise, Jews were denied full civil and political rights until the 1830s. After that they became increasingly politically active. Older Jewish families became prominent in government and business in the twentieth century. Many European Jews, fleeing Nazi persecution in Germany, sought refuge in the Caribbean (Martin, 1994).

Middle Eastern immigrants in the early twentieth century, mainly from what is now Lebanon, are generically called "Syrians" in the West Indies. They brought Arabic surnames with them but the majority of them were already Christians, and were absorbed largely into traditional churches, especially the Roman Catholic church.

Perhaps the most dramatic challenge in the twentieth century West Indies to the religious and secular status quo was the development of the Rastafari in Jamaica in the 1930s. The Rastafari have become a phenomenon throughout the Caribbean and, indeed, throughout the entire worldwide black diaspora. They are now commonplace to the extent that their dreadlocks, their wearing of the Ethiopian colors of red, gold, and green, their influence on reggae music, and their linguistic innovations have made them easily identifiable. But their worldview, which can be called a kind of African Zionism, has been deceptively oversimplified in popular understanding. Rastafari consciousness owes much to the religious worldview that was also fundamental to the more consciously sociopolitical movement of Garveyism, which was based in a black theology that overturned the negative valuations that colonialism had attached to the word "African." Marcus Garvey's pan-Africanism and his theology of a black God proved to have universal appeal throughout the African diaspora, foreshadowing the appeal that Rastafari style and consciousness would have later in the twentieth century. Rastafari is not only a legacy of Garveyism, however, but has roots in the Revival tradition that preceded it, as Chevannes (1994) has shown (pp. 21 & 120). The Rastafari theme of liberation from Babylonian captivity in the West and return to Africa also echoes a long established mythology in Afro-Caribbean folk consciousness in which motifs of spirit return are expressed in story, song, and religious metaphor (McDaniel, 1990). The African consciousness of the Rastafari goes deep in the Jamaican and West Indian past, and is a perfect example of the processes of continuity and change, of rooted consciousness and startling innovation, that have been characteristic of Caribbean history.

The mainstream Christian churches, such as the Anglicans, Roman Catholics, Presbyterians, Methodists, Baptists, Moravians, and Congregationalists, remained important in the twentieth century Caribbean. Their priests, pastors, and missionaries relied on Europe and, increasingly, on North America to replenish their ranks, although as the century progressed most of these churches gradually moved toward indigenization of leadership. They tended to maintain spiritual rationalizations for the sociopolitical status quo, propping up the colonial hierarchies of class and color, retaining patriotic links with the metropole, and becoming tentatively progressive when Creole nationalism led to movements for local leadership, autonomy and, in the 1960s and 1970s, independence. Even then their alliance was mainly with local oligarchies against mass movements for popular democracy or revolution.[8]

The mainstream churches in the twentieth century have not been universally conservative or oligarchic, however. There have been individuals and groups within the churches that have promoted a twentieth century version of the social gospel or a West Indian embodiment of liberation theology. These movements have been espoused and documented by the Caribbean Conference of Churches (not without controversy within the Conference) over the past quarter century, especially in that group's periodical, *Caribbean Contact*, which reported throughout its twenty-two year (1972–94) existence the progressive grounding of the European churches in Caribbean reality.

Important in the narrative of the history of religion in the twentieth century Caribbean is the tenacious growth of apocalyptic, fundamentalist, and pentecostal churches and sects originating in North America. These groups, such as the Jehovah's Witnesses, Seventh Day Adventists, and various representations of the Church of God in Christ, have made headway in conditions of post-colonial dependence and economic instability. Their emphasis has been on individualistic or in-group ideas of self-help, and they are sociopolitically quietistic. They represent an in-turning reaction against the frustrating pace of cultural autonomy and economic self-sufficiency in the Caribbean.

Diane Austin Broos, who writes on pentecostalism and gender issues, has analyzed the significance of pentecostalism in the Caribbean, specifically in reference to Jamaica (Austin Broos, 1996). She has demonstrated that the pentecostal organizational reliance on North American leadership maintains a neo-colonial situation of dependency. Yet she has also shown that certain aspects of pentecostalism developed indigenously, and that the Afro-Creole worldview, with its openness to a spiritual cosmology and its presumption that the real is whole and not split between the secular and the sacred, has begun to absorb pentecostalism into a process of Creole transformation.

Conclusion

In the larger historical picture, similar transformations have been taking place in the five hundred year encounter of diverse cultures in the Caribbean. The unseverable link between religion and West Indian sociopolitical history has been continued and confirmed in the twentieth century. The old world cultures of Africa and, in Trinidad and Guyana, of India, have been preserved in the mnemonic of religious ceremony and mythology, creating Afro-Creole or Indo-Creole alternatives to the dominating traditions of Europe and North America.

Endnotes

1. "Syncretism" remains a convenient catchword for the fusion of religious traditions and practices from different cultures. Because it includes in its meaning the notion of uncritical or failed synthesis, however, it has been increasingly rejected by scholars of Caribbean religion as being analytically inadequate for understanding cultural contact, continuity, and change. Brandon (1993), for example, argues that the term is irrelevant for explaining how individuals can claim to be members of a particular Christian church but have little difficulty in accommodating worldviews derived from multiple sources (pp. 167–71 and 180–81). Desmangles (1992) prefers the term "symbiosis" to "syncretism" in order to counter the notion of an impure fusion of traditions. He uses "symbiosis" in an ethnological sense, according to which diverse religious traditions are juxtaposed in space and time without fusion to constitute the whole phenomenon of a new religion, Haitian Vodou, in his example (8–11). Desmangles identifies Taino elements in Vodou. Other scholars have explored Taino retentions in Spanish Caribbean religious expres-

sions. See, for example, Anthony M. Stevens-Arroyo's essay, "The Persistence of Religious Cosmovision in an Alien World," in Stevens-Arroyo and Perez y Mena (1995, pp. 113–35). Historical archeologist Kofi Agorsah's research in Jamaica indicates cultural interaction between surviving Tainos and early African slave runaways on that island. He sums up his work in two essays, "Background to Maroon Heritage" (1994, pp. 1–35) and "Archaeology of Maroon Settlements in Jamaica" (1994, pp. 163–87).

2. The story of the Codrington experiment is an interesting and complex one, and there was lively disagreement within the SPG, and between abolitionists and pro-slavery propagandists, on what the church could accomplish on a plantation that depended on slave labor. See Chapter 7, "Sugar, Slavery and the Planters' Church," in Dayfoot (1998) for a full narrative. One of the most thorough surveys of the history of Codrington is Bennett (1958).

3. It should be noted that African Christian scholars such as Mbiti and Idowu have been criticized by other African writers for inventing a traditional religion that never existed by filtering African worldviews through distorting Western categories (Isichei, 1995, p. 325). One of their strongest critics was Okot p'Bitek (1970) of Uganda. "The African deities of the books," he wrote, "clothed with the attributes of the Christian God, are, in the main, creations of the students of African religions. They are all beyond recognition to the ordinary Africans in the countryside" (p. 88).

4. The two most noteworthy of Anglican clergymen who were critics of slave society were Morgan Godwyn in the seventeenth century and James Ramsay in the eighteenth. After witnessing the plantation system in Barbados, Godwyn published *The Negro's and Indians Advocate* (London 1680), in which he did not attack slavery as such, but argued against the "pretenses" of planters who maintained that blacks were inferior and incapable of participation in Christian civilization as he understood it. He reminded whites of Africa's traditional civilizations, "once famous for both Arts and Arms." The Rev. James Ramsay went beyond Godwyn's protest. After serving as a priest in St. Kitts and experiencing the conditions of the slave system, Ramsay became one of the prime movers in British abolitionism. He published his critique of slavery in *An Essay on the Treatment and Conversion of African Slaves in the British Sugar Colonies* (London 1784).

5. The influence of missionaries in the disintegration of slave society in Jamaica is the major theme in Turner (1982).

6. This issue is addressed by a number of essays in Bolt and Drescher (1980).

7. See Pulis (1998) for Baker, Liele, and black loyalists in Jamaica.

8. The experience of both mainstream and independent Christian churches in Africa during the era of decolonization in the 1950s and 1960s provides some interesting parallels as well as contrasts with the West Indian situation. See Isichei (1995) Chapter 12, "Independent Black Africa since 1960: Church, State, and Society."

References

Agorsah, E. Kofi., ed. 1994 *Maroon Heritage: Archaeological, Ethnographic and Historical Perspectives*. Kingston: Canoe Press.

Anderson, James S.M. 1845–56 *The History of the Church of England in the Colonies and Foreign Dependencies of the British Empire*. 3 vols. London.

Augier, F.R., and Gordon, S.C., eds. 1962 *Sources of West Indian History*. London: Longman Caribbean.

Austin Broos, Diane J. 1996 Politics and the redeemer: State and religion as ways of being in Jamaica. *New West Indian Guide* 70(1–2):59–90.

Bennett, J. Harry Jr. 1958 *Bondsmen and Bishops: Slavery and Apprenticeship on the Codrington Plantations of Barbados, 1710–1838*. Berkeley: University of California Press.

Berger, Peter L. 1973 On the religious sanctions of social fictions. In: *Ways of Being Religious* (eds., Frederick J. Streng, Charles L. Lloyd, Jr., and Jay T. Allen). Englewood Cliffs, NJ: Prentice-Hall.

Bolt, Christine and Drescher, Seymour, eds. 1980 *Anti-Slavery, Religion and Reform*. Folkestone, Kent UK: Wm. Dawson & Sons.

Brandon, George 1993 *Santeria from Africa to the New World: The Dead Sell Memories*. Bloomington: Indiana University Press.

Brathwaite, Edward 1971 *The Development of Creole Society in Jamaica, 1770–1820*. Oxford: Clarendon Press.

Brathwaite, Edward 1978 Kumina — the spirit of African survival in Jamaica. *Jamaica Journal* 42:45–63.

Brathwaite, Edward 1984 *History of the Voice: The Development of Nation Language in Anglophone Caribbean Poetry*. London: New Beacon.

Brathwaite, Edward and Kamau, Edward 1974 *Contradictory Omens: Cultural Diversity and Integration in the Caribbean*. Kingston: Savacou.

Brereton, Bridget 1981 *A History of Modern Trinidad, 1783–1962*. Kingston: Heinemann.

Burnside, Madeleine and Robotham, Rosemarie 1997 *Spirits of the Passage: The Transatlantic Slave Trade in the Seventeenth Century*. New York: Simon & Schuster.

Caldecott, A. 1898 *The Church in the West Indies*. London: Yates & Alexander.

Chevannes, Barry 1994 *Rastafari: Roots and Ideology*. Syracuse, NY: Syracuse University Press.

Chevannes, Barry, ed. 1995 *Rastafari and Other African-Caribbean Worldviews*. London and The Hague: Macmillan/Institute of Social Studies.

Clarke, John 1869 *Memorials of the Baptist Missionaries in Jamaica*. London: Yates & Alexander.

Claypole, William, and Robottom, John 1980 *Caribbean Story*. Jamaica, Trinidad, UK: Longman Caribbean.

Coleman-Norton, P.R. 1951 The apostle Paul and the Roman law of slavery. In: *Studies in Roman Economic and Social History* (ed., P.R. Coleman-Norton). Princeton, NJ: Princeton University Press.

Costa, Emilia Viotti da 1994 *Crowns of Glory, Tears of Blood: The Demerara Slave Rebellion of 1823*. New York: Oxford University Press.

Cox, Edward L. 1994 Religious intolerance and persecution: The Shakers of St. Vincent, 1900–1934. *Journal of Caribbean History* 28(2):208–43.

Dabydeen, David and Samaroo, Brinsley, eds. 1987 *India in the Caribbean*. London: Hansib/University of Warwick.

Davis, David Brion 1966 *The Problem of Slavery in Western Culture*. Ithaca, NY: Cornell University Press.

Dayfoot, Arthur C. 1998 *The Shaping of the West Indian church: The Formation of the Pattern of Church Life in the English-Speaking Caribbean During the Colonial Era, 1492–1962*. Kingston: The Press University of the West Indies.

Deismann, Adolf 1926 *Paul: A Study in Social and Religious History*. New York: Doran.

Desmangles, Leslie G. 1992 *The Faces of the Gods: Vodou and Roman Catholicism in Haiti.* Chapel Hill: University of North Carolina Press.

Dillenberger, John and Welch, Claude 1954 *Protestant Christianity: Interpreted Through Its Development.* New York: Charles Scribner's Sons.

Edwards, Paul, ed. 1967 [1789] *Equiano's Travels. Abridgement of The Interesting Narrative of the Life of Olaudah Equiano, or Gustavus Vassa, the African.* London: Heinemann.

Ellis, J.B. 1913 *The Diocese of Jamaica.* London: SPCK.

Glazier, Stephen D. 1983 *Marchin' the Pilgrims Home: Leadership and Decision-Making in an Afro-Caribbean Faith.* Westport, CT: Greenwood.

Gordon, Shirley C. 1996 *God Almighty Make Me Free: Christianity in Pre-emancipation Jamaica.* Bloomington: Indiana University Press.

Gordon, Shirley C. 1997 *Our Cause for His Glory: Christianization and Emancipation in Jamaica.* Kingston: The Press University of the West Indies.

Goveia, Elsa 1965 *Slave Society in the British Leeward Islands at the End of the Eighteenth Century.* New Haven, CT: Yale University Press.

Heuman, Gad 1994 *"The Killing Time," The Morant Bay Rebellion in Jamaica.* Knoxville: University of Tennessee Press.

Highfield, Arnold R. 1994 Patterns of accommodation and resistance: The Moravian witness to slavery in the Danish West Indies. *Journal of Caribbean History* 28(2):138–64.

Holzberg, Carol S. 1987 *Minorities and Power in a Black Society: The Jewish Community of Jamaica.* Baltimore: North-South Publishing Company.

Idowu, E.B. 1962 *Oludumare: God in Yoruba Belief.* London: Longman.

Isichei, Elizabeth. 1995 *A History of Christianity in Africa from Antiquity to the Present.* Lawrenceville, NJ: Africa World Press.

Lewis, Maureen Warner. 1977 The Nkuyu: spirit messengers of the Kumina. *Savacou* 13:57–78.

Lewis, Rupert and Bryan, Patrick, eds. 1988 *Garvey: His Work and Impact.* Mona, Jamaica: Institute of Social and Economic Research and Department of Extra-Mural Studies, University of the West Indies.

McDaniel, Lorna 1990 The flying Africans: Extent and strength of the myth in the Americas. *New West Indian Guide* 64(1–2):28–40.

Martin, Tony 1994 Jews to Trinidad. *Journal of Caribbean History* 28(2):244–57.

Mbiti, John S. 1970 *African Religions and Philosophy*. Garden City, NY: Anchor.

Mintz, Sidney and Price, Richard 1976 *An Anthropological Approach to the Afro-American Past: A Caribbean Perspective*. Philadelphia: Institute for the Study of Human Issues.

Neill, Stephen 1964 *A History of Christian Missions*. New York: Penguin.

Olwig, Karen Fog 1990 The struggle for respectability: Methodism and Afro-Caribbean culture on 19th century Nevis. *New West Indian Guide* 64(3–4):93–114.

Parrinder, Geoffrey 1969 *Religion in Africa*. Baltimore, MD: Penguin Books.

Patterson, Orlando 1967 *The Sociology of Slavery*. London: MacGibbon and Kee.

Patterson, Orlando 1972 *Die the Long Day*. St. Albans, UK: Mayflower Books.

p'Bitek, Okot 1970 *African Religions in Western Scholarship*. Kampala: East African Literature Bureau.

Pulis, John W. 1998 Bridging troubled waters: Moses Baker, George Liele, and the African-American Diaspora to Jamaica. In: *Moving On: Black Loyalists in the Afro-Atlantic World* (ed., John W. Pulis). New York: Garland.

Ramsay, James 1784 *An Essay on the Treatment and Conversion of African Slaves in the British Sugar Colonies*. London.

Rouse, Irving 1992 *The Tainos: Rise and Decline of the People Who Greeted Columbus*. New Haven: Yale University Press.

Sawyerr, Harry 1970 *God: Ancestor or Creator?* London: Longman.

Schuler, Monica 1980 *"Alas, Alas, Kongo": A Social History of Indentured African Immigration into Jamaica, 1841–1865*. Baltimore, MD: Johns Hopkins University Press.

Schuler, Monica 1991 Akan slave rebellions in the British Caribbean. In: *Caribbean Slave Society and Economy* (eds., Hilary Beckles and Verene Shepherd). New York: The New Press.

Simpson, George E. 1978 *Black Religions in the New World*. New York: Columbia University Press.

Stevens-Arroyo, Anthony M. 1988 *Case of the Jaguar: The Mythological World of the Tanis*. Albequerque: University of New Mexico Press.

Stevens-Arroyo, Anthony M. and Perez y Mena, Andres I., eds. 1995 *Enigmatic Powers: Syncretism with African and Indigenous Peoples' Religions among Latinos*. New York: Binder Center for Western Hemisphere Studies.

Stewart, Robert J. 1992 *Religion and Society in Post-Emancipation Jamaica*. Knoxville: University of Tennessee Press.

Taylor, John V. (1963). *The Primal Vision: Christian Presence Amid African Religion*. London: SCM Press.

Thompson, Vincent Bakpetu 1987 *The Making of the African Diaspora in the Americas, 1441–1900*. New York: Longman.

Thornton, John 1992 *Africa and Africans in the Making of the Atlantic World, 1400–1680*. New York: Cambridge University Press.

Tillich, Paul 1969 *What is Religion?* New York: Harper & Row.

Turner, Mary 1982 *Slaves and Missionaries: The Disintegration of Jamaican Slave Society*. Urbana: University of Illinois Press.

Vertovec, Steven 1992 *Hindu Trinidad: Religion, Ethnicity and Socio-Economic Change*. London: Macmillan.

Waddell, Hope Masterton 1863 *Twenty-Nine Years in the West Indies and Central Africa, 1829–1858*. London.

Walvin, James 1992 *Black Ivory: A history of British Slavery*. Washington, DC: Howard University Press.

Part I

ABROAD

INTRODUCTION
TO PART I

Kenneth Bilby

In 1953, when the anthropologist George Eaton Simpson carried out the first ethnographic study of the Rastafari movement in West Kingston, Jamaica, the world was a very different place.[1] Those peoples, cultures, and religions normally thought of as "Caribbean" were still more or less neatly contained within the Antillean archipelago and a few fringe areas of coastal South and Central America. Few outside of Jamaica had heard of the Rastafarians. Not long after Simpson left Jamaica, one of the Rasta brethren with whom he continued to correspond, a member of the United Afro-West Indian Federation, also left the island — not to repatriate to Africa, but to resettle in London.[2] This early transatlantic mission by a Rastafarian proselytizer was a sign of things to come. The immense wave of postwar West Indian migration that was just beginning would eventually remake not only the urban centers of Western Europe and North America, but the Caribbean countries themselves. Today, some four decades later, "home" and "abroad" represent two facets of a single Caribbean reality.

What has this displacement meant for the religions of those Caribbean peoples who now reside abroad? One thing that is certain is that in New York, Miami, Toronto, London, Paris, and Amsterdam, and in dozens of other cities on both sides of the ocean, spiritual traditions brought from the Caribbean are finding a new life. In these metropolitan crossroads, practitioners of transplanted Caribbean faiths are exposed to an array of spiritual alternatives of truly global proportions.

Never before have the possibilities for religious exchange and interpenetration been so great, and never before have such heavy demands been placed on the adaptability of Caribbean religion.

The contours of this spiritual terrain, this diaspora, remain largely uncharted. Only recently have ethnographic studies of religious life among Caribbean immigrants in Europe and the United States begun to appear.³ These studies have opened the way to more nuanced understandings of both the structural and experiential dimensions of Caribbean religion as practiced outside of the Caribbean. The chapters in Part I of this book represent a further step in this direction.

In the following chapters, we glimpse the working out of general questions of identity and faith common to the experience of most, if not all, devotees of Caribbean religions living abroad. When surrounded by new forms of difference, after all, received assumptions about the nature of the spiritual world — like those about society more generally — become problematic in new ways. As members of religious communities are inserted into new social and economic matrices, issues of identity, authenticity, and power arise or resurface in new guises, taking on new significance. Under such circumstances, religious contexts, like the social alignments, cultural values, and ethnic boundaries that are articulated within and through them, may become more fluid than ever, or conversely, they may harden in defensive reaction. Whichever of these eventualities results, the process of adaptation to a new social milieu is likely to entail a variety of challenges to religious ideology, with all this may imply for the individual psyche and the social body.

In her chapter on the problems of representation raised by the globalization of Rastafari, Carole Yawney provides some general indications of how this rapidly expanding African-Caribbean religious movement has had (and in the future may increasingly have) to contend with such challenges. To what extent, she asks, does Rastafari have "the capacity for developing a trans-cultural appeal beyond the confines of its local, Caribbean-based, specifically Jamaican, Afrocentric orientation, without fundamentally altering its basic premises"? Framing her question more specifically, she goes on to wonder how Jamaican-based root forms of Rastafari such as those embodied in Nyabinghi culture will "accommodate the many manifestations of Rastafari which have arisen locally" as the movement has spread.

The other chapters explore similar questions. In each of them, we encounter specific examples of transplanted Caribbean religions and their practitioners responding to new opportunities, challenges, and constraints. In the "multicultural arena" occupied by Surinamese immigrants in the Netherlands, described by Ineke van Wetering, Ndjuka and Saramaka Maroons who are unwilling to abandon their

African-derived traditional religions publicly contest the echoes of hegemonic Christianity that continue to influence the thinking of Creole adherents of the Afro-Surinamese Winti religion, thus bringing to the surface deep cultural contradictions stemming from the colonial past. In the encounters portrayed by van Wetering, these clashes between religious ideologies, transplanted to the Dutch context, are never resolved, and Maroon worshipers "have to be content with creating disturbances in the background."

Philip Scher's chapter on the famous West Indian Carnival of Brooklyn outlines the large-scale structural conditions that encourage the drawing of religious and ethnic lines between Caribbeans and other peoples in New York City. Focusing on the tragic "Crown Heights incident" of 1991, in which a car driven by a Hasidic Jew accidentally struck and killed the child of a Guyanese immigrant, he shows how the political-ideological machinery of the city of New York has led Caribbean peoples of diverse religious and cultural backgrounds to bridge their differences and develop a fragile, overarching "West Indian" identity — an identity that is defined in opposition to other essentialized identities, such as that of the Lubavitcher Hasidic community with whom West Indians compete for recognition and city resources. Brooklyn is also the setting for the religious encounters discussed by Wallace Zane, in which Vincentian Converted adherents are exposed to the related yet different practices of Trinidadian Spiritual Baptists, as well as those of various other faiths. The responses of the Converted to their new environment range from experimentation with "similar spirit-oriented religions from the Caribbean" to attempts by some congregations to "shield themselves from the challenges offered by contact with other religions by reducing the amount of visiting they do with other churches."

In the final chapter of Part I, John Homiak ponders the implications of the rapidly expanding Rasta "mediascape" for the boundaries of the "Rastafari Nation" as Rasta images, sounds, and themes continue to be disseminated across the world. Pointing out that new kinds of media representation have allowed the formerly marginalized Nyabinghi House (a traditionalist segment of Rastafari founded by some of the original elders) to increase its visibility within the larger movement, he anticipates a growing give-and-take between local and transnational versions of Rasta reality. The cultural and ideological exchanges spurred by this process of feedback, he suggests, "are likely to alter a number of traditional Rastafari attitudes on issues such as gender, death, and identity."

Carole Yawney, in her contribution to this volume, makes the important point that researchers engaging Rastafari in the future will need to be more sensitive to the ideological ramifications of their work. One might add that the messengers of Rastafari themselves, as they move into new territories and encounter new forms of difference, could perhaps benefit by attempting to do the same. Indeed, the long-term effectiveness of Rastafari as a vehicle of Pan-Africanist sentiment and a means of promoting solidarity in the face of shared oppression may depend on the flexibility of its proselytizers, and their ability to adjust their own convictions to those of the many millions in Africa and the diaspora who are likely, when challenged by imported Afrocentric ideologies, to stand firm in their devotion to the basic principles of the indigenous forms of worship passed down directly from their own ancestors.[4]

As we rapidly move toward the millennium, the world is clearly no longer what it was when Professor Simpson's Rastafarian interlocutors could propound their particular notions of African authenticity with little likelihood that these would ever be put to the test in other parts of the diaspora, not to mention on the African continent itself. Now that Rastafari, to an even greater extent than other Caribbean religions, is finding new life abroad, the challenges facing it will certainly grow, along with the opportunities. Given what we know of the adaptability of African-Caribbean religions, and their histories of resistance, resilience, and creativity, there is good reason to believe that not only Rastafari, but the various other Caribbean faiths that now flourish on foreign soil, will continue to rise to the challenges ahead.

Endnotes

1. For a recent and thoughtful look back at the circumstances of this pioneering fieldwork and the era in which it took place, see Simpson (1994).

2. George Eaton Simpson, personal communication, December 1993.

3. See, for example, Brandon (1983), Brown (1989), Brown (1991), Cashmore (1979), Derveld and Noordegraf (1988), Gregory (1986), Murphy (1988), Newall (1978), Palmié (1986, 1991), Venema (1992), van Wetering (1987)

4. In his study of the impact of Rastafari among the youth of Ghana and Senegambia, Neil Savishinsky (1993) indicates that when he discussed such questions with (non-Rasta) Africans who had substantial knowledge of the movement and its religious ideology, he found that the majority of them considered Rastafari — despite the fact that certain of its cultural components can be shown to derive genuinely from African sources — an "alien" and decidedly "Western" import; some Ghanaians even went so far as to describe Ghanaian Rastas as "anti-Ghanaian" or "anti-African" (p. 172). He also found that the appeal of Jamaican-style Rastafari theology (as opposed to the mere trappings of Rasta made popular through reggae) tended to be limited to those "alienated" individuals "seeking to escape from the narrow confines of ethnic or kin-based social relationships and establish wider, more inclusive networks of belonging and allegiance" (pp. 285–286). It is not surprising, thus, that those Rastas in West Africa who seriously attempt to abide by Jamaican-derived notions of Rasta "livity" — some of which conflict in fundamental ways with both traditional African religions and the syncreticistic spiritist churches that have drawn on them — are few in number, and tend to be concentrated in urban areas.

References

Brandon, G. 1983 *The Dead Sell Memories: An Anthropological Study of Santería in New York City*. Unpublished PhD dissertation, Rutgers University, New Brunswick, NJ.

Brown, D.H. 1989 *Garden in the Machine: Afro-Cuban Sacred Art and Performance in Urban New Jersey and New York*. Unpublished PhD dissertation, Yale University.

Brown, K.M. 1991 *Mama Lola: A Vodou Priestess in Brooklyn*. Berkeley: University of California Press.

Cashmore, E. 1979 *Rastaman: The Rastafarian Movement in England.* London: George Allen and Unwin.

Derveld, F.E.R., and Noordegraaf, H., eds. 1988 *Winti-Religie: Een Afro-Surinaamse Godsdienst in Nederland.* Amersfoort/Leuven: De Horstink.

Gregory, S. 1986 *Santería in New York City: A Study in Cultural Resistance.* Unpublished PhD dissertation, New School for Social Research, NY.

Murphy, J.M. 1988 *Santería: An African Religion in America.* Boston: Beacon Press.

Newall, V. 1978 Some examples of the practice of obeah by West Indian immigrants in London. *Folklore* 89(1):29–51.

Palmié, S. 1986 Afro-Cuban religion in exile: Santería in South Florida. *Journal of Caribbean Studies* 5(3):171–179.

Palmié, S. 1991 *Das Exil der Götter: Geschichte und Vorstellungswelt einer afrokubanischen Religion.* Frankfurt: Peter Lang.

Savishinsky, N.J. 1993 *Rastafari in the Promised Land: The Spread of a Jamaican Socio-Religious Movement and Its Music and Culture among the Youth of Ghana and Senegambia.* Unpublished PhD dissertation, Columbia University, NY.

Simpson, G.E. 1994 Some reflections on the Rastafari movement in Jamaica: West Kingston in the early 1950s. *Jamaica Journal* 25(2):3–10.

Venema, T. 1992 *Famiri nanga Kulturu: Creoolse Sociale Verhoudingen en Winti in Amsterdam.* Amsterdam: Het Spinhuis.

Wetering, W. van 1987 Quasi-kin groups, religion and social order among Surinam Creoles in the Netherlands. *Netherlands Journal of Sociology* 23(2):92–101.

3: WEST INDIAN AMERICAN DAY: BECOMING A TILE IN THE "GORGEOUS MOSAIC"

Philip W. Scher

> Identity — it's a psychic sense of place.... And it's a way of knowing that no matter where I put myself, that I am not necessarily what's around me. I am part of my surroundings and I become separate from them and it's being able to make those differentiations clearly that lets us have an identity.
>
> Ntozake Shange in *Fires in the Mirror*

> Ethnic identity and difference are socially produced in the here and now, not archaeologically salvaged from the disappearing past.
>
> M.P. Smith

On Labor Day, 1991, the motorcade of the Grand Rebbe Menachem Schneerson pulled out of the World Headquarters of the Lubavitcher Hasidic sect on Eastern Parkway in Brooklyn, New York. The car was mobbed by throngs of well-wishers and supporters eager to get a glimpse of the man thought by some Lubavitchers to be the Messiah himself. The Rebbe's car was led by an unmarked police vehicle as it attempted to make its way to a cemetery in Queens where the Rebbe's wife and father-in-law are buried. Suddenly the motorcade jerked to a halt. Towering over the cars, swaying lightly in the breeze, were the sun and the moon.

The sun and the moon, in this case, were two masqueraders from the West Indian American Day Parade, known more commonly as the "Brooklyn Carnival." The impasse was reported in the *New York Times*, a symbolic moment that capped a two week period of ethnic violence and tension between the West Indian and the Lubavitcher Hasidic communities in the Crown Heights section of Brooklyn.

This essay traces the events of this two week period in 1991, with special emphasis placed on the role of the Brooklyn Carnival. The Carnival has long been a showpiece of the West Indian American community in Brooklyn, as well as a point of tension between the Hasidic community (especially the Lubavitcher sect) and the Caribbean population. The leaders of the Hasidim had complained of difficulties in celebrating their holidays when the Carnival was being held. They had petitioned frequently for a change in the venue, a change of the dates and even the cancellation of the festival. The West Indians, the vast majority in the area, had frequently complained of the preferential treatment given to the Hasidim by the City of New York. Hasidic leaders were given police escorts, special parking was made available and, in general, many West Indian leaders claimed they had a greater influence on the City Council than their numbers merited. Yet for the greater part of the history of these two communities, there has been a general acceptance of and peace between neighbors. Disputes were often handled by local Community Boards, the Bureau of Ethnic Affairs or other bodies established by the city in conjunction with local leaders.

The events of late Summer 1991 provide a context within which to examine the relationship not only between these two communities, but between the "ethnic performance" of a transmigrant community and the structure of "identity politics" in New York. The very way in which the Carnival becomes positioned within the City's political-economic framework is in part determined by its reception as an "ethnic" event. To those in leadership positions within the Carnival's administration as well as members of the Caribbean cultural and political elite, the Carnival takes on a new significance as a political resource which is in part determined by the City's attitude towards such events.

Identity politics cannot be completely divorced from other kinds of political activity, of course, and this essay will highlight some of the ways the Carnival, which makes West Indian "culture" explicit and publicly available, serves as a kind of magnet for City politicians who are subsequently able to recognize the Caribbean community as a significant player in City politics. Former Mayor of New York David Dinkins described the City's multiple ethnic groups as forming a "gorgeous mosaic." The mosaic image is more than a colorful piece of speech-making. As a rhetorical device it speaks to the heart of a political philosophy that sees the City divided into marked and bounded cultural territories with which City administrators must negotiate, especially in regard to the allocation of resources.

The outcome of the Carnival of 1991 was of dire importance because it was something of a test case for the possibility of the West Indian community's political success. If the festival could come off without ethnic violence, then it could remain a positive symbol of West Indian solidarity and commitment to peace. If it disintegrated into disorder, it was feared that the festival would lose the political clout it had gained painstakingly over the years.

This was the primary concern of local Caribbean leaders, many of whom see the event as a legitimator of what they perceive as their "largely invisible community" (Yarrow 1991:B-1). For these leaders the Carnival plays an important role in their bid for a share in the City's ethnically based political and economic spoils as exemplified by such bodies as the Mayor's Ethnic Advisory Council responsible for community grants and other aid to communities.[1] In this sense, what is known in anthropology as a "resource competition" model of ethnicity is largely imposed upon the community through the contextualization of the festival vis-à-vis other groups and their relationships to City Hall.

Methodology

The Crown Heights disturbances took place in a community where I have been working for several years. The events of that late summer have been an important part of the Brooklyn Carnival ever since. In 1994, when a controversy arose concerning Rosh Hashanah, some of the ghosts of 1991 briefly appeared again. The strain on the Hasidic Jewish and West Indian communities has been great at times, as has the vigilance on the part of some community leaders to prevent further erosion in relations between these two groups. Most of the interviews I conducted on this topic were done well after the event and suggest that, while the memories linger, there is a great willingness to move on. I also spent a great deal of time looking at archival material such as newspaper accounts, editorials, letters, magazine articles, dramatic treatments and radio interviews. Because the subject matter was so intensely public, I found such materials vital to the ethnography and integral to it. In many cases issues of ethnicity and culture are extensively played out in public discourse, between groups, through comparison and the language of difference. In such cases I follow Arjun Appadurai's conception of culture as kind of boundary marker, or a set of distinct characteristics used to set off one group from another (1996:14–16). In that sense all public media which inform, are informed by and provide some incentive for strategies of cultural production and presentation are within the scope of the contemporary ethnography.

The Crown Heights Incident of 1991

On the evening of August 19, 1991, the motorcade of Menachem Schneerson was heading along Utica Avenue in Brooklyn on its way to the cemetery for his weekly visit to the grave of his wife and father-in-law.[2] Passing across President Street, the car rushing to bring up the rear of the motorcade allegedly went through the intersection late and was sideswiped. The car jumped a curb and killed Gavin Cato, the seven year old son of a Guyanese immigrant and injured Cato's seven year old cousin, Angela. A crowd of local African Americans and Caribbean Americans quickly surrounded the vehicles. Yosef Lifsh, the twenty-two-year-old driver of the car got out, he claimed, to help the children. He was immediately set upon, beaten and allegedly robbed. The police arrived and, a few minutes later, a private ambulance from a Hasidic company rushed into view. Officers hustled Lifsh into the Hasidic ambulance, as they later stressed, for his own protection and, as the van raced from the scene, a city ambulance came to care for the children. The crowd perceived this as yet another example of members of the Jewish community getting preferential treatment and they became angry, then violent. In addition to setting upon Lifsh, the crowd attacked the Hasidic ambulance drivers and the police. The accumulation of onlookers grew thicker as people emerged from a nearby B.B. King concert. Within a few hours there were reports of looting and general destruction of property. Members of the local media were assaulted as they tried to photograph the scenes of violence. Three hours after the accident a gang of approximately twenty black youths attacked Yankel Rosenbaum, an Australian student conducting research in New York, as he walked home, not far from the scene of the accident. Rosenbaum was not a Lubavitcher, but an ultra-Orthodox Jew. He was stabbed. Police rushed to his aid, and the gang of youths scattered. The authorities apprehended Lemerick Nelson, and, after finding a bloody knife and three bloodstained one dollar bills, they brought him to a local precinct where he allegedly confessed to the stabbing. He was later acquitted. Rosenbaum was taken to a hospital where two of his wounds were treated. A third wound went unnoticed, and he bled to death.

Over the next three days a storm of protest and devastation raged across Crown Heights. Crowds of protesters stood outside the Lubavitcher World headquarters and shouted anti-Semitic slogans such as "Hitler didn't do his job."[3] The violence would have seemed extreme if it were based solely on the accident that killed Gavin Cato. However, the long history of smoldering animosity between the two groups contributed greatly to the magnitude of the ensuing clash. Perhaps the greatest contribution to the tension between the groups was the West Indian belief that the City tended to be more responsive to the needs of the Jewish community than to their own. A report in *The New Yorker* magazine explained some of the West Indians' grievances towards Hasidic Jews (Logan 1991). Chief among these was the ongoing conflict that had arisen as a result of the desire of Lubavitchers to live as close to the Rebbe as possible. Lubavitchers often tried to secure homes for their families by pressuring their black Caribbean neighbors to sell their property to other Lubavitchers. The Hasidim also had a reputation for being insular, even to other Jews, and they continue, presently, to operate their own private, heavily armed security forces.

Jews and West Indians in Crown Heights

The Lubavitcher sect of the Orthodox Jews, founded in the mid-eighteenth century, moved almost en masse to Crown Heights from Poland in 1940. At the time the neighborhood was largely Eastern European Jewish and Italian. The massive migration of West Indian blacks began in the early 1950s, and increased steadily through the 1960s. "White flight" to the suburbs, with the exception of the Hasidim, marked the 1970s in Brooklyn. Within a relatively short span of time,

Crown Heights and the adjacent Flatbush and East Flatbush sections of Brooklyn became largely black West Indian enclaves. West Indians, who, in the earliest migrations had settled in traditionally African American neighborhoods such as Harlem, now avoided such areas. There may be several reasons for this, including an aversion to what was perceived as ghetto living and, as Kasinitz has pointed out, architecture (1992:57–58). The new West Indian immigrant populations preferred areas that offered small family homes for purchase rather than rentals from unscrupulous landlords. The purchase of homes by West Indians was often what ensured the capital base to provide for their children and the accumulation of more capital (Kasinitz 1992:58).

As the core Caribbean population has grown in Brooklyn, so have the external manifestations of this new "ethnic" presence. Now comprising approximately 300,000 people in this area alone, the main market strips along Flatbush Avenue, Utica Avenue and other streets have developed a strong Caribbean quality. Roti (a West Indian curry wrapped in a split pea flour pancake) shops, Caribbean music shops, travel agencies run by and for West Indians and markets with West Indian goods are now common sights. The center-piece of this strong cultural presence in Brooklyn is the West Indian American Day Parade. Begun as an indoor ball for Trinidadians in Harlem in the 1920s, the celebration grew and, in 1947, became a parade up Manhattan's Seventh Avenue. In the middle 1960s, Trinidadian costume maker Rufus Gorin brought the event to the flourishing West Indian communities in Brooklyn, where it exists today. Presently, the parade runs along the Eastern Parkway and attracts nearly two million spectators and participants. According to a study sponsored by the Caribbean American Media Studies Inc., the event brings close to forty million dollars to the city in taxable revenue (Forde 1990:1).[4] Many thousands of visitors come from the West Indies, the United Kingdom, Canada and other parts of the United States to see the event and visit with friends and relatives. In 1989 approximately 11,000 people came from the West Indies alone (Forde 1990:3). More than twice that amount came from New Jersey. Many of these travelers who come to see and participate in the Carnival are of West Indian origin. In short, Labor Day in Brooklyn has become "diaspora central" for many West Indians and a convenient way for families and friends separated by great distances to come together. This enormous flowering of the West Indian community surrounds the Lubavitchers almost entirely.

The Carnival

Although the event is called a parade, it is based on the Carnival in Trinidad and Tobago. The general organization of the event consists of a procession of "bands" which are not musical, but groups of masqueraders portraying or "playing" a "theme." The bands are generally subdivided into sections, with each section playing some aspect of the band's theme. The bands in New York are led by individuals or committees who are responsible for hiring costume designers, organizing the construction of the costumes, engaging the services of musical groups and/or DJs to accompany the masqueraders, throwing "fetes" and generally ensuring a good time to the participants. The participants themselves pay a general fee which provides a costume, a place in the Parade of the Bands and often includes some extras such as beverages on the road and breakfast on the morning of the Carnival.

The celebration is different from other ethnic parades in the City such as the Puerto Rican Parade or the St. Patrick's Day Parade in that it is not a festival highlighting a distinct, national-cultural group. If it were, it would be the Trinidadian Day Parade. It is, rather, the combination of many different West Indian groups some of whom share some kind of festival or Carnival traditions with the relatively smaller numbers of Trinidadians. Thus, the parade includes participation by Jamaicans, Guyanese, Grenadans, Barbadians and other West Indian groups such as Vincentians and St. Lucians. In recent years people from the French Antilles have begun to participate in greater numbers, and in 1995 I noticed a Belizean presence. The multinational make-up of the event is further complemented by the addition of African Americans, some of whom see this as a pan-African celebration and participate in that spirit.

The Carnival is unlike an ethnic parade in structural ways as well. The Carnival in Brooklyn has tried to capture the spirit of its Trinidadian parent by emphasizing a certain lack of order. This has been difficult to achieve in the New York setting because a fundamental city- or nationwide collective understanding of the Carnival tradition does not exist. In Trinidad, even if one does not choose to participate, one must acknowledge the presence of Carnival and the preeminence of Carnival on the days of its celebration. As the saying goes "The road made to walk on Carnival day." In New York, as a Trinidadian journalist put it, on the next street it's "business as usual" (T. Joseph, Personal Interview 1994). Most of the city, up until recently, had no idea of, or no interest in, the Carnival. And even today, with interest growing, many of those present at the festival in Brooklyn are purely spectators. In Trinidad, except for certain judging and spectating venues, most of the people on the street are participants in the Carnival in some way or another. In Port-of-Spain, Trinidad's capital, there is no clearly set route for any of the bands to follow. Although they must pass in front of three judging venues, they need not proceed to them in any particular order. Carnival bands tend to take over the city, and all else effectively stops. Oddly enough, in Port-of-Spain very few streets are officially closed or cordoned off, though there are parking restrictions and certain streets have special traffic laws for the days of Carnival. There exists a general understanding that during Carnival driving would be a folly. In New York, conversely, there is a set route along the Eastern Parkway from Utica Avenue to Grand Army plaza, although in some neighborhoods bands will roam about relatively freely.

Reconstructing Carnival in Brooklyn

The parade-like route of the Carnival is one restriction that Brooklyn West Indians have had to work with. The leaders of the West Indian American Day Carnival Association (WIADCA) have always stressed their desire to try to avoid a parade feeling to which such structured routes contribute. They have tried to approximate not just the Parade of the Bands, as it is called in Trinidad, but the whole complex of Carnival activities that make up the four main days of Carnival. Towards this end they have re-assembled and transplanted the various parts of the Trinidad Carnival in New York. There is a Panorama Steelband competition, a Dimanche Gras competition (in which the elaborate Kings and Queens of Carnival vie for prizes) and a Calypso

Monarch competition. Perhaps the most impressive element in the Brooklyn Carnival is the J'Ouvert (pronounced *joo-vay*).

J'Ouvert is the opening of Carnival during which masqueraders come out into the streets early in the morning dressed in costumes of their own devising or smeared with mud or oil. It is the most abandoned and purely ecstatic part of the Carnival in Trinidad, and it has managed to flourish and grow in Brooklyn with the general cooperation of the police and the city.

The many facets of the Carnival mean that it is not merely a parade or an ethnic showcase. Much of what happens is not directed outward, but inward, toward the community — serving the community directly. The Carnival spans most of Labor Day weekend, culminating on Labor Day itself. The day of the Parade of the Bands is obviously the most visible feature of the Carnival, and it is here that the event comes closest to being an ethnic parade.

Within the West Indian community the participation in and enthusiasm for the event are enormous and wide-ranging, cutting across national boundaries and class divisions. It is cited by many as the "centerpiece" of West Indian identity in New York City. It is the one major occasion during which Caribbean peoples, primarily Anglophonic but also including Haitians, Martiniqueans and others, make known their significant presence in the city. The unique position of the Carnival as a forum for the presentation of ethnicity, along with the growing size of the Caribbean community, has ensured that the Carnival will become the focus of intense political activity. Of the many different types of political activity that surround the Carnival the most salient in this essay is the role of the festival in the complex arena of identity politics.

The Carnival has not always been a high-profile political event. For many, especially in the Carnival artists' community, its political aspect is either ignored or resented. Certainly the Carnival was not devised as a political project in this way. Caribbean-style balls and mini-Carnivals have been held in New York at least since the twenties. Many older West Indians with whom I spoke remember these gatherings as a way for homesick West Indians to feel a bit of home, meet other expatriates and emigrants and solidify existing social relations. Very little reference is made, with regard to the early Carnivals, to the performance of "culture" for a wider or official audience. The political nature of the original Carnival balls was more directed to forming

networks within the community, establishing links with religious
organizations and pooling resources.[5] The emergence onto the street,
first in Harlem and later in Brooklyn, was the first step toward a more
public and self-conscious display of ethnicity. After the parade was
taken over and expanded by the current president of the West Indian
American Day Carnival Association, Carlos Lezama, the festival grew
in size as did the West Indian community itself. By the middle of the
1980s both the Carnival and the community were attracting serious
attention from City politicians. The West Indian vote could no longer
be ignored, and the event and the community were established as
permanent fixtures in the City's ethnic array.[6]

Resource Competition and Ethnicity: Some Background

The literature on ethnicity in anthropology was for some time dominated by the resource competition model (Williams 1989). This position holds, at one level, that a kind of political ethnicity results when
disempowered groups create informal, culturally based associations
in order to participate to greater effect in the political-economic process of the larger political unit (especially the nation-state). Brackette
Williams notes that resource competition theorists failed to take into
account the larger ideological foundations upon which the nation-
state is based, and therefore missed important elements which would
determine the structure of "ethnic" associations. Williams also points
out that resource-competition models fail to address the presence of
non-ethnic resource competition groups. She indicates that resource
competition models do not "address the knotty question of how
individuals or even immigrant cultural groups identify and rank their
interests" (1989:409). I would add that such models do not seem
concerned about the types of interests such groups might identify. In
other words, resource competition does not fully explain "ethnicity"
if it foregrounds economic interests over cultural ones. It does not
always demonstrate the relationship between economic necessity and
the social construction of a cultural group. For example, does the
charge that Hasidim in Crown Heights get special treatment on Holy
Days speak to their successes with economic or cultural benefits? It
seems clear that the two are intertwined, yet not always in mutually
productive or supportive relationships. The persistence of some cul-

tural forms, no matter how much they contribute to a sense of group solidarity, may result in negative attention from those who control access to services. Thus, for it to be true that the presentation of a distinct ethnic identity tends to yield greater access to goods and services within New York City, then the presentation of ethnicity must operate at both cultural and economic levels simultaneously and within acceptable boundaries.

Culture and Ethnicity in West Indian Brooklyn

It is largely the perception of the West Indian community (as expressed through its cultural and political leaders as well as through its editorial pages)[7] that a West Indian identity responsibly presented through the Carnival will lead to a much more advantageous position for West Indians within the City's ethno-political universe. An editorial comment in a widely read Caribbean travel magazine stated: "The single thing that unites West Indians in this country [the United States] is our Carnivals. Our leaders must now use the leverage provided by these circumstances to build and consolidate our political muscle and agenda. No more nice guys" (Francois and Hall 1995:95). In a thinly veiled reference to the Hasidim the editorial continues "Our lesson can be well learned from the very people who annually threaten this event. Politics and only politics is the means by which 4% can dictate to 96%" (Francois and Hall 1995:95).

The imploring quality of this editorial is echoed by other publications. Carlos Lezama, president of WIADCA, has written that a sense of community is "critical to us in maintaining our existence within the wider sphere of other ethnic groups" (cited in Kasinitz 1992:149). A major factor in the under-representation of West Indians in New York City politics has been the lack of voters registered from West Indian backgrounds. Although Una Clarke, a city council member originally from Jamaica, states that one-third of all recently naturalized citizens in New York are of Caribbean origin and that an even greater number of Caribbean Americans are participating in the electoral process, the nature of the Caribbean American community may still be called transnational in a very specific sense. From 1965 to 1975 the Caribbean population in New York doubled. Although the size of the population increased, the concerns of the immigrants tended to stay focused on their home countries. Frequent trips home, remittances and retirement to the Caribbean were all indicative of the fact that many immigrants were not interested in investing both mentally and physically (if not financially) in their adopted country.

The events surrounding the Crown Heights unrest of 1991 brought into relief many of the issues outlined above for local Caribbean leaders and activists. The highly organized and seemingly coherent Lubavitcher community stood in contrast to what was negatively characterized as the loosely organized, under-represented and politically apathetic West Indian community. The culturally uniform Lubavitchers could rally around their undisputed leader, the Grand Rebbe Schneerson, while the West Indian community was fractured along national lines.

Let us return to the previous question of how to understand the limitations of the resource competition model of ethnicity in a situation that seems to support such a model. The benefits bestowed upon ethnic groups in New York are largely dependent upon the ability of the collectivity to prove its status as a "group." The government of New York City, like much of the rest of the country, has responded to pressure to maintain and preserve ethnic heritages by implementing state and federal programs. Bilingual education, access to city services and influence in city decision making are examples of "rewards" available to the visible ethnic groups. There is no better way to become "visible" than through conspicuous displays of culture. The manipulation of overt cultural features produces the signposts of a viable ethnicity. What emerges is a situation in which ethnic groups petition, in one way or another, for recognition by the City that they are sufficiently ethnic to be considered legitimate. The result is that recognition becomes a City service in itself. Culture/ethnicity becomes something that the City has the power to bestow. In this sense there seem to be a number of "culture-criteria" to which groups must in some way conform. I am not making the argument that the fulfillment of these criteria in the public sector necessarily reflects on actual practice. Often practice is ignored or downplayed when it runs contrary to the kinds of official culture promoted by a group's own spokespeople. Innovation, assimilation and the creative manipulation of cultural forms in the immigrant setting is often frowned upon by representatives of the ethnic group because it creates the illusion of there being no culture there at all. Yet it is exactly such manipulation that keeps the cultural form alive and relevant to the majority of practitioners.[8] Thus changes made to the Carnival are always contested for many different reasons.

Williams stresses that one ignores the larger ideological underpinnings of the state (or in this case the City) at one's peril. In the case of New York, the power structure rewards cultural presence in digestible forms such as ethnic parades. The importance of Carnival to the West Indian community becomes its ability to impart ethnicity to West Indians. The West Indian leadership's public comments on the Carnival begin to revolve around the festival's power to confer political clout on the group. Although other factors are present in many individual West Indian's description of the event's value, public rhetoric is shaped by the ideological constraints of the larger polity. It is ultimately the City that is imposing a resource competition model upon the "gorgeous mosaic" of New York. The successful accomplishment of this awarded ethnicity status requires the active compliance of leaders within the West Indian community.

The importance, then, of the West Indian Carnival's survival is clear. Although the Carnival is not easily pressed into the service of political agendas, it remains a visible expressive act by a large group of West Indians and therefore is the perfect location for the superimposition of identity rhetoric. It is possible to suggest at this point that Carnival is not really the font of West Indian identity in New York, but rather that West Indian identity is required of, and laid over the festival. This too, however, would be overly deterministic. The idea of the Carnival as a source of Caribbean identity and as an expression of Caribbean culture ultimately shapes the way in which the Carnival is organized and the manner by which it is entered into by participants. The rhetoric does not merely hover over the event. To the degree that it has influence over individuals, it helps shape the event as well.

It is also clear that the Carnival's survival after the Crown Heights disturbances began to rest heavily on its ability to "patch things up." The great unifying potential of the Carnival was finally put to the test. Two weeks after Crown Heights, leaders of the Lubavitcher community were asked to march as guests of the West Indian American Day Carnival Association as a sign of goodwill. The Carnival went off peacefully. In the wake of the event, efforts were promoted by both sides to contribute to greater cultural understanding between the two groups. In 1994, the Carnival fell on Rosh Hashanah. As part of the on-going efforts by both groups to avoid conflicts, various meetings and symposia were organized.[9]

Also in 1994 a Korean cultural group was asked to join the parade in the wake of conflicts between West Indians and Korean grocers. The case of the Jews, the Koreans and even the African American community within the Carnival illustrates the precarious position that the festival plays in relation to West Indian identity production/reproduction and the resolution of local ethnic conflict. Carnival is a Trinidadian-become-West Indian affair and thus serves as a way of bringing together different members of the West Indian community. It provides an "authentic" cultural event, an ethnic display event. Yet the Carnival is also meant, according to Carlos Lezama, as a way to build bridges to other communities — most importantly to African Americans, but also to Jews and Koreans.[10] Other active members of the West Indian community have noted the economic benefits the Carnival has for the City. But as stated above, for most of these benefits to emerge from the event it has to be a West Indian affair. Most of the money spent by spectators — be they tourists or city dwellers, West Indian or not — is to experience not just a parade or a festival, but a **West Indian festival**.

The resource competition model which dominates the raison d'être of the Carnival for some of its organizers and some Caribbean leaders carries with it the burdensome quality of requiring cultural "purity." The event must continue to be "we thing," as many Trinidadians say, while at the same time not provoking animosity from other groups. It is difficult terrain to negotiate because actions of ethnic groups are often perceived to be exclusive and can have divisive repercussions, while, at the same time, fluid cultural boundaries can give the appearance of an intangible or weak cultural presence. The "gorgeous mosaic" ideology of Mayor Dinkins' administration appears to be, albeit inadvertently, a catalyst to strict sectarianism among the City's ethnic groups even as it stresses multiculturalism.

Of interest here is the relationship between a notion of identity as a means to an economic and political end and Mayor Dinkins' provocative metaphor of the "gorgeous mosaic." The Mayor here is clearly avoiding the problematic metaphors of the past to describe the co-existence of many cultural groups together under one administrative unit. The "melting pot," "salad" and "stew" metaphors all have come under fire for their various descriptive shortcomings. The mosaic has the advantage, presumably, of emphasizing the importance and beauty of cultural difference as each culture adds to an overall, unified "picture" that, upon "stepping back," is fully revealed. The mosaic metaphor implies the presence of neatly defined "tiles" placed cheek by jowl in the service of a grander order that no one tile may realize alone. The interesting aspect of this metaphor, as opposed to the others I have mentioned above, is its unique emphasis on spatiality and what is more, its reification of those spaces. In the mosaic tiles have special places reserved for them, they are in positions firm and fixed. It is the perfect metaphor for the kinds of essentialized identities required by an administrative bureaucracy such as New York City's which allots goods and services on the basis of ethnic identity.

Stasis and Identity Politics

The current literature exploring space and identity is growing with great rapidity (for instance see Keith and Pile 1993, Lash and Friedman 1992). Massey (1993) has contended that prevailing implicit or explicit dichotomies of space and time are inadequate. She claims that temporal metaphors and temporality in general have been given precedence over spatial metaphors and spatiality. Furthermore time has been defined at the expense of space, as presence to space's absence. Space has been generally conceived of as stasis and temporality as progress, as open, as the true location for the possibility of an emancipatory politics.

In New York, the mosaic metaphor resonates with the idea of space as stasis. Social identities that are constituted within such a framework of static principles ultimately yield governable polities. The metaphor seems to elicit comfort in the same way that city planning does in other ways. The comfort of the grid, of numbers intersecting, of places conforming to a predictable pattern is constantly threatened by the pirating of public or private spaces by the unruly minions of disorder. The ethnic group, moving into a space and transforming that space into a usable living space, into a place, potentially undermines the authority of the metropole at large. The mosaic gives the impression that all is in order, static, easy to locate. What constantly belies this image is the relationship of the "tiles" in the system. If the system is meant to impart "presence" and define identity in relation to others (that are not it), then such a system depends upon a notion of reified ethnic identities that persist through time and fundamentally cannot change lest they risk becoming meaningless. The mosaic requires tiles that not only sit in their assigned places, but that do not change "color." That is, the "tiles" do not change what is perceived to be their fundamental character, their essence.

But the "tiles" do change. The West Indian community is not marked by "cultural" attributes over which it has no power. It is made up of individuals who must have an active relationship to their locale through daily practices and negotiations. The "culture" that results from this is larger in scope than the limited definition offered at the beginning of this essay. This sort of Caribbean culture exists in New York because people make it so. But the actions of these many thousands of individuals — whether it be in Carnival or kinship relations — are not necessarily the same as what various interested parties claim those actions represent. Anthropologists may be sensitive to praxis and the performance of culture, but the City of New York, the various culture brokers and the leaders of the Caribbean population cannot found a relationship on the uncertainties inherent in praxis oriented approaches to culture. Such approaches de-essentialize culture, thereby making the mosaic fuzzy.

In many ways the Carnival's peacemaking role lends legitimacy to Caribbean leadership. It signals the presence of a responsible, coherent West Indian community. It indicates that West Indian identity exists, and that it is not a threat to the social order — essential qualities in becoming a tile. But there exists a tension in the constant shifts and changes that occur every year in the way the Carnival is actually undertaken.[11]

Conclusion

The West Indian American Day Parade presents some unique insights into the role of ethnic cultural display events. They must be made to walk a fine line *between forum for identity display* and *active event within the adopted community*. The presence of these events in the actual day to day life of the community-at-large means that they change in relation to new circumstances that confront them. It is this quality that threatens the required "authenticity" and exclusivity upon which solid "ethnicities" may be built. The future of research into Caribbean cultural change in diaspora must take into account the different pressures that cultural forms negotiate as a clue to the processes of change the forms themselves undergo. These changes radically reflect the conditions of power within which the transmigrants themselves must exist. For social scientists interested in these matters, the case of the Carnival in Brooklyn highlights the way primordial notions of ethnicity such as those utilized in the resource competition model and echoed in official policies of multiculturalism, can make an impact upon the cultural forms being studied even as they become part of the political environment of the City.

Endnotes

This essay began as a paper presented as part of a panel on Caribbean religion at the 1995 American Anthropological Association meetings in Washington, DC. Funding for this project was provided by a grant from the Wenner-Gren Foundation for Anthropological research. I would like to thank John Pulis for organizing this panel as well as Garth Green and Dallas Brennan for reading and commenting on earlier drafts. I would also like to thank the other panel members as well as discussants Richard Price and John Szwed.

1. Basch (1987:183) gives some idea here of the entrenched philosophy of ethnicity-based political policy in New York. As she states "[T]he ethnic structuring of New York City ... focuses attention on ethnicity and encourages groups to organize around, and thus reproduce, their ethnicity." NB: The Mayor's Ethnic Advisory Council was dissolved after the Dinkins administration. In Brooklyn, the Bureau of Ethnic Affairs, a branch of the Borough President's office, continues to handle such disputes as it has for eleven years.

2. The following account was pieced together from a number of newspaper accounts, editorials and academic articles that purported to describe the event. Their accuracy cannot, of course, be fully guaranteed.

3. It is not clear what percentage of protesters were West Indian, of West Indian descent, or native African Americans.

4. These numbers should be received with healthy skepticism, as there has been no serious study conducted to determine the actual revenue generated by the Carnival and such a study would be extremely complicated to implement.

5. See Irma Watkins-Owens (1996:60–61) on the role of the Church and other benevolent organizations in the West Indian community in Harlem.

6. It is not within the scope of this essay to detail the growth and changes in the political character of the Caribbean community in New York. See Kasinitz's excellent study (1992) for a detailed overview of these issues. It is worth noting, however, that Caribbean Americans have often acted like "traditional" immigrant groups and members of a "racial" minority during the course of their history in the United States.

7. I am referring here to public statements expressed by local leaders and editorialists in some of the leading Caribbean publications in New York. See, for example Sleeper (1988) for an overview.

8. It is not only the "people on the street" who manipulate the forms or practices of elements within the Carnival. Officials responsible for the presentation of the festival, despite some protests to the contrary, have actively changed the Carnival for their own purposes over the years. See Kasinitz (1992) for New York and Cohen (1993) for examples from London's Notting Hill Carnival.

9. One such symposium at Medgar Evers College featured guest speaker Rabbi Yisrael Francis, described as an "African-Caribbean-American-Hasidic Jew."

10. The case of the Koreans is problematic because it has resulted in the inclusion of another ethnic group within the Carnival, which, if even only minutely, begins to dilute the festival as a Caribbean event.

11. The scope of this essay does not allow for details regarding the erosion of the static cultural form described here, but see Scher (1997).

References

Appadurai, Arjun 1996 *Modernity at Large: Cultural Dimensions of Globalization*. Minneapolis: University of Minnesota Press.

Basch, Linda 1987 The Vincentians and Grenadians: The role of voluntary associations in immigrant adaptation to New York City. In: *New Immigrants in New York* (ed., Nancy Foner). New York: Columbia University Press.

Beck, Melinda, Shenitz, Bruce and Mabry, Marcus 1991 Bonfire in Crown Heights. *Newsweek*, September 9, 1991 118(11):48.

Blauner, Peter 1986 Islands in the city. *New York Magazine*, April 21, 1986 19:66–73.

Chaney, Elsa M. 1987 The context of caribbean migration. In: *Caribbean Life in New York City* (eds., Constance Sutton and Elsa Chaney). New York: Center for Migration Studies.

Cohen, Abner 1993 *Masquerade Politics*. Berkeley: University of California Press.

De Leon, Sherrie Ann 1996 West Indians make mas' in Brooklyn. *The Independent*, September 13, 1996.

Doyle-Marshall, William 1983 Bitter taste in Brooklyn. *Trinidad Guardian*, October 18, 1983.

Doyle-Marshall, William 1985 New challenge for Brooklyn carnival. *Trinidad Guardian*, July 24, 1985.

Evanier, David 1991 The lynching of Yankel Rosenbaum. *The New Republic*, October 14, 1991 205(16):21–26.

Foner, Nancy 1987a *New Immigrants in New York City: Race and Ethnicity Among Migrants in New York City*. New York: Columbia University Press.

Foner, Nancy 1987b West Indians in New York City and London: a comparative analysis. In: *Caribbean Life in New York City* (eds., Constance Sutton and Elsa Chaney). New York: Center for Migration Studies.

Forde, Donny 1990 *Report to Caribbean American Media Studies, Inc.* (unpublished).

Francois, David and Hall, Carlisle 1995 Carnival as politics. In: *So Yu Going To ... Carnival*, Vol. 6, pp. 19–21.

Goldberg, David Theo 1994 *Multiculturalism: A Critical Reader*. Oxford: Basil Blackwell.

Gonzalez, David 1991 Hasidim say they'll join parade line: good will gesture in Crown Heights. *The New York Times*, September 2, 1991.

Gourevitch, Philip 1993 The Crown Heights riot and its aftermath. *Commentary*, January 1993 95(1):29–34.

Gutmann, Amy 1994 *Multiculturalism*. Princeton: Princeton University Press.

Hall, Herman 1982 Inside Brooklyn's carnival. *Everybody's Magazine* 6:12–22.

Hill, Donald R. 1981 New York's Caribbean carnival. *Everybody's Magazine* 5:33–37.

Hill, Donald R. 1994 A History of West Indian Carnival in New York City to 1978. *New York Folklore* 20(1–2):47–66.

Hill, Donald R. and Abramson, Robert 1979 West Indian carnival in Brooklyn. *Natural History*, August–September 1979, pp. 73–85.

Jackson, P. 1988 Street life: the politics of carnival. *Environment and Planning D: Society and Space* 6:213–227.

Joseph, Terry. Interview on September 19, 1994.

Kadetsky, Elizabeth 1992 Racial politics in New York. *The Nation*, November 30, 1992 255(18):656–658.

Kasinitz, Philip 1992 *Caribbean New York*. Ithaca: Cornell University Press.

Keith, Michael and Pile, Steve 1993 *Place and the Politics of Identity*. London: Routledge.

Kifner, John 1991 Blacks march by Hasidim through a corridor of blue. *The New York Times*, August 25, 1991.

Kifner, John 1991 In Brooklyn, steel drums and a truce. *The New York Times*, September 3, 1991.

Klein, Joe 1991 Deadly metaphors. *New York Magazine*, September 9, 1991 24(35):26–29.

Lash, Scott and Friedman, Jonathan 1992 *Modernity and Identity*. Oxford: Basil Blackwell.

Logan, Andy 1991 Syzygy. *The New Yorker*, September 23, 1991 67(31):102–107.

Massey, Doreen 1993 Politics and space/time. In: *Place and the Politics of Identity* (eds., Michael Keith and Steve Pile). London: Routledge.

Moses, Knolly 1985 Brooklyn mas' still marked by petty feuding, disorganization. *Trinidad Guardian*, August 25, 1985.

Palmer, Ransford W. 1995 *Pilgrims from the Sun: West Indian Migration to America*. New York: Twayne Publishers.

Pryce, Everton A. 1985 The Notting Hill gate carnival — black politics, resistance and leadership 1976–1978. *Caribbean Quarterly* 31(2):35–52.

Purdy, Matthew 1994 Parade shows off West Indian political clout. *The New York Times*, September 9, 1994.

Reyes, Elma 1985 Carnival in Brooklyn: a chip off TT mas'. *Trinidad Express Newspaper*, September 13, 1985.

Scher, Philip W. 1997 *A Moveable Fete: Trinidad Carnival as Transnational Cultural Process*. Unpublished dissertation. University of Pennsylvania.

Sleeper, Jim 1988 Playing the ethnic card in New York City. In: *American Visions* 3:6–10.

Smith, Anna Deavere 1993 *Fires in the Mirror*. New York: Anchor Books/Doubleday.

Smith, Michael Peter 1992 Postmodernism, urban ethnography and the new social space of ethnic identity. *Theory and Society* 21:493–531.

Stafford, Susan Buchanan 1987 The Haitians: the cultural meaning of race and ethnicity. In: *New Immigrants in New York City* (ed., Nancy Foner). New York: Columbia University Press.

Stinner, William F., de Albuquerque, Klaus and Bryce-Laporte, Roy S. 1982 *Return Migration and Remittances: Developing a Caribbean Perspective*. Washington: Smithsonian Institution Press.

Sutton, Constance and Chaney, Elsa 1992 *Caribbean Immigrants in New York*. New York: Center for Migration Studies.

Sutton, Constance R. and Chaney, Elsa M. 1994 *Caribbean Life in New York City: Sociocultural Dimensions*. New York: Center for Migration Studies.

Sutton, Constance R. and Makiesky-Barrow, Susan 1987 Migration and West Indian racial and ethnic consciousness. In: *Caribbean Life in New York City* (eds., Constance Sutton and Elsa Chaney). New York: Center for Migration Studies.

Taylor, John 1992 The politics of grievance. *New York Magazine*, December 7, 1992 25(48):18.

Toney, Joyce Roberta 1986 *The Development of a Culture of Migration Among a Caribbean People: St. Vincent and New York*. PhD dissertation. Teachers College, Columbia University.

van Capelleveen, Remco 1988 "Peripheral" culture in the metropolis: West Indians in New York City. In: *Alternative Cultures in the Caribbean* (eds., T. Bremer and U. Fleischmann). Berlin: Bibliotecha Ibero-Americana, Vervuert Verlag, pp. 131–147.

Watkins-Owens, Irma 1996 *Blood Relations*. Bloomington: Indiana University Press.

Williams, Brackette 1989 A class act: anthropology and the race to nation across ethnic terrain. *Annaul Review of Anthropology* 18:401–444.

Yarrow Andrew L. 1991 Brooklyn prepares and braces, for a parade. *The New York Times*, August 30, 1991.

No Author: Newspapers and Magazines

Everybody's Caribbean Magazine 1994 Problems between Hasidim and community over the 1994 Caribbean carnival. *Everybody's Caribbean Magazine* 18:27–31.

Everybody's Magazine 1990 New York's Caribbean carnival 1990. *Everybody's Magazine* 14:4–14.

New York Times 1991 In Crown Heights, simmering tensions and a fragile peace. *The New York Times*, August 23, 1991.

4: CULTURAL ENCOUNTERS IN THE DIASPORA: SURINAME CREOLE RELIGION IN THE NETHERLANDS

Ineke van Wetering

This chapter explores a clash between representatives of two ethnic groups within one "minority" group: African-American migrants from Suriname in the Netherlands. At the manifest level, it is a discourse about religious tolerance in a multicultural society. Latently, ethnic politics are involved. African American culture is reproduced both by Creoles, descendants of one-time plantation slaves who were emancipated in 1863, and Bush Negroes or Maroons, whose ancestors fled these plantations since the end of the 17th century to build viable societies in the interior. These sub-groups share large domains of the African heritage, but have evolved different social systems over time.

Public disputes between adherents of African Surinamese cultures have been rare in the past. The groups have led separate lives for a long time; cultural negotiations were mostly handled individually, in disparate contexts and through variegated channels. During the last decades, however, frictions between Creoles and Maroons surfaced, both in the home country and in the diaspora. Paradoxically, state funding of cultural manifestations in the Netherlands is the catalyst for an open confrontation. To obtain a share of the spoils ethnic mobilization becomes imperative, and to be really effective the active cooperation of Creoles and Maroons is required. In order to qualify for subsidies, the cultural heritage should be cast as "culture," not "religion." Yet, culture and religion overlap considerably, which implies that a cultural program should have a theological foundation. It is here that problems surface, as a standardization of religious notions is hard to reach, as we will see.

Vagueness of key concepts in culture, and mystification as a means to create unity have been noticed as significant features in other "black" or Creole communities. Ulf Hannerz (1973) and Abner Cohen (1981) for instance have drawn attention to the ambiguousness of the cultural concepts endorsed by the groups they studied, "blacks" in the United States and the Creoles of Sierra Leone, respectively. They regard this as pivotal for a sociocultural analysis, and have based their argument on culture's very elusiveness. This approach seems worth following in the case of Suriname's cultural politics.

Transatlantic Migrants and Their Background

In the 1970s, upon Suriname's impending political independence, many of its citizens had fled the new state and opted for Dutch nationality.[2] In fact, about half of the population crossed the Atlantic to settle in the Netherlands. No severing of ties with the home country was intended, and indeed considerable efforts are made to keep relations intact, particularly with kin.

Among these migrants, a substantial number is directly or indirectly conversant with "traditional" culture, which is based on the African heritage. Most are urban-based Creoles, a minority was born in the hinterland. *Winti* is the most used term to refer to the Creole variety of folk culture; it is named after the invading spirits or "winds" that play a large part in belief and cult.[2] For an older generation, *Winti* is also the term used in the Netherlands to refer to the whole of the cultural heritage. To the young and modern, who are in search of their "roots," the term's connotation of backwardness is unpalatable; they will speak of "our culture" (*Wi kulturu*).

Segments of both the Creole and Maroon groups are actively engaged in the reproduction of what they regard as basic in their cultures. The groups' respective historical experiences have shaped and marked the way these sectors of the "black" population reproduce their worldview. After emancipation in 1863, the Creoles gradually managed to obtain strategic positions under Dutch colonial rule. Well before independence in 1975, the Creole group had become established as the politically dominant one. In close and direct contact with a governing elite and with the outside world, they regard themselves as successors of the colonial rulers, entitled to a leading cultural role. They claim hegemonic power over "the culture," and regard the hinterland as their backyard. Well-educated and prepared for public action in a modern western world, Creoles mostly act as spokesmen for the African-American segment, in the home country and abroad.

Creoles are Christians, whereas the majority of Maroons are open and militant adherents of an African-Surinamese religion.

The Maroons won their freedom two centuries earlier, and have lived in semi-autonomous communities in the interior, in what virtually were states-within-the-state. Their relations with the outside world have been largely determined by economic factors: in some periods the level of incorporation was relatively high, at other times, the Maroons fell back into a peripheral state. Social integration into a national society started only belatedly, to be blocked again by a civil war in the 1980s.

Ethnicity has been a marked feature in Suriname's political and social life. Students of Suriname society have mainly paid attention to the ethnic political rivalries between the major groups in the urban "Greater Paramaribo" area (Dew, 1978). Until recently, the groups living in the interior hardly counted as a political factor. Yet, by sheer numbers and by enfranchisement in 1963, their support became potentially significant. Creole attempts to recruit Maroons as political allies met with varying degrees of success. In the hinterland, distrust and ambivalence towards Paramaribo and its designs tends to be great: Maroons are fully aware that they are looked down upon socially (cf. Price, 1983; Thoden van Velzen, 1990).

Tensions between the two sectors have been exacerbated by the armed conflict that erupted in 1986 and lasted to 1990 (Thoden van Velzen, 1994). Hostilities have formally ended, but a redefinition of relations has not been achieved. Tambiah (1989, pp. 338–9) mentions the attacks on Maroons by the townsmen of Suriname as one of the worldwide incidents of resurgent ethnic conflict. Tambiah (1989, p. 346) points out that: "political moves may be made by a demographically dominant ethnic population to gain advantages over minority groups, and to introduce elements of sociopolitical and even religious discrimination and asymmetry, and thereby incorporating the groups into the polity on unequal terms." Tambiah's observation certainly holds water for Suriname. Discontent about second-class citizenship is rife among Maroons.

Marginalized in Suriname and less numerous in the new host society, the Maroons contest Creole aspirations of hegemony in cultural affairs. Ndyuka Maroons from the eastern part of Suriname in particular, among whom Christianity hardly has made any headway, lay claim to higher degrees of authenticity. Their religion, almost completely beyond control of either Christian church or state, developed openly and publicly according to its own dynamics. Those Ndyuka raised in the tribal heartland of the Tapanahoni River are familiar with African American notions which to them are "natural," legitimate and proper, not something to be ambivalent about. Nor do they feel any great need to search for "roots" or identity. Many Creoles, particularly those from the middle classes, frankly say that they have difficulty in finding out what *Winti* is. They admit that Maroon culture is "deeper," but they regard their own culture as more "civilized."

For Creoles, Christian religion and modern thought is hegemonic in a way it is not for Maroons. That is, hegemonic both in the standard, institutionalized form, understood as a law laid down from the top, and in the Foucauldian sense, as part of the realities of life, important as a way to achieve respectability and social advancement. Yet, as Eriksen (1992, p. 156) has reminded us, "facile assumptions about 'cultural hegemony' and the presumed dominance of bourgeois values in capitalist society may deserve further scrutiny." Among many Suriname Creoles, especially those of the less privileged classes, Christian religion is certainly not accepted as the only viable way of religious life; the ritual ties with kinsfolk, encoded in *Winti* rituals, also count. All Creoles accept some parts of the African heritage as a marker of identity.

For Creoles, the African heritage is part of informal group life and often a private affair, valued as a means to bridge oppositions. Ritual ties affirm a relationship of interdependence between an urban, westernized sector and the socially immobile. This implies that those better-off, whether Christian or not, pay respects to the unseen powers venerated by the "common people" who practice *Winti*. Implicitly, a synthesis with Christianity has been reached, but syncretism is denied. As cultural nationalists, the Creoles claim an authentic, not a syncretized culture, and wish to present a united front to the outside world. Open conflict over cultural matters is not in their interest. In order to promote their culture in a new setting and gain access to subsidies, internal differences connected with class and regional background are kept in the background.

Although striking similarities can be noted in religious views and practices of Creoles and Maroons, differences are no less significant. No more than internal discrepancies, these disparities in religious views and practices are part of public discourse. In any case, Creoles assume that their version of "the culture" is shared by all who trace descent from Africans. Most urbanized Creoles think that the type of plantation community their grand- or greatgrandparents lived in, is the model of all societies of "blacks" beyond the coastal area.

Creoles hold inconsistent views of the hinterland. Many are convinced that Africa lives on in the interior in a pure and unadulterated state, which they partly admire and envy. On the other hand, all that refers to *Winti*, and, even more so, all that pertains to the African American heritage in the interior, has served as an image of civilization's antipode, and is tainted with associations of backwardness and even barbarity. Moreover, the magical powers of Maroons are greatly feared.

The attitudes towards "Africa" are also highly mixed. The negative image of the interior and its inhabitants centers around its alleged "African" character; Herskovits' generalization (1936/1969, p. 3; 1966, pp. 52–3), though refuted (Mintz and Price 1992) lives on in a popularized, often denigratory mode.[3] Partly, this has been accepted as a mystification induced by colonialism and is thus rejected (Voorhoeve and Lichtveld, 1975). There has been a countermovement which still holds sway in literary circles, where the virtues of the past and the interior, far-off, are extolled. In an influential revision of colonialist historiography, Anton de Kom (1934/1971, pp. 72 ff.) brought the heroes of the eighteenth century Maroon guerilla warfare into the limelight and made them part of a new Creole ideology. Until the civil war marked the Maroons as a potential threat, the names of 18th century Maroon warriors Boni, Baron and Joli-Coeur were on every nationalist's lips. History was claimed as a resource in different ways by different parties, and ideologies change. In the coastal zone, these leaders' fame no longer was invoked as a source of pride, as soon as the Maroons of the interior started to intimidate the centre. In the hinterland, ambivalence about the role of the founding fathers had been the prevailing attitude among Maroon oral historians (Thoden van Velzen, 1995), as such heroes supported but also had posed a threat to the coherence of their fledgling societies.

Among middle-class Creoles, ambivalence prevails towards all that regards *Winti*. The other term denoting the religious complex, *Afkodrey* (literally "afgoderij" or idolatry), which has no pejorative connotations for believers, bears witness to the colonial background

from which the negative stereotype emerged. As the case-study
brings out, many are in two minds.

Creole opinions are rarely put to the test, though, so they linger. In
Suriname, it is considered bad form to discuss popular religion, as
this is part of implicit or covert culture. Individuals belonging to
different subgroups are often sincerely unaware of differences in
outlook. Yet, they cherish a conviction that there is such thing as "a
culture" and are inclined to assume that their own versions are
self-evidently right and true. Consensus about what African-American culture "really is" and how it should be represented to an outside
world is in abeyance. Although nationalists, young intellectuals, had
been active in the promotion of *Winti* or *Kulturu*, as part of a search
for "roots," and had obtained a repeal of the law prohibiting *Winti*
rituals in 1971, this was looked at askance by many, for different
reasons. Those Creoles who belong to the middle classes or elite do
not see *Winti* as quite respectable, and the lower classes who form the
mainstay of *Winti* adherents distrust any attempt to wring control
over "tradition" from their hands. These struggles take place in private, within the kin group, where attempts are made to bridge class
differences by ritual means. As far as public debate is concerned, not
much has changed since colonial times. Only when communal
"black" action is called for, in a new context, there is room for innovation. In this situation, to be described presently, we will see latent
conflicts surface.

In the country of the one-time colonizing power, social distance
between the two groups is maintained. The new citizens mostly
settled among peers. Creoles are usually found in the big cities, and
Maroons have concentrated in other places. For informal socializing,
each sector keeps within the bounds of its own cultural enclave.

The Politics of Culture

For an understanding of Suriname Creole politics in cultural matters,
a comparison with strategies employed by Creole groups in similar
situations is enlightening. For the present discussion, two studies of
cultural politics in other "black" social sectors and societies are highly
instructive: Hannerz's (1973) interpretation of the meaning of "soul"

in the United States, and Cohen's (1981) study of Creole culture in Sierra Leone.

Notions about "soul" have become relevant in the post-war period, Hannerz noted. The concept is extremely vague and defies attempts at a more precise definition. The very vagueness of the ideas is, however, not fortuitous, he persuasively argues, but rather makes them suitable as an ideology to bridge a growing social inequality within the ranks of the black population. These notions have become popular at a moment in history when differences in standards of living and success in the wider world threaten the solidarity so much needed by the less fortunate. Soul is, almost by definition, a quality the unsuccessful possess and which the rising middle class lacks. To make up for such deficiency, Hannerz argues, the upwardly mobile should not lose touch with the common man or woman. Yet, Hannerz (1973, p. 30) notes, culture in the form of "soul" is not politicized, in the sense of: made into a public issue. This is equally true of *Winti*. Many believers resent attempts to bring the cult into the open. Yet, there is one noticeable difference between "soul" and *Winti*: the acceptance of an element of popular culture like soul is noncommittal, and *Winti* entails ritual obligations.

The position of the Creole groups in Sierra Leone and in Suriname bears many resemblances and cultural politics also show marked similarities. The West-African Creoles had a comparable headstart, dating from colonial days, were numerically at a disadvantage and equally faced a threat from ethnic rivals. Cohen's (1981) fascinating study highlights the informal strategies employed to maintain a leading position, the notable efforts to bridge internal differences, and the cultural politics of making the most of the private aspects of social life for purposes of ethnic mobilization. Both Christian and selected elements of non-Christian or reinvented "African" religion served as an underpinning of the material and ideological base of their dominance. "African" notions, such as a belief in ancestral wrath, surfaced at a moment when they were in danger of losing control over landed property (pp. 54, 92, 164). In a rich ceremonial life, Creoles shifted back and forth from Christian to African ritual. Cohen (p. 186) speaks of a dualistic culture, mediating and mystifying contradictions. Quite striking in Cohen's account is, that the two worldviews were not merged deliberately, or presented as a new synthesis, which would set the Creoles off as a group over against others. Culture was very much politicized, not overtly but informally, as an assemblage geared to the purpose of recruiting in- and outsiders. In other words, ethnic policy forestalled overly syncretic tendencies. The cultural complex was, however, fully "creolized." The same appears to hold for the cultural endeavors of Suriname Creoles.[4]

The Multicultural Arena

To establish contacts with immigrants, the Dutch administration funds welfare organizations to represent group interests. Ethnic brokers are predominantly of Creole background. Many young Creole men and women, well-educated and versed in Dutch language, were gainfully employed in this social sector, a main channel of upwards mobility in the 1960s and 1970s. Some in this new middle class saw an opportunity to act as cultural brokers and pressed for a redefinition of the culture concept so that it might include forms of religious organization. The argument was that the separation of religion and culture is a modern, western phenomenon which is unknown in other social systems where culture and religion are synonymous: for the majority of migrants religion is embedded in a way of life. Moreover, the cultural transition was supposed to affect migrants deeply, and religion was presented as a resource enabling people to cope with and negotiate social changes. The brokers pointed out that other migrant groups, primarily those adhering to a world religion such as Islam, were not only recognized by the authorities and in civil society, but also managed to obtain privileges and material support (Van Wetering, 1990). As Baumann (1995) has noted in British politics, a purportedly secular state can yet be an active partner in the establishment of religious difference into quasi-corporate communities. The same is true in the Netherlands. So some opinion leaders in Surinamese circles started to act on behalf of popular religion, in pursuit of a recognition of *Winti*.

A *Winti* Seminar

The case-study discussed here is part of this action; it highlights one of the ways migrants from Suriname have chosen to form an alliance and strive for acceptance in Dutch society. The protagonists had singled out "health care" as a target where the *Winti* issue could be taken up. Alternative systems of health care, and their eligibility to receive funding from the Dutch National Health Service were widely discussed. The cultural brokers chose the ecumenical movement within the Protestant churches as a platform. The enterprise was subsidized by the Ministry of WVC (Welfare, Health Care and Culture), as the manifest goal was to enhance sympathy for and to promote the emancipation of an allegedly underprivileged minority. It was argued that many migrants suffer from maladjustment due to the confrontation with a different type of society, and are in need of support by those qualified by an understanding of their background. Pastors, case-workers and health care professionals had been confronted with manifestations of beliefs that seemed to them unacceptable — in fact, "pagan" or outright idolatrous — and asked for guidance. So it was concluded that all who were involved in the assistance of migrants should be given adequate information on a belief system unfamiliar to them, in order to facilitate communication. The Dutch branch of the Council of Churches, which has the promotion of religious tolerance for an aim, responded by organizing a seminar. The initiative had been taken by a group in the Dutch Reformed Church that hoped to solve smoldering conflicts lingering between indigenous Dutch members and migrants from Suriname. The event took place early in 1987 in Utrecht. The enthusiasm to participate had been overwhelming; in fact, many requests to attend had to be turned down.

Winti Out of the Closet

Utrecht, February 17th 1987. The meeting is chaired by a young, university-trained Creole intellectual. Two male Creole speakers — one anthropologist and one health care professional who both had published on *Winti* — had been invited, but both had declined the invitation. So two outsider anthropologists were asked to give some introductory talks in their place, which is not quite to the liking of the audience, either "black" or "white."[5] At the outset, reactions are restrained, though, and only some minor points are brought up for discussion. One clergyman however, a dignified elderly Creole with a standing reputation in the Community of Evangelical Brethren — the Moravian or Herrnhut Society and main Protestant denomination in Suriname — puts the cat among the pigeons. He asks straight away what the idea is behind this meeting: are the organizers perhaps heading for syncretism? He reminds the public that the Christian churches are not in favor of this. Do the participants perhaps support the pentecostal approach, and also wish to cast out the demons?

Another young Creole intellectual steps in to deplore the lack of openness and even hypocrisy among his fellows. Why can they not freely acknowledge that they are sympathetic to their own culture and do participate in *Winti* rituals? But he wants to stress simultaneously, that he has little patience with swindlers who abuse their fellows' credulity to their own advantage. Notoriously many of those are around, and it is high time that the sheep are separated from the goats.

In the meantime, the rank and file of believers who occupy the backbenches have got restless and shout loud interruptions. The few among them who raise points for discussion, happen to touch on marginal issues only: details in ritual practice or points of view. But the public does not care for such particulars; statements or testimonies of adherents are expected. A young Creole woman and a native Dutch hippy-like pastor both insist that it is high time that "the black voice" be heard. The last speaker, in search of appeasement, announces he wants to introduce a real traditional healer now, who can "tell it as it is." So peace is restored, if only for the moment.

The Creole ritual expert, apparently not privileged by formal education, opens by advocating the Bible as a way to *Winti*. He states that Jesus was moved by a Kromanti or African sky spirit, and compared the winti to angels. He goes on by differentiating between divine forces and demons, the realm of God and Satan, and winds up by denouncing the evil done by persons who call on the ancestors for help: the shades of the dead are demons!

This attempt at syncretism evokes much comment. Some Creoles will make an exception for the ancestors that had been baptized, the *kabra*. Others contest this, and, moreover, there is no consensus about the right terms for these classes of baptized and unbaptized forebears, the *kabra* and *profen* (cf. Wooding, 1981). Then a Ndyuka speaker interrupts; he dismisses the whole issue of baptism, proclaims himself a worshiper of ancestors and insists on offering up a prayer to these powers. In "cultural" terms, for most Creoles and Maroons this should have been the proper way to proceed: one should ask the permission of the forebears before referring to them, and, more precisely, cannot even mention the ancestors without offering a libation first. But the latter is not proposed: the idea of the invocation is enough to cause an outcry. Tumult breaks out.

The chairman intervenes by stating that some participants had announced beforehand that they would leave immediately upon such suggestions. A female native Dutch parson prefers to stay: otherwise it would seem that her savior was not strong enough to withstand the evil powers. A young Creole woman rises to say that there is no need for cautionary harangues about her religion. Another young Creole clergyman settles the matter by saying that the whole meeting is senseless when those present cannot respect other people's prayers.

The protagonist of Maroon religion stands up and invites the chairman to support him in traditional fashion, current in the interior to this day, by endorsing his words. The problem is that his phrasing is so "traditional" or "deep," as it is expressed, that the chairman is unable to react in style. So he resorts to a conciliatory move which, sensing the audience's mood, is called-for anyway, and closes the meeting's first round by calling upon the audience to say the Lord's prayer.

In the interval many participants in asides make it clear that they would have preferred a more open stand, that is, if others would be at the forefront. The afternoon session is dedicated to talks of two Creole health care practitioners, and discussions about their experiences. This is felt as a great relief by the majority in the audience, although it fails to satisfy the common *Winti* adept, let be the few Maroons present. The female health care worker addresses the day's main issue: the possibilities of an incorporation of *Winti* into the health care system. She is in favor of attuning treatment to a client's worldview. On the one hand, she distrusts the prevalent labeling of all psychic troubles in a psychiatric idiom, but is equally wary of the tendency to attribute all problems to *Winti*. She realizes that nationalism is involved. She recommends further research on a potential acceptance of *Winti* as an alternative form of treatment, and the

promotion of an organization of healers. Yet, she winds up by sketch-
ing her sense of awkwardness when she, of a family of staunch
supporters of the Moravian church, was confronted by a case of winti
possession in her job situation.

The male Creole psychiatrist sticks to his mainstream views, but
tries to mollify the public by using the current euphemisms for
alluding to "tradition." He does not quite get away with this, but
when asked whether he would consult a traditional healer for his own
benefit, he responds with: "My roots lie in Paramaribo, what more
should I say. I never said that I would not do so." In the ensuing
discussions, the same Creole clergyman who opened with a fierce
attack on any dabbling in *Afkodrey*, describes a case from his family:
one of his sons is seriously afflicted, allegedly by a curse from the
ancestors in the maternal line. He is not sure how to act, and asks the
psychiatrist's advice. The latter counsels a reconciliation with the
mother's relatives "if this is possible." The patient's well-being ought
to be the main consideration. This implies, as is well-understood by
all present although it is not spelled out, that a *Winti* ritual is due.
This outcome, or the speaker's turn, surprises no one. This is what
"the culture" is like.

The members of the day's steering committee, representatives of
the Federation of Suriname Migrants' Welfare Organizations (Sticht-
ing Landelijke Federatie van Welzijnsorganisaties voor Surinamers),
who enter the limelight when the meeting draws to a close, present
a list of desired policy measures. Not much is heard of this later,
however, as it becomes clear soon that all bills to promote alternative
systems of health care have been turned down by parliament.

Analysis

Notably, syncretism and nationalism are terms used in everyday
discourse, either to proclaim or discredit certain views and proposals.
So they are as much part of what is the object of study as a potential
instrument of analysis. Some terms, like ethnicity, are not so readily
used, though. This is perhaps fortuitous, but may also be looked upon
as too sensitive a topic to be broached in public. Discourses are as
interesting for what they explicitly say, as for what is left unsaid in
specific contexts.

What this case brings out is primarily the strong grip the Creoles have on public discourse in African American circles. The Maroon view hardly gets a hearing, nor do the common *Winti* adepts among the Creoles. These parties to the venture have to be content with creating disturbances in the background. At the same time, it suggests perplexity, entanglement and ambivalence of those in leading circles.

The role of the Creole ritual expert called upon to present the view of the "common believer" is interesting. He does not truly do what he is asked to do, but adapts to the expectations of the meeting's sponsors and presents a mixed view which makes him look like a quasi-traditionalist. He is co-opted, but is not openly criticized for this "defection" by the backbenches; it is an expected part of behavior dating from colonial times. In the inner circle, the expert will be appreciated for his cleverness, as true openness is appreciated by none. Therefore his move does not provide the breakthrough which was hoped for. The type of syncretism he presents — syncretism as defined by Stewart and Shaw (1994): a deliberate attempt at merging — is current in Suriname,[6] but is not politicized, neither informally nor formally. Not in the home country, nor again in the diaspora.[7] No social sector will publicly acclaim such views. To my knowledge, there is no syncretism in ritual practice. The hard core of *Winti* adepts prefers to keep Christian religion and *Winti* separate.[8] Members of the middle class take care to stick to conventionalized ways of dealing with the issue. The cue, implied in a compromise formula, is simply not taken.

Men display a greater reluctance to speak their minds than do women. The latter seem to be more open to innovation. Two factors may be involved here. Firstly, this may be due to the fact that women are restrained less than men by an interest in the status-quo. Public politics are mainly an affair of males, whereas women have a great share in the informal strategies of group mobilization (Herskovits and Herskovits, 1969; Van Wetering, 1987). Men do not for a moment lose sight of the potential danger to communal purposes implied in discussion over moot subjects such as popular religion, and set great store by the maintenance of a cultural code of evasion evolved over a long period. Yet, ethnic loyalties prevail over gender difference: Creole women who ask questions may defy received opinion now and then, but those women who have an occasion to present a view formally conform to accepted standards. Secondly, being to a lesser extent and less directly responsible, women may act in the same way as the Maroon traditional healer, as a vanguard in "testing the limits." As Scott (1990, pp. 149–50) suggested, "the marginal and apolitical status of women in a patriarchic order can be creatively exploited." Women can be effectively used for launching daring ideas which men, later, can suavely discourage as inopportune.

The open conflict over ancestor worship was extremely painful to Creole sensibilities. The Ndyuka spokesman was fully aware of this, but grasped the opportunity to challenge Creole pretensions of cultural leadership. He could afford to do so, as he had built up a reputation as a traditional healer among the common people. In fact, he acted as a religious entrepreneur and was referred to as a *poiman*, a person with the wherewithal to get his way or a "big man." He had also received the — tacit — support of the most powerful Creole welfare organization. In a sense, he exploited the dependence of the middle class on the lower class' and Maroons' allegedly untutored minds, who may be less versed in urban ways, but are nonetheless the mainstay of "tradition." His challenge was an outright refusal to be placed under Christian tutelage, and a claim for the autonomy of African American religion. In his own way, the Maroon opponent was engaged in "testing the limits." For Creole leadership, however, to make concessions would have been tantamount to a loss of control.

Class differences within the ranks of the Creole section are also manifest. Common *Winti* adepts distrust middle class constructions of "their" religion, all knowledge on this topic derived from books, and stress an acceptance of ritual experts' authority or the testimony of mediums as a hallmark of tradition. They frown on open discussions of religious knowledge. Yet, when such discussions cannot be avoided, they will throw in their weight, if only by filibustering, asking awkward questions or creating an uproar. Others stand to gain from acceptance by the outside world, and many feel ambivalent. This is most clearly shown by persons with a middle class background; on the one hand, they wish to express solidarity with other group members, but they realize that they do so at the peril of a loss of status. Differences of opinion which, partly for political reasons, had remained or been kept obscure and unacknowledged, flared into the open.

Ethnic Politics and the Curtailment of Syncretism

The fact that discussions are unwelcome and feared as disruptive, is related to the politics of ethnicity. The cultural code is, in itself, a compromise formula, a product of a creolization process that evolved where Christian supervision was relatively strict, and where opportunities for upwards mobility were only open to Christians. Over the centuries, however, *Winti* has been one of the main channels for informal contacts between the emergent middle class and commoners, the urban and rural sector, Creole and Maroon. As an informal system, it was part of a typically Creole lifestyle.

Winti is an outstanding example of a religion that, mainly by the sponsoring of healing rituals, serves as an umbrella, and an equalizer of social difference in Creole society. Rituals are notoriously costly (Voorhoeve, 1983), and participation prevents people from breaking out of existing networks. A new formula of religious synthesis — the compromise solution suggested by one of the meeting's sponsors, and brought forward by a quasi-traditionalist — would not have the required social effects. Intellectually, it would be acceptable to many in the rising new middle class. It would free them from the ritual obligations that often are experienced as a burden. The popularity of pentecostalism among migrants from Suriname — a fast-growing movement — that makes use of exorcism to liberate people from troublesome winti and stress-causing ties, testifies to this. The traditional accommodation between Christianity and *Winti*, however, keeps social ties intact. This is a latent, but major preoccupation of those who attend meetings like those described above.

Postscript

Ethnicity has been singled out as a factor that restricts syncretism, and is part of cultural nationalism. At the back of this is Suriname's economic situation, its peripherality in a world system. There is a manifest — and successful — attempt at covering up the internal class-based and regional differences, in order to present a united front to the outside world.

Not much has changed since Patterson (1973, p. 246) noted the enormous cleavages of class and ethnicity in the Caribbean, and the threat posed by dwindling economic opportunities to the realization of nationalist aspirations. Migration from periphery to centre was not halted by diminishing prospects. On the contrary, the rise of expectations drove many to the metropoles to try their luck. The urban drift presented problems for the new nationalist elites at home as much as for the administration of the one-time colonial countries. This factor may be behind the vigor of the ethnic enterprise, as the interdependence between classes, and the internal core and periphery, remains. At present, Creoles are confronted with greater differences than ever before, in opportunities, status and wealth within society, and with more rivals beyond their ranks. The task of bridging the deepening chasm is gigantic. Migration to Europe has only intensified this difficulty. Ethnic loyalties used to depend on clientelism, but as resources are reduced, chances of maintaining the system are dwindling. Yet, the demands of ethnic solidarity remain.

It is doubtful whether conventional ways of dealing with the situation will remain effective for long. Suriname is in bad straits, economically. Politically, the accumulated problems tend to topple a vulnerable democratic system; the country is on the verge of a relapse into a political dictatorship. Migrants have made tremendous efforts to help keep the mother country afloat, but relations between migrants and kinsmen back home are under great strain. Whether ethnic solidarity can last under such pressures is hard to foretell. We can hardly expect an ideology, propped up by ritual means, to run counter to the main drift of material forces for long.

Endnotes

1. Suriname counted around 400.000 inhabitants in the early 1970s, a number which has remained more or less constant since. In the Netherlands, the total number of immigrants from Suriname is assessed now at more than 220.000.

2. Wooding's (1981) authoritative study gives an encompassing overview and definition of the belief system as it was found in the Para

district, known to be a *Winti* hotbed. Herskovits and Herskovits (1936/1969) stress the centrality of the soul cult in popular religion. The latter is also marked in religious practice in the Netherlands (Van Wetering 1995b), but does not show in everyday speech.

3. Creole authors, Wooding for instance, are aware of cultural variety of African American religion in their country, but occasionally tend to equate "the interior" with "Africa." They evaluate this as positive, whereas in popular fantasy negative associations are intermingled with positive ones.

4. The role of ethnicity discussed here refers solely to Creole ethnicity, not to such processes among Maroons. These groups have their own, quite different, ways of maintaining group boundaries. But these did not become manifest in the case described below.

5. The texts of the day's presentations have been published in Dutch. My colleague's introduction was based on fieldwork work as an anthropologist and assistant of a ritual expert in the Para district, and I compared the African American systems as they have developed among the Ndyuka and Creole migrant women.

6. Stewart and Shaw (1994:, pp. 7, 17) have proposed to restrict the term syncretism to the processes and politics of religious synthesis, and to focus upon discourses of syncretism. Their approach is valuable but of restricted use in this case. If conscious attempts at synthesis are essential, *Winti* would be ruled out, as these are actively discouraged. Their observation that ethnicity, nationalism and multiculturalism promote claims of authenticity and a move towards an essentialist, anti-syncretic stand, is partly true of Suriname's "African American" religions, but the effects have been found as contradictory and paradoxical as they have been elsewhere (Van Wetering, in press).

7. There are some notable exceptions, such as public prayers to Anana at the opening of multicultural shows in the Netherlands now (cf. Van Wetering, in press). But the believers regard this as a more or less performative act, and this is not made part of private rituals.

8. This view is shared by nearly all authors who have published on African Surinamese religion: all prefer to speak of complementarity of the two systems. Nevertheless, a few note the attempts as described above.

References

Baumann, Gerd 1995 Religious migrants in secular Britain? The secular state as an agent of religious encorporation. *Etnofoor* 8(2):31–46.

Cohen, Abner 1981 *The Politics of Elite Culture: Explorations in the Dramaturgy of Power in a Modern African Society*. Berkeley: University of California Press.

De Kom, Anton 1934/1971 *Wij slaven van Suriname*. Amsterdam: Contact N.V.

Dew, Edward M. 1978 *The Difficult Flowering of Suriname. Ethnicity and Politics in a Plural Society*. The Hague: Nijhoff.

Eriksen, Thomas Hylland 1992 *Us and Them in Modern Societies: Ethnicity and Nationalism in Trinidad, Mauritius and Beyond*. Oslo: Scandinavian University Press.

Hannerz, Ulf 1970/1973 The significance of soul. In: *Soul: Black Experience* (ed., Lee Rainwater). New Brunswick, NJ: Transaction Books, pp. 15–30.

Herskovits, M.J. and Herskovits, F.S. 1936/1969 *Suriname Folk-Lore*. New York: AMS Press.

Herskovits, M.J. 1941/1958 *The Myth of the Negro Past*. Boston: Beacon Press.

Mintz, Sidney W. 1974 *Caribbean Transformations*. Chicago: Aldine.

Mintz, Sidney W. and Price, Richard 1976/1992 *The Birth of African American Culture: An Anthropological Perspective*. Boston: Beacon Press.

Patterson, Orlando 1973 Reflections on the fate of blacks in the Americas. In: *Soul: Black Experience* (ed., Lee Rainwater). New Brunswick, NJ: Transaction Books, pp. 201–54.

Price, Richard 1983 *First-Time: The Historical Vision of an Afro-American People*. Baltimore: Johns Hopkins University Press.

Scott, James 1990 *Domination and the Arts of Resistance: Hidden Transcripts*. New Haven/London: Yale University Press.

Stewart, Charles and Shaw, Rosalind 1994 *Syncretism / Anti-Syncretism: The Politics of Religious Synthesis*. London/New York: Routledge.

Tambiah, S.J. 1989 Ethnic conflict in the world today. *American Ethnologist* 16(2):335–349.

Thoden van Velzen, H.U.E. 1990 The Maroon insurgency: anthropological reflections on the civil war in Suriname. In: *Resistance and Rebellion in Suriname: Old and New* (ed., Gary Brana Shute). Williamsburg, VA: The College of William and Mary, pp. 159–188.

Thoden van Velzen, H.U.E. 1994 Priests, spirit mediums, and guerillas in Suriname. In: *Transactions: Essays in Honor of Jeremy Boissevain* (ed., Jojada Verrips). Amsterdam: Het Spinhuis, pp. 209–28.

Thoden van Velzen, H.U.E. 1995 Dangerous ancestors: ambivalent visions of eighteenth- and nineteenth-century leaders of the eastern Maroons of Suriname. In: *Slave Cultures and Cultures of Slavery* (ed., Stephan Palmié). Knoxville: Tennessee University Press, pp. 112–144.

Van Wetering, W. 1987 Informal supportive networks: quasi-kin groups, religion and social order among Suriname Creoles in the Netherlands. *The Netherlands Journal of Sociology* 23(2):92–101.

Van Wetering, W. 1990 Dissonance in discourse: the politics of Afro-Surinamese culture in the Netherlands. In: *Resistance and Rebellion in Suriname: Old and New* (ed., Gary Brana-Shute). Williamsburg, VA: The College of William and Mary, pp. 291–308.

Van Wetering, W. 1995a Demons in a garbage chute. In: *Rastafari and Other African-Caribbean Worldviews* (ed., Barry Chevannes). London: MacMillan, pp. 211–232.

Van Wetering, W. 1995b Transformations of slave experience. In: *Slave Cultures and Cultures of Slavery* (ed., Stephan Palmié). Knoxville: Tennessee University Press, pp. 210–238.

Van Wetering, W. In press. Some thoughts on syncretism in Suriname Creole migrant culture. In: *New Trends and Developments in African Religions* (ed., Peter B. Clarke). Westport, CT: Greenwood Press.

Voorhoeve, Jan 1960/1983 The obiaman and his influence in the Moravian parish. *Bijdragen tot de Taal-, Land- en Volkenkunde* 139: 411–420.

Voorhoeve, Jan and Lichtveld, Ursy M. 1975 *Creole Drum.* New Haven/London: Yale University Press.

Wooding, Charles J. 1981 *Evolving Culture. A Cross-Cultural Study of Suriname, West Africa and the Caribbean.* University Press of America.

5 : Movements of Jah People: From Soundscapes to Mediascape

John P. Homiak

Dem time (1940s–50s) Father send I-n-I into de wilderness wid only de Word. Naked, hungry, and shelterless, wi doan hab nuttin' left fi hold 'pon. Still, wi doan downhearted. Wi travel on wid a full heart an' do de works. Gradually wi bring in de people and teach dem 'bout der culture

Bongo Poro, St. Thomas, Jamaica, July 1980

The title of this chapter identifies two phases in the evolution of Rastafari as a community, a community in which "the majority of its members are unlikely to know or encounter each other, but whose sense of identity is sustained by an image of their mutual communion" (Anderson 1991:6). The frames of reference proposed here, those of soundscape and mediascape, track the development of the movement from a "cult" of protest in colonial Jamaica to its postcolonial reality as a transnational community and an international network of black cultural resistance. At first glance, this couplet would appear to suggest a simple contrast between the local and global. It is necessary, however, to appreciate that Rastafari has always involved a complex interplay between local developments and global events (see Austin Broos, 1987, 1991–2; Yawney, 1995).

As I use the terms here, soundscape and mediascape are sites of political struggle and community definition. While the two are inseparable within the reality of the Rasta movement, they represent different moments within its development and the dissemination of a message of the unity and common destiny of African peoples at home and abroad. Viewed historically, these terms reflect the difference between Rastafari as a pariah element in Jamaica in the early 1930s to its emergence as a form of popular culture in the 1970s deeply implicated in the formation of nationalist politics and identity. The reality of this distinction remains alive in the declaration cited above by Bongo Poro, a Nyabinghi patriarch (Figure 1).

The contrasts between these two sites, then, are not ones of cultural content, message, or philosophy, but involve differences in the structuring of social relations; in the distinctive images around which community is organized and experienced; and in the flow, frequency, reach, connectedness, and scale of social interactions. Within the local context of the soundscape is nested a roots culture with coherent symbolic boundaries and generational continuity. This includes a tradition of face-to-face mentoring through "reasonings" in which "teachment" is imparted from Elder to youth as well as larger communal "groundings" in which community is constituted by the use of the Nyabinghi drums to "praise Jah and chant down Babylon."[1] Several key images reside herein: the glowing herbs pipe or *chalice* passing from hand to hand, the prophet's rod, the standing 'binghi drums in tricolor, and the circular peaked-roof Nyabinghi tabernacle.

The mediascape, by contrast, is a globalized, diffuse, and deterritorialized site initially defined by the dissemination of reggae, a Jamaican-inspired music critical to the globalization of the Rasta message and to the emergence of Rastafari communities outside Jamaica. These communities in the Caribbean, North America, Europe, and Africa have become enmeshed in the global flows created by the communications and media technology of the late 20th century (Appadauri 1991). During the 1970s, popular expressions of Rastafari in the mediascape, through the recording, print and broadcast media, as well as through touring reggae artists, provided the basis for a global identification with the "rootical" expressions of Rasta and its redemptive vision. Here the key organizing images incline toward the flashing dreadlocks and the charismatic stage presence of Bob Marley and the other international ambassadors of the culture. Linking both sites, however, are the common symbols of Africa-Ethiopia — the tricolors, and, most important, the image of Emperor Haile Selassie I.

In the following pages I describe some of the ethnographic contexts of these spheres of interaction and illustrate some of the ways in which the local and global, rootical and popular have become enfolded within the contemporary Rasta movement. I argue that the

Figure 1. Bongo Poro, a Nyabinghi patriarch, in traditional posture of prayer and reverence. Emperor Haile Selassie was frequently photographed in this posture.

challenges of describing and of theorizing Rastafari in its current global reality are inseparable from one another. I believe that the forms of multi-site ethnography and collaboration advocated by Yawney reflect an experimental ethnography of social movements that is only beginning to receive attention. No single ethnographer can possibly hope to track the increasingly rapid and complex cultural flows among Rastafari globally, and this undertaking involves long-term commitment and flexible multi-site fieldwork, and active collaboration with Rastafari as well with other Rastafari researchers.

Word-Sound-and-Power: Under the Tambrin Tree

> Is de Word mon use fi explore earth. Yuh can tek de Word and ride de wings of de morning ta de farther reaches of Creation. Doan care how far yuh guh, de word is der. It is so high you cyaan't go over it, so low yuh cyaan't guh under it, so wide yuh cyaan't go around it. Yuh jus haffa stand and confront de word.
>
> Ras Timothy Hill, Lion Bay 1980

[March 2, 1986, Lion Bay, Jamaica]: "Hailie-I, Selassie-I! Black Ises [praises]. Kibir la amblak [Glory to God]." I am greeted by a chorus of sounds as I wind my way down a dirt road past a row of rude slatboard dwellings, sentinels for an off-the-beaten-track Rasta camp east of Kingston. I respond, in turn, "Rastafari, Selassie-I" and strike toward the center of the camp. As I break into a clearing a series of booming drumbeats echo from a hut notched into the rocky hillside. These sounds are followed by cries of "Lightening fi babylon! Weakheart a guh drop! Yuh a bloodklatt white bwoy. Move and guh way!" I recognize the source but I continue forward without acknowledging the sound.[2]

In virtually the same heartbeat, I am greeted by a chorus of sounds from a group of the brethren assembled in their customary spot for reasoning under the tambrin tree. "Love Iyah," "One heart, one Iyound!" "Blessed, Jah-son. Give thanks fi see de mon."

"One love in de House," I respond as I am greeted by Bongo Shephan, the leading elder of the group and a brethren who had mentored me during my first years of fieldwork. Rising from his perch on a gnarled root of the enormous tree, Shephan holds the herbs cup in his hand conspicuously aloft and then breaks into a recitation of Psalms. As he begins to speak, the other brethren stand and adopt a posture of prayer:

"Glory to word, glory to sound, glory to Iwah [power]. Behold how good and pleasant it is for bredrin to dwell together in Inity. It is like the precious ointment upon the head that ran down upon the beard, even I-mon's beard that went down to the skirts of my garment. It is like the dew that descended upon Mt. Imon and upon the mountains of Zion-I. For it is there that the Lord, Jah....

... Rastafari ...

... commanded his blessing ... even love and life forIver more. Blessed be the Living I ... Selassie I ...

... Selah."

With this blessing, the boundary around the sacred has been consciously elevated and I am incorporated into the communion of a half-dozen brethren. It has been more than a year since my last visit and there is, as usual, conversation to catch up with each other as well as those community members not present and significant events in Jamaica and elsewhere. I have just come from two weeks in Dominica and Guadeloupe and the brethren are keen to know how things are there, especially with Rasta. For several hours in the lengthening shadows of the late afternoon and into the early evening, the herbs pipe is blessed, lit and passed among the group. As darkness descends, only the glowing cup of the chalice is left to illuminate the dreadlocked countenances of the brethren. Bongo Shephan has opened a reasoning about the most notable event of the past few days, the disaster of the American space shuttle Challenger:

Shephan: De whole world suppose ta know wha gwaan — yuh nah see how Reagan's "seven-headed beast" [the space shuttle Challenger] burst and lick off him rattidcup! Hey, I wonder if mon really know what really happen ta dis space shuttle wha explode de other day?

Quallo: Yes, it a de same seven-headed beast wha crash!

Shep: Prophecy reveal it. For Revelation [...] show yuh about de
             seven-headed beast that will dwell ina de heavens and fight
             against de woman wid de man-child — dat is de Messiah
             — in de midsts of heaven, mon. Dis mon-child is to be de
             ONE ta fulfill de everliving Father, de Almighty Jah....

Chorus: Rastafari!

Jake: In de midst of heaven?

Shep: Yeah, in de midst of heaven. Look 'pon Reagan [with the
             space shuttle] now. Yuh did know seh him carry de mark of
             de beast — which is de same Lucifer.

Jakes: Mi know him name carry 6-6-6.

Shep: Natural. R-o-n-a-l-d W-i-l-s-o-n R-e-a-g-a-n (6 letters in each
             word). Dat is de mark of de Beast, de Anti-Christ. Which
             part him deyah? Him ina de midst of heaven [with the
             shuttle]. Mon haffa look ina word-sound feh know certain
             thing. Is de sound reveal itself — *Challen-Jah!* [pronouncing
             the name "Challenger"]

World: Wha yuh seh de name of it again?

Shep: *Challen-Jah, mon!* A yuh no hear? *"Challen-Jah,"* mi seh! Feh
             dem a guh "challenge Jah." A de Dragon!

Chorus: Aoooh!

Shep: A who did challenge Jah ina de heavens two thousand year
             ago come again. De same Lucifer mon!

Benji: De same Dragon wid seven head.

Shep: Yes. Is de same Dragon, ya know, wid seven head — feh
             dem have seven astronaut, nah true?

Jake: Yes-I.

Shep: Mi know dis who space shuttle 'ting is a next strategy to
             keep up arms race ina space. Dem wan colonize space wid
             weapon. Check de seven people dat guh ina dat shuttle and
             see if dem nah represent seven rass klatt mystery or "gov-
             ernment." It come like yuh hab one from every nation —
             black mon [an African American], Chiney mon, one from
             Japan [Asian American], Indian mon, woman....

World: ... a de most technical people him [Reagan] send up der in space. Teacher and all dem 'ting a turn de yout dem into stargazer....

Quallo: ... nah respect earth ... for de earth is de Lord and I-n-I art de fullness thereof. All de problem d'pon earth and dem have de people offa dem head. People dong here ina wickedness and poverty and Babylon gwaan wid dem same vanity. Pure war-and-crime d'pon earth.

Shep: Yes Iyah ... dat is why de heathen rage and de people imagine vain things. Rahab [America] try fi tek it pon a higher level now. Dat is why dem send de teacher-in-space.

Jake: Did that get much publicity here in Jamaica?

Shep: Yes mon. Dat is wha dem tek feh mek de whole Jamaica pickney run after dis ting. Is how dem look fi brainwash de [next] generation mek dem look ina de sky. People a bawl ina de ghetto every day feh food and likle shelter nobody nah badder bout dat. Yuh no see how de government use it and tek de people mind dem and de youth dem ... dem a cry out over dis catastrophe. Cause everyone "out der" [in babylon] a talk bout de teacher. Dat is de wickedness dem use feh brainwash black people....

Quallo: ... stargazers and multiprognosticators ... it is prophecy.

Shep: She gonna give lesson from space.

World: Yes, dat is de next Tower of Babel dem try and tek feh sow confusion. De Tower of Babel cyaan't reach ina space. A pure mischeif, ya know. Wha mi seh ... she think it so sweet going up. She nebber know!

Jake: So, Bongo Shephan. How you see this arms race side of the shuttle?

Shep: Yes, dat is a next portion. Feh mi know Reagan haffa push dis arms race. Him know 'Merica cyaan't win Russia 'pon earth, so him try a thing ina space. I-n-I know seh all dese nuclear [weapon] wha mek haffa use. Dat is a portion of the prophecy.

And a next portion again. Dis space shuttle haffa use rare mineral, some kinda rare minerals and metal wha dem mine in South Africa. Cyaan't work without dem ting, ya know.

So Reagon nah leggo dat. Is through dat him colonize space. So him haffa keep up de apartheid wid Botha.[3]

Quallo: Nah true ... Reagan and Botha is like chamber-and-batti (i.e., like a toilet seat and buttocks).

World: ... and dem keep up apartheid through dat. A pure blood klatt brutality dem keep up pon de I-n-I bredda and sista ina dem own "yard" [i.e., Africa/South Africa].

Shep: True Iyah ... Is colonialism in a neo-style. Is a more "technical" strategy dem use feh hold black people. Feh [Queen] Elizabeth did have Africans under de said system and now Rahab [America] come and tek it under Reagan. Dat is why yuh see only certain black mon can come a White House. Cause yuh see dis one mon — wha him name again — Jonas Swimbi [Savimbi]

Jakes: Savimbi you mean, the leader of UNITA.

Shep: Yes — de said one, give thanks. Dat one is puppet feh Reagon and Botha. Dem use him and him army feh fight 'gainst black people. Is de said divide-and-rule "polytricks" dem tek a rule black mon for a longer time. Still, nuttin can hidden from de sight of I-n-I. De said people who was wid de Father [Selassie] 2,000 years ago and who did fight certain battle is de said people who is wid him this day!

Quallo: ... an unchanging lineridge [spiritual lineage] through de Order of Melchizadec, de I seen?

Shep: ... yes, so wi haffa give thanks Inually [continually] ...

World: What was de sound again....

Shep: *Challen'-Jah*, Iyah! Dem a challenge de King. But de said Tower of Babel wha crash in dat time. It cyaan't stand again!

Quallo: ... for knowledge increaseth every day. Yes-I. Bless and sanctifull.

For at least four decades — beginning in places like Back o' Wall, the Dungle, Trench Town, Moonlight City, Shanti Town, Ackee Walk, and Wareika Hill — individuals have been socialized into Rasta culture and have reproduced a continuously meaningful Afrocentric worldview through participation in ongoing sessions of reasoning like the one described above. The above named sites are all "remembered places" that continue to serve as anchors for community among Jamaican Rastafari. Those of Shephan's generation and older continue to recreate community around more recent sites of dispersal like Lion Bay. Here, beneath the tambrin tree, they continued to explore the heights and depths of word-sound-and-power.[4]

Yawney (1975, 1977; 1983; 1994), Chevannes (1994:208–30), Pulis (1993) and I have all produced works which reveal the ways in which Rasta discourse is a site of political struggle. Of interest in the above example is the distinction which (Yawney, 1985:2–4) draws between iterative discourse, that which is codified and formulaic, and generative discourse, that which is creative and which produces far-ranging, unique and meaningful associations. Yawney makes the further point that these complementary aspects of Rasta discourse reflect the different, although not necessarily separate, roles which Elders play as "preachers" or as "teachers," the ability to effect these roles being determined by the relative intellectual and charismatic attributes of particular speakers.

These distinctions enable us to understand how the soundscape, in its local manifestations, functions simultaneously as an arena where individuals are socialized through ongoing exposure to the formulaic, as a context where Rastafari recognize insiders and outsiders based on criteria for speech competence and the ability to reproduce discourse, as a framework for the reproduction of meaning, and as a site for revelation that encourages a disciplined but free-wheeling exchange of ideas in order to yield new insights. It is the periodic production of generative discourse, as in the example cited above, that both affirms the revelatory potential of reasoning and authenticates the charismatic qualities of individual speakers.

What should be clear from the above is that reasonings, while locally situated and of limited duration, routinely draw upon both local and global events in relation to an understanding of a wider field of geopolitical relations (see Yawney, 1975). These understandings do not become doctrine; rather, they generate a provisional consensus. These working understandings, carried forward into reasonings among other circles of brethren have their own ripple effect as propositions are tested, refined, and reworked for further insights. Had any of us known at the time that the cause for the explosion of the shuttle was placed on its "seals," this no doubt would have called into play yet another set of biblical analogies and explanations.[5]

It would be misleading to present reasoning as a disembodied intellectual and "bloodless" activity. Rastafari are called, and their words and thoughts are impassioned. While "peace and love" are frequently reflected in their dealings with others, they demand "truth and rights" for black people without apology. For Rastafari, "the Word" is a two-edged sword — both "love" and "fire" — which makes the soundscape an arena in which moral and evaluative criteria are constantly brought to bear upon the attributes of speakers. Within the soundscape have evolved ritual means for dealing with disagreement and for stemming factionalism.

These protocols trace to life in the camps and yards of this era, which involved adherence to a disciplined code of behavior in which individuals were held accountable to community standards. Present-day Elders who became Rasta during this period often remark nostalgically that this was the period of greatest unity amongst Rasta. It was also, they acknowledge, a time of "combustible sounds" among the brethren. One Rasta leader who grew up in Back o' Wall characterizes this as a time during which "mon couldn't hide from reasoning" (i.e., adherents had to make themselves verbally accountable to the community).

This statement is a telling insight into the formative nature of the soundscape as a local face-to-face community whose members were not only fearless in confronting agents of colonial authority but, with respect to their own diverse ideas and opinions, could themselves be a litigious collectivity. Suspension of talk, however, has never been an option among the members of this community of self-identified exiles. This continues to be the case within the soundscape. Unlike other embedded egalitarian communities in which the cessation of talk is a critical indicator of conflict (Brenneis 1988:502), the Rastafari ritualize conflict in the service of community. The "true Rasta" is someone who cannot be offended by words.[6] He is one who, as noted above, "must stand and confront the word."

In this manner, Rastafari "test the Irits [spirit]" and come to "know a mon's heart." These protocols apply with added measure to researchers. They are an extension of the strategies by which Rastafari screen, control, and use the chalice to "sieve out" researchers. Regardless of how long one's involvement may be, it is always subject to negotiation across the width and breath of the soundscape. Because of the fluidity of Rasta social organization, I routinely find myself in situations with individuals I have not previously met and who feel the need to "check me out." This is invariably the case at island-wide Nyabinghi where the symbolic boundaries of the sacred and definitions of insiders and outsiders are maintained at their highest level. In such instances, the ethnographer must be prepared to deliver himself with sound:

[August 17, 1987, Bath, St. Thomas Jamaica. Nyabinghi Assembly celebrating the 100th birthday of Marcus Garvey] I have "trod" with Bongo Shephan, Bredda Benji, and Ras World to a major event commemorating the centenary birthday of Marcus Garvey. This is the culmination of a month-long round-the-island tour by the Nyabinghi House. Just days before my arrival, a binghi had "sealed" [closed] at Lion Bay under Shephan's sponsorship. Bath is to be the culminating event.

The binghi is being kept just behind the police station. A tabernacle has been raised in the center of an open soccer field and cricket green. As we walk down a narrow access road, we are greeted by Ras Headfull, the resident elder and the brethren charged with "keeping the duty." It is still early and "first night Ises" has yet to begin. Several hundred brethren and sistren are milling about in small groups, some caucusing informally, others clearly upon more serious reasonings. We are met by a hail of cries as we break into the opening, most directed at me: "Fiya bun de White House," "Death to de traitors," "White bwoy, yuh haffa move!" Shep and World respond with "Hotta flames," "Crash de Dragon!" As we move onto the compound, Shep, Benji, and World are hailed by other brethren and step off. Having experienced this a dozen or so times over the past years, I steel myself for the transition.

Almost immediately, I am surrounded by a dozen or so young Dreadlocks who form a tight circle around me screaming cries of "Fiya fi de white bwoy," "Lightening," "Oonu a slime, move and guh way." Within minutes, their antics have become the basis for a public drama that transforms the entire compound, cries emanating from every corner of assembly. As I scan the terrain, my eyes meet those of eight or nine Elders in whose yards I have grounded. A few direct cautionary sounds at the youth surrounding me, but none seek to intervene. I know all are watching to see how I will acquit myself.

Initially, I attempt to dismiss the youths, telling them that they know nothing about me and to "Allow me! I-mon free." I then step to Brother Vince, Shepan's son-in-law, a thirtyish brethren who is sitting next to the storehouse for the binghi. As I sit down next to Vince, he casually hands me a rizzler and a tat of herbs and invites me to pray. One of the young Dreads picks this up: "Is your friend dat?" and another, "You is a black traitor." Roaring back, Vince retorts: "Oonu is idiot! I-n-I doan deal wid "friends." De House of Nyabinghi doan know nuttin' 'bout friends. Nyabinghi call fe de righteous in every nation — black, white, brown, red, and yellow. Jah no partial." Undeterred, the group presses forward. Once again, I am isolated and the attack continues. After about a half-hour of this an Elder named Bongo Bud approaches the group and me. "Hold dong, Lions. Tek time, tek time" — momentarily, the Elder quells the confusion.

Although I have met Bud on several other visits and have reasoned with him previously, we are not well known to each other. Initially, I am uncertain of his intent. Having momentarily silenced the youth, he turns to me with a stern countenance and loudly demands at nose-end distance, "Who are you?" "I am a remnant of my nation come to give praises to His Majesty," I reply. "No!" he retorts, "Who are you?" Now confused, I seek to gauge his drift and try again: "I am one called by Rastafari." Again, "No!" I try a next tack: "I am Jah-son, I-mon." Again, Bud's reply is no. By this time, the youth have started again: "Spy, CIA, Blood klatt pirate!, murderer, Ku Klux Klan." The Elder is clearly searching for something specific and states, "White mon, who are you to the House of Rastafari?" Gauging his drift, I volunteer, "I art Esau, and you are my brother, Jacob" [see Genesis 27:1–55].

"Aaaaah," he exclaims, finally satisfied. "And what is it I have done to you, my brother." Smiling at his method, I reply, "You have taken away my birthright, brother, deceiving our father Isaac into thinking that you were I. Still, I-n-I are one family and we must live together. For Father did say that until the color of man's skin is of no more significance than the color of his eyes, there will never be peace in Creation."

"True sound, Jah son. You have learned your lesson well." Then, turning to the youth Dreads, the Elder declares: "Prophecy show I-n-I dat wi must careful wid strangers for Jah seh He will send I-gels to travel with I-n-I. So give the judgment to the King and render righteousness unto his sons. Young Lions, mind wha you a do. This mon knows more about your culture than oonu. Go back a school!" Dressed down and publicly rebuked, the youths disperse.

Through an impromptu social drama which drew upon biblical discourse (the brotherhood of the black and the white races as seen through the allegory of Jacob and Essau), the Elder simultaneously probed my level of consciousness and provided me with an opportunity to publicly "deliver myself with sounds." In so doing, he had temporarily opened a portal in the House for me to step through.

Like other primarily oral cultures, auditory space among the Rastafari is perceived and mapped as a physical field (Peek, 1981:21). The descriptions offered above are presented to evoke the textured and many-layered nature of the soundscape. This is a field of varied cadences, registers, and genres embodied in biblical poetry and moral criticism, of supremely confident and resolute speakers whose voices oscillate between uplifting praise and fiery sound, solemn preachifying and extended harangues, contentious "argument" and "conscious" reasoning. What Reisman (1974:56–9) has pointed out for other parts of the African and African-American world also holds for Rastafari. Community is based on the calling of a person's names, the act of uttering and naming variously implying a social relationship, sense of mutual commitment, or an invoking of qualities, either positive or negative. As implied by the idea of "living sound," speech is a live channel for action and feeling. In such a context, order is imposed and achieved amidst contending sound and "noise" by commanding voices that periodically bring the utterances of others into unity or for a common purpose.

The message of racial protest hammered out in this space is organically linked to the rhythms of resistance found in reggae — the popular expression of Rasta, which has been critical in its globalization. Understand, however, that there is no facile correspondence between this public and internationalized aspect of the soundscape and the "roots" culture from which it was birthed. The session, the reggae concert, and more recently the dancehall, do not map the same moral universe as reasonings or groundation.[7] We are talking about liminal space which is demarcated and given meaning through the Biblical chronicles of exile. God's Chosen People are wandering in the wilderness without permanent sites for spiritual ascension. They have been down in the valley, in the Pit of Jehosephat, for a very long time sustained only by the inevitability of prophecy and the knowledge that the God of Jacob will not forsake his people. It is the spoken word itself — "living sound" — that calls the community into being

and into the service of Jah Rastafari, God and King, who in due season
will call them home.

Within the soundscape, the moral capacities of the person are
defined by evaluative criteria applied to the workings of the voice.
A rich terminology of locational and corporeal qualities — resonate
with the metaphors of the Bible — are customarily used to describe
the manifest quality and impact of a speaker's word-sound. Rastas
refer respectfully to individuals who are "grounded," "seated," and
who can "hold their corner" (i.e., are resolute and can vigorously
defend an idea or position). These are brethren who "know themselves" or are "within themselves," having become Rasta through
years of reasoning; in effect, an extended and deliberate process of
communally supported self-examination. After having consecrated
themselves to Jah as "living sacrifices," they have chosen to "carry
locks" (grow dreadlocks) as their personal symbol of the faith. Recognizing both the isolation and danger of the sacred, these moral
guardians counsel others against hasty and ill-conceived steps without similar self-knowledge. "Tek time, tek time, mon," is their constant reminder to those "coming up." For in the counsels of Rastafari,
"the same word that is sweet to the mouth, may be bitter to the belly."
It is grounded brethren who are "heartical," "firm," and balanced.
Their personal testimonies form an important part of the oral culture
of Rastafari, and they are the ones who produce "conscious sound"
and "tangible" or "solid reasoning." As the principal expounders of
ideology, they enable other communicants to "step higher" in reasoning. Words cannot "bore" or "penetrate" them. They are incom-
bustible, they "pass through the fiya" in the midst of contentious
noise or heated argument. At the same time, these teachers and
preachers have a keen sense of the power of speech as a channel for
action, both positive and negative. More often than not, it is their
commanding voices in the midst of a congregation that transform
"noise" and chaos into orderly word-sound.

In contrast, the community recognizes individuals who "cyaan't
seated," who "circle" rather than "come into a reasoning," or whose
reasoning is "soft," without force or logical quality. Such individuals
may just be "coming up in the faith" and, because they are not yet
"seasoned," they try to "rush into a ting." They are often described
as "outside themselves," as prone to "taking counsel," or as ready to

"follow any sound" (i.e., are easily swayed). Such speakers tend to "chat folly." Because they are "outside themselves," they are frequently "off" or "missing" (in their reasoning) and tend to invite disorder and unnecessary argument.

In the "counsels of His Majesty," respect is accorded to speakers who are not only biblically fluent and who have intellectual qualities but who demonstrate spiritual resolve and psychological resilience. The brethren will poetically intone that "words without deeds is like a garden full of weeds." The "works" of heartical Rastas — their moral bearing, personal sacrifices, and communal deeds — are all manifestations that "make the word live." Those with longstanding commitment who have lived principled lives and who possess oratorical and intellectual skill are regarded as Elders and acknowledged as "coming from far."[8]

Visionary Discourse and Deterritorialized Space

> You see, far and near, a little while you shall see I and a little while yuh just can't see I because I art here, I art there, I art everywhere. I art in, I art out, I art all d'bout, to *no* ends of the earth through the I-wah (power) of Jah Rastafari.
>
> Ackee Mon, cited in liner notes, Bilby & Leib, 1983, *From Kongo to Zion*

Among Rastafari at home and abroad, the soundscape incorporates many "remembered places" which serve as anchors and sources of inspiration for ongoing community. The legendary camps and yards of West Kingston, places like Fire Key, the Dungle, Back o' Wall, and Salt Lane, are but the most notable. By and large, however, the soundscape coincides with no settled community, no church or organization, no fixed site for spiritual ascension. As echoed above in the words of Ackee Mon, it is its own kind of deterritorialized space, here, there, and everywhere to "no ends of the earth."

Community exists only in the act of a communal quest for meaning and inspiration; in the act of giving Jah praises. All else is simply what is required to survive and sojourn in Babylon. It is not surprising, then, that the "linguistic latitudes" of Rasta encode their own extension of metaphysical space which evoke their own liminality and diasporic outlooks.[9]

These are sensibilities encoded in the ubiquitous sound of I/as, which is not only the primary sound of Rasta dialect, but a metaphysical and mystical concept grounded in biblical logic. The "I" — first person, singular, a man — is the Creator, Jah Rastafari, who "lives" within the temple of every individual. For the Rasta, this is the concept and the mystery of I-n-I: that God is a man (in the person of Emperor Haile Selassie) who "lives within man." Attending to the homonomy between "I" and "eye," it is the "I/Eye" within man that gives rise to the notion of visionary communication, which bridges the dislocation between the black man in his condition in Babylonian captivity and his deliverance in Zion (see Yawney, 1979:170–72; Pollard, 1982:21; Homiak, 1995:162). This perspective underlies the reproduction and evaluation of inspired reasoning by Elders — charismatic and visionary discourse produced in the service of community.

Part of the genius of this self-referential discourse is that it inherently encodes resistance to the incarceration of the black man in Babylon. The forces and potentialities of the soundscape "burst the seals" of this containment. From a Rasta perspective, then, the communicative field extends "from earth to Zion," from a diasporic outpost to the heart of the continent — the direct visionary communication which each Rasta claims with Jah Rastafari, Selassie-I.[10] The nature of outreach here is both figurative and literal. Rastafari typically have social networks that reach well beyond what one might associate with their humble gates.

In my own case, it was several years before I began to pay sufficient attention to the implications of these links. "I-n-I are here as international brethren to greet visitors from abroad." This was a statement which I frequently encountered among the brethren at Lion Bay during my first period of fieldwork. Initially, I assumed this to be pure hyperbole. However, during my first year of fieldwork and subsequent revisits, I had the opportunity to engage Rastafari who visited this camp from Guyana, Grenada, Ethiopia, Trinidad, Senegal, England, and North America. Bunny Wailer had built a house that was nested in the steep hillside above this camp. One afternoon, while standing next to this gate, I witnessed the launching of one of what was perhaps the first tour of traditional Rastafari abroad (involving Ras Mortimo Planno and Arthur Kitchen), a precursor to "missions" and international "trods" of Elders that would follow in the mid-1980s and 1990s.

Well before the advent of Marcus Garvey, the Jamaican context was part of a wider African world open to external ideas and flows of information. In this regard, the soundscape was its own kind of imagined community even though it developed within a context of colonial containment and control. The first preachers of Rastafari doctrine were well-traveled individuals who returned to Jamaica in the early 1930s after experiencing the circumstances of black people in North America and the Caribbean Basin (see Austin, 1983). If one is looking for a model of "traveling culture" in the early annals of Rasta, simply consider Leonard Howell's 1936 publication of the *Promised Key*. The element in this text that served to underwrite his authority was Howell's account of his travels to the Gold Coast and Ethiopia where he was allegedly witness to the coronation of Haile Selassie I.[11]

During this same period, other parts of the African diaspora, the continent, and Ethiopia came more sharply into focus. Out of the emerging music industry in Trinidad during the 1930s came several calypsos that expressed support for the plight of a besieged Ethiopia. This music and other songs with African themes circulated among Jamaicans and West Indians throughout the Caribbean Basin and North America via black seamen and other travelers. There was outreach through the Ethiopian World Federation which, while headquartered in New York, created branches in Jamaica, Trinidad, and other islands. Through this organ came news of Emperor Selassie's gift of a landgrant in Ethiopia to peoples of African descent who had assisted his nation during the Italian-Ethiopian conflict (Smith, Nettleford, & Augier, 1978).

The 1960s, in particular, was a period of increasing exchange and feedback between the movement and proponents of black nationalism. The case of Walter Rodney and the linkage with Rastafari and the Abeng movement are among the most notable. Other linkages are part of a subaltern history, what Rasta might call "the half that has yet to be told." Only during the late 1980s, after I assisted several delegations of Elders to travel to the United States, did brethren feel free to discuss with me some of the contacts that they had in West Kingston and elsewhere. In 1963–1964, Stokeley Carmichael and Miriam Makeba, on a visit from apartheid South Africa, visited several of the Rasta camps in West Kingston, including Back o' Wall. At least one of George Simpson's Rasta informants migrated to England and remained in contact with the group in West Kingston about which Simpson wrote. Similarly, Jah Bones, initially grounded in West Kingston, writes about the connections between Rastafari in Jamaica and England that developed during the early 1960s. In 1961, Mortimo Planno met with Malcolm X in New York where the two were interviewed for a TV spot. And in the late 1960s, many of these Elders also reasoned with both Walter Rodney and Maurice Bishop who drew upon the support of Rastafari in Grenada in his overthrow of the Gairy regime. Individual Rastafarians, of course, could no doubt expand considerably upon such linkages and their significance. It is worth noting that all of these connections to the wider African world existed prior to recent globalization at a time when the Jamaican response to the movement was one of repression and containment.

From Strength to Strength:
Rastafari in Transition

As a segue from the soundscape into the mediascape, we can consider some of the changes in Rastafari during the 1970s and 1980s. What I term the soundscape changed dramatically in the postcolonial period, especially in the 1970s when cooptation, rather than repression, became the primary response to the movement. This decade witnessed the popularization of Rasta through reggae music, an organic extension of the soundscape which, when allied with the socialist politics of the Marley era, served to legitimate aspects of Rasta message and culture. Reggae was certainly central to the spread of Rasta into the ranks of the middle class and the principal means by which Jamaican society has embraced selected aspects of Rasta ideology.[12] At the same time, reggae was promoting the globalization of Rastafari.

Any detailed discussion of the mediascape — those cultural flows and connections which are part of Rasta's globalization — would necessarily have to track the dissemination of reggae throughout the Caribbean, Europe, North America, and Africa (see Savashinshy, 1995; Gjersat, 1994; Bilby, 1996). This would include its reception among expatriate West Indian communities and its appeal to a youth culture in the cities of Europe and North America where the policies of the state continued to marginalize and discriminate against peoples of color.

By the mid- to late 1970s, Rastafari communities had developed in nearly all of these sites, not to mention South Africa, Ghana, Senegal, Tanzania, and Zimbabwe. The tours of musicians such as Marley, Burning Spear, and others were critical to the spread of the message, along with travel by traditional Elders. All of these developments in the 1970s laid the groundwork upon which the traditional roots expressions of Rastafari have been grafted.

During the same decade that Rasta "burst" the confines of its Jamaican Babylon via reggae, Rastafari in the more traditional terrain of the soundscape were engaged in a phase of retrenchment. I am referring to developments within the House of Nyabinghi (see Homiak, 1997). Because of constant pressures to coopt Rastafari during the 1970s, Nyabinghi celebrations during this period need to be seen as a site of struggle concerning the definition of the movement and its vision of repatriation. During the late 1960s and early 1970s Nyabinghi emerged as a communal event staged almost exclusively in specially prepared rural venues. Nyabinghi became, in effect, a ritual pilgrimage "out of Babylon," which served to re-emphasize the status of Rastafari as African "exiles" and to mark their separation from the wider contexts of postcolonial Jamaica. Each 'binghi became a rehearsal for repatriation and underscored the cultural and spiritual qualities required to realize this goal. These developments must be seen in the context of political strategies that threatened the cultural autonomy of the movement and the ability of Rasta to define their own sense of community and identity. It is the House of Nyabinghi that serves to reinforce the traditional aspects of the movement's moral imagination: the Rastafarian as exile, pilgrim, sojourner, visitor, a stranger in a strange land, and a prophet who will "never bow before force."

Even though Rasta had become physically dispersed within Jamaica, this part of the soundscape has acted as a stabilizing influence. Anchored by two generations of Rastafari who entered the faith in the 1950s and 1960s, the House perpetuated the same kind of face-to-face traditions of reasoning and grounding that characterized the culture in West Kingston.[13] During this same time, Rasta had already entered the realm of popular culture and "gone international."

Island/I-land Roots, Metropolitan Branches

In proposing the concept of mediascape to describe and explore the globalization of Rastafari, I am not simply concerned with the products created by telecommunications, recording, VCR technology, and cyberspace as a means to represent and disseminate Rasta culture. Rather, I wish to direct attention to the accelerated pace at which people, information *and* various related media now circulate within the portals of Rasta. Due to these developments, the House has now emerged as a deterritorialized site in which separate places — New York, Toronto, London, D.C. and Jamaica — are becoming a single "community" through a continuous flow of people, information, and cultural resources (see Clifford 1994:303). These flows not only serve to exponentially increase the volume and frequency of networking among Rastafari globally, they require new strategies on the part of Rasta to monitor and shape them. In this regard, it is necessary to recognize the way media has shaped the popularization and commodification of Rasta culture. While the media has sometimes sympathetically represented the fundamental message and culture, it has more frequently distorted, criminalized, or trivialized the culture. It is precisely for this reason that Rastafari have become increasingly self-conscious and critical about how and by whom they are represented. This emergent Rasta intelligentsia seeks to claim and control their own space within the mediascape through a host of independent initiatives. These include newsletters and publications such as *Rastafari Speaks* (originally published in Trinidad) or *Jahug* (published in London), *Uprising* published out of Toronto, *Sound-Bytes*, a recent venture out of Washington, D.C.; independent film and video production units like CEDDO co-founded in London by Menelik Shabazz, a Barbadian-born Rasta, or I-Vision Productions founded by Ras Moya (also in London); and distribution ventures like Frontline Distributing in Chicago, cable television (such as Lioness Productions in Maryland), and an array of radio programs devoted whole or in part to reggae and Rastafari.

These developments also need to be appreciated in terms of the importance that Jamaica has acquired for the global Rasta community as the birthplace of the movement. While Ethiopia is unquestionably the movement's geography of desire, Jamaica remains a "site of attachment" of growing importance to an international community.[14] There are several aspects of "traveling culture" at work here. The first is that the Nyabinghi House, during the past decade, has become closely connected with Rastafari communities in North America, most of the small islands in the Caribbean, as well as in Africa. These linkages derive from various international "trods" or missions undertaken by Elders traveling abroad and the effect these have had on the consolidation of Rastafari communities in North America and elsewhere.[15] The enhanced international profile that the House now enjoys derives, in part, from the fact that these movements and connections have been a prime focus in publications such as *Rastafari Speaks, Jahug*, and other ephemeral papers. Both Yawney (1995) and I (Homiak, 1994) have reviewed elsewhere some of the reasons for and impacts of these missions. Suffice it to say that the Elders chose to trod internationally to provide guidance and "grounding" to Rastafari abroad, the majority of whom embraced Rasta through the inspiration of reggae music rather than through traditional Elder-youth interactions. The international impact of reggae, therefore, must be recognized as making possible the subsequent global spread of rooted forms.[16]

But still another aspect of Rastafari as a traveling culture has became wrapped up within these flows: increasing numbers of reggae artists similarly feel the need to record in Jamaica.[17] Examples of these include Alpha Blondy from Cote d'Ivoire, Lucky Dube from South Africa, Nico, the most well-known Rasta artist from Cayenne, French Guiana, and, more recently, Nasio Fontaine, a rising star from Dominica. Lesser known, but no less significant for our purposes, are performers such as Denroy Morgan, an artist who has recently returned to Jamaica from living in the United States and Toronto, artists and community activists such as Ras Leon and Sister Makeda (publishers of *Uprising* magazine).

What is doubly significant about these movements in terms of the enfolding of the local-global/rootical-popular is that many of these artists also activity seek out the Nyabinghi roots of their culture and the opportunity to "ground" with the Elders. This is simply one manifestation that brethren and sistren, in both local and global contexts, are increasingly attuned to opportunities for international networking. On my most recent trip to Jamaica, Brother World, a Nyabinghi brethren I have known for over 15 years, made a special point of carrying me to the yard of Ras Denroy Morgan where we spent an evening reasoning. World did this because he perceived us as having mutual interests in the international development of the movement. Neither of us knew at the time that we both contributed to a common project dealing with the history of the movement (see note 19).

Denroy, a brethren affiliated with the Twelve Tribes of Israel who, after 21 years as a Rasta, recently relocated to Jamaica was preparing to attend his first Nyabinghi. Ironically, this binghi, in Hayes, Clarendon, was being sponsored by Everton Blender, another reggae artist who has a close identification with the House of Nyabinghi. The particular irony of these movements is that, even as they combine to further globalize and transform the movement into an increasingly deterritorialized site, they also elevate the significance of Jamaica ("Jah-mek-ya") as a "place."

Another striking example of this kind of intertwining is Nasio Fontaine's music video "Wanna Go Home" (1996), which was shot in Jamaica to promote his album of the same name. This video was shot in Jamaica in front of the Nyabinghi tabernacle in Scotts Pass, Manchester, using Nyabinghi drummers and dancers. This is significant given the longstanding prohibition that the House has regarding photography and film/video for commercial purposes. Equally significant, from the perspective of how such productions serve to blurr the roots/popular genres of expression, are the visual and musical elements in this video. The video uses the traditional Nyabinghi tempo, with a combination of Ethiopian and Nyabinghi iconography and three sistren (garbed in Ethiopian *shammas*), as background for a Marleyesque Nasio Fontanine.

Rooting/Routing the Mediascape: The Indigenization of Modernity

From its inception, Rastafari has entailed an indigenization of the modern. From a Rasta perspective, this has meant a remodeling or reinterpretation of contemporary symbols and events as signifiers of "anciency" and as a means to authenticate the process of culture-building. Looking for an example of the use of the popular in early Rastafari, one might turn to the "street meeting" era of Rasta in Kingston. During the early 1950s, Simpson encountered public meetings of the brethren, which the January 1931 issue of the *National Geographic* used to illustrate the prophecy of Emperor Haile Selassie's coronation. Perhaps no social movement aside from Rastafari has cobbled together such an unlikely assemblage of signifiers steeped in "anciency" and "naturality" while at the same time making use of the popular, the modern, and the technological in disseminating itself.

For over a decade now, the "roots" of Rastafari have been following the routes traced by its popular reggae "branches." In the current moment of the mediascape, the combination of roots-popular content and high production values must be seen as another way in which the globalization of Rastafari is consciously being effected and its culture authenticated. This process can be discerned in the willingness of traditional Rastafari to experiment with forms of communication other than the spoken word to communicate their message. Most of the works to which I am referring are a result of the travel of traditional Elders and of their collaboration with Rastafari communities in second diasporas. *Rastafari Elders* (1991), a CD and audiocassette of Nyabinghi chants and speechifying is one example, produced by Ras Records with seven of the Elders who traveled to the eastern United States in 1988 and 1989. Ras Sam Brown's two CDs of dub poetry and preachifying, *Teacher* (1991) and *The History* (1997), and the CDs/tapes of Nyabinghi poetry by Ras Pidow, *Modern Antique* (1992), and Sister Farika Birhan, *Rainbow Dawning* (1994), are other examples. While these are examples of media generated through contacts in New York, Baltimore, Washington, D.C., Philadelphia, and Atlanta, the *Ark of the Covenant: Nyabinghi* by Ras Ivi and the Family of Rastafari (1994) is an example of work done in England in the aftermath of the Centenary networking. All of these productions express how traditional reverberations from within the soundscape have become part of a traveling culture.

Yet another production that reflects this complex networking is the double-CD released by Ras Everton McPherson, a Rasta activist and author, *Kalunga: Traditional Rastafari Kumina Songs, Prayers, and Reasonings* (1995). This effort to bring a little-known piece of Rasta history to light involved field recordings of remnant members of Leonard Howell's Pinnacle community performing early Rasta chants on kumina drums (see Bilby and Leib, 1983), as well as the collaboration of Rastafari from several communities in Jamaica and abroad. The production circumstances of this CD — which involved Ras MacPherson, but this writer, and contacts facilitated by Mortimo Planno with a brethren in Brooklyn — attest to the unexpected and serendipitous contacts that shape the mediascape.[18]

Finally, we note of the highly aestheticized revision of the traditional Nyabinghi chant "Tell Out Rastafari Teachings around the Whole World" by Harry T, a 'binghi drummer who grew in the yard of Ras Mortimo Planno (personal communication, Carole Yawney, July 1997). This chant, released around the centenary of Haile Selassie's birthday, while based on a classic chant, lacks the dominant presence of the drums and the raw and unbridled energy so common to Nyabinghi. It is, by at least one knowledgeable opinion, closer to Jamaican gospel than Nyabinghi (Ken Bilby, personal communication, 1996). However, because of the way that it features a very gifted singer, Sister Tynsi, a traditional Rasta message is given a broader appeal.

The Mobilized Gaze: From Vision to Videography

> Dis is not de same movement today as in Back o' Wall days. I-n-I are now d'pon a more ambassadorial tradition. Mon haffa know how ta deal wid people differently dis time.
>
> Bongo Shephan, 1994, Cypress Hall, St. Andrew, Jamaica

My own experience in moving with Rastafari outside Jamaica and in moving with the Nyabinghi House "in yard" confirm these intertwining and deterritorializing flows between Rastafari who are geographically distant and often of different social backgrounds yet motivated by the same ideals and concerns. The kinds of reciprocal flows noted above — of Elder trods abroad and "pilgrimages" to Jamaica — position the House as a transnational space. In North America and elsewhere, cosmopolitan Rastafari have achieved a measure of authority and influence based on their groundings with the Elders. Conversely, many of the Elders now affect a wider field of social relations through the social links they maintain with cosmopolitan Rastafari outside Jamaica. This has brought video, radio, local and cable television, as well as print media, increasingly into the picture with respect to the circulation of visual media about — as well as by and for — Rastafari.

Over the past seven or eight years, an increasing number of my interactions with Rastafari have centered around the exchange and circulation of videotaped materials. Indeed, recently I participated in taping a cable television program (entitled "Reasonings") with several local Rastafari in Washington, D.C.; provided videotape documentation to a Jamaican brethren recently returned from London via Ethiopia and South Africa; exchanged several items of "historic" videotape documentation with a local brethren; and sent additional videos to the House in Jamaica where a number of Nyabinghi centers maintain their own "archives."

In my view, one of the ways the House seeks to bring participants into the culture and adapt its roots traditions to metropolitan contexts is through increasing use of VCR technology and the circulation of videotapes that document the cultural and spiritual life of the House. This medium has extended the boundaries of this imagined community by providing a "mobilized gaze." That is, these visual documents serve to artificially extend the boundaries of the "nation" through generating discussion about a wider network of individuals — some of whom are only present via representations of their performance in the events being documented. Circulation of these second-order representations is actually well adapted to pre-existing networks of communication among members of a community that has always been dispersed.

I first became aware of this process in the mid-1980s following a number of major international conferences on Rasta. It is hardly surprising that the Rastafari would turn to VCR technology since they have always been communicators. Later, in 1988, 1989, and 1990 I became involved in the process, assisting a number of delegations to travel to the United States in my role as an anthropologist at the Smithsonian. These missions were mounted in direct response to a call from members of Rastafari communities who felt themselves to be under siege by the state and its agents of authority.[19] The result was a series of public programs, which sought to educate the public about the authentic spiritual traditions and culture of Rastafari. These events were widely videotaped both by Rastafari in these communities and others to document the unprecedented and historic nature of these occurrences. The production and circulation of these media within selected social networks has, coupled with publishing initiatives cited above, been central to the elevated profile that the House has assumed.

Bear in mind that we need to distinguish between commercial media flows, which are promoted in magazines such as *The Beat, Dub Missive, Reggae Times*, and *Reggae Review* and videotapes which, in effect, circulate within the House.[20] We are talking about video shot by and for Rasta that is not commercially distributed. These are videos of Elders' "trods" (recently to Ethiopia); of Nyabinghi sessions in Jamaica, Toronto, Washington, D.C., and elsewhere; preachifying and oratory of Elders; reasonings on Rasta livity, repatriation, black history, gender relations, personal testimony, and the struggle of Rastafari for dignity, cultural autonomy, and economic development in Jamaica and elsewhere.

With respect to videotape media, my own experience with the first delegation of Rastafari Elders who visited the U.S. in 1988 is illustrative. It was not merely that the venues at which the Elders presented were videotaped — the Elders' delegation arrived with videotape documentation. During their visit they were lodged in at a brethren's residence in Baltimore where they remained for over six weeks. This site served as a kind of "open house" for local Rastafari and other members of the black community where, almost nightly, there were reasonings, 'binghi chanting, and screenings of videos shot at Nyabinghi around Jamaica. The Elders had indeed traveled with their culture — themselves, their oratorical skills, their drums, *and* video representations of their traditional ritual and cultural life "in yard." Over the course of that month, the contents of these videos were the subject of considerable direct elaboration through reasoning and personal testimony.

As a gateway into the roots traditions of the movement, these videotapes need to be appreciated within the social context of Rastafari communities outside Jamaica. By and large, Rastafari in these settings find it necessary to maintain a lower profile with respect to their ritual life than is possible in Jamaica, due to the illegal status of their sacrament, police surveillance, and the economic realities of metropolitan life. Rastafari ritual and ceremonial life, therefore, is necessarily truncated and tailored to the rhythms of a more regimented life in the urban centers of North America. Nyabinghi assemblies, when they are held, are typically limited to one-night assemblies rather than the three- or seven-day celebrations found in Jamaica.

A number of points on the Rastafari use of videotaped materials to extend community within the transnational sphere are useful here. While the very existence of these media — video images — is a reflection of modern technology, it is necessary to point out that the Rastafari are not of one mind about this process. The issue of who can videotape, under what circumstances, and with what audience in mind tends to be a matter of ongoing debate worked out in terms of what Rastafari call "collective security" (i.e., with a course of action taken only after prolonged and democratic debate in which all voices are heard).

It has been my observation that control over the dissemination of these tapes reflects a very traditional Rasta pattern of carefully managing relations of trust and reciprocity. They do not circulate willy-nilly. Rather, they pass between and within communities by brethren or sistren who share personal relationships of trust and a long-term commitment to the faith. This kind of exchange of communicative media is roughly equivalent to the way the Rastafari in the Kingston slums managed to create an alternative space for cultural communication. In this sense, the flow of this medium remains embedded in received understandings about who can "call" or assemble the House and about how the collective security of its members — those present spiritually as well as physically — will be ensured.

Even in the heyday of the camps and yards, it was impossible for a given individual to know and interact with everyone. At the same time, a strong sense of community resulted from the fact that virtually all brethren were "grounded" in small face-to-face groups of individuals who reasoned and chanted together. This has always enabled Rastas to keep abreast of the affairs and concerns of a far wider collectivity of people that those with whom they have actual ongoing interaction. The frequently and volume of face-to-face interactions within the mediascape, while differently structured, now provide an alternative for traditional patterns while continuing to give brethren and sistren a sense of involvement with a much larger collectivity of individuals.

From my perspective, video — and the social contacts it facilities — now constitutes a mobiled gaze by which global connectedness is effected within the House. Through the use of visual technology, brethren and sistren gain a feel for Rasta life elsewhere — or the reach of Rastafari elsewhere. An interesting example involves an American-born brethren living in Washington, D.C. with whom I am familiar. Recently, he traveled to the U.S. Virgins Islands. There, among other Rastas, he was greatly impressed by the reasoning of Ras Boanerges, a Jamaican patriarch. It was on videotape, however, that he witnessed the Elder's reasoning, which had been shot during a mission to the V.I. by members of the House. This experience generated an exchange of videotape materials between this brethren and members of the St. John community.

The example raises another point about the use of videotape as a form of communication. Both in face-to-face interaction and on video, Elders have become increasingly self-conscious about the House's construction and dissemination of Rasta history. The amount of critical discussion I have heard about these visual documents suggests to me that at least some 'binghi brethren and sistren see the House reflexively in terms of their own representations. This suggests that delegates on these missions (and the media they beget) increasingly circulate within a symbolic economy of performance (cf. Knight, 1992:242).[21]

Videotaped documentation of the personal testimony of various Elders who have "pass through" the persecution of the early years of Rasta is an example. This makes the testimony meaningful to those in Rasta communities abroad who are the targets of state sponsored repression or media attempts to criminalize or trivialize their culture. Hearing Elder Rastas describe their experiences of bearing many "crosses" on their personal journey and having come "from way down in the valley" serves to inspire others and validate the faith and vision of Rastafari.

Invariably, when Elders, either in Jamaica or abroad, comment on such visual documents they frame a contrast between the former outcast status of the movement — to which they bear living testimony — and its present state of international recognition. Once, while visiting Ras Pidow, a Washington, D.C. Elder, I watched a tape of him performing in Washington's Freedom Plaza at JAMFEST (a celebration commemorating 30 years of Jamaican Independence).

This elder opened the first day of festivities with his poetry accompanied by an ensemble of 'binghi drummers. Then on tape he described what he was actually doing 30 years prior on Jamaican Independence Day, August 1, 1962. He provided a testimony of his arrest, jailing, and trial on an herb charge as well as of his trial, at which "Father [Selassie I] delivered him" by putting the right words in his mouth to speak to plead his case to the judge.

Within the context of social relations of brethren and sistren who know each other, videos sustain the idea of community as an expanded field of social relations — one by which speakers/viewers can assess the contents and "consciousness" of what other speakers say and how they present themselves. In this sense, video can reinforce a traditional aspect of the culture. This raises a related point — that video often circulates in contexts where it is subject to further contextualization, critique, and dialogue. These flows continue to be enmeshed within a community of "speakers who speak to each other and about each other." Set within these social linkages, the communications on video elicit feedback from other members of the House who bring their own critical and aesthetic perspectives to bear upon how successfully 'binghi culture and the core premises of the movement are being represented.

Another change that these flows seem have promoted are more visible linkages between the Elders and Rastafari who are reggae artists. The House has described its relationship to reggae through an arboreal metaphor: "Reggae is the branch, Nyabinghi is the root. In order to know Rastafari you have to take it from the root." At the same time, it is probably fair to say that considerable ambivalence has existed among traditional Rastafari toward the commercial, not to mention "slack," aspects of this music. My own view is that the transnational flows have closed the distance between the two considerably. A number of the tapes circulating both inside and outside Jamaica reveal the dependence that traditional Rastafari in places such as Washington, D.C. and New York have on reggae promotions, artists, and venues (e.g., Bob Marley celebrations in Washington, D.C. are now regularly opened by chanting, drumming, and testimony by Nyabinghi Elders). Conversely, in Jamaica a growing number of reggae artists are involved in the House and some now sponsor the annual celebrations held by the House. Finally, it seems that many

Rastafari who make pilgrimages to Jamaica time these to coincide with Reggae Sunsplash, an international reggae event, and the House's celebration of Ethiopian New Year (Maskaram) and Marcus Garvey's birthday.

Conclusion

Inasmuch as this chapter is based on long-term ethnography conducted in multiple locations, it implicitly raises issues about how to evaluate current scholarship on the Rastafari. The diversity of opinion, belief, and practice that is a feature of the Jamaican context makes generalization about the movement problematic. The enfolding of the local and global spheres in the contemporary movement makes this more difficult. I agree with Yawney that work on Rastafari in the global context requires a long-term research strategy, attention to multiple sites, and collaboration with other scholars and with Rastafari brethren and sistren themselves.

It should be apparent from this discussion that the terms local and global with respect to "versions" of Rastafari cultural are potentially arbitrary and raise the issue of whose definition of "local" is in play. What I call soundscapes and mediascapes intertwine both roots versions as well as cosmopolitan versions of Rasta tradition. In large measure, the impetus that has brought Rastafari "out of yard" (i.e., Jamaica) has involved coordination between not only traditional Nyabinghi Elders, but also Rasta community activists, artists, and educated Rastafari who write about and represent the movement. This latter cohort, as observed above, has been keenly aware of the cultural capital represented by the House. They have clearly drawn upon the symbolic value of the Elders to authorize an orthodox version of Rastafari that confers a legitimacy upon Rastafari in the diasporas of the North American and European metropolitan areas. The reciprocal media flows, moreover, have repositioned the House in Jamaica, transforming it from a position of obscurity on the postcolonial periphery to the symbolic center of a geography of black resistance.

Indeed, the narrowing between center-periphery and local-global seems almost at the point of implosion. Any search of the World Wide

Web for Rastafari will turn up nearly a hundred hits, and most browsers register into double digits in a search on Nyabinghi. Recently, while surfing the Internet, I spent time "passing through" some of my favorite Rasta websites, which include the Virtual Nyabinghi, Nation On-Line, and Abyssinian Cyberspace.

Endnotes

1. Insofar as it is organized around Elders as nodal points in the creation and dissemination of ideology, the soundscape is a resident/resonant archive of popular memory that traces continuity with the history of African-Jamaican and pan-African struggle.

2. The soundscape is very much an evaluative environment in which individuals are called upon not only to make ongoing discriminations between ambient babble and "conscious" sounds but to maneuver in a context of linguistic indirection. Previous writings on Rasta speech have virtually ignored this social aspect of speech behavior despite the conspicuous importance which the Rastafari themselves attach to it. In the Rasta doctrine of "word-sound-and-power," words are always a two-edged force. They carry the uplifting force of "life" and "love" as well as the purifying but potentially destructive force of "fire." Because the word is regarded as inherently life-affirming, it is held that there are no words which can offend the true and heartical Rasta. Words that lack substance or which are off the mark are said to simply "pass through," being dismissed as "void" and "burned" within the heartical fire of the intended addressee. Rastafari continuously monitor each other's consciousness according to the sounds which individuals may "take unto" or "follow" and those which they ignore or "dash away."

3. From the early to mid-1980s, the Republic of South Africa conducted a vigorous propaganda campaign to influence American and European foreign policy and minimize external pressures on the reform of apartheid. Propaganda materials were available to U.S. citizens upon request. After returning to Washington, D.C., in March 1986, I requested materials and was sent, among other items, a pamphlet, "The Vital Role of South Africa's Minerals." This pamphlet was

particularly informative in light of Bongo Ketu's reasoning. It included a representation of the space shuttle Columbia accompanied by the statement: "South Africa is a valuable source of strategically scarce minerals used in the high technology construction of the U.S. space shuttle Columbia, seen here" (Publications Division of the Department of Foreign Affairs and Information, Republic of South Africa, March 1982).

4. In his biography of Bob Marley, White (1983) makes reference to this camp as the headquarters for the Theocractic Government of Rastafari and as "founded" by Bongo Shephan and Bongo Gabby. While this site did serve as such a meeting place between 1974 and the early 1980s, its history actually attests to the more complex relations between the soundscape and an emergent mediascape in Rastafari during the late 1960s and early 1970s. Oral accounts have it that a handful of Rastafari first began to settle in this community in the late 1960s when Coxsone Dodd traveled with his sound system to keep dances out on the main road, a movement which was further encouraged by the general displacement of Rastafari from West Kingston during the mid-1960s. During the early 1970s, Bunny Wailer built a house on the hillside overlooking this camp and Chris Blackwell, possibly with Marley's encouragement, funded the erection of a community center in which Rastafari held their meetings. For a brief time, Bob and Rita Marley lived in the housing scheme about a half-mile from this camp. In 1974, during a Nyabinghi celebration, this camp was formally recognized as a "headquarters" for the Emperor Haile Selassie I Theocratic Government, also known as the House of Nyabinghi.

5. For the Rastafari, the concept of the seal is central to the scriptural authentication of the divinity of Emperor Haile Selassie (see *Revelation* 5:5–7), since only His Majesty, as the returned Christ, was seen worthy to open or "burst" the seven seals leading to the final judgement and redemption of the faithful. In Rastafari discourse, the bursting of the biblical seals is, among other things, intimately related to the idea of the judgement and destruction of the oppressor.

6. As noted above, the Rastafari (like other Jamaicans and West Indians) have elaborated techniques of linguistic indirection to comment upon the state of existing social relations.

7. For other accounts which provide insight into the diversity and creativity within the local Jamaican soundscape, see Bilby (1996), Homiak (1995), Owens (1975), Pulis (1994), and Yawney (1987, 1990).

8. The multiple metaphors and evaluative frames which Rastafari apply to speaking and speech abilities are an indication of the profound agency which they attribute to words. Thus, speech is, for them, "the works," the work that Jah calls upon them to perform as part of their divine duty. Among other prophetic sources, Rastafari draw upon the language of *Hebrews* 7 to express the timeless and unchanging duty that is expressed through their faith, "a priest forever after the order of Melchisedec."

9. This field encompasses a cosmology mapped onto the socialized body of the Dreadlocks Rastafari. In the process of reasoning, the brethren will, for example, refer to the locks as "telepathic antennae" or "mystic magnets" which "draw up communication with Zion." With respect to their own subjectivity in reasonings, an individual may state: "I guh up ina mi heavens (head)" or "I seat up ina mi heavens and reason wid de Fadda (God/Selassie)." Coupled with other aspects of discourse (e.g., the terms "Jah-mek-ya" (Jah makes here) and "I-thiopia"), such statements express the view that there is a special geographic relationship between Jamaica and Ethiopa. The former, an outpost of European colonialism, is "the Valley of Decision" where "all nations will be judged by Jah Rastafari, ruler of Zion and earth."

10. This correspondence between I/Eye emerged at a time when colonial surveillance of Rastas and definitions of social space emerged as strategies by the state to contain, discipline, and control the movement. It is surprising, therefore, that no scholar has yet remarked on the inherently counterhegemonic aspect of this linguistic register. The Rasta claims to be able to "stay in and look out" or to "seat up in his tatu [dwelling] and look out at wha gwaan ina Babylon."

11. On the verso of the postcards of Haile Selassie which Howell allegedly sold in 1934 as "passports" to Ethiopia was inscribed: "Leonard Perceival Howell, Traveled the world through."

12. Through reggae, many Jamaicans have come to acknowledge the necessity for a strong Afrocentric component to their national identity. The demands for social justice inherent in much of reggae music have not, however, been translated into political action. In this regard, reggae has allowed Garvey and Marley to be assigned to a "safe" niche within the pantheon of national heroes without significantly altering the status quo.

13. During the 1970s, the House of Nyabinghi became both a traveling culture and a deterritorialized space. The latter was achieved through the increasing use of recorders at islandwide binghi celebrations and the subsequent circulation Nyabinghi chants, testimony, and reasoning on audiocassettes among the brethren and sistren in both Jamaica and abroad. Within wide networks that constitute the House, this became a way of providing a niche for music which had virtually no commercial acceptance. During my first few years of fieldwork, I found that many Nyabinghi brethren and sistren had their own personal archives of tapes and would frequently play these tapes for hours on end as a way to revisit the occasion of the actual 'binghi and/or to critique the quality of "the work" or the "Ises" (praises) produced by the congregation at that event. In this way, the House maintained an ongoing presence in the experience of its members which transcended the time and space of a specific celebration.

14. The contemporary international movement might be considered to have bifurcated centers — Ethiopia and Jamaica. From this perspective, the Rasta diaspora is now characterized by a tension between the dystopic and utopic elements of its localization in Jamaica. Jamaica, once exclusively a "living hell" (e.g., "Egypt" or "the Pit of Jehosephat") to the Rastafari, is now also extolled as a "Blessed Land, Jah-mek-ya," the site of the movement's religious revelation.

15. These events include a delegation of Elders who traveled through the Eastern Caribbean in 1982. The first official missions outside the Caribbean, known as "The Voice of Thunder: Dialogue with Nyabinghi Elders," was organized in Toronto in 1984. In 1986, an international Rastafari conference, "Rastafari Focus," was held as part of Caribbean Focus at the Commonwealth Institute in the United Kingdom (see Yawney, chapter 8, this volume).

16. Yawney (personal communication 1990) has described the travel of traditional Rasta culture during the 1980s as involving a "second wave of missionization" atop the influences of reggae which began in the 1970s.

17. There is clearly a dual draw to Jamaica based on the elevated visibility of the Nyabinghi House in recent years and the heightened activity of Kingston's recording studios. Ken Bilby (personal communication) has noted that there is an economic component to this

movement in that employment is provided for traditional Rastafari drumming ensembles as backup for musicians who record in Jamaica. These traditional roots musicians have probably fared poorly during the dancehall era with its emphasis on computer-generated rhythms.

18. In 1994, I provided Ras E.P. McPherson an audiocassette of my own research with the Howellites, a tape which had been recorded during a meeting of three members of Howell's remnant community and five of the Nyabinghi Elders who were preparing to travel abroad to represent the House in 1988. The tape I recorded was combined with earlier recordings done by Ras McPherson in the early 1980s. Ras Mortimo Planno subsequently put McPherson in touch with Ras Denroy Morgan in Brooklyn who, in turn, arranged the production facilities for this CD in 1995. Only subsequent to my reasoning with Ras Denroy in September of 1996 did I realize our mutual connections to the CD.

19. Rastas in metropolitan communities have found themselves periodically under siege, having to deal with forms of oppression and racism around the criminal justice system, immigration practices, and the like. A number of these missions abroad have been designed to educate the public about the true nature of Rastafari practice and to enable local Rasta communities to more effectively represent themselves. As Yawney (1995:3) argues, Rastafari under such circumstances "may quite possibly rely increasingly on the more orthodox forms of livity for religious and cultural protection."

20. In the former category I am speaking about productions inspired by reggae-driven Jamaican popular culture. This includes Jamaican films such as *The Harder They Come* (1973), *Rockers* (1978), *Countryman* (1982), and *The Land of Look Behind* (1981).

21. The focus on Nyabinghi traditions which can travel has, I believe, had an impact upon "reasoning" as a ritualized, intensive, and time-consuming communicative event. Over the last ten years, the circles of brethren with whom I move in the Nyabinghi House expend visibly less time and energy on this activity than I witnessed during my early years of fieldwork. More focus is given to preachifying, counsels of Elders, and activities in Nyabinghi centers. I say this with some caution as an impressionistic view based on much shorter periods in the field since my initial fieldwork.

References

Anderson, Benedict 1991 *Imagined Communities: Reflections on the Origins and Spread of Nationalism* (revised edition). New York: Verso.

Appadauri, Arjun 1990 Disjunction and difference in the global cultural economy. *Public Culture* 2(1):1–24.

Appadauri, Arjun 1991 Global ethnoscapes: notes and queries for a transnational anthropology. In: *Recapturing Anthropology* (ed., Richard G. Fox). Santa Fe, NM: School of American Research Press.

Bilby, Kenneth 1995 *Caribbean Currents: Caribbean Music from Rhumba to Reggae*. Philadelphia: Temple University Press.

Bilby, Kenneth and Leib, Elliott 1983 *From Kongo to Zion: Three Black Musical Traditions from Jamaica* (liner notes). Heartbeat Records.

Brenneis, Donald 1988 Talk and transformation. *Man* (NS) 22:499–510.

Chevannes, Barrington 1995 *Rastafari: Roots and Ideology*. Syracuse, NY: Syracuse University Press.

Chevannes, Barrington 1981 The Rastafari and the urban youth. In: *Perspective on Jamaica in the Seventies* (ed., Carl Stone and Aggrey Brown). Kingston: Jamaica Publishing House.

Clifford, James 1992 Traveling cultures. In: *Cultural Studies* (eds., Lawrence Grossberg, C. Nelson, and P. Treichler). New York: Routledge.

Clifford, James 1994 Diasporas. *Cultural Anthropology* 9(1):302–338.

Frankenberg, Ruth and Mani, Lata 1993 Crosscurrents, crosstalk: race, "postcoloniality" and the politics of location. *Cultural Studies* 7(2):292–310.

Gjerset, Heidi 1994 First generation Rastafari in St. Eustatius: a case study in the Netherlands Antilles. *Caribbean Quarterly* 40(1):64–77.

Homiak, John 1994a From yard to nation: Rastafari and the politics of eldership at home and abroad. In: *Ay Bobo: Afro-Karibische Religionen* (ed., Manfred Kreamser). Vienna: Universitatsverlag.

Homiak, John 1994b Rastafari voices reach Ethiopia. *American Anthropologist* 96(4):958–63.

Jah Bones 1985 *One Love: Rastafari History, Doctrine, and Livity*. London: Pearson & Brunlees, Ltd.

Jan van Dijk, Frank 1995 Sociological means: colonial reactions to the radicalization of the Rastafari in Jamaica, 1956–59. *New West Indies Guide* 6(1–2):67–101.

Knight, John 1992 Globalization and new ethnographic localities: anthropological reflections on Gidden's *Modernity and Self-Identity*. *JASO* 23(3):239–51.

Owens, Joseph 1975 *Dread: The Rastafarians of Jamaica*. Kingston: Sangster Publishers.

Peek, Philip 1981 The power of words in African verbal arts. *Journal of American Folklore* 94:19–42.

Pulis, John 1993 "Up-full sounds:" language, identity, and the worldview of Rastafari. *Ethnic Groups* 10:285–300.

Reisman, Karl 1974 Noise and order. In: *Language in Its Social Setting* (ed., William Gage). Washington, DC: The Anthropological Society of Washington.

White, Timothy 1983 *Catch a Fire: The Life of Bob Marley*. London: Elm Tree Books.

Yawney, Carole D. 1994 Rastafari sounds of cultural resistance: Amharic language training in Trenchtown, Jamaica. In: *Ay Bobo: Afro-Karibische Religionen* (ed., Manfred Kremser). Vienna: Universitatsverlag.

Yawney, Carole D. 1995 Tell out King Rasta doctrine around the whole world: the Rastafari in global perspective. In: *The Reordering of Culture* (eds., Alorna Ruprecht and C. Taiana). Ottawa: Carleton University Press.

Yawney, Carole D. 1987 Who killed Bob Marley. *Canadian Forum*, December 1984, pp. 29–31.

6: SPIRITUAL BAPTISTS IN NEW YORK CITY: A VIEW FROM THE VINCENTIAN CONVERTED

Wallace W. Zane

Introduction

Spiritual Baptists are found throughout the Eastern Caribbean and in places to which people from the Caribbean have migrated. Henney, who studied the Vincentian Spiritual Baptists, described them as a form of fundamentalist Christianity (Henney, 1971, p. 219; 1974, p. 23). Glazier, who has written more than anyone else about the religion, has identified the beliefs of the Spiritual Baptists in Trinidad as polytheistic (Glazier, 1983, p. 4; 1992, p. 143). While these two views seem irreconcilable, they do in fact reflect the very wide variation that occurs in Spiritual Baptist belief and practice. Spiritual Baptists from the island of St. Vincent, also called *the Converted*, have a different tradition from those on other islands.

This chapter examines what happens when the (more) fundamentalist Vincentian Converted meet up with the (more) polytheistic Trinidadian (and other) Spiritual Baptists in Brooklyn, New York, where Trinidadians and Vincentians and people from every Caribbean nation have migrated. Converted practices in New York change in response to contact with others. Besides religions from the Caribbean, the Converted interact with American churches in Brooklyn, who present further inducements to change. I begin with a description of the Spiritual Baptists of St. Vincent. Then I present the challenges faced by the Converted in living and worshipping in New York, along with the ways the religion has changed in response to those factors.[1]

The history of St. Vincent has been characterized by massive migration (voluntary or involuntary), into and out of, from its first settlement. The British and French, who controlled the island at various times, imported scores of thousands of slaves from Africa. The British deported thousands of Garifuna (descendants of African

maroons and the aboriginal Caribs) to Central America. After emancipation, many of the former slaves began migrating to Trinidad and
Guyana where wages were higher than in St. Vincent. That pattern
continued into the twentieth century with Aruba and Trinidad, then
England, Canada, and the United States as destinations. Trinidad,
always of high importance, has persisted as a destination for Vincentian workers since the 1830s (Basch, Schiller, & Szanton Blanc, 1994,
p. 60).

By the 1850s, police reports indicate that the Converted religion
was established in St. Vincent (Fraser, 1995). Sometime in the early
1900s, Vincentian migrants had carried the religion to Trinidad, where
it acquired the name Spiritual Baptist, and altered in the process
(Hackshaw, 1992, p. 78). The exact origins of the Spiritual Baptists are
debated, but all agree that the religion is composed of African and
European elements and developed its own form in the West Indies
(see Houk, 1995, pp. 71–76).

As part of a colonial effort to eliminate Africanisms in Vincentian
society (Cox, 1994), the religion of the Converted was illegal in St.
Vincent from 1912 to 1965 by the provisions of the Shaker Prohibition
Ordinance (St. Vincent, 1927, 1965). Although it was acknowledged
as long ago as 1907 that they preferred the name Converted (Cox,
1994, p. 214), colonial authorities persisted in calling them Shakers.
That name is only used derogatorily today.

Although sharing numerous features with religions elsewhere in
the Caribbean, many characteristics of Converted religion, including
the beliefs attached to the practices, are significantly different. While
most religions developing in the African diaspora are characterized
by possession — "working the spirit" (J. Murphy, 1994) — Converted
religion is characterized by travel in spiritual lands. It is not just a
motif; it is an experience normatively expected of all believers. Travel
to different lands is a familiar event in Vincentian life in various
forms, physically by the transnational nature of the culture and spiritually by the practice of Converted rituals.

The Converted in St. Vincent

The Converted are not unique among diasporan religions in their
emphasis on travel over possession (see Seaga, 1982, for Jamaican

Pukkumina; and Chaumeil, 1992, for Brazilian Daime), but by all published accounts no spiritual landscapes in the Caribbean are elaborated as much as the Converted and other Spiritual Baptists. The spiritual world is perceived as a spiritual aspect of the physical earth. Places to which the Converted regularly travel are a spiritual version (or the spiritual aspect) of Zion, Africa, China, India, Jerusalem, Bethlehem, Canaan, the Valley of Jehoshaphat, the Desert, the Jungle, as well as various places on top of and under the sea, and a large number of other cities, countries, and islands. They (spiritually) meet the people who live in those places, learn their songs and dances, as well as other useful knowledge.

The Vincentians who become Converted are those least likely to travel physically. They tend to be the poorest on the island. Most Converted I talked to in St. Vincent had never been outside of St. Vincent and the Grenadines. For the Vincentian Converted, the is-land-bound world is articulated with an ability to transcend the barriers (poverty, sea, air) that keep them from first-hand knowledge of other places.

Where they travel in the spirit is a wonderful and varied world of people and spirits and spiritual lands. As spiritual workers, each with her and his own task, the Converted (especially the more experienced and dedicated ones) are expected to spend quite a lot of time in the spirit realm. This is perhaps the most astonishing feature of the Converted as Christians and as a religion in the world — regular travel in spiritual realms for all members of the religious community, not just the leaders as in the shamanic model (cf. Winthrop, 1991, p. 256). Travel in the spirit is not a vacation; it is undertaken for the acquisition of knowledge for spiritual work.

Vincentian Converted identity is enhanced by the concept that spirits (other than God) need not be supplicated for favors in the spiritual world. The Converted can go to the spiritual world and do the work themselves. This contrasts with most Caribbean religions, where the emphasis is on spirits coming to the site, to the person, to the aid of the situation. However, the Converted do work "with spirits." Each Converted person has a saint. The saint acts as a spirit helper, pointing the way or imparting knowledge in the spiritual realm. Saints in Vincentian Converted cosmology are not iconic be-ings like the Catholic saints with highly specialized niches. They are more like generalized spirit helpers. Some Converted people do not know the name of their saint, but can give a vivid description based on the encounter with the saint in the spiritual world. The most commonly named saints (e.g., Catherine, Philomene, John the Baptist, Michael) are the same as those recognized in Shango (Herskovits & Herskovits, 1947, p. 331). However, rather than a saint possessing someone's body, as in Shango or Orisha (e.g., Houk, 1995) the Converted person meets with the saint in the spirit world for instruction and guidance. The Converted person "works with" the saint; the saint does not work through the Converted person. It is the Holy Spirit that does that.

In spite of the presence of saints, the emphasis of the Converted is always on travel (cf. Parks, 1981, p. 49; Herskovits & Herskovits, 1947, pp. 271–272). They are always going somewhere. "They [*or* We *or* I] ain't going nowhere" is an often-heard metaphor for failure in Converted religion. The Converted person becomes Christian in *The Pilgrim's Progress*, traveling the heavenly road, with lessons to learn and work to do on the way.[2] Many tunes sung in church are called *roads*, *keys* (to spiritual cities), and *ships*. The church itself is called a ship. The song leader is frequently named the *captain*, directing the ship of the church by his selection of songs. The captain also leads *doption* — formalized rhythmic movements akin to dancing that denote travel in the spiritual realm. This is usually participated in by several in the congregation during the service who, by the doption, travel together to specific spiritual locales.

While traveling is a metaphor that organizes experience in the Converted church, the stated purpose of the meetings is the worship of God. Prayers, singing, and preaching (or other public speaking) take up most of the service. Without the doption and the distinctive uniforms and paraphernalia of the Converted, one may mistake Converted worship for that in a Pentecostal church. When I asked Converted ministers and church members which church was most like them, Pentecostals (for their similarly ecstatic worship) and Methodists (because the Converted use the Methodist Order of Service) figured equally in the responses.

Unlike the Pentecostals and Methodists in St. Vincent, the Converted are strongly identified with Africa. Africa is believed to be the source of the spiritual techniques of the Converted, which were turned to Christian purposes when the enslaved Africans converted to Christianity. Some African traits found in a general way in other islands are associated exclusively with the Converted in St. Vincent. For instance, head-ties, commonly worn by women throughout the African diaspora, are, in St. Vincent, a distinctive mark of the Converted. Other Vincentian women do not wear them for fear of being identified as a member of the religion that is still stigmatized thirty years after legalization. An ornamental plant imported from West Africa known as *the dragon* (*Dracaena* spp.) is planted on the graves of Converted people and on no others. I was told a number of times about the Converted religion that "the work came from Africa." That work entails the performance of rituals, as well as travel in the spiritual world.

Mourning and Baptism are the defining Converted rituals (cf. Simpson, 1966). *Mourning* is a period of ritual seclusion in the *mourning room* during which the Converted person talks to God and expects to travel spiritually. Introduction to the experience of the spiritual lands usually occurs at this time. Mourning is also called the *pilgrim journey* or *spiritual journey*. After having traveled to the cities during mourning the pilgrim is said to belong to the cities to which she has traveled. It is common to hear reference to a church member as, for instance, an "African woman," or as belonging to the "Chinese tribe," or as a "Canaanite." The Converted person may go to the cities to which she belongs by means of doption in the church service. Most of the people I knew who mourned in St. Vincent stayed in the room (ritually blindfolded, praying, tended by others) for 12 to 15 days.

Baptism is by immersion. Most Converted were christened in another church as an infant. Although the Anglicans, Methodists, and Roman Catholics (called *the established churches* by Vincentians) refer to christening (or infant baptism) as baptism, the Converted consider immersion to be the only Biblically recognized baptism. Being baptized by immersion is a symbol of conversion to the Spiritual Baptist faith. Converted baptism in St. Vincent is preceded by three days in the mourning room. This is called the *baptismal journey*. Travels occur during this period and normally one obtains a role or task in the church as well. The two key rituals, mourning and baptism, are reflected in the name Spiritual Baptist, mourning being the means by which the Converted enter and work in the spiritual world, and immersion as their form of baptism. The name also reflects the two primary historical influences on the religion, the spiritual work from African sources and baptism from Christianity.

Every time one mourns, as well as during one's baptismal journey one may acquire ritual roles in the spiritual realm which are then performed in the physical setting of the church. These are called *spiritual gifts* or *spiritual names* and everyone is expected to have one. One's gift may be as humble as *florist* (who cleans and decorates the church), or more elevated like the *shepherd*, who is responsible to morally guide the church. Other spiritual gifts (e.g., *watchman*, *warrior*, *leader*, *diver*, *prover*, *teacher*) each carry a specific ritual task (cf. Glazier, 1983, pp. 52–54; Henney, 1974, pp. 30–31). The *pointer* is the highest grade of spiritual gift and a pointer is usually the head of the church. The primary role of the pointer is to "point the pilgrim on" to the spiritual world. The spiritual journeys of the Converted are directed by the pointer of the church (under the guidance of the Holy Spirit). The status of pointer, like all of the gifts in the spiritual hierarchy, is obtained by mourning. The pointer is usually the one in the congregation who has mourned the most.

Women are essential to the work of the church. Many of the spiritual gifts and ritual roles are exclusive to women. There are female pointers, called *pointing mothers*, and a woman may head a church as well as a man. Each church must have a father and a mother. They perform different tasks (but this varies considerably according to the tradition in each congregation). If a small church lacks one of either a pointing father or a pointing mother, neighboring churches assist in important rituals. Sometimes this is referred to as "borrowing" the individual(s) from the other church.

The ritual work the Converted do is not confined to the church. In St. Vincent, the Converted are the spiritual workers of the island. They both "work in the spirit" (that is, travel) and work with spirits. For a good proportion of the non-Converted in St. Vincent, the Converted are who to call when it comes to spirits. In fact, in St. Vincent, they are used by the general population to conduct wakes (cf. Gullick, 1971, p. 10; Young, 1993, p. 164). "Most people use them [...] because they are good with spirits," I was told by a non-Converted Vincentian. They can "put the spirit [of the loved one] to rest." The local Converted pointer will be contacted to *clean a house* (from evil spirits) or to dispense a *spiritual bath* to remove feelings of oppression or sickness, and like operations. The Converted are alone, or nearly so, in performing these sorts of services in St. Vincent.

In a number of ways Vincentians who are not Converted rely on the Converted because of their spiritual powers. Concordant with the belief in the power of the Converted is some amount of fear of the Converted among the general population. Spiritual power is not restricted to pointers. All Spiritual Baptists are believed by most Vincentians to have special powers. The spiritual work the Converted do is sometimes confused with *obeah* (sorcery) by many Vincentians. The Converted respond that obeah is the use of spiritual power for bad, while they use their spiritual power for good purposes. Time and again during my field work, I was warned by non-Converted to be careful because the Converted might "put a spirit on you" — that is, work obeah. Accusations of obeah are often directed against pointers and other Converted.

Other Religions in St. Vincent

Converted see themselves as alike and different from other religions in St. Vincent and the Caribbean. These can be divided into Africa-oriented religions and Euro-Christian religions. In St. Vincent, the only other religion with an African orientation is Rastafarianism. However, to the Vincentian Converted, not much about the Rastas is seen to come from Africa (as the spiritual work of the Spiritual Baptists is said to do). Most Converted see the Rastas as very dedicated people trying to live as people did in Biblical times, but who delude themselves that Haile Selassie is the focal point of worship and power instead of Jesus Christ (of course the Rastas would say that Selassie *is* Christ). Both in St. Vincent and in Grenada, I did encounter Rastafarians at Spiritual Baptist (Converted) events who told me they were Spiritual Baptist and Rasta at once (see Littlewood, 1993, who describes a comparable juxtaposition in Trinidad). Rastas are not found in this sort of association with other religions in St. Vincent. That some Rasta individuals worship freely with and as Spiritual Baptists is a consequence of the African orientation of both religions and of the spiritual flexibility of Converted religion.

From the Vincentian point of view, all other African religions exist elsewhere. In St. Vincent, three types of religions with an African orientation are talked about by the Converted: Haitian Vodun, Shango/Orisha, Revival/Spiritual Baptist. In St. Vincent, the word *voodoo* is a synonym with obeah. *Voodoo* is talked about as having overrun Haiti. It is not understood to be a religion (as Vodun) in its own right. To the average Vincentian, Vodun is voodoo and that means sorcery.

Shango/Orisha poses a similar problem to the Converted. Shango is thought to be somewhere between pure obeah and Spiritual Baptist work. Stories about Shango (from Vincentians returned from Trinidad) are often on the agenda in St. Vincent for visiting, church socials, moonlight nights, etc. For the Converted emigrating to Brooklyn, where Shangoists/Orisha worshippers also live and work and worship, the association (from Trinidad) of Shango with Spiritual Baptists is noted with apprehension.[3]

The Converted view (from St. Vincent) of Spiritual Baptists in other islands is mixed. Some, especially those returned from sojourns in Trinidad, claim all foreign Spiritual Baptists are really *Shango Baptists*. Others report that the Trinidadians do spirit-filled "God's work" as the Converted themselves do. Because ritual innovations are revealed by God during mourning, Spiritual Baptists on different islands are expected to have slight ritual differences — as are individual congregations in St. Vincent. Spiritual Baptists say, "Each house cooks its food different, but it's still food." However, because of the possible association of Trinidadian Spiritual Baptists with Shango, many Vincentians in St. Vincent, and in Trinidad, are wary of Trinidadian Spiritual Baptists.

From the beginning, the Converted have been different from the established churches on St. Vincent. However, the Converted must address the many Christian religions reaching St. Vincent from North America — namely, Southern Baptists, Pentecostals, and the Seventh Day Adventists. Departures that each of these denominations represent from mainstream Christianity on St. Vincent were formerly distinguishing features of the Converted alone. First, these three are quite visibly millenarian religions — a position the Converted held exclusively before.[4] Second, they all baptize by immersion — a defining feature of the Spiritual Baptists. Third, in the case of the Pentecostals, "they rejoice like us." Converted respondents in St. Vincent discussed practices that the other religions share with the Converted in such a way as to indicate substantial identity threats (e.g., "They took [this or that practice] from us"). But the threat is small. The Converted in St. Vincent are so long established and so much a part

of local culture compared to the intrusive religions that the Converted mainly consider the others to be failed imitators. In answer to
what it means that the Converted are called Baptists and the "American" (Southern) Baptists are also called Baptists, I was told, "They
carry the name, but they don't do the work."

The Converted see themselves as separated from other religions
by their closer adherence to the word of God and responsiveness to
the will of the Holy Spirit. Their concept of spiritual work (both as
travel and as the performance of distinctive rituals), as in the quote
above, also sets them apart. A large part of Vincentian Converted
identity is organized around experiences in the mourning room —
mainly consisting of travels in the spiritual lands. These are marked
by external symbols in the church such as flags representing various
spiritual cities, flowers, and *seals* (chalk drawings) that have specific
meanings revealed in the spiritual world. Symbols are also contained
in the uniforms the Converted are expected to wear to church. The
uniform of each Converted is different according to her experience in
the spirit world. Different aspects of the uniform — the manner in
which the head-tie is tied, colors in the uniform, the presence of
sashes, cords or belts — communicate to others in the congregation
regarding the spiritual city to which the Converted person belongs,
her spiritual gifts, and the saint with whom she works.

Much of Converted cosmology (e.g., the spiritual lands), many
ritual goods (such as flags and uniforms), and most of the ritual
practices are different from other religions in St. Vincent. Nonetheless,
Converted in St. Vincent primarily note two practices for self-definition, mourning and baptism. With the increasing presence of other
adult-baptizing religions in St. Vincent (specifically, Pentecostals, Sev-
enth-Day Adventists, and "American" Baptists), and the predomi-
nance of them in Brooklyn, mourning is stressed as the distinguishing
feature. The two prominent colloquial names for Spiritual Baptists in
St. Vincent, the Converted and *the Penitent*, imply the historical association of the religion and the practices. Conversion is exhibited by
adult baptism, repentance is evidenced by the mourning for sins.

Converted in New York

Population movement under colonialism (by the slave trade and
indenture) is a chief historical factor in the development of Caribbean

cultures. Currently as well, migration is the major factor in the creation of societal norms in the Caribbean (Jolivet, 1985). Not only are
Vincentians part of the larger African diaspora, but they sometimes
refer to the dispersal of Vincentians to other parts of the world as a
"Vincentian diaspora." An important destination in this diaspora is
Brooklyn, New York. It is estimated there were about 5000 Vincentians living in New York City in 1980 (Basch et al., 1994, p. 56). By
1996, the number had certainly increased, including large numbers of
illegal immigrants and long term visitors from St. Vincent. A Vincentian reporter I interviewed (who had lived most of his life in Brooklyn
before returning to St. Vincent in 1995) estimated the number of
Vincentians resident in Brooklyn at 40,000. The Vincentians I checked
with in Brooklyn agree with the 40,000 number, although the actual
figure is probably between five and forty thousand.

According to Gearing, two factors tend to push people out of
St. Vincent — the colonial preference for all things foreign over
things Vincentian and emigration as the "preferred response of the
Vincentian people to harsh economic conditions and political control"
(Gearing, 1992, p. 1279). The pressures for emigration from St. Vincent
are increasing (cf. Thomas-Hope, 1992, p. 155). To look at only one
factor, unemployment in St. Vincent rose gradually from 13.5 percent
in 1960, 13.8 percent in 1970, 23 percent in 1980 (Marshall, 1984), to
44 percent in 1990 (Miller, 1992), and 52 percent in 1995 (*The Vincentian*
newspaper, June 2, 1995, p. 19).

In New York, there are between 400 and 800 Vincentian Converted.[5] The percentage of Converted among Vincentians in New
York is probably around 3 percent. In St. Vincent, the ratio of Converted to the larger population is a minimum of 10 percent out of a
population of 106 thousand (St. Vincent, 1993, p. 14). Nearly everyone
I talked to in St. Vincent, from a Roman Catholic priest to ministers
in government, told me that there are far more Converted than are
reported in government records. The reason for the lower rate of
Converted among Vincentians in New York is simple. Converted
religion is a religion of the poor. Vincentians who travel abroad,
especially to America, tend to be those with the most money and the
most contacts (Thomas-Hope, 1992, p. 138). They are not the poorest
in the island.

This factor affects the congregational make-up of the Converted in
Brooklyn. Converted in New York are better off financially than those

in St. Vincent, they can afford to mourn more often, and receive more spiritual gifts. There is a higher number of mothers, teachers, and pointers in the Brooklyn Converted churches compared to those in St. Vincent.

There is a focal point to Vincentian identity (Converted and non-Converted) in New York and that lies in St. Vincent. Converted churches are a symbol and a reproduction of that core in the alien place. The fact that many of the Converted in Brooklyn joined the faith after moving to Brooklyn may be an expression of that feeling — of the need for a connection with home. Chaney (1987, p. 4) writes that "Caribbean migrants do not appear to leave their homelands definitely, even though they may never return except for visits. Their insertion in New York City retains a provisional quality."

In a way, all of Spiritual Baptist locality is temporary. This stems from the frequent relocation of meeting places necessitated by (former) state persecution, the requirement that spiritual work must often be done in people's houses (e.g., wakes), and the spiritual focus of the religion (the physical world is not as important as the spiritual world). As Glazier indicates for other Spiritual Baptists, it is the presence of the Converted who make the site sacred (Glazier, 1992, p. 143). They carry the sacredness with them. The site is far less important than the fact that the Converted are there. As an example of this idea, every service, whether in the church, at a home, in the market square or beside the road, requires a fresh consecration of the ritual space.

The provisional quality of Vincentian life in New York can be detected in a typical service in a Brooklyn church, most likely in a basement or a storefront. The service begins with a rite known as *consecration* or *surveying*. It accomplishes the same end as physical surveying — establishing boundaries — in this case, of a sacred space. While the congregation sings a hymn, designated members proceed to the four corners of the church (making a cross by their movements). Each *surveyor* is in charge of one element used in the consecration. One person has a bell, one a glass of water, one a bottle of perfume, one a calabash of grain. At each corner, a prayer is said, the bell is rung, and water, perfume, and grain is spilled on the floor. Then a trail is made (of rung bells and spilled water, perfume, and grain) from the doors of the church to the center, where the surveyors shake hands.

In St. Vincent, the heat evaporates the water quickly, but in Brooklyn the water tends to stay on the floor. In some churches, the poured water is mopped up after the consecration. One church has done away with the rite entirely. Another concession to the climatic differences between St. Vincent and Brooklyn is that the bare feet required at services in the tropics may be covered with slippers. I was present one night when a pointer denounced this practice. Those under his charge, however, were allowed to wear socks as protection from the cold concrete floor.

The service is opened by the *leader* or *leadress* who recites the liturgy of the (Methodist) Order for Morning Prayer (used morning and evening). Most people in the church carry (British) Methodist Hymn-Books, from which the majority of hymns are taken. The words to the hymns are still called out by the leader, as they are in St. Vincent where few can afford hymnals. After the liturgy is performed, a few members are invited to offer prayers — which they sing to tunes they have been given in the spiritual world. The rest of the congregation joins in the prayers by singing antiphonal responses.

After the prayers, the leader turns the service over to the pointer or the pointing mother. The pointer may make announcements or invite members or visiting Converted to speak. At some services, everyone present is expected to say something. *Visions* (dreams containing a message for the congregation) are reported at this time by the pointer or other members. The pointer may preach, although, as in St. Vincent, some churches rarely have a sermon. Singing is the most important part of the service and that is emphasized over speaking.

If an important ritual is called for (relating to mourning or baptism) it is commenced and occupies the rest of the evening. A *thanksgiving* may be given at this time as well. A thanksgiving is an offering of thanks from an individual for a particular grace from God. It involves supplying a table covered with food and candles (distributed to the congregation afterwards). The congregation is also usually fed a full meal by the thanksgiver. A thanksgiving is expensive and one seldom sees one in St. Vincent. In some Brooklyn churches they occur almost weekly.

Whether the occasion is an important ritual or a normal service, *doption* (also called *rejoicing*) is a usual part of the service. Doption is the term for special rhythmic movements accompanying journeys to spiritual lands in the church service. These movements and the vocalizations associated with them are physically similar to "labouring" or "trumping" in Jamaican Revival Zion churches, but the Converted give a very different meaning to the movements (cf. Chevannes, 1978, p. 8). Doption is contrasted with the journeys during mourning in which the person is usually lying down. The captain takes over the service at this time, guiding those doing doption to whichever lands the Holy Spirit directs him. Not everyone can do doption. There are different doptions for different cities, and one may only do the doptions for the cities to which she belongs (that is, the cities to which she has traveled during mourning). The rest of the congregation sings choruses and hymns to help the travelers along. Doption is the same in St. Vincent and in Brooklyn, but each congregation has its own tradition regarding the meaning of specific doptions. Doption may occur at different times in the service (depending on inspiration by the Holy Spirit), but it often signifies a climax to the meeting.

To end the meeting, the entire congregation recites a series of doxologies. In St. Vincent and in Brooklyn, church services usually last five hours. Many last longer.

In spite of numerous pressures for change, there is a close correspondence between rituals and ideas in St. Vincent and those in Vincentian churches in Brooklyn. In large part this is due to a high level of contact between Brooklyn and St. Vincent, including, for one Brooklyn church, a yearly pilgrimage to St. Vincent.

Changes in Vincentian Converted practice between St. Vincent and Brooklyn primarily relate to differences in economic and environmental conditions as well as the influence of culture contact. Some economic and environmental changes were noted above. However, the relative wealth does not necessarily make it easier to be a Converted. All who had something to say on the matter told me it is harder to be a Converted in Brooklyn than in St. Vincent. One reason is the lack of a sense of place in the larger community. Another is the different lifestyle required in New York. These changes affect all Caribbean religions. The difficulties negotiated by Haitian Vodunists in Brooklyn — "[w]ork pressures, distance, the problems of late-night travel in New York City, even a different sense of time" (Brown, 1991, p. 47) — apply equally well to the Converted.

Environmental and economic conditions have led to differences between Converted life and worship in New York and that in St.

Vincent. Exposure to other religions, however, motivates the greatest changes in the practice of Converted religion in New York.

Other Spiritual Baptists in New York

Although New York contains over one million West Indians (van Capelleveen, 1993, pp. 132–133), those from Trinidad affect the Vincentian Converted the most. Many Vincentians in New York spent time working in Trinidad before moving to America. Vincentians in Trinidad find a stigma attached to their nationality. "The Vincentians and Grenadians are small islanders [...] In Trinidad they are viewed as clients, a status tinged with an aura of inferiority" (Basch, 1987, p. 189; cf. Courlander, 1996, p. 103). This association carries over to the relation between the Vincentian Converted and the more numerous Trinidadian Spiritual Baptists in New York.

Trinidadian Spiritual Baptists offer some confusion to the Vincentian Converted. The term "Spiritual Baptist" originated in Trinidad. In St. Vincent, the official government name for the Converted is Spiritual Baptist. This changed from Christian Pilgrim or Pilgrim Baptist and Wesleyan Baptist two decades ago. The two ordaining denominations in St. Vincent (the Archdiocese and the Organization), covering about half of the churches there, have Spiritual Baptist in their full denominational name and nearly every Converted church is known as Spiritual Baptist. In St. Vincent, however, and among the Vincentians in Brooklyn, "Converted" is the word which evokes the most passion and identity. To differentiate the Vincentians from the Trinidadians, who have a different ritual tradition, I refer to the Vincentian Spiritual Baptists as Converted (as they do themselves — but not with the same frequency as Spiritual Baptist, or simply Baptist). The problem with names is more complex, however, as the Trinidadians will also sometimes refer to themselves as Converted. I do note that for the Trinidadians in Brooklyn, the name Spiritual Baptist carries more emotion, probably because that name is deeply rooted in Trinidad (and less well-rooted in St. Vincent). While terms of reference can be superficial in other circumstances, for the Converted in Brooklyn the subject is vital. Discussion of these matters take up large amounts of their time (cf. Hackshaw, 1992, pp. 77–98).[6]

The Spiritual Baptists in Barbados and Grenada (and Tobago and Venezuela) originated with migrants to Trinidad returning to their home countries. Some Vincentian presence is found among the Spiritual Baptists in other islands, but the influence is small. Every Vincentian Converted has been told since childhood that the religion emerged in St. Vincent and traveled to wherever else it is found. Many, maybe most, of the Trinidadian pointers and bishops discount the idea of a Vincentian origin (Hackshaw, 1992; Thomas, 1987), although some do admit to me that the Vincentian tradition is well-grounded in the spirit. Vincentians, coming from a small, poor country with few resources already have to contend with strong prejudice from Trinidad. To assert their country as the birthplace of one of the important religions in the Caribbean, a position of which they could be rightly proud, is difficult to do in the face of assertions to the negative from large, rich, better-educated Trinidad. Added to that is the fact that the Spiritual Baptists in all of the surrounding islands are practicing the Trinidadian tradition. Vincentians have been told that slaves in secret prayer and fasting in the Vincentian mountains established the techniques that make the Spiritual Baptists special among all Christians. In the face of Trinidadian claims to the contrary, Vincentians may be inclined to wonder if their religion is not after all a species of African Christianity (Aladura) rooting itself in Trinidad and spreading to St. Vincent as one important Trinidadian bishop in Brooklyn communicated to me (see also Brathwaite, 1982, p. 45).

Trinidadian rituals differ mainly in access to and acceptance of elements of ritual goods and symbols from other religions, notably Shango and Hinduism, although any observable tradition is fair game (for example, Buddhism and Confucianism [see Glazier, 1983] and Freemasonry — sources which do not yet have a notable presence in St. Vincent). This does not make the Trinidadian Spiritual Baptists any less Christian; not-Christian elements are simply additional routes of power and knowledge given to the Spiritual Baptists by God. Elements taken from Shango/Orisha and other religions among the Trinidadians vary by congregation and denomination (among at least eight Spiritual Baptist denominations in Trinidad [Hackshaw, 1992, p. 24]), but generally amount to a greater use and variety of physical symbols and ritual goods than in the Vincentian churches. Every physical item in the church has a spiritual counterpart. In addition, many spiritual items in the church are only visible to those

with "spiritual eyes." A steel sword which one might find in a Trinidadian church would be considered too strong a reliance on a physical symbol in St. Vincent, where the spiritual sword for which the
physical stands should only be seen by those who have (spiritual)
eyes to see it.[7]

The Trinidadian Spiritual Baptist churches I visited in Brooklyn
have a greater emphasis on the presence of spirits at the church
meetings than do Vincentian churches. Spirits other than the Holy
Spirit may come to a church service in St. Vincent and be entertained
(in some churches) by the lighting of candles, pouring of water, and
waving of specific flags on occasion. However, the interaction with
spirits that is so prominent in the Trinidadian churches in Brooklyn
(and some of the Vincentian ones there) is at least secondary in the
Converted churches. In St. Vincent, the primary spiritual activity is
travel in the spirit — either in journeys to the spiritual lands, or by
gazing (the ability to see people and places in the spiritual world
without traveling there). In other words, the Trinidadian churches
participate in the Caribbean-wide pattern of spiritual beings "coming
to" the believer rather than the Vincentian pattern of believing practitioners "going to" the spiritual beings — wherever they may be.
Spirits do come to the Converted churches, but the emphasis is
different.

Trinidadians travel, too, through gazing or doption as well as by
mourning, but the emphasis on the presence of spirits, with precisely
the same saint names as those emphasized by Shango, makes many
of the Trinidadian churches feel ideologically different from the Vincentian ones. Furthermore, the syncretic influences from other Christian denominations are mainly Roman Catholic (Trinidad being
primarily a Catholic country) — including saints' images (in 5 of the
7 Trinidadian Spiritual Baptist Churches I visited in Brooklyn). This,
visually at least, puts the Trinidadian churches at odds with the
Vincentian ones, who, coming from a Protestant tradition, tend to
eschew images of saints as idolatry. In the seventeen Converted
churches I visited in St. Vincent, only two had any representation of
saints — one had a six-inch statuette of St. Francis, and one, whose
pointer had spent many years in Trinidad, had two 18-inch statues on
the altar. Acknowledging the saints is fine to the Vincentians — they
see and converse with saints in the spiritual world frequently and
each Converted person usually has one saint they work with closely.

Keeping a statue of a saint, however, seems improper to most of the Converted who voiced an opinion. That said, one Vincentian shrugged her shoulders when I asked if she was offended at Trinidadians praying to saints. She said, "Everybody has a saint they work with. Why shouldn't you ask them for something?"

In addition, many of the Trinidadian churches in Brooklyn also have Hindu images, and in two I was able to observe a statue of the Happy Buddha, representing the spiritual city of China. Some of the ritual movements and spiritual dances among the Trinidadians are too different for the comfort of my Vincentian respondents; the influence of Shango, they said. A further "Shango" influence is found in that some of the Spiritual Baptist churches in the Trinidadian tradition will at times sacrifice a pigeon or dove.

Drums, never found in the Spiritual Baptist churches in St. Vincent, are present in most of the Trinidadian churches. While this is apparently a Shango influence, it does not bother the Vincentians as much as other differences. In their own churches, the Vincentians "play the drums" spiritually — that is, they imitate the instrument with their voices. The Trinidadian Spiritual Baptist churches I visited do not consider themselves Shango, and for the most part will not even acknowledge the term *Shango Baptist* (colloquially applied to all Spiritual Baptists by non-Spiritual Baptist Trinidadians I met in Brooklyn and to all Trinidadian Spiritual Baptists by many Vincentians). Those who the Vincentians consider Shango Baptist are sometimes called merely "Shango" and shunned as such by the Vincentians — even in circumstances where those same Trinidadians would have shunned Shango or Orisha religion themselves.

Despite some differences, the Trinidadian church service is in most respects identical to the Vincentian norm. Vincentian respondents with whom I visited the Trinidadian churches explained the Shango-like variances as errant knowledge on the part of the Trinidadians. Shango (Orisha), like voodoo (Vodun), is often conflated with obeah by the Converted. The perceived connection of obeah with Shango and Shango with the Trinidadian Spiritual Baptists forms part of the uneasiness some Converted feel in approaching a Trinidadian church. Trinidadians are believed by many Vincentians to be potential workers of obeah.[8] Pointers in New York make frequent reference to this belief (and the belief in obeah in general) in their sermons, trying to convince their congregations that the misfortunes they experience are the result of their own shortcomings, not from someone applying the powers of "bad" to them. The pointers' common aphorism: "You say somebody do you; but you do yourself."

In spite of a belief that there are some bad individuals among the Trinidadians, the Trinidadian Spiritual Baptists are seen as "fellow workers in the vineyard" trying to do good spiritual work for Christ. They are considered to be part of the same communion and denomination as the Vincentian Converted.

To make matters more confusing, Trinidadian Spiritual Baptists are not the only Spiritual Baptists in Brooklyn. While most of the Spiritual Baptists from the Caribbean appear to have historical connections to the ones from St. Vincent, the "Spiritual Baptists" from Jamaica and Guyana have an independent development and seem to have taken (or had ascribed to them) the name out of a sense of affinity, as the Converted themselves did (Hackshaw, 1992, pp. 78–82; cf. Pitt, 1955, p. 386). The identification of the Jamaican (Revival Zion) and Guyanese (Jordanite) religions with Spiritual Baptists is natural. They are each religions of the poor in their own countries; they are perceived as strange in their own countries; they wrap their heads with cloth, and work with spirits. They rejoice in a lively "pentecostal" fashion, and keep good fundamentalist doctrine — emphasizing the grace of Jesus Christ and justifying their actions with Biblical references. They are considered Spiritual Baptists by the Vincentians I was with. Again, the features which distinguish them from other churches in their home country — baptism by immersion and working with spirits, following the command of Christ in the third chapter of the gospel of John that one must be born of the water and the spirit — make these a natural ally of the Vincentian Converted (and Trinidadian Spiritual Baptists). Given the red letter injunction to baptize, it is not surprising that disparate Christian groups sensing in themselves a greater spirituality than others would use the words "Spiritual Baptist" as an identifying marker. Yet the Jamaicans are different from the Converted. Tellingly, the Vincentian pointer I was with told me in a low voice as we entered a Jamaican Spiritual Baptist church in Brooklyn, "They don't mourn."

Several of the Trinidadian churches have Vincentian heads (pointers or pointing mothers), but they practice the Trinidadian traditions and learned their ways in Trinidad (that is, the individual migrated from St. Vincent to Trinidad and then, eventually, to the United

States). Some do return to St. Vincent, but on return the least Vincentian of the traits are de-emphasized or are not practiced at all. A pointer in New York who had noticed this explained the reason for the conformity by saying, "The people wouldn't like it [the Trinidadian rituals]." The pressures to change abroad are countered by pressures for conformity at home (cf. Abrahams, 1983, pp. 83–87).

Other Caribbean Religions

Caribbean influences apart from other Spiritual Baptists have little influence on Converted practice. Language differences account for some of this, as does the visibility of other religions. While Converted in St. Vincent are aware of Haitian Vodun (as voodoo), it is little talked about in New York. When I asked why, I was told that voodoo is not an issue because Haitians are generally avoided (because of their association with voodoo). The same is true of Santeria from the Spanish-speaking Caribbean.

Converted also have little contact with Shango/Orisha. Both Shango from Trinidad and Pukkumina from Jamaica are avoided due to their practice of sacrifice. Because Shango is practiced by English-speaking West Indians, Vincentians show a rather high awareness of it. Many of the traits of the Shangoist (head-tying, working with spirits, Africa-orientation) are shared by the Converted. "Catching spirit" — the shaking behavior of spirit possession — for both looks nearly the same. However, the Shango practice is diabolical because they catch a spirit while the Spiritual Baptists catch the Spirit (a distinction made much of by the Spiritual Baptists).

The Converted in St. Vincent have no opportunity for contact with Shango practices, except for those individuals who might go to Trinidad or Grenada to work. Even then, prolonged direct contact with Shango is unlikely. In New York, the situation is the same. The Shango ceremonies tend not to be community affairs open to all, but accessible only by invitation. Nonetheless, the Shangoists in Trinidad (and Grenada) are associated more with the Spiritual Baptists that with any other religion. Shango does influence Vincentian Converted practice in that effort is sometimes expended by Converted to distance themselves from possible identification with Shango.

American Influence

As in St. Vincent, American religions in Brooklyn are influences for change. Although the Converted note with interest the big churches, flashy preachers, and radio and television exposure of the Euro-American and African-American churches in New York City, the Caribbean churches are more or less invisible to the Americans. In the recent book *The Black Churches of Brooklyn* (Tylor, 1994) there is not one mention of a West Indian church or of the Caribbean at all — in spite of the presence of hundreds of thousands of Black Caribbean church-goers in Brooklyn (see also L. Murphy, Melton, & Ward, 1993). The West Indian religions, whose appeal is limited to West Indians, present no threat to the American churches. The overwhelming presence of the American churches does present a challenge to the West Indians, however.

Once in the United States, multiplied varieties of Pentecostal and Baptist sects present themselves with features approaching more closely the Spiritual Baptist norms than do the Pentecostal and "American" Baptist versions in St. Vincent. Many of the Black Baptist churches in Brooklyn have similar singing rhythms (not found in any of the other churches in St. Vincent) and some, referring to the spiritual baptism believed to accompany water baptism, describe themselves as "spiritual baptists." One can see that people coming from a small island, trying to find their place in the world, and believing themselves to be a part of a larger religious communion, may be tempted to conform to the predominating forms as an attempt at legitimacy in a foreign country.

Conclusion

The outward symbols that make the Converted special in St. Vincent are shared by many groups in New York, groups by whom they are sometimes drawn in admiration, sometimes repulsed in antipathy. The influx of ideas and images from other religions are accompanied by pressures for change. The motivators arise from the need to fit in to the new place, as well as to preserve the sense of connection to St. Vincent.

The dual nature of Converted identity — Spiritual/Baptist (African/Christian) is a natural divider. Alterations in practices and in outward symbols depend on who the Converted, as individuals and as congregations, consider themselves most to be and most not to be. Bases on which the changes are made can be found in St. Vincent and in the pattern of Vincentian imagination about the world. St. Vincent suffers the stigma of being seen as "backward" by other Caribbean nations — an unpleasant label for a developing nation. The Vincentians, especially those who have been to Trinidad, feel the sting of being "small island." On top of that, other Vincentians criticize Converted as "backward." Those who make it to Brooklyn tend to be the most mobile, the most forward-looking Vincentians, a large number having worked in Trinidad before traveling to the United States. One common response in Brooklyn is a tendency to present one's self/congregation as less "backward," less African, more like the American churches in style and form, although the essential Converted elements of mourning and work in the spirit are not given up. Reflecting an appeal to urban sophistication, the pastor of one Converted church explained his lack of candles and lack of spiritual flags, absence of a bell, and use of the hymnal of an American denomination in his church as preferred because "more modern."

Although acknowledging itself as Spiritual Baptist, this particular church had removed "Spiritual" from its name, the sign indicating only that the storefront church is one of any scores of "Baptist" churches of any provenance or denomination in Brooklyn. Converse to this, many Converted churches drop "Baptist" from their name. The signs over their church doors read "Spiritual Temple" or "Spiritual Church" — stressing difference from the American churches that carry the name Baptist. As in St. Vincent, many churches have no signs at all, members knowing which building to go to (or, more likely in Brooklyn, which basement). Selection of which symbols to accent is situational. Stressing "Baptist" or "Spiritual" is not an abnegation of either. The pastor of one of the more "Spiritual" churches told me that when people ask him what he is, he just says, "West Indian Baptist." If people respond, "Shango Baptist?," he replies, "No, Vincentian Converted Baptist."

Experimentation is another response to the proximity of similar spirit-oriented religions from the Caribbean. The Converted recognize the sharing of African and/or spiritual traits in their religion with other Caribbean religions and may adopt practices that will enhance their knowledge and power to do the work of Jesus. Most Vincentians are, at the very least, wary if not outright afraid of the Trinidadian churches — so dangerously close to Shango, with statues of saints and representations of Indian gods (perceived as saints). In spite of the potential danger, the Converted are skilled spiritual experts. They are able to detect good and combat evil. For the Converted churches that selectively accept foreign practices, some qualities change, but the substance of the religion remains the same. That does not prevent "purer" Converted from complaining about Shango, Orisha, or Hindu influences.

Individually, some members, directed by vision or by personal inclination, turn completely to the Trinidadian styles, or even to working with the orisha spirits — who, according to my few Vincentian respondents who work with them, are seen as powerful helping spirits serving the cause of Christ, not as possessing deities. Those Vincentian Spiritual Baptists who follow the Trinidadian tradition or practice the Shango Baptist rites (that is, praying to saints and sacrificing doves) are usually those who have spent time in Trinidad and have had direct contact with Shango/Orisha in its Trinidadian setting.

Resistance to change is a third strategy. Some congregations shield themselves from the challenges offered by contact with other religions by reducing the amount of visiting they do with other churches. This represents a major change. In St. Vincent, visiting between churches is a cherished and joyful institution. One pointer in St. Vincent told me, "You hardly stay home a Sunday." Visiting is a mixing of different church families, a time to see how different churches perform certain rites, to learn new songs, to see new faces, and it is one of the means by which churches in St. Vincent stay fresh and vibrant in a way that the conventional churches cannot approach. For churches in New York, not to visit with other Spiritual Baptist churches is different, but protects the members from confusing influences. A Converted church, already a refuge of Vincentian homeliness in the chilly and foreign social atmosphere of New York, can become a fortress of spiritual immunity from dangerous forces.

The history of Converted religion is one of rapid response to changes. In Brooklyn, this pattern continues. While the changes vary by congregation, the religion remains substantially intact. In spite of the colonial effort to eliminate Africanisms from the descendants of Africans, a sense of African-ness has remained in St. Vincent in the form of Converted religion. In spite of the buffets of in-island prejudice as well as out-island prejudice, legal persecution, lowly origins, and challenges from other religions in Brooklyn and elsewhere, the Converted remain spiritual workers dedicated to their Christian purpose. The relatively simple spiritual equation in St. Vincent — with the Converted poor and powerless in the physical world but rich and powerful in the spirit — is more complex in Brooklyn. Other religions are rich in the spirit as well. American Pentecostals and Baptists as well as Spiritual Baptists from other islands force a sharper definition of Converted religion than in St. Vincent. Vincentian Converted, individually and as congregations, address this problem variously by speedy adaptation to external influences, by the alteration of external symbols, by adaptation of useful strategies for power, and by reclusion for protection.

Endnotes

1. This chapter is based on data gathered during fourteen months of fieldwork among the Vincentian Converted in St. Vincent (April–September 1995) and Brooklyn (October 1995–June 1996). The Converted is the religion identified in legal documents in St. Vincent as Spiritual Baptist, and formerly as Shakers, Christian Pilgrims, and Pilgrim Baptists. General statements of practice or belief reflect the view reported most often by my respondents or what I observed most often in churches I visited. While norms can be identified, the revelatory nature of the religion leads to a wide range of variety in practice. All unattributed quotes are from my fieldnotes and were said by one or more Converted. Converted or Vincentian terms are italicized the first time they are used. Quotations around a word or a phrase are not to indicate that I think it is specious, but to denote that while I heard it from one or more Vincentians, it is not a term in general use. I capitalize the word *God* to refer to the Christian god, as Converted and other Christians use the term. Uncapitalized, *god* refers to an unspecified deity.

2. When Converted tell me that their journeys are like those of Christian, the character in *The Pilgrim's Progress*, they are not merely using a convenient metaphor. For the Vincentian Converted, *The Pilgrim's*

Progress by John Bunyan is a major source of inspiration, a holy
scripture secondary to the Bible. In some churches, members are
instructed to study the book so that they "will know where to go"
in the spiritual world. It is a "true and good story" and if the
Converted "walk right" they will go on the road that Christian
walked and they will arrive where he did (Heaven).

3. For a description of the relationship between Spiritual Baptists and
   Shango/Orisha in Trinidad, see Houk (1995) and Glazier (1985).

4. I use "millenarian" in Worsley's (1957, p. 12) sense of "those movements in which there is an expectation of, and preparation for, the
   coming of a period of supernatural bliss." The Converted, along with
   the Southern Baptists, Pentecostals, Seventh Day Adventists and
   other fundamentalist Christians, believe in an imminent return of
   Jesus to earth. A spiritual urgency not found in the mainstream
   churches attends the actions of these denominations.

5. It is difficult to estimate the number of Converted in New York at
   any one time since the Vincentian population in New York includes
   a large number of visitors who may stay a few weeks or a few
   months. My figure is based on those who regularly attended Converted churches during my field work in Brooklyn. I did meet some
   people who consider themselves Converted but attend Pentecostal
   churches in Brooklyn. Also, some Vincentians in New York attend
   Trinidadian Spiritual Baptist churches. Ministers, in addition, sometimes inflate the membership numbers for their churches and may
   include all those who have undergone baptism or mourning at the
   church rather than just active members. One Converted minister told
   me that he had two hundred members in his church but, when he
   one day showed me a list of the members, there were only 32 names.
   Some of those on his list told me their membership was in another
   church but that they attended both. The smaller number is more in
   line with congregation size in St. Vincent (and with what I observed
   in that church). Converted tell me that with very large numbers (over
   100) it is difficult to do the spiritual work.

6. For instance, one respondent who had been baptized as a Converted
   in the 1960s told me that she never heard the term Spiritual Baptist
   until years later: "It was only when I went to Trinidad I learned about
   this Baptists."

7. Almost all of my visits to Trinidadian churches were made accompanying Vincentian Spiritual Baptists who were visiting as fellow
   Christians. The Vincentians were as curious as I to see how the
   practices differed and on several occasions Vincentians went with

me because I was going anyway. I was able to check on the spot or shortly thereafter how the Vincentians felt about the differences they had observed. Discussion of differences is very common. My questions about attitudes towards differences in practices among the Caribbean religions, but especially about the Trinidadian Spiritual Baptists, altered very little the streams of conversations in which the Vincentian Converted were already intently engaged.

8. This is the same sorcery believed by non-Converted to be practiced among the Converted in St. Vincent. Converted say the pointers have the power to do the bad magic, but they never would because they are working for God and not the devil or themselves.

References

Abrahams, R.D. 1983 *The Man-of-Words in the West Indies: Performance and the Emergence of Creole Culture*. Baltimore and London: Johns Hopkins University Press.

Basch, L. 1987 The Vincentians and Grenadians: The role of voluntary associations in immigrant adaptation to New York City. In: *New Immigrants in New York* (ed., N. Foner). New York: Columbia University Press, pp. 159–193.

Basch, L.; Schiller, N.G.; and Szanton Blanc, C. 1994 *Nations Unbound: Transnational Projects, Postcolonial Predicaments, and Deterritorialized Nation-States*. Langhorne, PA: Gordon and Breach.

Brathwaite, E.K. 1982 *Native Language Poetry (English in the Caribbean: Notes on Language and Poetry)*. Savacou Working Paper 5. Mona, Jamaica: Savacou.

Brown, K.M. 1991 *Mama Lola: A Vodun Priestess in Brooklyn*. Berkeley: University of California Press.

Chaney, E.M. 1987 The context of Caribbean migration. In: *Caribbean Life in New York City: Sociocultural Dimensions* (eds., C.R. Sutton and E.M. Chaney). New York: Center for Migration Studies of New York, Inc., pp. 1–14.

Chaumeil, J.P. 1992 Un Nouveau Testament pour un Troisième Millénaire: La religion du Daime au Brésil. *Cahiers d'Études Africaines* 32(1):151–155.

Chevannes, B. 1978 Revivalism: A disappearing religion. *Caribbean Quarterly* 24:1–17.

Courlander, H. 1996 [1976] *A Treasury of Afro-American Folklore.* New York: Marlowe and Company.

Cox, E.L. 1994 Religious intolerance and persecution: The Shakers of St. Vincent, 1900–1934. *Journal of Caribbean History* 28(2):208–243.

Fraser, A. 1995 Unpublished transcript from radio address in series "From Whence We Came" on April 20, 1995. NBC Radio, St. Vincent and the Grenadines.

Gearing, J. 1992 Family planning in St. Vincent, West Indies: A population history perspective. *Social Science and Medicine* 35(10):1273–1282.

Glazier, S.D. 1983 *Marchin' the Pilgrims Home: Leadership and Decision-Making in an Afro-Caribbean Faith.* Westport, CT: Greenwood Press.

Glazier, S.D. 1985 Syncretism and separation: Ritual change in an Afro-Caribbean faith. *Journal of American Folklore* 98:49–62.

Glazier, S.D. 1992 Pilgrimages in the Caribbean: A comparison of cases from Haiti and the Caribbean. In: *Sacred Journeys: The Anthropology of Pilgrimage* (ed., A. Morris). Westport, CT: Greenwood Press, pp. 135–147.

Gullick, C. 1971 Shakers and ecstasy. *New Fire* [Oxford] 9:7–11.

Hackshaw, J.M. 1992 *The Baptist Denomination: 1816–1991.* Trinidad: Amphy and Bashua Jackson Memorial Society.

Henney, J.H. 1971 The Shakers of St. Vincent: A stable religion. In: *Religion, Altered States of Consciousness, and Social Change* (ed., E. Bourguignon). Columbus: Ohio State University Press, pp. 219–263.

Henney, J.H. 1974 Spirit-possession belief and trance behavior in two fundamentalist groups in St. Vincent. In: *Trance, Healing, and Hallucination: Three Field Studies in Religious Experience* (eds., F.D. Goodman, J.H. Henney, and E. Pressl). New York: John Wiley and Sons, pp. 6–111.

Herskovits, M.J. and Herskovits, F.S. 1947 *Trinidad Village.* New York: Alfred A. Knopf.

Houk, J.T. 1995 *Spirits, Blood, and Drums.* Philadelphia: Temple University Press.

Jolivet, M-J. 1985 Migrations et histoire dans la «Caraïbe Française». *Cahiers ORSTOM, séries Sciences Humaines* 21(1):99–113.

Littlewood, R. 1993 *Pathology and Identity: The Work of Mother Earth in Trinidad*. Cambridge: Cambridge University Press.

Marshall, D.I. 1984 Vincentian contract labour migration to Barbados: The satisfaction of mutual needs? *Social and Economic Studies* 37(3):63–92.

Miller, S. 1992 Nurse-midwifery in St. Vincent and the Grenadines. *Journal of Nurse-Midwifery* 37(1):53–60.

Murphy, J.M. 1994 *Working the Spirit: Ceremonies in the African Diaspora*. Boston: Beacon Press.

Murphy, L.G.; Melton, J.G.; and Ward, G.L. 1993 *Encyclopedia of African American Religions*. New York: Garland Publishing, Inc.

Parks, A.V. 1981 *The Conceptualization of Kinship Among the Spiritual Baptists of Trinidad*. PhD Dissertation. Princeton University.

Pitt, E.A. 1955 Acculturative and synthetic aspects of religion and life in the island of St. Vincent and other predominantly Protestant islands and areas of the West Indies and the Caribbean. *Actes of the Fourth International Congress of Anthropological and Ethnological Sciences* 1952:385–390. Vienna: Verlag Adolf Holzhausens Nfg.

St. Vincent 1927 *The Laws of St. Vincent: Containing the Ordinances of the Colony in Force on the 4th Day of May 1926*, Vol. 2 (revised edition). London: Crown Agents for the Colonies.

St. Vincent 1965 *Ordinances for the Year 1965*. Kingstown, St. Vincent: Government Printing Office.

St. Vincent 1993 *1991 Population and Housing Census Report*, Vol. 2. Kingstown, St. Vincent: Statistical Office, Ministry of Finance and Planning.

Seaga, E. 1982 [1969] *Revival Cults in Jamaica*. Kingston: The Institute of Jamaica.

Simpson, G.E. 1966 Baptismal, "mourning," and "building" ceremonies of the Shouters in Trinidad. *Journal of American Folklore* 79:537–550.

Thomas, E. 1987 *A History of the Shouter Baptists in Trinidad and Tobago*. Tacarigua, Trinidad: Calaloux Publications.

Thomas-Hope, E.M. 1992 *Explanation in Caribbean Migration: Perception and the Image: Jamaica, Barbados, St. Vincent*. London: Macmillan Caribbean.

Tylor, C. 1994 *The Black Churches of Brooklyn*. New York: Columbia University Press.

van Capelleveen, R. 1993 "Peripheral" culture in the metropolis: West Indians in New York City. In: *Alternative Cultures in the Caribbean* (eds., T. Bremer and U. Fleischmann). Frankfurt am Main: Vervuert Verlag, pp. 131–147.

Winthrop, R.H. 1991 *Dictionary of Concepts in Cultural Anthropology*. New York: Greenwood Press.

Worsely, P. 1957 *The Trumpet Shall Sound: A Study of "Cargo" Cults in Melanesia*. London: MacGibbon and Kee.

Young, V.H. 1993 *Becoming West Indian: Culture, Self, and Nation in St. Vincent*. Washington: Smithsonian Institution Press.

7: ONLY VISITORS HERE: REPRESENTING RASTAFARI INTO THE 21ST CENTURY

Carole D. Yawney

Rastafari is a religious movement that began in Jamaica in the 1930s, but which now can be found in many other countries. The title of Emperor Haile Selassie I of Ethiopia before his coronation was Ras Tafari. This is the origin of the name of the movement. For Rastafari, Emperor Haile Selassie I is the Divinity and Ethiopia is considered the promised land of Zion.

Rastafari consider themselves spiritual warriors who "chant down Babylon" through "word-sound-power." Babylon, according to Rastafari is the secular, materialistic, unjust society, which dominates the world. While some chants are used to subvert the negative energies and oppression associated with Babylon, other chants use the Power of the Sound of the Word to give thanks and praises to Jah Rastafari, Emperor Haile Selassie of Ethiopia, the Godhead.[1] Chanting and praising Jah Rastafari is primarily accomplished or performed together in assemblies. In the early 1970s when I first went to Jamaica to do fieldwork, I frequently heard the following chant at Rastafari celebrations:

We are only visitors here
And we have to time to fear.
For when we reach Ethiopia land,
His Majesty going to take us by the hand.
We are only visitors here.

This chant not only points to repatriation to Africa, which in Rastafari is both a redemptive and a collective movement, but it also emphasizes the theme of ephemerality, being-in-transition, which pervades the Rastafari world view. Rastafari may well be visitors here, but they are involuntary exiles, with a strong determination to return to Africa. Rastafari often say that "without a vision the people perish." This means that as descendants of people forcibly removed from Africa, they must maintain the goal of returning to Africa. In the meantime, until full-scale repatriation is possible, Rastafari actively promote both an interest in African culture and history, and communication with African people everywhere. In addition to chanting and drumming, known as Nyahbinghi, Rastafari have also developed a distinctively Jamaican musical form known as reggae to spread this message well beyond the confines of the Caribbean.[2]

In this chapter I discuss the influence that local culture has had on the spread of Rastafari, and more particularly, on the scholars who research the movement. In my own case, from the first time that I heard this chant, it has spoken to my personal experience as a researcher of Rastafari. As a white woman and a non-Rastafari I too was only a visitor here. Over the years this chant has reminded my that the opportunity to move among Rastafari is not one to be taken for granted, and I suggest that the globalization of Rastafari has not only challenged Rastafari culture itself, but has placed particular demands and responsibilities upon researchers.

I make the case for long-term multisite field work, which takes into account the larger political context within which we work. Since no one individual is capable of covering the entire field of Rastafari, especially in its global manifestation, I will also advocate collaboration between researchers of Rastafari and Rastafari themselves. While these concerns should apply to fieldwork, they are especially important in the case of Rastafari, which has experienced a history of misrepresentation in both academic studies and the popular media. Because what we write as ethnographers of Rastafari is open to so many readings, and because Rastafari themselves call into question the nature of any ethnographic generalization, we need ethnographic reportage of Rastafari that constantly triangulates from multiple perspectives. Globalization serves to make the issue of generalizations about Rastafari and Rastafari identity even more problematic. As Mortimo Planno has stated:

> I and I in the Western world, in the Diaspora, we have our contribution what we can do for Africa. And we are doing it in our own way. We want to link it with understanding. Get your Bible and read it, read it with understanding. And tell out the Rasta doctrine round the whole world. And that is what is going on today. I mean, this is a living proof

to find other Rasta man in South Africa today can hear from a Rasta man in the Caribbean or in Jamaica or wherever outside in the Diaspora. The link what we intend to have in Africa. For that is what His Majesty give us as a guideline: international cooperation quicken progress. So in our cooperation internationally and the telecommunication we are using now that links us together is a reality of one of the mystic. You get the idea? The mystic breeze that blow from here to Africa, this is one of the mystic now that international cooperation quicken progress. (Ras Mortimo Planno, 1997)[3]

The Globalization of Rastafari

In this section I briefly review the history of the globalization of Rastafari as a counter-hegemonic culture. By this I am suggesting that Rastafari have always resisted dominant cultural assumptions about the meaning of being African in the Diaspora. By declaring that Emperor Haile Selassie I of Ethiopia is God and demanding their right to repatriate, Rastafari have challenged everyday notions in colonialist and post-colonialist societies that Africans are no longer Africans but are Jamaicans or the nationality of the country in which they reside. I discuss this issue, because while self-representation is critical to Rastafari, such African nationalist identities are often seen as retrogressive in postmodernist thinking.

Being in forced exile does not automatically result in the loss of connection to one's roots, despite the many attempts by Europeans to wipe out the memory and inheritance of Africa. The history of the struggle of African people in the Caribbean Diaspora to keep their cultures alive is well documented (cf. Alleyene,1988; Bush,1990; Warner-Lewis, 1991), as are the efforts to deny and suppress these cultures (Brathwaite, 1993:190–204; Spencer-Strachans, 1992). Since its inception, Rastafari has been concerned with images and with their representation in the media and have learned to distrust or at least question outsiders who wrote about them. Leaders of Rastafari pressured the University of the West Indies in the 1960s to issue a report in order to dispel what they regarded as dangerous myths about the movement. In describing their first meeting with the university team at the Jonestown Primary School, Ras Mortimo Planno, one of the strategists who played a key role in motivating the university to do the research, recounts:

Dr. Lewis (principal of the university) say: Now, Mr. Planno, what do you want? And me explain it to him. Me say: well, out of the blue the Premier [of Jamaica] accuse us of being subversive and want to take away Jamaica. We don't have that as out intention. What we want is repatriation to Ethiopia. We are not interested in taking away the colony Jamaica. We want to leave the country Jamaica for Ethiopia. We have our land in Ethiopia His Majesty give we. Things like that. (Ras Mortimo Planno, 1984)

Just how contentious these notions of African identity and repatriation were in the Jamaican context is described in regard to the University report on Rastafari:

The first and second recommendations in the Report ... invited strong criticism from the wider society at large; and understandably so, for these recommendations turned on those very tenets of the Rastafarian doctrine which posed fundamental threats to Jamaicanism. First there is the implied allegiance to a foreign (albeit friendly) Head of State. Secondly, the emphasis on Africa brought uneasiness to a country which had never regarded itself as black. (Nettleford, 1970:44–45)

Ras Mortimo Planno addressed the perception of Rastafari by the wider society in 1960 in the following way:

It was during the time when Black uprising, the time of Congo change, with Lumumba and Tshombe. The whole of that coming to America, the United Nations. You know, Nkrumah, the African Renaissance. So we were more in seeing Africa on this wide scale (and) not just coming along with just Ethiopia, Ethiopia, Ethiopia — which some misinterpret me love for Ethiopia and the reason why we say Ethiopia more than anything else.
   So you had various types of delegations coming around the West here. And some even come to Jamaica from Ghana, you know. And they wasn't too much agree with Rasta. For all the writers, the whole media was saying, Rasta fanatic. We just deal with Haile Selassie and Ethiopia and no deal with no other Africa. And the type of, kind of prejudice the African leaders them mind against Rasta that anyone of them don't look upon Rasta as anything. So we know ourselves as Rasta now going to have to gain the respect by blasting you writers, journalists, sociologists. (Ras Mortimo Planno, 1984)

Generally speaking, Rastafari have always had to defend their claims concerning Selassie, as well as their right to repatriate to Ethiopia, against charges by the wider Jamaican public of foolishness and idealism. Because the media often portrayed them as fanatics devoted to Emperor Haile Selassie and Ethiopia, Rastafari have had to ensure that their more general concern with Pan-Africanism and African liberation movements is recognized by outsiders. This could be regarded as a Rastafari public relations issue. Below Ras Mortimo Planno describes the role that he played in an effort to internationalize Rastafari's call for African unity. He refers to his functioning as an Elder and advisor to Bob Marley, who became an international reggae superstar in the 1970s:

> Now, there was a Bob Marley who was a rude boy which is a different Bob Marley from the Bob Marley that I and I know. Yes, I. So, we're going to mould Bob Marley from the Bob Marley the rude boy into Bob Marley the Rasta messenJah who carry Jah message throughout the whole world. So that was the purpose of having Bob Marley in Trenchtown, that we use Bob Marley as our messenJah who carry the messages around the whole world that today I can fe able be talking to my brethren and sistren in South Africa about Bob Marley being today is his birthday.
>   Good. So we want Africa to know from our perspective the purpose of using Bob Marley as a messenger who have done us great to link Africa with us in the Caribbean and in the West Indies and throughout the whole Western Diaspora with Africa. So I think you have done a great work in linking us in the Western Diaspora to the African in Africa. (Ras Mortimo Planno, 1997)

The history of Rastafari can be regarded as the product of a dynamic relationship between local and global influences. Chevannes provides a summary of the contributions of Ethiopianism, Garveyism, and Pan-Africanism to Rastafari thought (Chevannes, 1994). Homiak has pointed out that many of its early leaders, such as Leonard Howell, Joseph Hibbert, and Archibald Dunkley, also traveled outside of Jamaica, not to mention the extensive international experience of Marcus Garvey. The fact that Selassie is regarded as His Divine Majesty has served to keep them abreast of international currents. Moreover, Caribbean people and Rastafari themselves have always been travelers, more as workers than as tourists, but on the move nevertheless (Yawney, 1995).

At the same time, local developments within Rastafari resulted in the formation of groups with slightly different orientations. Rastafari are fond of saying "My Father's house has many mansions."[4] While some developments have incubated locally, they have spread globally in that members of these groups can be found throughout North America, Europe, and Africa, and elsewhere.

Background

Since the 1970s, and particularly since the Centennial Celebrations in Ethiopia of Emperor Haile Selassie's birthday in 1992, we have witnessed a major spread of Rastafari internationally. This chapter charts the first diaspora of the movement, which occurred during the 1950s and 1960s through immigration, and a second diaspora that began in the 1970s with Bob Marley, and other reggae musicians. The most recent phase of Rastafari globalization has been facilitated by international travel and communications technology such as access to the internet.[5]

As we approach the 21st century, we observe that Rastafari has managed to export itself and its message of African unity around the globe. In fact, there may be more Rastafari living outside of Jamaica, or even the Caribbean, than in the country of origin. At the very least, in the 1990s we have seen a concerted effort by Rastafari to promote their own internationalization through a series of conferences and cultural programs held in the Caribbean, North America, the United Kingdom, and various states of Africa.[6]

Moreover, Rastafari has generally lacked established institutional support which could have made proselytization easier. It has relied heavily upon ad hoc organizations, networking through travel, and the recording media to spread its message. In most societies, Rastafari has been persecuted by the state, criminalized by the press, and commodified by popular culture (Yawney, 1995:60). Despite all this, and by overcoming its own internal contradictions and sectarian politics, Rastafari continues to be a vibrant and dynamic force and presents a positive vision of Afrocentric culture that directly challenges the cultural hegemony of white supremacy and racism.

Rastafari have established a community presence in the United States, Canada, Britain and other parts of Europe, Brazil, Japan, and New Zealand (Campbell,1987; Keita,1991; van Dijk, 1993). While it remains to be determined in these locales to what extent their members are of African descent, such developments illustrate the contention that Rastafari are "twice removed from their homeland in Africa and from their adopted home in the Caribbean" (Campbell, 1987:8). Doubly displaced then, Rastafari are singularly redeemed by their increasing presence on the continent of Africa, where they join energies with nationals of several states (Campbell, 1987; Savishinsky, 1994; Turner, 1994).[7]

The fact of a double diaspora leads us to ask to what extent can Rastafari develop a trans-cultural appeal beyond the confines of its local, specifically Jamaican, Afrocentric orientation without altering its basic premises? How do the various cultural attitudes and practices that Rastafari encounter in these local communities of the second diaspora feed back into Rastafari society? Having reached home to Africa, how do Rastafari relate to African communities? These latter two issues have been raised by Campbell (1987:71) Homiak (1996:3), and by myself (Yawney, 1993; 1995:69). Savishinsky (1994a) has written an intriguing and provocative account of possible links between Jamaican Rastafari and the Baye Faal of Senegambia, which supports the argument that this line of inquiry must be pursued if we are to appreciate Rastafari in its global context. Below I discuss the different kinds of strategies that researchers and ethnographers need to consider in order to examine these issues.

Researching Diasporas: Methodological Problems and Conceptual Considerations

His Majesty has left with us the realization that international communication quicken progress. And international cooperation quicken progress. So we are trying now to use that link of international communication to quicken the progress of our people. We know of all who scramble for Africa have all different versions of our history. The Belgians, they have their own version, Italian have their version, the Germans have their version of African history. So we African are going to have to print or paint our own history. Look, I went to Nigeria and in discussing their mass communication of Nigeria we make then

know that twenty-six books written on Bob Marley as a Rasta but we
don't write any book of it. Then twenty-six sociologists writing them
own version of who them think is a Rasta and how them think Rasta
should really operate.

Now Rasta is the earth's most strangest man, and that go for all Africa
too. And that go for all Africa too. For Africa going to realize now that
we are one brother and not as the European teach them that Rasta are
fanatic only deal with Ethiopia and His Majesty Haile Selassie. We
Rasta is for all Africa. And that is something we want to get across to
the African leader who prejudices against Rasta through the Western
propaganda that them laid against Rasta. And we think we have done
not enough but we have done much to really bring that link. (Ras
Mortimo Planno, 1997)

In this extract Ras Planno reiterates a sentiment quoted previously,
that non-Rastafari scholars and the media have distorted the truth of
Rastafari. In this section I list several research considerations that the
globalization of Rastafari raises. Then I present two extended examples which illustrate my concerns.

In the seventy years since the inception of Rastafari, new conceptual models in the social sciences and literary criticism have developed, which directly address some of these research concerns. Here
I refer to postmodernism, feminism, and anti-racism. At first, in
scholarly writing on Rastafari, class analysis dominated efforts
to explain Rastafari from the perspective of the religions of the oppressed and protest movements of the poor (Barrett, 1977; Campbell,
1987; Simpson, 1955; Wilson, 1973). But now we have moved from
models of millennialist cults to prototypes of traveling cultures as
possible perspectives on Rastafari.[8] Given the complexity of the Rastafari global community and forms of cultural expression within it,
we can no longer presume any one interpretive perspective. We need
to develop multifaceted frameworks to reflect this changing situation.

It is beyond the scope of this chapter to discuss the contributions
of postmodernism, feminism, and anti-racism to scholarship. However, I need to briefly define what I mean by anti-racism research
because it informs much of my thinking on the subject of Rastafari
ethnography. Although postmodernism and then feminism gradually
found their ways into mainstream academic discourse, anti-racism is
not as well established as a frame of reference. There is a growing
body of literature on anti-racism pedagogy but there is no corre-

sponding source on anti-racism research (Das Gupta, 1993; Dei, 1996; Gill, Mayor, and Blair, 1992; McCarthy and Crichlow, 1993).[9]

Anti-racism research shares much in common with feminist research.[10] Skeggs argues that "issues of principles and power will inform any research project. Feminist ethnography forces the researcher to confront these issues, rather than ignore them" (Skeggs, 1994:88–89). This understanding also applies to anti-racism ethnography and can be applied in several ways. Collaborative research projects, however negotiated, begin to approach the problem of unequal power between the researched and the researcher. This allows community needs and priorities to influence the research agenda, especially where the community in question continues to experience various forms of racism. A long-term research commitment also means the researcher is available and two-way accessibility serves to redistribute power in an unequal relationship.

Anti-racism research also addresses the question of representation. One researcher has discussed how his own anti-racism work as an African cultural activist is concerned with learning how people survive and liberate themselves. He has argued that we need to de-mystify postmodern discourse, which too easily masks the reality of people's suffering, partly through its obscurist language (Marshall, 1996). In addition, Marshall cautions that as anti-racism researchers we also must take responsibility for not making the vulnerable even more vulnerable. From an anti-racism perspective, we need to ask ourselves if we are contributing to further negative stereotyping of the community we are studying. For example, interpretations of Rastafari as a "cult" passed over into popular culture and reinforced media images of Rastafari such as "Rasta, the bizarre cult suspected of violent crimes" (*Globe and Mail*, 1975, quoted in Yawney, 1984:326).

A historical review of the academic literature on Rastafari would expose how dominant academic frameworks can serve as a means of social control, particularly when they cross over into popular culture. It would also raise questions about the politics of the social construction of "experts" and the legitimization of "expert" knowledge.[11]

In its Jamaican context Rastafari has always presented a challenge to researchers. As a global culture these challenges are compounded by new ones. Most Rastafari have been extremely distrustful of outside investigators, such as scholars and reporters, who are consigned to the disparaging category of "pharisees and scribes." It remains to be seen how Rastafari in various diasporic communities structure their relationship with researchers. Because I have been doing this work for twenty-five years I travel with the baggage of a prior reputation, for better or for worse. It will be interesting to observe how the next generation of Rastafari accommodate the upcoming generation of researchers.

At least in Jamaica Rastafari have both political and ritual strategies for "testing" and "controlling" researchers. Frequently, for example, they will offer a copious amount of ganja to smoke to study its effects and to interview the researcher under its influence. Rastafari also engage visitors in strenuous dialogues in an effort to tease out any hidden agendas or assumptions. If the researcher is not prepared to participate without reservation, it can be an uncomfortable experience, and Rastafari who have no other means to check on a visitor's background, simply say, "we just take this chalice and sieve them out."[12]

These kinds of field work pressures may help account for a burgeoning literature on Rastafari but few long-term ethnographers, of whom few are women.

Writing from the perspective of someone with sustained field experience, I would argue that this confers a tremendous advantage when researching the globalization of Rastafari from a comparative viewpoint. Like the Elders of Rastafari who travel on missions abroad, experienced ethnographers can also step forward into the international Rastafari community with a sense of grounding. Having had an extended period of research experience in Jamaica, when I do visit other Rastafari communities in the diaspora I can plug into existing networks and accomplish a good deal in a short period of time. Marcus and Fischer have argued that multilocale ethnography "may entail a novel kind of fieldwork. Rather than being situated in one, or two communities, the fieldworker must be mobile, covering a network that encompasses a process, which is in fact the object of the study" (Marcus and Fischer, 1986:94). While the heterogeneity of Rastafari in Jamaica is extensive, its range of expression becomes even more complex as the process of globalization proceeds. Does this make it more difficult for researchers who are just beginning to study Rastafari? On the one hand, there are mentoring relationships in Rastafari, which can provide one with a teaching lineage of sorts that can make introduction into new communities smoother. Jah Bones, a well-known Elder based in the United Kingdom, who recently passed over, described his own coming up in the faith in terms of brethren who served as his teachers (Bones, 1985:22–37). This holds true for ethnographers as well. These frames of reference can be helpful when meeting Rastafari outside of Jamaica whom one does not know through an established network. For example, I met several prisoners during the prolonged struggle for the recognition of Rastafari religious rights in New York state. We all told stories of our experiences in Jamaica, the Rastafari bases we visited regularly, the Elders who were a formative influence on us, and so on. This helped establish a common ground, and in fact, some of us contacted each other's Elders.

On the other hand, if a brethren or field worker is identified too closely with a specific orientation or Elder, he or she tends to be regarded as being in that particular camp. In the international arena this may open doors as well as keep them closed.

Oral history too, as with good ethnographic work, is founded on long-term relationships established in good faith. Many Rastafari follow very closely accounts of themselves written by others and do not hesitate to give critical feedback. Scholars such as Chevannes and Hill have devoted much energy to collecting oral histories and documenting the course of Rastafari. Both interviewed the first generation of Rastafari practitioners. Chevanne's book on Rastafari ideology is a case in point. A large part of it is based on interviews with older Rastafari who provide data, which would otherwise have been lost (Chevannes, 1994).

Will the succeeding generation of Elders be as cooperative, or will Rastafari research their own history and culture? Will there continue to be two parallel literatures, one academic and one Rastafari? For example, Ras E.S.P. McPherson has documented a number of Rastafari meetings and events in which he was involved (McPherson, 1991). Yet his work is rarely cited in the scholarly literature. This example raises the question of ownership of research material, particularly when scholars are working with oral histories in the form of tape recordings, and when the communities they are researching have a long history of being misrepresented.

One of the most challenging aspects of the globalization of Rastafari involves the collapse of the temporal and spatial dimension between the field and the place the ethnographer calls home. Such experience has enriched not only my ethnography but my life as well. Rastafari with whom I worked in the early 1970s who have moved to Toronto are now only a phone call away, and Toronto itself has developed a significant Rastafari community. A researcher may be called upon to assist Rastafari interests in a variety of ways. One of my roles has been to circulate Rastafari materials that I have acquired on various field trips to an international network of Rastafari, as well as to put people I meet in touch with each other.

When the field comes to the anthropologist there may be a blurring of professional and personal roles. Because I have conducted research without the use of questionnaires and have rarely used a tape recorder, how do people know when I am being an anthropologist? There is an increased responsibility for ethnographers to conform to ethical guidelines, which state that in the absence of any informed consent one must assume confidentiality and anonymity.

Clifford argues that traditional ethnography "has localized what is actually a regional/national/global nexus" (Clifford, 1992:100). In so doing, it privileges settled communities as fieldwork sites. However, Clifford argues that traveling cultures, a term he uses to refer to the hybridity achieved when a locally developed culture moves into a global context, are equally important research interests. They pose "representational challenges" for researchers, which require a range of responses, including "innovative forms of multi-locale ethnography" (Clifford, 1992: 101–2).

Gilroy has attempted to do just this by exploring the notion of "the black Atlantic world" built upon countless numbers of "diasporic conversations," which have taken place through cultural exchanges, involving face-to-face communication and remote exchanges (Gilroy, 1993:199). Rastafari are a significant part of this black Atlantic world. This raises the question of how we are to research video and cybernetic communities, which are increasingly part of the Rastafari experience. Since 1990 there has been a marked increase in group travel by Rastafari to international gatherings, which in themselves are temporary manifestations of community, and ethnographers need to recognize the legitimacy of such fieldwork sites, however short-lived.

Collaboration and sharing of data and perspectives between researchers of Rastafari and Rastafari researchers would greatly facilitate our understanding of Rastafari. As noted above, globalization has coincided with the coming of age of a generation of Rastafari scholars, cultural activists, and critical artists. As experts on Rastafari, they have an international presence as much as Elders, and play key roles in national and international assemblies. They are also part of Rastafari as a traveling culture, and their input also challenges the intellectual hegemony of outside researchers in a way that raises issues of responsibility and representation.

My point is to illustrate the value of triangulating several kinds of source materials in order to develop a perspective on Rastafari. It is imperative that we situate our analysis of Rastafari within the context of the more critical literature on race, class, and gender, if we are to appreciate the kinds of strategies which Rastafari adopt over time.

The following two case studies serve to illustrate several of the points made above. The first sheds light on the value of conducting ethnographic fieldwork in a temporary site and the second demonstrates the complexity of focusing on Rastafari as a traveling culture by following international networks and traveling with Rastafari.

Rastafari Focus 1986 and the Role of Rastafari Women

By discussing this example at some length, I hope not only to illustrate the value of first-hand ethnographic research, but also to partly fill a gap in the literature on the subject of gender and the challenge that globalization presents to the role of women in Rastafari. In July, 1986, a major international Rastafari conference was held as part of Caribbean Focus, a year-long cultural celebration of Caribbean arts and culture in the United Kingdom. The Rastafari Focus was convened for two weeks in London under the coordinating auspices of the Rastafarian Advisory Service (RAS).

In this discussion I focus specifically on one part of the two week program, the panel, "Women, Rastafari, and the Family". This was a significant event in the history of international Rastafari gatherings because it was the first time that so much of the program was devoted to women's issues. The panel was chaired by a Rastafari woman and all three presenters were women. Here I base my account on my own notes made at the time, but, RAS also published a report that has summaries of these presentations (RAS, 1988: 26–35).

The session began with male Elders on stage in the main auditorium of the Commonwealth Institute playing the drums and chanting. There was a capacity audience, with many women and children in attendance. The first presentation was made by a Rastafari sister who reasoned "On the Building of the Nation" by turning to Biblical instructions for all African women, who in the context of Rastafari are seen as "nation builders," the foundation for which is the African family. The next speaker who was from the Ethiopian Orthodox Church gave an account of her life as a Rastafari woman. She presented a model for male–female relations and the family from the church's point of view, which is based on the monogamous nuclear family. She also emphasized that woman is made to be a man's equal, neither over or under him.

Following her presentation, a Rastafari sister addressed the difference between European and African families. She defended the right of Rastafari to chose the type of family organization that suited them, based on African patterns, if they so desired. However, she went on to say that most Rastafari women want to live in the tradition of King Alpha and Queen Omega, which involves one man and one woman. In this context she discussed the role of the woman as protector of the family institution and the behavioral code assigned to her. She then discussed the life circumstances of Rastafari and other black women that make it difficult to achieve this life. When the panel finished, there was a poetry reading by a Rastafari sister and dub poet who addressed in a very direct way several of the stresses and strains in male–female relations, much to the delight of the audience. The chair of the panel then opened the discussion to the audience.

At this point the senior Elder came center stage to reason and to answer questions as well. He explained how in Rastafari religious assemblies in Jamaica "dawtas" (a Rastafari term of address for sisters) are not allowed to be around altars or to even speak in the assembly. He noted that, while in Jamaica dawtas have no power in the organization of the assembly, here in the United Kingdom this would be embarrassing. He suggested that the local dawtas now had the opportunity to reason with the Elders and to get their teaching "straightened forward."

A discussion developed around monogamy versus polygamy, which involved the audience. There was a lot of jostling for the opportunity to speak. One of the brethren said women should not be allowed to wear pants into the assembly as they did in the United Kingdom. A lengthy discussion on dress codes followed. This triggered another sister to suggest that these concerns were trivial compared with what African people are struggling for in Africa. There were several calls for action. Finally a Rastafari sister in the audience suggested that they take up a collection there and now to purchase sanitary supplies and medicines for women in refugee camps in Africa. The hat was passed not once but twice. Ironically, the collection for sanitary supplies, among other things, touched on the delicate issue of a serious tabu in Rastafari around women's power to contaminate through menstruation. Yet here were women taking the most initiative seen at this point in public at the conference to mobilize the entire assembly in a act of Pan-African solidarity despite the fact they were under siege at that very moment.

At the same time as the collection was being organized, some Rastafari sisters initiated a discussion about how Rastafari Focus could support the struggle against apartheid in South Africa. Eventually a series of resolutions were drawn up, to be affirmed later in the conference. These included strongly restating the Rastafari antiapartheid position, calling for an economic boycott of South Africa, and petitioning the British and Caribbean governments to enforce more anti-apartheid measures.

This vignette demonstrates the way in which issues of gender and power intersect and how women carry on with their agenda despite efforts to undermine their authority. There were also other themes during this conference that provided continuity with the earlier international assemblies: repatriation, Rastafari economic development, and ways of dealing with various forms of repression and attacks on the movement. As in previous international conferences, Nyahbinghi played the central spiritual role. At the end of the conference, a new initiative, the Nyahbinghi Project, generated a series of workshops that were held in several communities in the United Kingdom over the next months.

Rastafari Focus was a major event in the history of Rastafari. It was held at the Commonwealth Institute, a rather prestigious venue, and it continued for two weeks, longer than any other Rastafari international gathering before or since. Ethnographers need to recognize the role that such conferences play in the development of Rastafari as a global phenomenon. It is important that researchers maintain communication with Rastafari networks and to attend such events because their significance cannot be understood solely by reading the available literature.

For example, a case in point is found in van Dijk's major study of Rastafari, which devotes only five pages to a discussion of the role of the international Rastafari conferences yet concludes that "there were no tangible results" (van Dijk, 1993: 271). Here one can only guess at what van Dijk means by results. Moreover, he argues that "they [international conferences] once more demonstrated the inability of the Rastafarians to organize themselves effectively and to overcome their internal differences" (cf. van Dijk, 1993:271). The fact that, without any long-term institutional support, Rastafari have organized numerous international gatherings and missions since the early 1980s speaks to the need for alternative interpretation. As critical ethnographers it is our responsibility to seek out alternative sources became such comments are, at the very least, misleading.

In addition to contributing to the development of a global community, international gatherings provide opportunities for women to assume responsibilities and leadership roles not traditional in Rastafari. A number of younger women researchers are beginning to focus exclusively on women within Rastafari, a topic which has been neglected, documenting the life experiences of Rastafari women and their aesthetic, spiritual, and material contributions to "Rastafari as a globalized practice" (cf. L. Collins, personal communication, July 3, 1997).

Weaving the Threads of Multisite Ethnography

Although the next example illustrates the complexity of doing multisite Rastafari ethnography over time, it is based on commonly practiced ethnographic methods involving networking and commitment to sustaining relationships. It also illustrates some issues discussed above as they pertain to Rastafari. I have made a decision not to reveal certain details that would make my case stronger in order to protect the personal security of some individuals. Although ethnographers make these choices all the time, in the case of Rastafari and its history of persecution and criminalization, we have to be especially cautious.

I have tried to represent this sequence of events as I experienced them mirroring how Rastafari themselves would draw significance from the way in which these interconnections manifested. I attempt to demonstrate the way in which Rastafari networks function over time and space.

In multisite ethnography and traveling cultures, although one can plan for definite research projects, field workers have to be open to unexpected opportunities, in the Rastafari sense of moving with the spirit, or being attuned to serendipity.[13] I describe a series of ethnographic moments in which I participated over the period of two years, from July, 1995 to early 1997. I pick up the thread of this particular sequence of events in the summer of 1995 with an International Rastafari Gathering in Toronto, which peaked on the occasion of Emperor Haile Selassie's birthday celebration, July 23. Several Jamaican-based Elders attended (Ras Boanerges, Bongo Time, Ras Sam Brown, Ras Irie Irons, and Ma Ashanti), as well as members of a younger generation of Rastafari from the Caribbean, United States, and United Kingdom (Sister Desta Tonga, Sister Yvonne Gayle, Ras Abraham Pettie, Ras Ibo, Ras Ivi, and Bongo Spear). Many of these brethren and sisters had attended and organized international events and were focal points in local and global networks, gathering and disseminating information throughout the global Rastafari community.

During this time frame a black American dreadlocks journalist, Mumia Abu-Jamal, was sitting on death row, scheduled to be executed in Pennsylvania on August 17, 1995. The Rastafari noted that the execution date coincided with the birthday of Marcus Garvey, a significant figure in Rastafari history.

Mumia had been in prison since 1981 and by the summer of 1995 his cause had become an international example of racist and political injustice. Protests were held in Germany, Italy, United Kingdom, France, Japan, and South Africa. In Toronto there were vigils and demonstrations at the United States consulate. I started reasoning with some brethren about Mumia's case. Mumia is not a Rastafari, nor a member of the MOVE organization, based in Philadelphia, and as a former Black Panther actively protested some of the same oppressive conditions with which Rastafari are familiar.

I had some facts about Mumia's case but was less knowledgeable about MOVE. One brother recalled that in the late 1970s and early 1980s American Rastafari had been harassed by the police on the suspicion that they were MOVE members, who also wear their hair in dreadlocks and take the last name "Africa." Confusion between the two occurred between 1977 and 1985 when MOVE had a series of confrontations with the police, and when Rastafari were being criminalized by the media, resulting in tension between the two groups.[14] For example, the Church of Haile Selassie I, with active branches in Jamaica, New York and London, headed by Abuna Ascento Foxe, a Jamaican Rastafari Elder, did not support Mumia in the summer of 1995, with the concern that such protest activity might cause a backlash against members of this congregation (Hepner, 1996:43).

A different atmosphere prevailed in Toronto. In early August, Starliner Productions, a media organization inspired by the African and Rastafari struggles, sponsored a benefit concert by Mutabaruka, a Jamaican dub poet with a Pan-Africanist orientation, in support of Mumia Abu-Jamal. Fortunately, Mumia's execution was stayed just a few days before August 17 in order for the appeal process to take place.[15] By the fall, Mumia's case was still unresolved. I decided to visit Philadelphia on my way to Washington, D.C., to find out more about Mumia's situation. I was accompanied by two Toronto-based Rastafari who wanted to drive to Philadelphia and Washington via New York City. They wanted to attend the 2nd Annual Rastafari Awards Banquet sponsored by the International Rastafari Advancement Seminary (IRAS) on the occasion of Emperor Haile Selassie's Coronation, November 2nd. The awards banquet resembled a mini-Rastafari international gathering, with several hundred people including some who had attended the gathering in Toronto the previous summer. Guests came from primarily the United States, Canada, and Jamaica.

Not only did the banquet facilitate international networking, but organizers[16] told me that they felt it was important, from the perspective of building cultural and community pride, to host such an elegant occasion not typically associated in the public's mind with Rastafari. The banquet was advertised by both flyers and formal invitations. It opened with a Divine Assembly and a Royal Salute, followed by a vegetarian dinner. One of the organizers was known for the exquisite "tajj" (Amharic for honey mead) he makes only for this banquet using an Ethiopian recipe, served in bottles with labels sporting Ethiopian motifs. Such a beverage, while generally not part of orthodox Rastafari foodways, certainly seems to reflect the cosmopolitan ambience of New York and is eagerly anticipated.

During and after dinner there was Rastafari-inspired entertainment before the speeches and awards. The banquet honored well-known Elders and other Rastafari who made significant contributions to the community. Scholarships for Rastafari youth were also awarded. The annual banquet is designed as a truly *royal* occasion, which celebrates one of the most important days in the Rastafari calendar in a grand style appropriate to this world capital. By contrast, in Jamaica or elsewhere in the Caribbean, week-long Nyahbinghis would be held in rural areas while camping out under the stars. Be it banquet or binghi, however, such occasions serve to mobilize the Rastafari community for religious, cultural, and political ends, as well as facilitating international networking.

Following the banquet, we traveled to Washington in order to attend the American Anthropological Association meetings before going to Philadelphia. There I presented an earlier draft of this paper. Part of my research commitment is to distribute my writing that I do to Rastafari for comment as well as to invite members to attend such meetings. It is important that Rastafari have the opportunity to attend such scholarly events and represent themselves. In fact, at the meetings we linked up with a Rastafari sister who is also a professional anthropologist. We had both done fieldwork in Jamaica in the early 1970s. The sister with whom I was traveling also knew her in another context and this was an opportunity for me to receive feedback.

After the meetings we visited Rastafari in the area before moving on to Philadelphia. One of the brothers who offered to house us had stayed during the gathering in Toronto with the sister with whom I was traveling. The details of how Rastafari accommodate each other — and even the ethnographer — while traveling are important. Most Rastafari are vegan and prefer chemical-free foods, and many travel with their own cooking and eating utensils, which they know are not contaminated. They take their own supplies with them as they do not eat in restaurants or on airplanes. They often prefer to stay with other

Rastafari in a culturally supportive environment, rather than with non-Rastafari relatives.

In Philadelphia we managed to make contact with the International Family and Friends of Mumia Abu-Jamal, which invited us to return to attend a conference in early December, 1995. Three weeks later we returned to attend the conference and met members of the local Rastafari community and the MOVE organization. Following our return to Toronto after this second trip, the Toronto Rastafari House of Nyahbinghi and I as a representative of various constituencies at York University, decided to organize a campus-community program in solidarity with Mumia and MOVE.

The program was co-sponsored by: the African Canadian Legal Clinic, the Atkinson College Certificate in Anti-Racist Research and Practice, the York University Centre for Race and Ethnic Relations, and the Ontario Public Interest Working Group, to name a few (see Yawney, 1997, for more detail.) At the public talks, press conference, and radio shows, Lydia Barashango (Mumia's sister), I Abdul Jon (a MOVE supporter), and Ras Iration I (a writer and dub poet) worked as a team. Ras Iration I would introduce the similarities in the struggle of black people and Rastafari in Toronto and Philadelphia, while the others covered the details of MOVE's history and Mumia's case.

Although the relationship between Rastafari and MOVE has been tense in some ways, there has been demonstrated support for MOVE by Rastafari in the United States. A Rastafari journalist and MOVE supporter, who has lived and worked in the Philadelphia area for years, told me that Mumia interviewed Bob Marley when Marley was in Philadelphia on tour during his career as a radio journalist. I was told that in the unaired section of the tape, when asked by Mumia what he thought of MOVE, Marley responded "MOVE IS Rasta!" Marley went on to state that the same persecution that MOVE experienced in 1977–1978 was similar to what happened to Rastafari in the late 1950s. When some of us traveled again to Philadelphia in May, 1996, to attend an international Mumia/MOVE support conference, the U.K. representative was a Rastafari activist and reggae performer who had given concerts in Europe in support of Mumia.

Following another trip to Philadelphia to attend a MOVE event in August, 1996, I decided to visit Jamaica in the first week of September, 1996 to participate in a study session with Ras Planno and some of his brethren. We spent ten days sharing information, listening to tapes, viewing videos, and reading articles pertaining to both Rastafari and MOVE. Their reaction was supportive of MOVE and efforts to free Abu-Jamal and to challenge racism in the United States. As an ethnographer it was important to me to receive feedback from Rastafari with whom I had worked in Jamaica about the MOVE activities in which I was involved.

These two threads, Rastafari and MOVE, have become unexpectedly interwoven in my ethnographic practice. During another visit to Philadelphia in December, 1996, I had the opportunity to collaborate with the MOVE organization in order to prepare a research paper on it. I was planning to make a presentation on MOVE's approach to health care at a conference on primary health care sponsored by the International People's Health Council and South African health organizations, at the University of the Western Cape, January 29–31, 1997. When I learned that I would be traveling to South Africa in January, I immediately telephoned a Rastafari brother with whom I had worked on the Rastafari freedom of religion prison initiative in New York State. This brother had been concerned about the bombing of MOVE in 1985 and maintained an ongoing interest in MOVE's politics. He also had traveled extensively in Africa, and, as he kept me on one line, he called Cape Town on the other and arranged a contact in the Rastafari community. The marvels of telecommunication![17] I immediately sent copies of my research materials to South Africa so the local Rastafari could check me out before my arrival.

Considering that the South African Rastafari community first came into existence in the late 1970s, it has developed a phenomenal presence. The role of reggae music in this process was critical. Although the Rastafari community presence in South Africa was sufficiently significant to be courted by the African National Congress (ANC) during the 1993 election campaign, it continues to be under siege by the South African state in various ways.[18]

Shortly after I arrived I met members of the Rastafari Burning Spear Movement in Cape Town who were preparing a constitutional challenge to have cannabis use recognized as a religious right under the new constitution of South Africa. They documented for me repeated instances of police interference with their use of cannabis. Their leader, Ras Bernard Brown, had been charged with cannabis possession seven times in recent years. They had been unable to locate an expert witness to testify on Rastafari as a religion and the use of cannabis. Several months earlier, in 1996, they had secured an interview with a reporter from the *Mail and Guardian*, a South African weekly newspaper, who put out an international call for expert witnesses specifically naming Horace Campbell. Campbell, a Jamaican, had written a history of Rastafari, and had traveled and lived in Africa during the 1980s. Campbell later contacted Burning Spear's lawyer. Eventually I met with the same lawyer and agreed to be an expert witness. The day following this meeting, Ras Bernard was arrested again and I accompanied brethren to the police station to post bail. They drew my attention to the fact that at midnight the new constitution of South Africa went into effect and their grievances had not been addressed.

When in South Africa, I was contacted to do some media work on behalf of Mumia Abu-Jamal. Members of the Rastafari community gave me leads for radio and newspaper interviews and public talks. They arranged for the same reporter from the *Mail and Guardian* to interview me about Mumia. In the course of this, I was asked to be a guest on a special reggae tribute on Bush Radio, the oldest community radio station in Africa, for Bob Marley on his birthday.

I arranged for Ras Mortimo Planno, as Bob's Rastafari mentor, to be interviewed directly from Jamaica, which was enthusiastically welcomed. The few extracts I have included from that interview cannot do justice to the emotional impact of the occasion. As we were celebrating in the studio, however, Ras Bernard was arrested again for cannabis. Very early the next morning some of us were back in court to post bail again. Ironically, that was also the opening of the first Parliament under the new constitution. Ras Bernard and the rest of us left the court house for Parliament because we had formal invitations to be in the visitors gallery. At the same time approximately forty Rastafari who were demonstrating outside the Parliament to free cannabis were arrested for unlawful assembly. The manager of Bush Radio and one of the station's Rastafari broadcasters were bailing them out well into the wee hours of the morning.

It is interesting to note that Rastafari in South Africa are passing through some of the tribulations that Rastafari in Jamaica have experienced. Shortly after I left South Africa police stormed a Rastafari settlement in Cape Town, known as the Marcus Garvey Camp, which had been the focus of the Nyahbinghi mission several months earlier. Ten days after Bob's birthday, an article appeared in the *Cape Metro Sunday Times* about a twelve-year old Rastafari boy was refused entry to a Cape Town school because he would not trim his locks (Vanga, 1997). A couple of weeks later Ras Garreth Prince, whom I met during my stay, a dreadlocks Rastafari who had qualified for a lawyer, was denied registration of his Articles of Clerkship because he had previously been convicted of possession of cannabis. Ras Prince could be South Africa's first Rastafari lawyer if he is called to the Bar. But now he too has a constitutional challenge pending on the grounds that cannabis use is a religious right of Rastafari. I submitted an affidavit and accompanying exhibits for the first round of the challenge.

Because I was subsequently asked to serve as expert witness for two other constitutional challenges, one in Guam, and the other in Jamaica, I have put the lawyers and plaintiffs in touch with each other. Since then, statements, supporting documents, relevant case law, and written judgments have been circulating between us.

These various threads continue to weave a fine ethnographic fabric. The above example illustrates the challenges that face researchers of Rastafari in the global context. On the occasion of Marley's birthday celebration at Bush Radio, when the interviewer, Ras Elphy, asked Ras Planno to say his last words to the South African nation, Planno responded:

I and I want and desire the same thing. We say Africa Unite! For if Africa don't unite in this time we won't have any Africa. Right now we are looking at Rwanda, we looking at Liberia. From one end to the other of Africa and the problems that is going on there. In Central Africa. In South Africa too for South Africa problems don't yet solve although you get some independence and whatever. And if Mandela move now and younger people come try use radical attitude towards taking over the ANC government then we know is a different thing gonna happen in South Africa. We want to be here and there and everywhere to try and stop that. We don't want the race between Black and white to really go on any longer in South Africa. We would like to can solve that. And we would like what we are saying may be meaningful to those thinking otherwise. (Ras Mortimo Planno, 1997)

Endnotes

I wish to acknowledge the Social Science and Humanities Research Council of Canada and York University for providing financial assistance for some of the work described in this chapter. I wish to thank John Pulis for a free-wheeling exchange of ideas and infinite patience. As usual, I have benefitted greatly from an on-going dialogue with John Homiak, whose support and insights I value highly. I am also indebted to Professors Tania Das Gupta, George Dei, and Clem Marshall for sharing their experiences and ideas on the subject of anti-racist research so freely. And finally, I wish to thank all my Rastafari sistren and brethren who have shared their faith with me over many years.

1. John Homiak in this volume describes another manifestation of word-sound-power to which he refers as "soundscape."

2. Rastafari themselves will tell you that the term Nyahbinghi means "Death to Black and White oppressors." This is an orientation that developed in Jamaica in the late 1940s–early 1950s out of the House of the Youth Black Faith. See Barry Chevannes, 1994, and John Homiak, 1994a and 1995, for more detailed discussions of the history and culture of Nyahbinghi. Nyahbinghi embodies a way of life or "livity" based mainly on Old Testament practices. Thus orthodox Nyahbinghi practitioners do not cut their hair or "locks," follow vegan nutritional guidelines, and generally live as natural or as "ital" as possible. Men are expected to keep their locks covered by a tam or "Crown" except when attending to religious duties, while women are to keep their heads covered at all times. Moreover, women are expected to follow a modest dress code and to avoid certain responsibilities, such as preparing food, when menstruating. At the 1983 Second International Rastafari Conference held in Kingston, Jamaica, the Rastafari International Divine Order of the Nyahbinghi was recognized by the Assembly as the spiritual foundation for Rastafari.

3. The several quotations from Ras Mortimo Planno described later in this chapter were taken from the radio interview with him. Ras Planno is generally acknowledged as a Rastafari intellectual and the Elder who was Bob Marley's mentor.

4. See Chevannes, 1994,and Homiak, 1994, for discussion of sectarian variation within Rastafari.

5. See discussion by Bilby and Homiak in this volume about use of contemporary telecommunications technology by Rastafari.

6. On the subject of international Rastafari assemblies see: Chevannes, 1994:275–277; Homiak, 1994; Van Dijk, 1993:267–271; and Yawney, 1993; 1995. As well, there were International Rastafari Gatherings in Miami, 1994; Toronto, 1995; Atlanta, 1996; and St. Croix, 1997, organized by the International Community of Rastafari.

7. I have also seen home-produced video tapes on the activities of Rastafari in both Zimbabwe and Azania, particularly in the Capetown area. Representatives of several Rastafari collectivities reside in Ethiopia, as well as other parts of Africa. On field trips to Jamaica I have met Japanese Rastafari and have viewed home produced videos of Japanese Rastafari in Japan. Another source of information on the international Rastafari presence are the Rastafari-inspired newspapers such as *Dread Times*, based in Philadelphia, or *Rastafari Speaks*, published in Chicago. The Rastafari Economic Development Directory (First International Rastafari Entrepreneur Press) has a listing of international Rastafari organizations.

8. See Yawney, 1995:61–62, for a discussion of Rastafari as a traveling culture, modeled after the work of Clifford, 1992.

9. My experience with Rastafari was responsible for my professional interest in anti-racist work. I was one of the founding faculty members of the Certificate in Anti-Racist Research and Practice (CARRP), which is housed in the Department of Sociology, Atkinson College, York University.

10. See Kirby and McKenna, 1989, and Maynard and Purvis, 1994, for feminist research methodologies.

11. I am indebted to John Homiak for raising the issue of the social construction of expert knowledge with me.

12. While non-cooperation is almost a tabu topic, I think it does need to be raised. I do not want to give the impression that at a certain stage the ethnographer passes all the tests and then is somehow seamlessly

incorporated into the Rastafari community. This has not been my experience. While I have developed some long-term mutually respectful relationships with Rastafari, I continue to be criticized and questioned by Rastafari whom I have known for a long time. It would also be worthwhile exploring how different the experience of women researchers is from that of men.

13. Researching globalization of a culture has definite demands. Travel costs can be expensive. Unplanned research ventures often cannot be funded by granting agencies that require advance notice. Such research also requires flexibility in terms of work and other responsibilities.

14. In 1977–1978 a MOVE house was the target of a prolonged police siege. In 1985 a MOVE home was bombed by the city, resulting in eleven deaths and the destruction of sixty homes. See Chevannes 1994:265–269 for a discussion of the criminalization of Rastafari in the media during the same period.

15. Ironically, Robert Hill, a Garvey scholar and historian of Rastafari, met with me on August 17, 1995, Garvey's birthday and the original date of Mumia's execution. We recorded much of our conversation about Rastafari research experiences. Long-term ethnographers are repositories of all kinds of data, which may never get into print. A good case in point is George Simpson's reflections on field work in West Kingston, published nearly forty years later (Simpson, 1994).

16. Two members of the IRAS executive were also known to me from working to organize for Rastafari religious rights in the New York State prison system.

17. This brother and I had linked up in the United Kingdom two years previously. Another sister who had been peripherally involved in some of these events was also present. We actually tape recorded our recollections and made copies for all of us.

18. During the election campaign, the ANC distributed flyers with the salutation "Greetings I-N-I" prominently displayed alongside three photographs of Marcus Garvey, Bob Marley, and Nelson Mandela, with the statement, "The ANC recognizes that Rastas are part and parcel of the oppressed masses. We all know of the important role of the international Rasta movement has played in the Liberation Struggle in bringing to the attention of the World the message of our struggle through music."

References

Alleyne, M. 1988 *Roots of Jamaican Culture*. London: Pluto Press.

Barrett, L. 1977 *The Rastafarians*. Boston: Beacon Press.

Bones, Jah 1985 *One Love*. London: Voice of Rasta Publishing House.

Brathwaite, K. 1993 *Roots*. Ann Arbor: University of Michigan Press.

Campbell, H. 1987 *Rasta and Resistance*. Trenton, NJ: Africa World Press.

Chevannes, B. 1994 *Rastafari: Roots and Ideology*. Syracuse: Syracuse University Press.

Chevannes, B., ed. 1995 *Rastafari and Other African-Caribbean World Views*. London: MacMillan Press.

Clifford, J. 1992 Traveling cultures. In: *Cultural Studies* (eds., L. Grossberg, C. Nelson, and P. Treichler). New York, Routledge, pp. 96–112).

Clifford, J. 1994 Diasporas. *Cultural Anthropology* 9(3):302–338.

Das Gupta, T. 1993 Towards an anti-racist, feminist teaching method. *New Horizons In Adult Education* 7(1):33–50.

Dei, G. 1996 *Anti-Racism Education*. Halifax: Fernwood.

D. Gill; Mayor, B.; and Blair, M., eds. 1992 *Racism and Education*. London: Sage Publications.

Gilroy, P. 1993 *The Black Atlantic*. Cambridge: Harvard University Press.

Hepner, R. 1996 (June 12) *The House that Rasta Built: Church-Building Among New York Rastafarians*. Unpublished manuscript.

Hill, R. 1981 Dread history: Leonard P. Howelll and Millenarian visions in early Rastafari religions in Jamaica. *Epoche* 9:30–71.

Homiak, J. 1985 The Mystic revelation of Rasta-far-eye. In: Dreaming (ed., B. Tedlock). London: Cambridge University Press, pp. 220–245.

Homiak, J. 1994 From yard to nation: Rastafari and the politics of eldership at home and abroad. In M. Kremser (Ed.), Ay BoBo: Afro-Karibische Religionen (pp. 49–76). Vienna: Universitatsverlag.

Homiak, J. 1995 Dub history: soundings on Rastafari livity and language. In: *Rastafari and Other African-Caribbean Worldviews* (ed., B. Chevannes). London: Macmillan, pp. 127–181.

Hooks, Bell 1994 *Outlaw Culture: Resisting Representation.* New York: Routledge.

Kirby, S. and McKenna, K. 1989 *Experience, Research, Social Change.* Toronto: Garamond.

McCarthy, C. and Crichlow, W., eds. 1993 *Race and Representation in Education.* New York: Routeldge.

McPherson, E.S.P. 1991 *Rastafari and Politics.* Clarendon, Jamaica: Black International Iyahbinghi Press.

Marcus, G.E. and Fischer, M. 1986 *Anthropology As Cultural Critique.* Chicago: University of Chicago Press.

Marshall, C. 1996 Video as a vehicle for popularizing anti-racist research. Paper presented at Critical Perspectives On Anti-Racist Research Symposium. York University, Toronto, May 16.

Maynard, M. and Purvis, J., eds. 1994 *Researching Women's Lives From A Feminist Perspective.* London: Taylor and Francis.

Nettleford, R. 1970 *Mirror, Mirror.* Kingston: William Collins and Sangster.

Planno, Ras M. 1984 [June] Interview with author.

Planno, Ras P. 1997 [February 6] Interview on Bush Radio, Cape Town, South Africa.

Pulis, J. (this volume) Citing(sighting)-up: words, sounds, and reading scripture in Jamaica.

Pulis, J. 1993 Up-full sounds: language, identity, and the world-view of Rastafari. *Ethnic Groups* 10:285–300.

RAS 1988 *Focus On Rastafari: Selected Presentations From Rastafari Focus '86.* London: Rastafarian Advisory Service.

R.E.D.D. 1994 *Rastafari Economic Development Directory.* Washington, DC: First International Rastafari Entrepreneur Press.

Savishinsky, N. 1994a The Baye Faal of Senegambia: Muslim Rastas in the promised land? *Africa* 64(2):211–219.

Savishinsky, N. 1994b Rastafari in the Promised Land: the spread of a Jamaican socioreligious movement among the youth of Africa. *African Studies Review* 37(3):19–50.

Simpson, G.E. 1994 Some reflections on the Rastafari movement in Jamaica. *Jamaica Journal* 25(2):3–10.

Simpson, G.E. 1955 Political cultism in West Kingston, Jamaica. *Social and Economic Studies* 4(2):133–149.

Skeggs, B. 1994 Situating the production of feminist ethnography. In: *Researching Women's Lives From A Feminist Perspective* (eds., M. Maynard and J. Purvis). London: Taylor and Francis, pp. 72–92.

Spencer-Strachan, L. 1992 *Confronting the Colour Crisis in the Afrikan Diaspora: Emphasis Jamaica*. New York: Arikan World Infosystems.

Turner, T. 1994 Rastafari and the new society: Caribbean and East African feminist roots of a popular movement to reclaim the earthly commons. In: *Arise! Ye Mighty People* (eds., T. Turner with B. Ferguson). Trenton, NJ: Africa Wolrd Press, pp. 9–55.

Warner-Lewis, M. 1991 *Guinea's Other Suns: The African Dynamic in Trinidad Culture*. Dover, MA: The Majority Press.

van Dijk, F. 1993 *Jahmaica: Rastafari and Jamaican Society 1930–1990*. Utrecht: ISOR.

Vanga, S. 1997 [February 16] *Cape Metro Sunday Times*, p. 1.

Wilson, B. 1973 *Magic and the Millennium*. London: Heinemann.

Yawney, C. 1984 The Rastafarian community. In: *The Spirit of Toronto* (ed., L. Holton) Toronto: Image Publishing, pp. 321–327.

Yawney, C. 1993 Rasta mek a trod: symbolic ambiguity in a globalizing religion. In: *Alternative Cultures in the Caribbean* (eds., U. Fleischmann and T. Bremer). Frankfurt/Main: Vervuert Verlag, pp. 161–168.

Yawney, C. 1995 Tell out king Rasta doctrine around the whole world: Rastafari in global perspective. In: *The Reordering of Culture* (eds., A. Ruprecht and C. Taiana). Ottawa: Carleton University Press, pp. 57–73.

Yawney, C. 1997 In solidarity with Mumia. *Academics For Mumia Abu-Jamal Newsletter* 3(1):2–3.

Part II

HOME

INTRODUCTION
TO PART II

Carole D. Yawney

The chapters in this section challenge any notion we might have that Caribbean religions are local, static, and bounded phenomena. The authors are all experienced field workers and ethnographers with decades of research between them. Instead, the authors treat us to several case studies which demonstrate how an ongoing and dynamic cultural dialogue in the Caribbean and elsewhere contributes to the evolution of the area's religions.

Though each contribution is concerned with a discrete religion, the discussion reveals the ways in which the relationship between any one religious expression and another tends to be more seamless than fixed. The chapters also demonstrate just how permeable the membrane can be between religious and secular culture. The examples discussed call for a new model of understanding religion which emphasizes process and practitioner over form and content. We see how creatively and innovatively Caribbean religions respond to changing national and international context, and the role they play in negotiating cultural and national identities.

Aisha Khan states directly that her Trinidad research has lead her to appreciate religions not as "self-contained wholes" but as "living continuities" where identities are forged. Khan describes how "jharraying," a ritual whereby individuals are swept clean by an iman of any negative influences from the influence of the "evil eye," has been reconstituted as meaningful not only to Islamic practitioners, but to Hindus and Christians as well. Here, at the level of the local community, religious identities cut across the culturally constructed national identities of Indo-Trinidadian and Afro-Trinidadian in a way that makes sense in daily life.

Houk's chapter on Orisha in Trinidad provides an insight into the dynamic process of religious renewal through the incorporation of outside influences in what has been traditionally perceived as an Afro-Caribbean religion. Houk argues that the mourning ritual in

Orisha on the individual level generates creativity on the community level by introducing Hindu, Catholic, Kabbalah and other elements into the practice. Houk also describes how this tendency is balanced by a countervailing dynamic to Africanize Orisha shrines, which can be best understood in the context of constructing national identities in Trinidad. This perspective encourages us to focus on religion as an arena in which political as well as spiritual discourses take place.

This point is also illustrated by Green's chapter. Here we see how blurring the boundary between religious and popular culture resulted in a national crisis of representation. In fact, Green's analysis might lead one to conclude that the role of Carnival as a national institution in Trinidad takes on religious significance itself.

Another way that Caribbean religions express national identities is by indigenizing religious cultures from outside the region. Austin-Broos reminds us that the Caribbeanization of imported Christianity is a process that continues to this day, as pastors and practitioners alike struggle to achieve a balance between metropolitan and local influences. Central to the practice of Pentecostalism is Spirit baptism and the experience of speaking in tongues which confirms the potential for personal transformation by being bodily possessed by the Holy Ghost. These individual experiences are collectively redefined in a uniquely Jamaican way, using orality and the poetics of the Bible, to imagine a community beyond the poverty and violence of the local social environment.

This section also includes other examples of religions as "living testimonies" with an emphasis on personal growth and social change. Pulis's describes how this very enterprise of socially constructing the individual Rastafari worldview as "work in process" is mediated. He focuses on the activity of "citing up," an oral performance practice of subjecting a Bible reading to an interpretive commentary which re-appropriates the text to serve Rastafari ends. This is another example in which extensive ethnographic experience attunes the researcher to cultural nuances involved in the social production of discourse. Pulis demonstrates how not just the content of Rastafari teaching is counter-hegemonic but also the very process whereby the Rastafari worldview is constructed in an ongoing and dynamic way that subverts the dominant print-based culture. This Rastafari tradition of aurality shares much in common with that described by Austin-Broos and taken together both chapters illustrate the importance of the politics of interpretation in sustaining vibrant and dynamic religious cultures.

Glazier's study of Spiritual Baptist music also highlights the contribution of aurality as well as orality to the continued regeneration of religious culture. In much the same way that Khan's work challenged our notion of bounded religions, Glazier argues that we need to expand the scope of what constitutes "music." He shows how the boundary between sacred and secular music is not absolute, partly because religious performers also play in popular settings.

One is reminded of the role played by the high degree of mobility of the Kumina practitioners and performers discussed by Bilby in this volume. In fact, traveling and visiting by both humans and spirits contribute greatly to flexibility in Kumina and Convince. Both Kumina and Convince constitute African Nations in the Jamaican context. Bilby's account sheds further light on the process of indigenization, only in this case it is an African cultural identity which is being adapted to the particular needs of the local but diverse "creole" community.

Chevannes's chapter describes how the international attention focused on the death of reggae musicians has forced a religious culture to alter its approach to one of its most fundamental of premises. Traditionally Rastafari deny death and have nothing to do with the dead. Chevannes shows us how, with the aid of the Ethiopian Orthodox Church, the Rastafari negotiated this dilemma and relied on Jamaican folk behaviors in order to deal with the funerals and burials of these favorite sons. Chevannes's chapter clearly demonstrates the capacity of this Caribbean religion to make major adjustments in its worldview in a changing global context.

All in all, the chapters in this section challenge readers to re-think what constitutes religion. We are disabused of any notions we night have held that religions constitute spheres of behavior somehow separate from everyday life. We see how religious communities provide the ground for negotiating cultural identities at both the individual and national level. At the same time as far as the Caribbean is concerned the historical process of reshaping, reformulating, and reconfiguring outside influences continues to provide a source of innovation and renewal.

8: BLASPHEMY, SACRILEGE, AND MORAL DEGRADATION IN THE TRINIDAD CARNIVAL: THE HALLELUJAH CONTROVERSY OF 1995

Garth L. Green

Introduction

Debates about the composition and content of national culture reveal tensions inherent in the process of nation-building in post-colonial states especially those with multi-ethnic populations. National festivals such as the Carnival in Trinidad and Tobago[1] provide an arena in which different and conflicting ideas about national identity and the principles of inclusion in the nation may be expressed, contested, and resolved. In this chapter I discuss the controversy surrounding the name of a masquerade band for the 1995 Carnival in Trinidad and Tobago. Days after the band "launched," that is formally announced its theme and presented its costumes to the public in mid-November of 1994, a group of evangelical Pentecostal pastors protested that the name of the band, *Hallelujah*, constituted an act of disrespect of their religious beliefs. They attacked the designer of the band, Peter Minshall, and his associates for "hav[ing] decided to mockingly desecrate "Hallelujah" by dragging it into what is widely considered as easily one of the worst devil-glorifying festivals in the universe" (*Express* 11/13/94). In December, the Body of Concerned Pastors (BCP) comprising two hundred and eight pastors and led by Winston Cuffie, presented a petition to the Prime Minister, the Attorney General, the Police, and the National Carnival Commission, the administrative body that oversees the Carnival, asserting that the name of the band associated the name of God with the drunkenness and vulgarity of the Carnival. Invoking the Public Holidays and Festivals Act, the pastors argued that the band should not be allowed to parade under the name of *Hallelujah* since the Act prohibits any masquerade portrayal or representation which may bring any religion practiced in Trinidad and Tobago into disrepute. Despite threatening court action, the pastors did not succeed in getting Peter Minshall to change the name nor did they provoke the government to take any action on their behalf. *Hallelujah* participated in the Carnival and eventually won the coveted Band of the Year title.

Public response to the controversy was tremendous: hundreds of letters to the editor, newspaper columns by religious leaders and prominent public figures, editorials, and debates on the radio and television. The controversy provoked a wide range of responses and served as an opportunity to explore the role of the state in mediating the claims of groups in the society to full citizenship in Trinidad and Tobago and how those claims are evaluated and disputes about them resolved. As the Carnival season progressed from early November through February the issues raised by the controversy proliferated and precipitated a national debate about religious and artistic freedom, the constitutional protection of minorities, and tensions between a publicly expressed and promoted form of national cultural identity espousing inclusiveness, celebrating diversity, and promoting tolerance on the one hand and a religious identity that does not wish to be associated with the cultural forms associated with that cultural identity on the other hand.

The events discussed in this essay provide an excellent example of the forms of competing concepts of spirituality and religiousness that I often encountered when I was in Trinidad. Shortly before the Carnival of 1994, I attended an ecumenical conference on Carnival in which representatives of the Anglican, Catholic, Muslim, and Hindu faiths as well as scholars and performers examined the place of the Carnival within Trinidadian culture and society. The presentations and discussions revealed that Muslims and Hindus did not understand how the Carnival they had seen and read about could possibly have any deeper spiritual significance. While they ultimately acknowledged that such a spirituality was possible, they wanted to make sure that the Carnival was not presented to the rest of the world as the *primary* form of spirituality and religious expression in the country. They were concerned that their form of faith would be ignored and subsumed within, what to them, was an alien form of expression of faith and joy in God's creation.

News of the controversy reached me through email and letters with friends and acquaintances closely tied to Peter Minshall's mas band. Newspaper clippings can be a valuable resource into the ways current events crystallize public representations of identity and the public forums in which such debates take place.[2] Anthropologists should not be reluctant to draw on such sources of information when conducting ethnography for the voices heard and perspectives obtained through such materials are as valuable, especially for questions of identity, as those obtained through the standard anthropological practices of gathering information: interviews and participant observation.

Why did this conflict between the leaders of a small yet rapidly growing and vocal religious movement and one of the most respected, albeit controversial, artists in the country, so captivate the national imagination and elicit such intense national self-examination? Part of the answer lies in the ways the Carnival has been, throughout its two hundred year history in Trinidad, an arena in which emergent social groups have asserted their claims for inclusion in the political and cultural life of the country (Wood 1968, Brereton 1979, Trotman 1986, Liverpool 1993). While this is not the place to detail that history in full, since independence in 1962, the Carnival has held an important place in dominant narratives of Trinidadian national identity.

Throughout the history of Trinidad the Carnival has come under attack from colonial officials, religious authorities, and other self-appointed guardians of the public morality.[3] During the colonial era the Carnival became the center of controversies about public order, lewdness, morality, criminality, and even loyalty to the Empire. The anticolonial political movement that eventually led Trinidad and Tobago to independence portrayed the Carnival as the essential cultural expression of the people whereas it had been the target of repressive legislation during much of the British colonial period. While the Carnival had been the occasion to protest against what was seen as a culturally and religiously foreign regime, it became, after independence, invested with the significance of being "the national festival." What was once a highly charged moment of protest against the state gradually became subject to appropriation by the ruling forces in the newly independent Trinidad and Tobago as a marker of the ruling group's legitimacy.

The intensity of the *Hallelujah* debate and the wide range of issues and concerns that it provoked compels us to re-consider what we may

mean when we speak of "national" festivals and their relationship to
national identity. If we see national festivals as celebrations of the
nation, then how are we to interpret extreme opposition to such
events from a social group claiming to be a part of that nation? What
are the reactions to that opposition from those who have an interest
in perpetuating the representation of certain cultural forms as national? Are these events national cultural forms because they successfully incorporate divergent voices? Or is the status of any national
festival to be found in how it is deployed in arguments about what
national culture is rather than in its alleged capacity to represent and
incorporate various cultural forms? I argue that the Carnival, which
is so heavily burdened with the nationalist project of cultural identity
formation, and the social conflicts and tensions surrounding it, constitutes a prime arena for investigating how national identity is constructed and modified through ongoing social practices in a
post-colonial multi-ethnic state in which the composition of national
culture is highly contested.

Religion and the Carnival

According to the 1990 census, Trinidad and Tobago has a population
of 1.17 million persons. The five largest religious denominations are
Roman Catholic (29.4 percent or 330,655 people), Hindu (23.7 percent
or 267,040 people), Anglican (10.9 percent or 122,789 people), Pentecostal (7.5 percent or 84,066 people), and Islam (5.8 percent or 65,732
people) (Central Statistical Office 1993:xv). In 1980 only 3.5 percent
of the population identified themselves as Pentecostal, so the movement has grown rapidly in the last ten years.

   There has always been and continues to be religious opposition to
celebrants' behavior, especially that of women, during the Carnival.
While the primary concern of religious leaders has been with the
effects of prolonged periods of feting, drinking, and sexually suggestive display, there has also been concern over the depiction of religious iconography and the portrayal of religious themes deemed
unsuitable for inclusion in the Carnival. However, most religious
leaders are content to make yearly cautionary statements about the
need to behave more circumspectly during the Carnival and, in a
spirit of resignation, they plan alternative activities such as church

retreats to the beach (Stewart 1986: 310). Such general exhortations and denunciations constitute a regular part of every year's Carnival and are so customary that they are now part of Carnival "tradition."

In past years there have been controversies surrounding the depiction of Hindu deities in masquerades and the representation of East Indians in calypsos (Rohlehr 1990:251–257; Trotman 1991). These conflicts were usually amicably resolved through discussions between government officials, the offending artist, and leaders of the Hindu community. For example, in the 1995 Carnival, the Hindu community expressed some concern with the depiction of Lord Nataraja, the incarnation of Lord Shiva as the cosmic dancer, in the headpiece of a costume in *Hallelujah*. Satnarine Maharaj, the leader of the Sanatan Dharma Maha Sabha (SDMS), perhaps the most powerful Hindu organization, diplomatically refrained from attacking Minshall and *Hallelujah* in public. In an interview with the *Trinidad Guardian* (1/1/95:1) a representative of the SDMS stated:

> This is a very sensitive issue and we will prefer to talk with Minshall before we adopt a position in public. We believe taking a stand before adequate discussion will send a message of confrontation. This is not the message we would like to send.

This is an example of a model protest: private meetings, established organizations with recognized leadership, and careful negotiations conducted in an atmosphere of mutual respect away from the glare of public scrutiny eventually yielding an acceptable compromise. There is no flurry of advertisements, radio appearances, or televised attacks. Perhaps as proof of the effectiveness of such a moderate strategy, Minshall modified the headpiece of the costume so that it would depict a generic "cosmic dancer" and even agreed to develop a design to mark the 150th anniversary of Indian Arrival Day, the day commemorating the landing of the first indentured servants from India in Trinidad.

The case under discussion here differs from the Hindu situation because the Pentecostal pastors, as Christians, could not claim to speak for all Christians, most of whom expressed no objection to the name. Nor could Cuffie and the Body of Concerned Pastors claim to be speaking on behalf of the Pentecostal movement as a whole for there is no well-established hierarchy within the movement itself, each pastor having a great degree of authority over his own church. Finally, although the BCP's opposition was focused specifically on the name of the band, it was making a more general argument in opposition to the Carnival and its effects. Even though the pastors would be appeased if Minshall were to change the name, their general opposition to the Carnival would remain.

The Prime Minister, a born again Christian who also served as the minister for ecclesiastical affairs, chose not to intervene or mediate as requested in the BCP's petition. He commented that the parties to the dispute seemed rather entrenched in their positions and suggested that the courts would be the best place to resolve the issue (*Trinidad Guardian* 2/23/95:1). The pastors argued that the government's failure to take any action constituted an act of discrimination and indicated that the government did not take the Pentecostals' concerns as seriously as those of the other major religious groups in Trinidad and Tobago. So the whole affair quickly shifted from a concern with the name of the band as such to recognition in public of the right of the evangelicals to be acknowledged as legitimate representatives of a particular social group; to be granted the same rights and privileges as the other state-recognized religious organizations.

In criticizing Peter Minshall, Cuffie drew upon the fame and notoriety of the most controversial figure in the Carnival (Trinidad Express Newspapers, Ltd.: 1992). For the past twenty years, Minshall has been an eloquent and vocal defender of his own vision of the Carnival as well as an ardent analyst, critic, and commentator on contemporary social issues in Trinidad. Minshall is a Euro-Trinidadian who, although born in Guyana, grew up in Trinidad and became involved in the Carnival at an early age. He ultimately took his love of Carnival and studied theatrical design and art in England. He is an internationally renowned artist who has had exhibitions of his work in numerous museums around the world and has served as an artistic director of the opening ceremonies of the 1992 Summer Olympics in Barcelona, the opening ceremonies of the 1994 World Cup Soccer Tournament, and the opening and closing ceremonies of the 1996 Summer Olympics in Atlanta. His technical and artistic contributions and innovations to the Carnival are numerous and there is not space here to detail all of the controversies which have arisen out of Minshall's work. However, he has challenged the

Carnival authorities, expanded the dramatic possibilities of masquerade, and provoked very strong reactions, both positive and negative, among Trinidadians.

The BCP's attack on Minshall is ironic because he has consistently positioned himself in opposition to those elements in the Carnival which were most roundly criticized by Cuffie and the BCP. Minshall describes his Carnival presentations as a unique art form in which he can express the fundamental struggles of the human soul between good and evil while also commenting on current social conditions. His work has never been associated with the presentations of some of the larger masquerade bands which may have up to 4000 people, nearly eighty percent of them young women, dressed in colorful and suggestive costumes. These bands are commonly referred to by both critics and supporters as "jam and wine" bands because they highlight the more hedonistic aspects of the Carnival: drinking, dancing, and having a good time.

Pastor Winston Cuffie is the leader of the Miracle Ministries, a Pentecostal religious congregation located near Couva in central-western Trinidad some twenty miles south of the capital city, Port of Spain. For several years he has placed a weekly advertisement in a major daily newspaper in which he declaims on a variety of pertinent social issues. His recurrent diatribes against the Carnival are as familiar as the other markers of the return of the Carnival season: the sounds of the steel bands practicing in the panyards, the introduction of new calypsos in the tents, and the launching of the masquerade bands. It is through these advertisements that he carried out his campaign against *Hallelujah*, the Carnival, and the government.

In order to assert his claim as a leader in the Pentecostal community and the growing significance of the Pentecostal community as a whole within the larger religious community in Trinidad, Pastor Cuffie gambled that the government would respond favorably to his protest. At stake was the respectability of the movement. If Minshall and the government acceded to his requests, then that would indicate that the Pentecostal's religious beliefs were respected and taken seriously. Cuffie, as the leader of the protest, would be looked to in the future as the spokesman for this wing of the Pentecostal movement. Should Minshall not agree to the BCP's demands and the government refuse to intervene, then the road to respectability would be less smooth. In response, Cuffie would have to take the position that he was a part of a maligned and ignored religious movement in order to save face. The key to his success would be in not violating the unstated assumptions regarding protests against the Carnival and ideas about religious respectability. At issue here is Cuffie's ability to speak appropriately in this situation and to be recognized as worthy of speaking by those authorities able to confer legitimacy.

In attempting to gain recognition of the Pentecostal movement Cuffie appealed to the state authorities for action to be taken according to the Constitution and laws of the land. By following such a legal and institutional protocol, Cuffie argued that he was seeking redress for grievances through established channels. At the same time, by using the media to publicize the protest, Cuffie was also appealing to the disaffected and attempting to tap into their frustrations with the government. Cuffie had to plead the case of the disaffected yet without offending the authorities in the media, the state, and the religious community who would confer upon him the mantle of respectability he sought.

Hallelujah As Blasphemy

In their letter to the Prime Minister, reprinted in the *Express* on November 18, 1994, the BCP stated that they were "extremely hurt and offended," by the band and that they objected "categorically, unambiguously, and unequivocally" to its being granted a license to parade on Carnival Monday and Tuesday. They stated:

> For someone to take this emblem ... and drag it in the wanton vulgarity, drunkenness, wining, cussing and all — the debauchery of illicit sex, unwanted babies, abortions, AIDS, etc., to us, constitutes the worst type of mockery, ridicule, contempt and desecration of our religion.

"Hallelujah," which they said means to praise God, is one of the most sacred words in scripture, they argued, and to use the word is to invoke the name of God. The Pentecostals' voiced their protest, so they believed, in a manner which resonated with the standard form of protest. They measured their discourse against the model established historically by the Hindu and Muslim communities. As such they could claim that their concerns were of the same type as those expressed by religious groups seeking respect for their religious beliefs and iconography. Yet it was up to the authorities to whom they appealed to evaluate not only the legal validity of their protest but also the Pentecostals' legitimacy to speak for and to an audience, to be deemed worthy of speaking and of being heard.

To illustrate the gravity of the choice of the name Cuffie told the story of King Belshazzar from Daniel 5 who held a carnival-type fete and used the holy vessels of God in his revelries. At one point during the feast, Cuffie relates, the fingers of a man's hand mysteriously appeared on a wall and wrote "thou art weighed in the balance and found wanting." Belshazzar was slain that same night. Cuffie solemnly concluded, "Maybe the writing is on the wall for you, your friends and the children of you all, Minshall." Whether this "warning" refers to the consequences Minshall and his supporters are to experience in the hereafter or in the here and now is unclear. What is clear is the gravity of the situation from the perspective of the Pentecostals.

Minshall's initial response was to avoid any confrontation. He stated in an interview that both the artist and the minister seek to provide illumination of the human condition. He eschewed being drawn into the "dark shadow of public debate" (*Express* 12/28/94). In defending himself, Minshall readily adopted the biblical rhetoric used by Cuffie. No stranger to controversy and opposition, Minshall vowed to continue doing his work in his way.

The intensity of the conflict increased in January as the Carnival season began in earnest. Cuffie continued to express his opposition to the name in his weekly ads (*Express* 1/5/95; 1/27/95; 2/2/95; 2/3/95; 2/9/95; 2/10/95; 2/16/95; 2/17/95; 2/24/95) and proclaimed that he had been receiving complaints about the name from all over the country. In resubmitting their petition to the government, the pastors cited the complaints of the Hindu community over the depiction of Lord Nataraja that had been rapidly redressed and expressed the hope that the Pentecostals would receive the same treatment (*Express* 1/5/95:5). Attempting to deflect criticism for his attack upon Minshall and to focus more squarely upon the responsibility of the government to mediate such disputes in the name of national harmony, Cuffie praised Minshall for his artistic abilities and achievements and acknowledged his good intentions, but chided him for his lack of religious understanding. Cuffie hoped that Minshall would acknowledge the sanctity of their beliefs and change the name to something more appropriate such as *Celebration*, but continued to rely upon the government for satisfaction.

On January 27, 1995, Cuffie's rhetoric became sharper and more confrontational as his pleas to the government proved ineffective. Cuffie (*Express* 1/27/95) denounced Minshall's "mocking discrimination" and "hypocrisy" and expressed great anger at Minshall's willingness to appease the Hindu community while ignoring the Pentecostals' requests. He asked, "who can now doubt the ... evidence of a deliberate, calculated attack on Pentecostals and Evangelicals" and pronounced that the government's attitude constituted a "massive national scandal." In turning up the rhetorical heat, Cuffie began to withdraw from the somewhat conciliatory position he had taken earlier in the conflict.

Pastor Cuffie's ads used more and more scriptural references and adopted an increasingly strident tone. His ads contained extensive use of all capital letters, italics and boldface as though he were attempting to transpose the rhythms of an evangelical sermon into typescript.[4] On February 3, 1995 (*Express* 2/3/95:5) Pastor Cuffie challenged Minshall to "explain these spooky gods, spirits, and happenings" in his band. He dismissed Minshall's claim that he sought to improve the tone of the Carnival and denounced him as a "false apostle" and "deceitful worker" who possessed "spirit powers" with which he made people blind to his control and denigrated the "true and living God."

The following week, Pastor Cuffie (*Express* 2/9/95:4) complained of the "unprecedented prejudice against us." He cited a number of instances in which the government had responded to religious controversies surrounding the Carnival such as calypsos which mocked Hinduism. He also injected an element of class rhetoric into his argument by stating that this was the first time that the "multitude of simple, salt of the earth Pentecostal/Evangelical people are crying out to the Government in such a cause." He portrayed the Pentecostals as tolerant and quiet people who had never before called upon the government to act on their behalf. Cuffie (*Trinidad Guardian*

2/23/95:1) argued that the Pentecostals had followed the legitimated form of public protest regarding the Carnival and portrayed the government as denying them their due rights as members of the nation:

> With much concern, we wonder why a Government policy which was perfect for Hindus, Catholics, Baptists, Orishas and others in the past, is now a complete taboo for Pentecostals/Evangelicals. With all due respect, an acute case of discrimination appears to stare us in the face.

Having failed to command the audience that he acknowledged as having the authority to legitimate his protest, Cuffie chose to continue his verbal assaults. The rhetorical shift in the ads and other public statements marks a shift in the intended audience and as such a recognition of the failure of their quest for inclusion.

Each week thereafter until the Carnival on February 27 and 28, Pastor Cuffie reiterated his position calling for a change in the name of the band, attacked Minshall's pride and arrogance, and denounced the government for its irresponsibility and "high-handed mockery of the nation's laws, constitution, and freedoms of its citizens" (*Express* 2/17/95:5). In an ad entitled, *"The Big Minshall Secret/Satan's Tricks and Traps Never Change"* (*Express* 2/24/95:5), Cuffie continued to associate Minshall with the occult and Satanic rites of blood, accusing him of enticing and seducing the gullible and innocent.

On March 8, 1995 (*Express* 3/8/95:5), after the Carnival was over and Minshall's *Hallelujah* had received praise from the media and won the Band of the Year title, Cuffie launched his final salvo:

> Whether or not Minshall's mas or theatre on Carnival day was "nice" or all the Carnival Lovers in town "roared" or cheered or whether he placed first or last was never the issue in our protest.... It was extremely clear ON THE STREETS that the band members had their full share of involvement in the debauchery of wining, cussing, alcohol, beers, wantonness, vulgarity — and you name it — all in the name of *Hallelujah*. A plain case of hypocrisy and mockery.... Was it that spooky and nonsensical presentation Minshall expected us to believe can "clean up" Carnival and make it holy?.... Where was the holy praise of God? ... The whole thing was very clearly a total farce.... It's clear that the masman chose the name *Hallelujah* merely for attention and/or provo-

cation. God and Carnival just CANNOT mix: What fellowship hath
righteousness with unrighteousness and what communion hath light
with darkness? (emphasis in original)

Minshall's Response

On January 18, 1995, one week after a television appearance by Pastor
Cuffie, Minshall appeared on the same television interview program
and explained the rationale behind the name of the band. He said that
after watching the 1994 Carnival he was in despair (*Trinidad Guardian*
1/19/95: 1). He dramatically related how he had felt marginalised by
"the naked commerce" of Carnival. Minshall confided that after
watching the 1994 Carnival on television he became depressed. He
felt that the festival to which he had devoted his adult life and in
which he had sought to express himself artistically, had become "the
Mother of all Rot. It was as though the people had nothing left to
celebrate." Describing himself as feeling forlorn and alone, Minshall
stated that he wanted to do something positive. Although he was ill
in bed with despair, he scribbled the word "celebration" on a sheet of
paper. But mere celebration did not capture the spirit he suddenly felt
returning to himself. He then thought of:

> "hallelujah" as a word which epitomizes the joy of life and existence....
> I simply thought that "hallelujah" was a word that said much more
> than just "Praise God." It is a word of praise for the absolute joy of
> creation, a word that I should share with the people. (*Trinidad Guardian*
> 1/19/95:1)

Minshall explicitly likens his moment of artistic inspiration to a spiritual revelation.

Responding to Cuffie's charges that he was mocking the word of
God, Minshall defended his religious credentials:

> I am a Christian and I thought that the word was mine to share, to offer
> up with joy. There seems to be, in this blessed land of ours, a division
> between masman and a man of the cloth. The feeling is that a masman
> does not deal with God. I have been making mas with God for the past
> 20 years. An artist is something of a priest to his people. (*Trinidad
> Guardian* 1/19/95:1)

Minshall draws upon the idea that the creative act of the artist, the artist's sensitivity to the world around him, enables him to express the spiritual yearnings of his public. The idea of "making mas with God" suggests a collaboration of the spirit in which God inspires Minshall to create a masquerade band that captures the joys and fears hidden in the soul of all Trinidadians.

Continuing with the metaphor of spiritual revelation, Minshall (*Express* 1/19/95:7) explains,

> I didn't go to a Biblical theme.[5] The theme came to me. The most fitting word to epitomise celebration is hallelujah.... *Hallelujah* is to be used as a vehicle to show people that "we are beautiful," and "we have something to teach the world."

Minshall suggests that the band is not only for Trinidadians but also for outsiders, the rest of the world. The band is meant to instill a sense of pride, dignity, and self-respect that will also place Trinidad and Tobago on the world stage. He appeals to national pride, and his statement echoes the tourist brochure which lauds Trinidad's multicultural diversity and harmony and portrays the Carnival as a time in which racial, ethnic, and class antagonisms are temporarily displaced by a sense of equality and unity.

Minshall continues with the religious imagery by suggesting that the reinvigoration of *his* spirit will allow him to bring to Carnival a celebration of life and the joy of existence. And then, so Minshall argues, those who will participate in the band and those who will see the band will achieve a spiritual re-awakening. There is a clear link made between the condition of the Carnival and that of the people of Trinidad. And Minshall further suggests that what ails Trinidad cannot be cured through politics.

> We have lost our way. The politicians have lost the map. We are fragmented, lost. We've got to find our way. Carnival is the place where Hallelujah is needed. (*Express* 1/19/95:7)

This is Carnival as redemption.

Rhetorical Postures

The rhetoric of the controversy is of particular interest because it illustrates the fervor and passion which characterize public debate about the Carnival. Both Cuffie and Minshall adopted a set of biblical metaphors of loss and redemption to describe the Carnival and its present condition. While Cuffie and Minshall agreed that there were serious problems with the Carnival, each offered a different way of approaching them. For Cuffie, the Carnival is not just a symptom of social problems, it is a social problem. For Minshall (*Trinidad Guardian* 1/19/95), the Carnival reflects social conditions.

> Don't blame Carnival [for its present form and people's behavior]. Like all great art, Carnival is like a mirror of what we are [as a people] the rest of the year.

Each combatant felt compelled to educate his opponent as to the true nature of religion and the Carnival. For Pastor Cuffie and the BCP, it was necessary to express concern for Minshall's immortal soul, to forgive him for his ignorance, and to plead with him to change the name of the band as evidence of having seen the light and understood the word of God. For Minshall and his supporters, Cuffie and the BCP failed to understand the celebration of life, beauty, and deep spirituality which lies at the heart of the Carnival, all of which are part of the African heritage in Trinidad and Tobago, yet in which all people of the nation may take part.

After failing to convince his opponent, each resorted to a more absolutist position. Cuffie denounced Minshall as a "false apostle." Minshall and his supporters condemned Cuffie for attempting to censor their right to worship and to express themselves freely. The Carnival can be seen then, in the situated context of this controversy, as having a potent metaphorical connection to critical sources of cultural and social identity especially in relation to ideas of spirituality, nationality, citizenship, ethnicity, and morality.

Narrations of the Nation

Daniel Segal (1995:224) outlines positive and negative visions of the Trinidadian nation. In the positive vision, Trinidad is depicted as a "cosmopolitan" society in which people with vastly different ways of life, religious beliefs, and forms of celebration live together in relative harmony. In tourist brochures, guides for potential international investors, and popular literature, this vision of heterogeneity is celebrated and an ethos of toleration expounded. In the negative vision, these "narrations of conflict" (Segal 1995:228), ancestral differences between Trinidadians of European, African, and East Indian descent, products of the rigid class and color system of stratification of the plantation era, undermine any potential national unity and cause social discord and tension. In this vision, Trinidadian history is the product of moments of social conflict and Trinidadian society is depicted as always near the boiling point, as marked by grievances and animosities that cannot be resolved politically or symbolically. The attitude of tolerance lauded in the positive vision becomes one of barely veiled contempt or disdain in the negative vision. It is only through daily acts of self-control that Trinidadians are able to refrain from bursting forth in a riot of race and class warfare.

I would add to Segal's analysis that it is also important to identify explicitly the source of any particular narration of Trinidadian nationalism whether positive or negative. It is not just that there are positive and negative visions of Trinidadian nationalism circulating in the social imagination. These nationalist visions have particular social locations, are propagated by particular social actors, and resonate with particular political projects. So when we identify conflicting ways of narrating not only the nature of Trinidadian identity and national culture, but also of particular events and moments of crisis, we must be careful to mark how multiple narratives are deployed in the specific conjunction of circumstances and actors.

Carnival as the National Festival

These contrasting visions of the Trinidadian nation suggest the ideological context within which claims about the Carnival as a national festival are evaluated and contested. If, in a positive vision of the nation, the Carnival is praised as the national festival, then it should have certain qualities that embody this ethos of toleration and harmony. If the Carnival is to be emblematic of the nation, somehow inclusive of all of the groups which compose it, then it must occur within in an environment in which legitimate grievances about it are rapidly redressed. The Carnival must not offend. It must be, at some level, acceptable to or at least tolerated by all groups. The conundrum facing the state and ardent supporters of the Carnival which have sought to portray it as a national festival is how to reduce the potential for social divisiveness. Protests about some aspect of the Carnival may question this positive vision of the festival as representative of the nation.

The rhetorical deployments of the various meanings of the Carnival and the ways in which Trinidadians of different social groups understand the behavior of themselves and others during the Carnival: the way they speak about it, portray it, and enact it, indicate the difficulty of mobilizing the Carnival in this nation-building project. To tug on the thread of Carnival is to begin to unravel the complex tapestry of Trinidadian history for what may be teased out of a Carnival controversy reveals the uncertainties of the direction of a post-colonial state undergoing dramatic social, economic, and political changes.

The *Hallelujah* affair demonstrates how Carnival is important as a national festival not because it encapsulates some essence of Trinidadian culture and society, but because it serves as such a potent metaphor for the condition of the nation. It is impossible to avoid taking some kind of position toward it. While criticism is acceptable within a strictly defined discourse that allows one to withdraw from or not to participate in the event, any effort to cancel, eliminate, or outlaw it is interpreted as a form of cultural treason.

It is partly through extensive public discussions about the Carnival that ideas about what constitutes Trinidadian national identity are articulated, contested, and worked out. The Carnival's status as a "national" festival does not rely upon any general agreement as to its historical development or its representativeness of Trinidadian culture but rather on its polyvalent meanings and multiple metaphorical extensions in the service of distinct political agendas. In Trinidad, I argue, it is more important to enter into public debate and to be reckoned as a legitimate social group than it is to agree with or to acquiesce to some kind of putative national identity. What it means to be a Trinidadian is still in the process of being worked out. Through social conflicts like the *Hallelujah* controversy, these very different visions and beliefs come to be expressed, disseminated, and debated. During the Carnival ideological lines are drawn, positions are taken, and perspectives are established on social, cultural, and economic priorities in Trinidad. The Carnival may be the ideal national festival because it is as much about living with contentiousness and conflict as it is about national unity. This is the paradox of Carnival as a national festival in Trinidad and Tobago.

There are a number of rhetorical positions taken toward the Carnival. The positive view of the Carnival sees it as the basis of the unified nation, an egalitarian moment in which many of the barriers of race, class, and color are broken down. The Carnival is highlighted in popular discourse as a joyous time of celebration and as the exemplary manifestation of multicultural harmony. Carnival becomes the centerpiece of a national culture and its associated art forms, masquerade, steel band, and calypso, are taken as the unique cultural forms of Trinidad and Tobago, its contribution to a world culture. The Carnival becomes part of an objectified Trinidadian culture which then legitimates the idea that Trinidad has a national culture. Having a national culture is one requirement of being part of the international order of nation-states, which also requires political sovereignty and economic autonomy in addition to specific, tangible cultural forms (Williams 1991). Carnival has been described as the creative outpouring of the people, as a "mandate for a national theater" (Hill 1972), as the symbol of the struggle against colonial domination and cultural oppression, and as a unifying force capable of bringing the disparate elements of the Trinidadian social world together (Liverpool 1993). The Carnival is the enactment of the ideal of cultural fusion for it's essential characteristic is innovation and change. Carnival promotes an egalitarian ethos of communal work for a common goal and celebrates the creativity and vitality of the human spirit. The spirit of the Carnival is of incorporation, novelty, and innovation.

The negative vision of the Carnival sees it as a debauched orgy of materialism marked by drunkenness, lewd behavior, and sexual promiscuity and leading to violence, immorality, and disease. The Carnival distracts people from work, encourages a "live for the moment" mentality, and undermines respect for authority, morality, and religion. While the importance of the Carnival in Trinidadian history as a means of protest against colonial authorities is acknowledged, the current Carnival is seen as a despoiled version of this once vital expression of the dominated peoples of Trinidad.

The Carnival is, in yet a third vision that I call the reformist, still worthy of being restored to its place as a form of cultural and spiritual expression. The problem is that there is no agreement as to how to accomplish this task. There are calls from religious and political leaders to make the Carnival "morally uplifting," to purge it of its mindless "free up" characteristics that celebrate nothing more than having a good time. Hedonism does not make for a solid, respectable national culture. In the reformist vision, the Carnival has been disfigured and its current form is but a shadow of its heroic past. Nostalgia marks descriptions of the Carnivals of the past. Attention to detail and skillful craftwork in costume making has given way to shoddy construction, cheap materials, and artless design, so the nostalgists complain. Furthermore, the Carnival is now dominated by administrators, designers, and bandleaders who are more concerned about making money than they are about art and creativity.[6] It is only through a steady program of public education and exhortation about the noble history of the Carnival that the population will realize what the Carnival should be and change their behavior and attitudes accordingly.

Spirituality and the Carnival

While the Catholic Archbishop refused to comment, other Catholic priests praised Minshall for his efforts to praise God and His creation through the Carnival. They hoped that this spirit of celebration would raise the moral tone of the Carnival. Father Harvey wrote in the *Express* that the band "rather than take away from God's glory, [would] ... be a kaleidoscopic witness to the creative power the Almighty has shared with us all." For Father Harvey the controversy was not about religious belief or moral behavior but rather about power and national self-definition. He stated, "The numbers are increasing of those who, driven by their own radical insecurity, would impose their own definition of self, God, and country on the whole society in the name of religion." Father Harvey contended that to change the name would damage the artistic integrity of Minshall's vision which is clearly the product of inspiration.

Anglican ministers also supported Minshall's choice of the Carnival as a sphere in which to praise God arguing that no one sect has any monopoly on God and Truth. Dean Knolly Clarke, an ardent Carnival enthusiast, found nothing wrong with Minshall's attempt to salute the joy of existence but was concerned that the country's fascination with the controversy would distract it from contending with rising unemployment, inadequate education, increasing crime, and poverty. He suggested that perhaps an analysis of what the Carnival is becoming or has become might be more important than the name of the band.

These interpretations of the controversy explicitly deny the Pentecostals' claims to legitimacy by emphasizing the peculiarity of their position. For established and authorized religious leaders it is more important to recognize and acknowledge the multiplicity of concepts of spirituality that exist in Trinidad. What is more dangerous for them to do is to sanction those views that they consider to deny the legitimacy of those diverse concepts. The Catholic and Anglican commentators on the controversy while disputing the Pentecostals' claims of proprietorship over a Christian religious concept, can, in the name of ecumenical respect, simultaneously acknowledge the legitimacy of other religious groups, the Muslims or the Hindus, for example, to protest the representation of iconography or religious concepts that are unique to those groups, that is, that can in some sense be seen as "their" cultural/religious property.

The Afro-Trinidadian Nationalist Perspective

Perhaps the most formally argued and articulated position on the spirituality of the Carnival was put forth by Hollis Liverpool, known popularly by his calypso sobriquet, Chalkdust, in his defense of Minshall. Liverpool earned a doctorate in history from the University of Michigan writing on the Carnival as a ritual of rebellion and protest (Liverpool 1993). Liverpool approached the controversy from the perspective that it was yet another in the long line of misreadings of the forms of celebration characteristic of the African influence in Trinidad. In a lecture given at a government school in February 1995, Liverpool stated, "The essence of Carnival is to praise God in a way best known to Africans" (*Trinidad Guardian*, n.d.). Liverpool explained that the Carnival was the African's way of praising God for all that He provided: food, clothing, life itself. He cited incidents during the

nineteenth century in which the Roman Catholic Archbishop participated in Carnival parades. Liverpool, who until recently had been a
teacher in a secondary school and is now the Director of Culture,
argued that the Carnival has always been about praising God. He
highlighted the need for better public education about the history,
origins, and social uses of the Carnival. Were the public more informed about their own history, he suggested, there would not be
these kinds of controversies.

Liverpool's analysis of the conflict points to the ongoing project
of creating a common base of understanding of cultural forms which
would yield greater understanding of and respect for the contributions made to cultural practices found in Trinidad by those of African
descent. In his dissertation, "Rituals of Power and Rebellion: The
Carnival in Trinidad and Tobago," Liverpool (1993:xx) argues that
the Carnival has served as a form of cultural resistance to the imposition of European patterns of behavior and belief. One aspect of
colonial domination was the symbolic denigration of anything having to do with African cultural forms. Part of the recurrent opposition
to the Carnival, Liverpool suggests, is the incorporation of European
attitudes towards things African by Trinidadians of all backgrounds.
His purpose in writing the dissertation is to document the re-inter-
pretation and re-adaptation of African cultural beliefs and practices
within the environment of European domination in which those
forms were denigrated. Liverpool (1993:xxi) contends that Africans
did not simply adopt European values, but rather Africanized them.
He concludes that he wishes to give Africans their rightful place in
the creation of the current Carnival and, by extension, the cultural
identity of Trinidadians (Liverpool 1993:xxii).

Liverpool's analysis of the *Hallelujah* controversy, when seen in the
light of his intellectual and political project as outlined and undertaken in his dissertation and frequent public statements on the Carnival and its history, underscores the significance of the Carnival as
an arena for debate about national identity in Trinidad. Any opposition to the Carnival immediately becomes interpreted as a denial of
the contribution of Africans to Trinidadian culture, a symbol of disrespect and therefore the occasion to restate long-held grievances.
For Liverpool, the only legitimate criticisms of the Carnival are those
that speak to the dilution of the African spirit of the festival, and this

despite his acknowledgment of the European and East Indian contributions to the Carnival throughout its history. Liverpool validates Minshall's criticisms of the current state of the Carnival since Minshall has the proper credentials as a Carnival insider whose pedigree is largely unquestioned. Liverpool seems to imply that attacks on the Carnival from outsiders unfamiliar with its history and significance constitute a form of cultural ignorance to be remedied through reeducation. If you do not respect the Carnival and its traditions then you are guilty of siding with the colonial oppressor and of undermining the integrity of the still fragile national identity of Trinidad and Tobago

Liverpool's faith in the power of education to change people's ideas about the Carnival assumes that a history of contribution legitimates the present and that the current politics of the Carnival and the relations among the social forces in Trinidad today are similar to those in the past. While Cuffie might be able to acknowledge the history of resistance and rebellion that Liverpool documents, it is not certain that he would withdraw his opposition to *Hallelujah* after addressing the gaps in his historical knowledge.

Conclusion

The *Hallelujah* controversy, as it played itself out, reveals that Pastor Cuffie and the BCP were not concerned so much with the name of the band but more with how the government, the larger Pentecostal community, and the public at-large responded to their demand for recognition of their beliefs and their legitimacy as representatives of the group they claimed to represent. Pastor Cuffie appears to have wanted to gain for the Pentecostal movement and himself, the same moral, critical status accorded to the Catholic Archbishop, the Anglican archbishop, and the leaders of the major Hindu and Muslim organizations. When the Prime Minister refused to intervene or mediate, Pastor Cuffie immediately seized upon that as evidence of religious discrimination on the part of the government. The locus of the controversy shifted from the Carnival to the issue of constitutional freedoms and the equal protection of all religions under the law.

Minshall and Pastor Cuffie were engaged in a struggle over the meaning attributed to the Carnival as a form of spiritual expression and its place within the larger Trinidadian culture. But not only was the Carnival at stake. The very nature of religion and spirituality in general in Trinidad and Tobago was being discussed, as well as how cultural identity could be truly inclusive and representative in the face conflicting notions of spirituality. The Carnival was seen as both an indicator of all that was wrong in Trinidad and as the way to correct what was wrong. For Cuffie, the Carnival could not be spiritually redeemed and remain in any form similar to what it currently was. For Minshall, the Carnival had been appropriated by the forces of market rationality, crass materialism, and hedonism. It had fallen from its once prominent place as a celebration of the creative spirit. *Hallelujah* was a conscious effort to recapture the sense of joy and exuberance that once characterized the Carnival and to resurrect the profound spirit of life that the Carnival celebrates.

The *Hallelujah* controversy illuminates how diverse nationalist projects in Trinidad and Tobago are placed in mutual relief. The Carnival, so fundamental to a particular Afro-Trinidadian vision of the nation, becomes one of the most significant markers of inclusion in the nation. While from the perspective of an Afro-Trinidadian nationalism acceptance of, participation in, and contribution to the Carnival is the test all citizens must pass in order to be counted as part of the nation, another vision of the nation that celebrates pluralism and tolerance compels recognition of opposition to the Carnival. Emergent elements in Trinidad, such as the Pentecostals, can submit their claims for inclusion through appeals to the nationalist rhetoric which celebrates diversity and thereby subject it to the ultimate test: how can the nation mediate what appear to be competing and mutually exclusive claims? It is clear then that we must pay close attention not just to the rhetoric of competing nationalisms as Segal does, but more specifically to how those rhetorics are deployed in specific social contexts by specific social actors. It is through arguments, public debates, and confrontations, like the *Hallelujah* controversy, that the ongoing project of nation building is carried out. As one commentator stated, "Carnival will always be a subject of controversy. The day we get complacent and stop arguing about it, that will be its end" (*Trinidad Guardian* 1/29/95: 7).

Endnotes

An earlier version of this paper was presented at the 1995 Annual Meetings of the American Anthropological Association in Washington D.C. on November 15, 1995 as part of the panel "Caribbean Religions: Culture, Consciousness, and Community at Home and Abroad." I would like to thank the panel organizer, John Pulis, the discussants John Szwed and Richard Price, and the audience for their comments. I am indebted to Kevin Yelvington, Diana Wells, and especially Philip Scher for their comments and suggestions on earlier drafts of this essay. I would also like to thank Dr. Robert Lee for providing me with his insights and generous research assistance in the preparation of this essay. My research was conducted in Trinidad from September of 1992 to March of 1994 with grants from the Wenner-Gren Foundation and the Fulbright IIE Fixed Sum Program.

1. Trinidad and Tobago is a two-island republic found at the tail end of Caribbean archipelago, just off the northeast coast of Venezuela. It has a population of about 1.2 million persons. Approximately 40% of the population identify themselves as of East Indian descent, that is descendants of the indentured servants who came to Trinidad after the emancipation of the slaves in 1838. Another 40% identify themselves as of African descent, that is to say descendants of enslaved Africans, Africans "liberated" from slave ships captured by the British after the end of slavery in the British West Indies in 1838 and repatriated to Trinidad, or migrants from other West Indian islands; another 18% identify themselves as mixed, less than 0.7% identify themselves as white, and even smaller percentages identify themselves as Chinese (0.4%) or Syrian (0.1%) Trinidad and Tobago achieved independence in 1962 and became a Republic in 1976. It is a parliamentary democracy.

2. I do not think that I would have understood what the stakes were in the controversy had I not known the background of the participants and the details of the history of the Carnival I obtained during my eighteen months in Trinidad. During the summer months when there was little Carnival activity going on, I spent many hours in the National Archives and the Public Library reviewing the Carnival coverage in the two major daily newspapers, the *Trinidad Guardian* and the *Daily Express*, during the ten years preceding my fieldwork, to chronicle the debates and controversies that had occurred in those years.

3. Alonso (1990), Brereton (1979, 1981), Cowley (1996), Campbell (1988), Wood (1968), Pearse (1956), Liverpool (1986, 1993), Trotman (1986), and Rohlehr (1990) all explore how the Carnival was subject to various kinds of attempts at reform or repressive legislation to rid it of those elements that the ruling elites considered objectionable.

4. I am indebted to Philip Scher for this observation.

5. Minshall's mention of a "Biblical theme" carries within it a sly historical reference to the popularity of masquerade bands with biblical, usually Old Testament, themes from the mid-1930s to the mid-1950s. At that time there was even a special judging category, variously titled "Sacred History," "Jewish History," and later "Biblical Bands," for which bands with such themes as "Joys of the Ark," "The Good Samaritans," and "Joseph and His Brethren" competed (Anthony 1989:107, 231). Oddly enough, the precedent of numerous masquerade bands with biblical themes was never mentioned in any commentary on the controversy.

6. Powrie (1956), Hill (1972), Stewart (1983), and Liverpool (1993) examine and describe this sense of loss for golden age of Carnival in which the contemporary form of the festival is taken as a degraded version of the past. What is interesting is how one period's degraded version becomes a later era's "golden age."

References

Alonso, A. 1990 "Men in Rags" and the devil on the throne: a study of protest and inversion in the Carnival of post-emancipation Trinidad. *Plantation Society in the Americas* 3(1):73–120.

Anthony, M. 1989 *Parade of the Carnivals of Trinidad 1839–1989*. Port of Spain: Circle Press.

Brereton, B. 1979 *Race Relations in Colonial Trinidad 1870–1900*. Cambridge: Cambridge Univ. Press.

Brereton, B. 1981 The Trinidad Carnival 1870–1900. *Savacou* (11–12).

Campbell, S. 1988 Carnival, calypso, and class struggle in 19th century Trinidad. *History Workshop Journal* 26:1–27.

Central Statistical Office 1993 *1990 Population and Housing Census, Vol. II*. Port of Spain: Office of the Prime Minister, Central Statistical Office.

Cowley, J. 1996 *Carnival, Canboulay and Calypso: Trasitions in the Making.* Cambridge: Cambridge Univ. Press.

Hill, E. 1972 *The Trinidad Carnival: Mandate for a National Theater.* Austin: Univ. of Texas Press.

Liverpool, H. 1986 *Kaiso and Society.* Diego Martin, Trinidad: Juba Publications.

Liverpool, H. 1993 *Rituals of Power and Rebellion: The Carnival Tradition in Trinidad and Tobago.* PhD dissertation. Ann Arbor: Univ. of Michigan.

Pearse, A. 1956 Carnival in nineteenth century Trinidad. *Caribbean Quarterly* 4(3–4):4–42.

Powrie, B. 1956 The changing attitude of the coloured middle class towards carnival. *Caribbean Quarterly* 4(3–4):91–107.

Rohlehr, G. 1990 *Calypso and Society in Pre-Independence Trinidad.* Port of Spain, Trinidad: Author.

Segal, D.A. 1995 Living ancestors: nationalism and the past in postcolonial Trinidad and Tobago. In: *Remapping Memory: The Politics of Time and Space* (ed., J. Boyarin). Minneapolis: University of Minnesota Press, pp. 221–239.

Stewart, J. 1986 Patronage and control in the Trinidad Carnival. In: *The Anthropology of Experience* (eds., V. Turner and E. Bruner). Champaign-Urbana: University of Illinois Press, pp. 289–315.

Trinidad Express Newspapers, Ltd. 1992 *Minshall: The Man and His Mas'.* Port of Spain, Trinidad and Tobago: Trinidad Express Newspapers, Ltd.

Trotman, D.V. 1986 *Crime in Trinidad: Conflict and Control in A Plantation Society, 1838–1900.* Knoxville: University of Tennessee Press.

Trotman, D.V. 1991. The image of Indians in calypso, 1946–1986. In: *Social and Occupational Stratification in Contemporary Trinidad and Tobago* (ed., Selwyn Ryan). St. Augustine: ISER and the University of the West Indies.

Williams, B. 1991 *Stains on My Name, War in My Veins: Guyana and the Politics of Cultural Struggle.* Durham, NC: Duke University Press.

Wood, D. 1968 *Trinidad in Transition: The Years after Slavery.* New York: Oxford University Press.

9: PENTECOSTAL COMMUNITY AND JAMAICAN HIERARCHY

Diane J. Austin-Broos

Introduction

Stephen Glazier's 1980 collection entitled *Perspectives on Pentecostalism*, that brought together a number of essays on Pentecostalism in Latin America and the Caribbean, should have marked the beginning of a diverse and expanding discussion of the religion by a growing number of Caribbean scholars. Charles Chordas (1980, p. 166) proposed in that collection the imminent emergence of a field of "Pentecostal studies," which has developed for the Latin American area. The same cannot be said for the Caribbean where writing on this phenomenon has been fairly sparse despite Anthony LaRuffa's early entry into the field (1969, 1971) and references to Jamaican Pentecostalism in the work of Moore (1953), Simpson (1956, 1978), Hogg (1964) and also Wedenoja (1978, 1980) who all focussed nonetheless on Zion Revivalism. The influential presence of Pentecostalism has been noted in Puerto Rico, Haiti, the Bahamas, Bermuda, Barbados, Jamaica and Trinidad (Conn 1959; Glazier 1980; also see Brodwin 1996). Yet the impact of Pentecostal religion on the Caribbean remains a subject of fairly diffident discussion.

In his concluding essay to the 1980 collection, Frank Manning put a spirited argument to the effect that Pentecostalism in the Caribbean should be seen as a part of folk religion, as integral to the world of "reputation" rather than "respectability," and not as a part of the hegemonic cultural powers brought to the region through the expansion of British and American capitalism. In a vein quite contrary to Mintz's (1960) early reading of Pentecostalism as a protestant phenomenon, Manning contested its protestant credentials. He saw Pentecostalism, rather, as an accommodation to the "magic" of the world, "more episodic than methodic, more ritualistic than rational," a religion involved with "competitive performance" that might bring "modernizing influences" but also became in the Caribbean "an expression of the native ethos, a symbol of reputation" (Manning 1980, pp. 183, 186; also see Wilson 1973). He suggested that there is in Caribbean Pentecostalism a notable "ludic" dimension which I have sought to capture in my own account of Pentecostalism in Jamaica. I interpret Pentecostalism as part of a tradition characterized by a debate between the ethical rationalism of protestantism (see Weber, 1958) and the magical healing and trickster tradition of a New World African ritualism. It is the tension between these orders of being that shapes the Pentecostal world (Austin-Broos 1997, pp. 34–50). Both Manning's and my accounts differ from Mintz's characterization which emphasises guilt and modernization and suggests a Marxist-Freudian approach when he describes Don Taso's Pentecostal conversion as "the waste of a mind that stands above the others as the violet sprays of the *flor de cana* tower above the cane" (Mintz 1960, p. 277).

Yet it is probably a part of Pentecostalism's enigma for the Caribbean that Mintz's characterization cannot be dismissed however much Caribbean peoples have worked to make Pentecostalism their own. Indisputably the rise of Pentecostalism in the region is linked intimately with the rise of Northern American economic and political influence. At the end of the twentieth century, without a doubt Pentecostalism signals a new, mainly American dynamic of cultural incorporation that followed the initial European dynamic of the eighteenth and nineteenth centuries. It is the tension between these countervailing trends to indigenization on the one hand, and to metropolitan incorporation on the other, that makes Pentecostalism an awkward phenomenon difficult to render in convincing ways. Within the Jamaican milieu, especially, it seems to carry neither the indigenous conviction of the African Christian Zion Revival that emerged in the nineteenth century, nor the worldly critical thrust of twentieth century Rastafarianism. Though Pentecostalism for some time has been Jamaica's largest, single, religious affiliation, the paucity of comment on it, in comparison with Rastafarianism for instance, belies a marked disinclination to acknowledge it as part of a Jamaican world (but see Wedenoja, 1980; Austin, 1981; Austin-Broos, 1987). Its origins as a mission religion, its growth, and links with the metropolitan world seem to many to disqualify it from the status of a *Jamaican* phenomenon.

In this chapter I propose that Pentecostalism in Jamaica, like Orthodox Baptist practice before it, should be seen as integral and important to the articulation of Jamaican culture (see also Austin-Broos, 1984, 1987, 1991–2, 1993, 1996, 1997). My argument will be that Jamaican Pentecostalism deploys healing and the poetics of the Bible in ways that allow Jamaicans to imagine a community beyond racial hierarchy. My contention will be that for many people in Jamaica, and especially for Jamaican women, these poetics are more engaging, even real, than the poetics of "history" and political and economic "progress." Not only the imagery of the Bible as it is deployed in a Caribbean milieu, but also the trans-national links of Pentecostalism to the metropolitan world mean that the domain of religious practice makes a real difference in peoples' lives. Although this difference is circumscribed it is sufficiently significant, in comparison with the limited potential of politics to realize its more ambitious claims, to move and engage large numbers of people. That forms of popular religion rather than political creeds should be the medium for "utopias" (see Ricoeur, 1986) within Jamaica is a fact of considerable significance. This fact is not so much a reflection of a particular "consciousness" as it is a reflection of the historical experience of Jamaicans in the modern world. This argument proposes, then, that popular, institutionalized religion and especially Pentecostalism is specifying for Jamaican culture as much as the smaller cults and sects. It is specifying in its role as a medium for utopic critique, a form of critique that is not exclusive to Revival or Rastafarianism.

Pentecostalism in Jamaica: An Overview

It was during the period of the 1920s and 1930s that Pentecostal churches secured themselves in Jamaican society. They came as a series of individual initiatives, mainly from churches on the American eastern seaboard, beginning in the 1910s and expanding in the next two decades. Revivalism as a Christian mode stemming mainly from America had been established in Jamaica since the Great Revival of 1860 to 1861. In the early twentieth century, the mode spawned other indigenous movements including those of Raglan

Phillips, "Warrior" Higgins, and Mother J. C. Russell (see Austin-Broos 1997, pp. 87–92).[1] The early Pentecostalists were recruited from these previous movements, from Orthodox Baptists and from the Congregationalists. They also drew additional followers from other foreign missionary sects including the American Church of Christ and the British Salvationists. Rudolph Smith and Henry Hudson, both from upper Clarendon parish, and George White, from St. Elizabeth, were possibly the three most prominent early Jamaican Pentecostal evangelists. Smith and Hudson each headed for a time the Jamaican branches of major American trinitarian churches, the Church of God of Prophecy and the New Testament Church of God respectively. George White founded Jamaica's first Pentecostal Union of apostolic or unitarian churches.[2] From this movement developed the Jamaican branch of the American United Pentecostal Church, Jamaica's largest unitarian group. All three evangelists were active in Jamaica in the late 1920s and 1930s. Of the three, Rudolph Smith maintained the longest career which stretched into the 1970s.

These three churches have remained Jamaica's most prominent Pentecostal organizations with numerous churches in major urban centres and in most of the parishes. Other major trinitarian Pentecostal groups include the International Foursquare Gospel church that Aimee Semple Macpherson established in 1923 as a break away group from the American Assemblies of God (Anderson, 1979). A more modest group of Elim churches are loosely affiliated with the English Elim that separated from England's Apostolic church in 1921 (Gee, 1949; Calley, 1965:150–8). There is also a significant variety of indigenous Pentecostal churches both trinitarian and unitarian. Among the more interesting of these are the Kingston City Mission which grew from Raglan Phillips' Light Brigade, and two unitarian churches Rehobath Church of God in Christ Jesus and Shiloah Apostolic Church of Jamaica that grew out of the early Pentecostal Union. A third prominent unitarian church is the Pentecostal Gospel Temple, an indigenous break-away group from the United Pentecostal Church that came to prominence in the 1970s through the work of its female pastor. Another trinitarian church, with a television ministry developed in the 1980s, is the Deliverance Centre based in West Kingston. The list could be extended almost endlessly in order to underline the variety, pervasiveness and dynamism of

Pentecostalism within Jamaica, a dynamism indigenized during the early decades of Pentecostalism's growth.

By the time of the 1943 census this process was clearly registered especially in the parishes of Kingston and Clarendon. With postwar prosperity at home and abroad the movement expanded further so that, by the 1980s, Pentecostalism had become the espoused faith of roughly half a million Jamaicans in a population of around 2.3 million (see Austin-Broos 1997). Two Jamaican census categories, "Church of God" and "Pentecostal" address the Pentecostal world. The relative size of these categories suggests that Pentecostal trinitarian churches of God have become the most common religious organizations in Jamaica, the predominant folk church of a people that once defined its religious commitment in terms of an Orthodox Baptist faith and its unorthodox companion, Zion Revival. Pentecostals of one variety or another constitute a quarter of the entire census count, and roughly one-third of those with an expressed religious affiliation. As the census categories reflect only nominal religious affiliation, it is probably fair to say that where once a Baptist affiliation was the standard nominal religious affiliation in Jamaica, that standard is now Church of God. This phenomenon reflects regional changes in the Caribbean that have proceeded throughout the century. The legacies of Britain's colonialism gradually have been eroded as American influence has become more expansive. But with this new incorporation has also come a religious discourse that remains distinctively Jamaican.

The Construction of Jamaica's Pentecostal World

Jamaican Pentecostals generally believe that above and beyond conversion to the word of God there is a process of sanctification whereby a believer is rendered morally pure and capable of leading a "holy" or sinless life. In the Pentecostal view, to be sanctified is in fact to become a saint and Pentecostal congregations often are described as "communities of saints." Some church leaders regard sanctification simply as an empowerment to pursue the holiness state which will be established over many years. Among rank and file believers, however, and many of their local pastors, the idea that sanctification is a completed work is prevalent and seen to bear an intrinsic relation to being a saint. This is the case especially among older Pentecostalists who cherish the idea of moral perfection. In the trinitarian churches, the initial conversion and this second stage of spiritual empowering are referred to as "justification" and "sanctification" (see Stone, 1977, pp. 234–5). Where water is the baptismal medium that justifies people in faith, the Holy Spirit is the baptismal medium that sanctifies people for holiness. Pentecostals so sanctified refer to themselves as "saints." A process of "tarrying" or seeking for the Spirit through constant prayer and supplication often conjoins the two ritual stages (Stone, 1977, pp. 234–5; see also Anderson, 1979:180).

For all Pentecostal churches, sanctification or Spirit baptism is and only can be confirmed by "speaking in tongues." This is also the specific phrase employed by Jamaicans to describe the ecstatic experience. They mean by it, sometimes, "glossolalia" or a language unintelligible to man that is conferred by God so that saints can address Him. They also can mean "xenoglossy," or the instantaneous mastery of foreign tongues for the purpose of evangelism (Anderson 1979, pp. 16–19), though in Jamaica it is more common for "tongues" to be understood as glossolalia. The use of tongues is associated with notions of purification by fire. A preacher who evokes widespread glossolalia from a congregation is said "to have set the church alight." A lively preacher can also be known as a "lightening conductor." In the course of testimony, individual saints who break into glossolalia are often said to be "on fire." These expressions evoke the Biblical Pentecost where the blessing of the Holy Spirit descended on the apostles as fire and gave them the gift of tongues.

In Jamaica it is common for Pentecostal women to dress in white for communion services. Some churches have their women dress in white every Sunday. This use of a white garb to signify purity is shared with practitioners of Zion Revival, Jamaica's older revival religion (Chevannes 1971a, 1971b; Curtin 1970; Hogg 1964; Simpson 1956; Wedenoja 1978). Unlike Revivalists, the Pentecostal women do not wear turban wraps to cover their heads. Nonetheless, the emphasis on white, in conjunction with ecstatic services that proceed for many hours, lead many Jamaicans to assume that Pentecostal practitioners have very close relations with Revival religion. They are grouped by observers as "clap-clap" churches, the churches of the poor and "ignorant." This view also is confirmed by the fact that both religious forms sustain vocal male pastors with large female followings (Austin-Broos 1987; see also Cucchiari 1990; Gill 1990; Hollenweger 1969) The motif of a male religious leader with a large female band juxtaposes for Jamaicans ideas of holiness and "rudeness," or sexuality, that inform the humor of everyday life. For the purveyors of this humor, Revival and Pentecostal modes are one.

Within their own world, however, the two groups are quite antagonistic. Pentecostals view Revivalists as trucking in magic, the work of devil, in their practice of curing techniques related to rural folk healing with a repertoire of herbs and oils (see Barrett 1976; Long 1973). Healing is a central component of Pentecostal practice, but this is a healing from the Holy Spirit. Pentecostal healing is more often rendered as a cleansing that makes the body a vehicle for Spirit. A clean body signifies a thoroughly cleansed soul so that only a person justified in faith and seeking sanctification can be healed completely. A person who is so healed will be or become Pentecostalist (see also Brodwin 1996, pp. 188–9). Revival healing, on the other hand, can be realized on Revivalists and non-Revivalists alike. It signifies more the power of the healer than the purity of the person healed. Revival also can address forces of evil beyond the person including the forces of "*obeah*" or witchcraft. These different interpretations of healing reflect more or less emphasis given to personal sin in renderings of Christian cosmology. For the Revivalists, malign forces are there in the world to be contained by greater and opposing forces for good. Pentecostals, by comparison, place much more emphasis on the power of personal sin, through the wrath it elicits in God, to place malign powers in the way of a sinner. The view is that a "full, full cure" will only be secured through a redemption that also transforms the substance of the body. Redeeming from sin is curing the body and curing the body requires "cleansing" from sin. This process can be realized only when the Holy Spirit makes a body its vehicle and becoming such a vehicle is signified by speaking in tongues. From the Pentecostal point of view Revivalists, like other Christian groups, lack the revelation of speaking in tongues. They are debarred therefore from the cleansing from sin signified by Holy Ghost possession.

If Pentecostals on this account propose themselves as superior, Revivalists have their own critique of Pentecostal practice. They see Pentecostals as part of the growing "church business," as part of a commodified religious world issuing from America. They point to Pentecostalism's relations with the metropolis, and also to the emphasis on tithing in the churches that forms the basis of institutional funding. Their observation is that anyone may come to a Revival church for healing, and even "balm," or Revivalist specialist healing, though it requires a payment, does not require the continuing contributions involved in Pentecostal tithes.

Notwithstanding these points of conflict, the popular view of these churches as related is in fact quite correct. Their respective entries into Jamaica have both been indicative of major moments in the development of revival religion in the metropolitan world. If their construals of sin and healing vary, in both groups there is a focus on redemption and on the realization in the person of a transported or transformed state. Believers try to "get right" with God through the healing ministry of Jesus Christ in order to embody heaven come to earth, either in the form of possessing angels or in the form of the Holy Ghost (see Dayton 1980). Along with the considerable influence of Adventist Christianity, which came to the island in the 1890s, these groups purvey throughout Jamaica a climate of eudemonic hope in the present and millennial expectation for the future. They allow practitioners to imagine a spirit-filled world and experience its presence both within and beyond the milieu they identify with unsaved life.

Two major aspects of practice frame the Jamaican Pentecostal world: one is the practice and experience of healing and, by extension, exorcism. This complex convinces saints that when they are sanctified by the Holy Ghost, they actually experience a change of bodily substance that infuses their being with spiritual power and thereby renders them as saints. The other is a Biblical poetics that is used as the medium for interpretations of life. The passage from slavery to freedom in Jamaica is seen as an analogue of a passage from sin to a state of redemption, embodied in being a saint. History, then, is assimilated to a notion of personal transcendence. For the Jamaican Pentecostalists both the personal and public poles of human experience are rendered in a Biblical mode thereby making their status as saints a "uniquely real" circumstance (Geertz 1973; Turner 1967). I deal with each of these aspects in turn to underline the manner in which Pentecostalism is a lived experience that speaks to a Jamaican knowledge of the world.

Healing in Jamaican Pentecostalism

Jamaican Pentecostal healing which is always a healing of malaise that is spiritual and physical reflects among Pentecostals a Jamaican cultural acceptance of sin. Sin is at the heart of malaise for the Pentecostalist and healing is the way in which the person who remains unsaved begins a path to redemption. Observed from another vantage point, however, the Jamaican cultural acceptance of sin also reveals the historical transformation of West African notions of affliction and suffering. It is not only sickness but historical suffering that can be traced to the fact of sin and alleviated by sin's repudiation. Responsibility for human malaise thereby lies with individuals who serially bear the burden of sin. No accidental outcome of life's events, the evil that brings malaise is the product of a person's very being. But for the Pentecostal saint, benign and malign spiritual forces no longer reside beyond the person as inherent aspects of a New World African environment. Rather, they are stretched between the poles of God's transcendence and the immanence of man. In this New World Christian scheme, it is man's fallen state that confirms the inherent humanness of suffering, and history as a process of redemption. This "morality of being," as John Mbiti calls it, was first introduced to Jamaica by the missionaries of the slavery period (Mbiti 1969). It has been brought to fruition in Jamaica through the practices of Pentecostalism.

With this securing of sin in the cosmos has come a new interpretation of healing. The spiritual in-filling that creates a saint also creates a healed person who becomes a person of sound, healthy body and also a joyous being. Comaroff (1985, p. 210–11) has proposed that in Botswana, the suffering body is also a sign of the experience of a suffering society. Healing the body among the Tshidi is thereby healing their tortured social world. It is one of Pentecostalism's most interesting features that in the midst of modernity, it still renders cosmology as ontogeny and thereby inscribes moral order on the body. Jamaican Pentecostalism proposes that the cleansed and healed body is indicative of a union with Christ that inevitably re-orders the world of the saint. Yet when they cleanse and heal, Jamaican Pente-costals do not reconstitute their whole social world but rather enter a heaven on earth sustained only in saintly practice. Their practice does not obviate suffering in a larger Jamaica but only the suffering of the saved. It is therefore imperative that saints evangelize the many unsaved and seek to heal them too. This central call for every saint, to heal the multitude of the unsaved, is the principal ritual dynamic of the religion. Though embraced by all Pentecostalists, it is also a call that brings different orientations in men and women saints.

The male perspective on healing is articulated mainly from the authority position of a pastor or elder and concerns the duty of all church members to make themselves "clean vessels" for the Lord. In this, Jamaica's Pentecostal men show a concern to sustain the virtue of their women that is not peculiar to them alone but integral to creole religion. Among the Pentecostals, however, the moral malaise of fallen women also is represented in a physical mode as forms of malady requiring exorcism. Both men and women exorcise. In fact, as one of the "signs that follow" being saved, this ability is potentially there for every saint. It is principally among male pastors, however, that a mythology of exorcising women is deployed as an indication of special powers that sets them apart from other saints. Exorcism is a radical extension of the "laying on of hands," a mundane healing practice that occurs every Sunday in any Pentecostal church. The "laying on of hands," sometimes with oil, involves praying for a person who is ill or in pain, and transmitting through bodily touch one's own spiritual infusion to the person. The Spirit thereby cleanses the person, purifying body and soul through the blood, and dissolves the illness or relieves the pain. Exorcism is a magnified form of this practice that drives a manifest devil from a body that generally is perceived to be greatly disturbed (see also Csordas 1994, pp. 25–56; Kapferer 1979a, 1979b). Exorcism is the most dramatic act in which a pastor can be seen to heal and thereby allow a person to become a saint. Interestingly, most neophytes who are exorcised are women.

The maladies assumed to indicate an exorcism are generally psy-chological or gynaecological. The former include cases of depression and mild schizophrenia and presumably other forms of evident psychosis. Temper tantrums and other even fairly minor variations in demeanour also can be placed in this class however. The gynaecological cases often involve menstrual flux over many months, acute and regular abdominal pains, and swollen bellies or "bad belly," often assumed to be peculiar pregnancies (see also Sobo 1993, p. 286). Descriptions of the relevant cases of flux emphasize the viscous, clotted nature of the blood, its dark color, its evil smell, and the difficulties of dispensing with the substance. Flux can be a sign that a woman has become a breeding ground for devils which slip out through the contaminated blood to become troublesome agents in the world. The cases of pain and swollen bellies are cured when women eject the cause: a worm, a serpent, or perhaps a snake, in each case understood as an embodiment of evil. This is the pastor's most dramatic expression of power with regard to his following. His spiritual power is here embodied in real and dramatic physical process. Both the practice and mythology of exorcism are spread throughout Jamaican Pentecostal life.

A feminized engagement with healing is more likely to emerge in a Jamaican urban setting where a number of women, not necessarily related but living in adjoining yards, become mutually supporting sisters in a church. This group will include at least two and possibly three generations of women who assist each other in child-minding and illness, keep a "partner" together, and occasionally help with marketing. They will attend their church on a Sunday morning and possibly nightly twice a week for evangelism, tarrying, or women's prayer. Most will read their Bibles every day. Saints sustain not merely relations of "mutual dependency" but a relational life of holiness within a larger urban milieu (Austin 1984, pp. 41, 46–7). The moral order that saints create and their heavy reliance on the guidance of Jesus, as it is revealed through prayer and the Bible, gives these lives a sense of completeness that is different from other neighbourhood lives. The absolute grounding of Pentecostal faith is socially embodied in everyday being, made real through circumscribed social interaction within the bounds of a neighbourhood.

This constitution of community is also a healing for Jamaican women. As they live their created moral order, they revel in a healed and healthy body (see Csordas 1994, p. 26). The power of the force that transformed this body is revealed by the saints in two different ways. One is in the constant and successful experience of "laying on

of hands" for minor ills. Women frequently come to church with back
pains and pains in joints and muscles. Very often, these pains indicate
muscular or spinal strain from heavy work or the early onset of
arthritic pain that often comes with repeated and prolonged coldwa-
ter laundering. Saints have headaches as well, some of which clearly
come from stress. To this repertoire of pain that is integral to environment is added the cultural construction of pain as an obligatory
manifestation of saints' need for the Lord. Feeling pain and requiring
its cure are a manifestation of holiness that has not become arrogant
and over-confident. The curing that comes to terminate pain is a
major sign of saintly status, albeit in a human form. It signifies a
physical body governed by the power of the Spirit.

A healthy woman in Jamaica is also a woman who brings forth
children. And one of the disciplines of being a saint is that only
married women can procreate. Part of the health of saintly women
and of the community of which they are a part involves the substitu-
tion of spiritual mentoring for the saints' physical procreation. Saints
believe that through their vigorous evangelism, more and more Jamaicans will be reborn to populate their heaven on earth. In Jamaican
Pentecostal churches that sustain the larger women's congregations,
these ideas produce a striking imagery of the church itself "birthing"
new saints. Here the imagery of woman as vessel is transferred from
the locus of individual saints to their community and congregation.
The healed Pentecostal saint is a person without pain, often a woman,
in her alternative community who, through her Pentecostal congregation, produces saints who are born again.

The practice that can be dramatically individualized by the pastor
in exorcism is also made a collective practice in Pentecostal congregations. Spectacular exhortation and exorcism become the pastors
typical expression to assert his authority over other saints. Women
saints, on the other hand, draw attention to their efficacy and numbers through ritual statements of community. More inclined to witness than to exhort, they bring others to God through their practice
that re-affirms, like the pastors' acts, that the Holy Spirit is a real
presence in the body dissolving human malaise. But the Pentecostal
world of saints is anchored not only in the person and body but also
in that larger order of Jamaican history and everyday life. Through
the use of Biblical poetics, Pentecostals tend not only to the body but
to wider parameters of Jamaican experience.

The Poetics of Pentecostalism in Jamaica

Jamaican Pentecostals deploy the Bible to construct a landscape of experience. In this the dynamic of the world is seen to be a dynamic of redemption. Rather than seeing history as "progress" or as a movement to "freedom," Pentecostalists see Jamaican history as a course of transcendence from the "slavery" of sin. This was evidenced time and again during the course of fieldwork that I undertook in Kingston and the countryside (mainly Clarendon) during 1986–7 and in 1990–91. The following examples of Pentecostal preaching and comment give some indication of this dramatic rendering of experience. In a comment I discuss at greater length elsewhere, a Kingston pastor made this observation (see Austin-Broos 1996, p. 78–80).

> We will always undervalue ourselves until through God's grace we identify our roots. We would go to Africa lookin' where we came, and they in Africa lookin' to trace where they came, until they trace their roots to Adam.
>
> We are all his offspring. The great Creator, the universe declares, we are his offspring. There are certain principles that govern his [Adam's] offspring: I'm a child of God. I have to live like a child of God. I'm born again. I must live free from sin. Holiness must be our watchword, righteousness our password. Repentance must be our aim. That's the only thing that can bring us back to our roots.
>
> This day I ask you again. Who are you connected to? Who are you an offspring of? Have you found your roots?

This interpretation of a New World African historical experience through the Bible's account of genesis and redemption carries with it an important ambiguity. Whilst African sin often is evoked as the reason for New World enslavement, the suffering of that enslavement also is seen to create or reaffirm a marked capacity for redemption. In his famous essay, *The Muse of History*, Derek Walcott gives voice to a sentiment that is equally Jamaican when he observes that "the subject African had come to the New World ... with a profounder terror of blasphemy than the exhausted, hypocritical Christian. He understood too quickly the Christian rituals of a whipped, tortured, and murdered redeemer " (1974, p. 11). Walcott also proposes that in addressing Christianity, "the captured warrior and the tribal poet had chosen the very battleground which the captor proposed" not in order to experience "defeat" but, rather, through "conversion" to reconstitute the cosmology of a European world. "What was captured from the captor was his God" (Walcott 1974, p. 11). This was a revolution from within (see also Austin-Broos 1992, 1997). In these forms of comment in Pentecostalism, slavery is seen as a white institution. It is taken to demonstrate among whites a proneness to evil beyond the capacity of African Jamaicans. Africans, in turn, are often portrayed as a "spiritual" people in the sense that, having been a ritually oriented people more engaged with an animated world, they always were more disposed than whites to take up a New World Christian message. The power and autonomous dynamic of this message is proclaimed from a position of socioeconomic disadvantage in a fashion that is familiar in the colonized world.[3] The high valuation of African spirituality is reflected in the words of another pastor speaking not of initial Christian conversion, but of the progress of Pentecostalism,

> Jamaicans accepted Pentecostalism because they already lived in a spirit-filled world. They were African themselves. They were emotional. They liked rhythm in their worship, pipe and drum, and they knew what it was to be Spirit-filled from the days of the Great Revival. The whole world of Jamaica was busy with spirits, so the message of the Holy Spirit was welcome. Americans didn't need to tell Jamaicans that.

The importance of Christianity to Jamaican culture has not been, however, simply as an idiom of experience. It also has resided in the Bible's role as a principal medium for grounding a world made fragmentary and painful by the legacies of slavery and especially the racial hierarchy of slavery's colonial aftermath. In medieval times the Bible was viewed as the book in which "all mysteries of the universe [were] written," not merely a compendium but a master work that placed everything in the shadow of its order. For Jamaicans proselytized by dedicated missionaries who were nonconformists with a Biblical bent, Dante's claim for God through His book might have seemed especially apt: that He "ingathered, bound by love in one volume, the scattered leaves of all the universe" (Dante 1965). Certainly, the Bible's affirmation that all "differences are ... unified in God" would have been a tantalizing truth for a scattered people whose difference was disparaged in the larger colonial order (cf. Hart 1989, p. 91). Right from its beginnings in Jamaica, mission Christianity spoke not only to diversity but also to hierarchy and to a powerful view within Jamaica that felicitous being correlated with the whites.

In a Jamaican Pentecostal world, it is Jamaica's mainly black saints who command spiritual power in their heaven come to earth. This, they pronounce, is a colourless world but nonetheless a world where those who are poor and of African descent encounter fewer impediments than others in their passage to holiness. Moreover, aspects of Jamaican performance make Pentecostal rite not simply a prayer to a distant God but, rather, an embodied demonstration of His presence. This experience convinces saints that they are transformed and also empowered. Hopkin comments,

> The importance and significance of [Jamaican] worshipping lies in the worshipper's being filled by the religious spirit.... It is in the manner in which the worshippers bring on the experience and the surrounding circumstances that are conducive to it, that a difference between America and Jamaican Pentecostal styles of worship becomes manifest. In the Jamaican church music, rhythm, and movement of the service take on a religiously potent quality in themselves. Where white Pentecostals bring on the experience of the Holy Spirit by concentration and prayer, the Jamaican church members bring it on by cultivating religious fervour and excitement through these sense-oriented forms of self-expression, and through losing themselves in their active participation in the communal events of the church.... Where for the Americans singing a hymn is an act of praise, for the Jamaicans the song and all the dancing and rhythm that accompany it *are* a religious experience in themselves. This experience does not come about independent of the God that the songs praise; rather, the songs act as a vehicle of the God's power, and the means of experiencing Him. (Hopkin 1978, p. 25, emphasis added)

This experience of God within the believer allows Pentecostals to see in the Bible a compendium of lived accounts that are also stories in their own lives. Two further examples of pastors' narrative use of the Bible show how the Bible becomes real as a rendering of the lived, and historical, experience of saints.

In early 1991, a pastor addressed his West Kingston congregation comprised mainly of women on the theme of the care of "outside" children or children born out of wedlock. He observed that women who have children as an outcome of "fornication" or unsanctified sexual relations often then conclude that they need to live "in sin" either with the father of the children or with another man who will offer some support and protection to the fledgling family. The pastor observed, however, that any such support and protection was ne- gated by the fact that the child or children would thereby be placed within a sinful environment. Children would "grow" like the man so that when they became "big people" they, too, would not know "to stay under your own figtree and under your own vine." The alterna- tive for women with "outside" children was to come into the "Church of God" where support would be found through praising the Lord and sustaining a life in the service of God. Jesus would become the women's "friend" and they would be able to lean on Him in a way that would allow them to flee the experience of "Babylon." The pastor then enjoined his women saints, "Tek the child han' run! Yu mus' tek the baby in yu arms han' run!" He likened the situation to that of Mary and Joseph after the birth of Jesus. Fulfilling the prophecy of Jeremy, they were forced to flee from Bethlehem to Egypt in order to avoid Herod's vengeance on new born infants in response to the news that a Messiah had been born. Reference to the intermittent violence of the West Kingston area, which has involved the razing of some neighborhoods, here was proposed as a continuous milieu with that from which Mary and Joseph fled. They fled, the pastor proposed, from the same type of violence between competing gangs with politi- cal affiliations that has sometimes caused West Kingston residents also to flee their abodes. The pastor read from his Bible,

the angel of the Lord appeareth to Joseph in a dream, saying, Arise, and take the young child and his mother, and flee into Egypt, and be thou there until I bring word: for Herod will seek the young child and destroy him.

When he arose, he took the young child and is mother by night, and departed into Egypt: ...

Then Herod, when he saw that he was mocked of the wise men, was exceeding wroth, and sent forth, and slew all the children that were in Bethlehem, and in all the coasts thereof, from two years old and under, according to the time which he had diligently inquired of the wise men. (Matthew 2:13, 14, 16)

The pastor then re-iterated his call, "Tek the child han' run!" Women were to run both from the sin and the violence of their milieu, the sin, in the pastor's eyes, being a root cause of the violence. He referred not only to the church itself and its congregation as a haven for the mothers, but also to the church's extensive pre-school centre in which places might be found for children over three years old. These centres are a prominent feature of the larger Kingston Pentecostal churches and especially churches with large female followings. The pastor positioned himself as a Joseph leading women from a violent and dangerous milieu into one where they could be both safe and empowered. He proposed for women who were as yet unsaved an alternative milieu to the "sweetheart" life in which, with some assistance from the church, they might become both saints who were transformed beings and also women who might aspire to regular employment and an autonomous life. The utopia of a Pentecostal heaven come to earth in this Jamaican environment offers not only spiritual experience beyond the mundane, and one that reverses Jamaica's status hierarchy, but also a domain of practical empowerment for some of the Jamaicans who are most vulnerable in the conditions of downtown Kingston life.

The experience of violence in everyday life and the release from violence in God's domain represent for Kingston Pentecostals, especially, a contrast between powerlessness and a state of empowerment. Subjection to violence and powerlessness also are associated closely with the experience of being black in a New World order that began in slavery. Listening to the deployment of Old Testament verse in the course of Pentecostal services often evoked for me, as an observer, a scene from the Jamaican film, *The Harder They Come*, in which a youthful downtown cinema audience cheered the violent action of an "Italian" western. The film presented a reality to the audience that it seemed to recognize albeit in a shy and sometimes disbelieving way. I have been in such an audience myself. Similarly in Pentecostal churches, the violence of Old Testament tales of Biblical conflict and the wrath of God brings to the congregation a perceived touchstone in experience for people who have come from a history of slavery and contend with dispossession as a daily event.

When a pastor pronounces, therefore, that the community of saints is on the "victory side" she can describe directly in Biblical terms the awesome power of God to constitute an alternative world through His saints. In an East Kingston service in 1986 a pastor said to the saints,

> We feel that circumstance is going to put us under. We feel that the demands of life are pressing on us today. I'm going to tell you about some of God's victories so that you can know in truth and in faith that today you're on "the victory side."

The pastor's style was both urgent and intimate drawing the saints into her own engaging theme. She began to read from her massive Bible:

> Finally, my brethren, be strong in the Lord and in the power of his might.
> Put on the whole armour of God, that ye may be able to stand against the wiles of the devil.
> For we wrestle not against flesh and blood, but against principalities, against powers, against the rulers of darkness of this world, against spiritual wickedness in high places.
> Wherefore take unto you the whole armour of God, that yet may be able to stand.
> Stand therefore, having your loins girt about with truth, and having on the breastplate of righteousness;
> And your feet shod with the preparation of the gospel of peace;
> Above all, take the shield of faith, wherewith ye shall be able to quench all the fiery darts of the wicked.
> And take the helmet of salvation, and the sword of the Spirit, which is the word of God. (Ephesians 6:10–17)

The pastor enjoined her saints not to become embroiled in disputes within their yards. She suggested that when a fellow tenant taunted a saint she should simply draw away. She should not put herself at risk by employing "bad words" and physical assault. She should remember above all that her fight is a fight of the Spirit. Similarly, the pastor continued, the saints should not fight with the landlord. Even when he demanded rent that could not be paid, the saint should not argue but simply be contrite and give the worry "over to Jesus." At work, the pastor pointed out, it was foolish to fight a boss. At least a boss paid a person money (a muted reference to slavery). Every injustice in the world, she proclaimed, was an injustice that God could see. He had always fought for His people and He fought for His saints as well. The aim of the saint should be simply to fight the devil. "We wrestle not against flesh and blood, but against the evil day." The pastor then observed that there were many other victories of the Lord in the Bible, the victory of Joshua, for instance.

> And the Lord said unto Joshua, See, I have given into thine hand Jericho, and the king thereof, and the mighty men of valour.
> And ye shall compass the city all ye men of war, and go round about the city once. Thus shalt thou do six days....
> And it shall come to pass that when they make a long blast with the ram's horn, and when ye hear the sound of the trumpet, all the people shall shout with a great shout; and the wall of the city shall fall down flat, and the people shall ascend up everyman straight before him. (Joshua 6:2, 3, 5)

And the victory of Gideon over the Midianites,

> And Gideon sent messengers throughout all mount Ephraim, saying Come down against the Midianites, ...
> And they took two princes of the Midianites, Oreb and Zeeb; and they slew Oreb upon the rock Oreb, and Zeeb they slew at the winepress of Zeeb, and pursued Midian, and brought the heads of Oreb and Zeeb to Gideon on the other side of Jordan. (Judges 7:24–25)

And the victory of David over Goliath,

> Therefore David ran, and stood upon the Philistine, and took his sword and drew it out of the sheath thereof, and slew him, and cut off his head therewith. And when the Philistines saw their champion dead, they fled. (I Samuel 17:51)

In the midst of the cries of enthusiastic saints, the pastor emphasized that in the war of "flesh against flesh" the meek could never really triumph. The only victories to be had in life were through the Spirit of "our Lord" and the glorious encouragement of "our great God." Her closing injunction to the saints was to "Just give God the glory and forget the creature." She followed this injunction with another victory:

> And the Syrians fled before Israel; and David slew the men of seven hundred chariots of the Syrians, and forty thousand horsemen, and smote Chobach the captain of their host, who died there. (II Samuel 10:18)

> He arose, and smote the Philistines until his hand was weary and his hand clave unto the sword: and the Lord wrought a great victory that day. (II Samuel 23:10)

In the Pentecostal world of heaven come to earth through the Holy Ghost's transformation of sinners into saints, black and poor Jamaicans, who are most of the saints, become the highest achievers and the most empowered. This is also a colorless world, a world in poet Claude McKay's words "where black nor white can follow to betray" and a world where saints through the power of their God are invested with real material force to deflect the predations of their enemies (McKay 1953). This utopian world of victory for the righteous, with its sometimes lurid portrayals through the Bible, is given additional force by its positioning within a New World experience. Notwithstanding the achievements of Jamaican and other local nationalisms, this is a history that is destined by regional constraints to appear always as a history of injustice sustaining a racialized regional order. Not simply in Jamaica and the Caribbean itself, but also in Britain, North America and West Africa, the African component of a trans-Atlantic world seems too often disprivileged and underrated. The lived transformation of Pentecostal saints articulated through a Biblical poetics constitutes a utopic space in which saints are able "to expose the credibility gap" in an organized political domain that is limited in its power to intervene in the reproduction of this regional history. Both the Jamaican state and its political parties often lack credibility for ordinary Jamaicans. Promises that "better must come" are often disappointed not so much through the fault of the state, or the parties, but by virtue of a larger regional order. Within this milieu, many Jamaicans and especially poor Jamaicans experience a life which perforce they order in terms of an immediate daily practice they believe is guided by a transcendent God. They experience through bodily healing that the Holy Spirit can alleviate suffering and know that with release from the slavery of sin they, and other Jamaicans, may lead a felicitous life. In this milieu the "history" of a nation state promoting "progress" through "development" that never quite comes, often captures less the experience of life than the familiar and uplifting poetics of the Bible. From this perspective it is important to note that Pentecostalism in Jamaica is not simply an island-wide filigree of numerous tiny country churches. It is also in Kingston, Spanish Town and Ocho Rios, as well as in other major urban centres, weekly gatherings that are hundreds and sometimes a thousand strong cheering and clapping these vivid affirmations of utopic community propagated in the sermons of Pentecostal pastors. Pentecostalism in Jamaica is not only the intimate community. It is also a movement that supports regular gatherings and rallies as large as any promoted by a political party.

Pentecostal Enthusiasm, Its Conditions

So far I have suggested that Pentecostalism, like other popular Jamaican religions, provides a healing for individuals that is experienced as physical and moral as well. It also provides a utopic space from which Jamaicans, especially those who are poor and black and those who are also women, can question the power and applicability of secular accounts of their life (see Austin-Broos 1987). This questioning concerns not the political process as such, but the forms of power that are real in the world and the values and practice that define persons as felicitous beings in a Jamaican milieu. This is a politics of moral orders, a politics of the personal rather than a politics of governance (see Austin-Broos 1991–2, 1997). The experience of a healed body and a world that is consistent with the Bible's suggests to the saints that they have the means to control and improve the environment. Talking of violence in Jamaica, a Kingston pastor said to me in December 1990, "We need to stop this rubbish in our country. We cannot live much longer in this way of life. God has blessed our nation. God has given us strong and capable leaders. But while we praise them, it is to us that God has entrusted the task of rousing people spiritually."

In their Pentecostal congregations and in the course of daily life saints actually experience the spiritual empowerment of God and in their readings of the Bible see the victories of God's people as analogues of their own victories both accomplished and anticipated.

The Jamaicanness of Pentecostal practice lies at least in part in the way that Biblical poetics engages with and becomes the idiom of everyday life. But it is also the connection that Jamaicans draw between Christian aspiration and the legacies of slavery that makes a Pentecostal practice specific in Jamaica's environment. Pentecostalism is seen by saints as a practice beyond racism and it is as a route to a world beyond Jamaica's hierarchical order that Pentecostalism has enormous appeal to the poor.

In his discussion of Jamaica's "culture" of race, Jack Alexander is careful to state that although his Jamaican friends subscribed to various ideas about hierarchy they did not espouse racist views. They did not believe that whites in Jamaica or the region are biologically superior to blacks or, presumably, blacks superior to whites. Rather, Alexander proposes, they believed that "racial hierarchy is the result of a historical association of race with social dominance and style of life" (Alexander 1977:428). Styles of life, he seems to suggest, are judged as superior or inferior not in terms that are simply their own, but also to the extent that they conform to sets of positively valued norms related to life among the powerful (Alexander 1977:433–4 (fn 7)). I would add from the viewpoint of my own observations of daily life in Jamaica, that the life style of the powerful is sometimes seen as superior because it seems better able to control or command everyday exigencies. The issues of education and remuneration are crucial in these forms of perception. This is a rather different matter from proposing that a life style is superior because it is "white" or purportedly derived from a European model. Alexander makes a further point. He observes that in Jamaica "the link between appearance and race is conceived [as] biological" whereas the link between race and social position is conceived to be "historical." However, what remains less clearly defined is whether or not "the association of races," albeit always in historical contexts, is intrinsically hierarchical. Alexander proposes that in Jamaica the cultural scheme endorses this view. People of the "same 'blood' [are seen] to stick together" as an historical fact. The consequence of a multiplicity of "bloods" situated in the same social space inevitably generates social hierarchy, not as a biological principle but rather as an inexorable law of history which also has privileged whites.

These distinctions discussed by Alexander were ones he found implicit in the words of his middle class associates. They are consistent with my own field observations to the extent that lower class Jamaicans, though they discuss race in different ways, never entertain notions of a biological inferiority though they do dwell at great length on social disadvantage, as evidenced in poverty and lack of education, conferred by the intersection of colour discrimination and various relations of social reproduction (Austin-Broos 1994a, 1994b). Moreover, my friends often voiced a scepticism concerning how different life could be either between nations in the world, or between colours and classes in Jamaica. The weight of trans-Atlantic history often bears on their observations, for people compare situations in Jamaica, North America, Britain and sometimes a projected image of Africa itself, as if these were indeed "the world."

Notwithstanding these views of history, lower class people with whom I have worked also had an acute sense of their own humanness or spiritual being (cf. Jayawardena 1968–9). That being was understood to involve perennial tension between "natural" wants and a nascent or realized power of transcendence. Some, who were also Pentecostals, would refer to this property as their "blessedness" or to the fact that each was a "child of God" or "one of God's creations" or simply "a saint." Consistent with the religious view that Africans are inherently "spiritual," it was common to propose that black Jamaicans retained this humanness to a superior extent because they had passed through a history of suffering. Jamaicans' reference to themselves as "sufferers" is not here simply an abject description but rather one that links humanness and suffering to the propensity for superior spiritual being.

Along with this sense of self went also an acute sense among the poor that they were "not recognized" by the more fortunate. The remark would be made that a person in a certain position would not "recognize" a manual worker, a domestic, or one who was simply black and lower class. The view was often put to me that it was better to avoid certain circles because you would not be recognized: "If you ask for help, you would not be recognized," or, "Me doan buck up wid dem dere!" These comments were not so much complaints as observations on the everyday pragmatics of life. The sense of the comments was that one should not place oneself in such a position. (A black child "not recognized" in the classroom became a particular dilemma for this involved social relations it is hard to circumvent without some cost.) The marked disdain of women for domestic service in all but acute economic circumstances also is related to this view. Service within some households can involve an almost permanent non-recognition (see also Higman 1983; Lobdell 1988). Avoiding this "menial" work, and the term "menial" is commonly used, is integral to strategies that circumvent the need to request recognition.

"I am justified through the grace of God. I am sanctified by the Holy Ghost. I am recognized by Jesus. He is my friend." That these words and others like them are spoken over and over again as testimonies in Jamaican Pentecostal churches is not surprising. I have described elsewhere the historical role of churches in Jamaica, acting to constitute forms of social life and to define collective experience in a circumstance for the Caribbean where colonialism and neo-colonialism, in addition to the very small size of nations, has limited the salience of the state (Austin-Broos 1991–2, 1996). Three factors are important here: the uneven capacity of Caribbean states, including Jamaica's, to act as a structuring power in social life; the expanding structures of foreign churches partially funded from abroad; and the corresponding forms of collective life in which Jamaicans have been involved. The Orthodox Baptists secured a role for the church and for religion in Jamaica when they with other mission groups encouraged free villages. Although this process was fairly shortlived, the churches sustained their commitment to education and to some local services. As the twentieth century proceeded, the state assumed responsibility first in primary education and then increasingly in secondary education (Eisner 1960:326–7; Gordon 1963; Miller 1990). Nonetheless, the notion that churches should sustain a pastoral role was firmly established in Jamaica. Pentecostalism entered this milieu, already established in the nineteenth century, and has grown, all the while expanding this role, even as Jamaica became an independent nation. Not so active in education as were the Orthodox Baptists, in a more prosperous century, the Pentecostal churches themselves provide significant organizations in which ambitious saints can become involved. For many Pentecostalists, the church is a total way of life, a comprehensive "plausibility structure" that sustains coherence in their lives. It also reaches out to America and Britain to define the full extent of Pentecostalism. This trans-national and metropolitan world, rather than Jamaica's nation state, becomes the Pentecostal milieu. And this is a place for Jamaicans from which some sustain a utopic critique of the hierarchy of the region.

The church can become, in significant part, an imagined community for Jamaicans (Anderson 1983). And this is achieved at least in part because the modern state has continued to have an uneven presence in Jamaican life and even as an independent nation state, with its attendant political parties, has appeared unable in the view of some to transform the hierarchy of Jamaican daily life (see also Stone 1991, p. 93). The Pentecostal churches thereby bring an alternative order to political parties. Where the latter construct a reality based on the power of humankind and its legal institutions to arrange the goods of social life, Pentecostals propose God's spiritual power as a way to address personal sin seen as the cause of suffering. All these factors, made real for saints through Holy Spirit healing and the poetics of the Bible, come together to create a world in which saints seek to transcend hierarchy and confirm the reality of Jesus as friend. They do this from a local church, but also from one that often connects with significant trans-national organizations (see Basch, Schiller Blanc 1994).

Conclusion

The growth of Pentecostalism in Jamaica in the course of the twentieth century has been quite phenomenal. Undoubtedly, the religion's entry to Jamaica and its early missionary efforts were precipitated by the rise of North America in the region as a political and economic force progressively reducing the influence of the British. Pentecostalism has grown rapidly in Jamaica, however, because it became an indigenous force at a very early stage in its development, within a decade of its first introduction. To address Pentecostalism within Jamaica, is not simply to address American hegemony, then, but also the cultural dynamics of a twentieth century Jamaica. This discussion has pointed to at least four pertinent factors here: a long standing Jamaican practice of utopic responses to hierarchy that was there in earlier forms including the Orthodox Baptists and is also present in contemporary smaller sects including Zion Revival and Rastafarianism; a highly developed poetics of the Bible in which Jamaican Pentecostalists deploy the Bible in a discourse about their daily lives and their historical experience; an embodied practice of healing that makes real the notion of spiritual power and ties it to an empowering from the African past; and, finally, the institutional connections of churches that underpin this ritual experience of power with connections to a larger world that stands at a tangent to the state. But for the defining experience of embodied transformation involved in being healed and "born again," these characteristics of Pentecostalism are also characteristics of a wider religious discourse linked intimately to the geo-politics of the region. This discourse is not simply indigenous in the sense of being a self-contained whole. It is a discourse lived in a trans-national world that informs the tenor of experience.

This property of "in-betweenness" or "boundary" experience is a permanent property of Jamaican culture and perhaps this is why Pentecostal practice has spread so rapidly in Jamaica (Bhabha, 1994). In a world where "politricks" and the grand narrative of European developmental history commands less than full plausibility, organized religions from abroad are taken up and indigenized with alacrity. Pentecostalism reflects, then, not simply American influence but also a Jamaican response to a particular and enduring world of trans-Atlantic experience.

Endnotes

1. Raglan Phillips was born in England and migrated to Jamaica at around the age of 17. He remained as resident in Jamaica and evangelized with a Jamaican woman, Mary Coore. See Austin-Broos (1997).

2. Trinitarian Pentecostalists baptize in the name of "the Father, Son and Holy Ghost." Unitarian or "oneness" or "Jesus name" Pentecostalists baptize only in the name of "Jesus" as they take Him to be the embodiment of God. Also see Austin-Broos (1997).

3. With their complex relations to country, Australian Aboriginal groups, for instance, also claim to be more "spiritual" than European settlers in Australia. This concept of the spiritual is as much a product of the post-colonial process as it is a product of pre-colonial culture. For people who lack power in a national arena, it becomes a way of claiming an alternative form of power.

References

Alexander, J. 1977 The culture of race in middle-class Kingston. *American Ethnologist* 3:413–35.

Anderson, B. 1983 *Imagined Communities*. London: Verso.

Anderson, R. 1979 *Vision of the Disinherited: The Making of American Pentecostalism*. New York and Oxford: Oxford University Press.

Austin, D. 1981 Born again ... and again, and again: communitas and social change among Jamaican Pentecostalists. *Journal of Anthropological Research* 37:226–46.

Austin, D. 1984 *Urban Life in Kingston, Jamaica: The Culture and Class Ideology of Two Neighbourhoods*. New York and London: Gordon and Breach.

Austin-Broos, D. 1987 Pentecostals and Rastafarians: cultural, political and gender relations of two religious movements. *Social and Economic Studies* 36(4):1–19.

Austin-Broos, D. 1991–92 Religion and the politics of moral order in Jamaica. *Anthropological Forum* 6:287–319.

Austin-Broos, D. 1992 Redefining the moral order: interpretations of Christianity in post-emancipation Jamaica. In: *The Meaning of Freedom* (eds., F. McGlynn and S. Drescher). Pittsburgh and London: Pittsburgh University Press, pp. 221–45.

Austin-Broos, D. 1993 Hierarchy and Jamaican religion. Paper presented in the panel "Culture, Ideology and the Politics of Gender, Race and Class" at the annual meeting of the American Anthropological Association, November, Washington.

Austin-Broos, D. 1994a Race/class: Jamaica's discourse of heritable identity. *Nieuwe West-Indische Gids* 68:213–33

Austin-Broos, D. 1994b Talking race: the violence of words and silences. Paper presented in the panel "The Violence of Words and Silences" at the annual meeting of the American Anthropological Association, November, Atlanta.

Austin-Broos, D. 1996 Politics and the Redeemer: state and religion as ways of being in Jamaica. *Nieuwe West-Indische Gids* 70:59–90.

Austin-Broos, D. 1997 *Jamaica Genesis: Religion and Politics of Moral Orders.* London and Chicago: University of Chicago Press.

Barrett, L. 1976 *The Sun and the Drum: African roots in Jamaican folk tradition.* Kingston and London: Sangster's Bookstore and Heinemann.

Basch, L.; Schiller, N. Glick; and Blanc, C. Szanton 1994 *Nations Unbound: Transnational Projects, Postcolonial Predicaments and Deterritorialized Nation-States.* New York and London: Gordon and Breach.

Bhabha, H. 1994 *The Location of Culture.* London and New York: Routledge.

Brodwin, P. 1996 *Medicine and Morality in Haiti.* Cambridge, New York and Melbourne: Cambridge University Press.

Calley, M. 1965 *God's People, West Indian Pentecostals in England.* London and New York: Oxford University Press.

Chevannes, B. 1971a *Jamaican Lower Class Religion: Struggles Against Oppression.* MSc (Sociology) thesis. University of the West Indies, Mona.

Chevannes, B. 1971b Revival and black struggle. *Savacou* 5:27–37.

Chordas, T. 1980 Catholic Pentecostalism: a new word in a New World. In: *Perspectives of Pentecostalism* (ed., S. Glazier). Washington, DC: University Press of America, pp. 143–76.

Comaroff, J. 1985 *Body of Power, Spirit of Resistance.* Chicago: University of Chicago Press.

Conn, C. 1959 *Where the Saints Have Trod: A History of the Church of God Missions.* Cleveland, TN: Pathway Press.

Csordas, C. 1994 *The Sacred Self.* Berkeley: University of California Press.

Cucchiari, S. 1990 Between shame and sanctification: patriarchy and its transformation in Sicilian Pentecostalism. *American Ethnologist* 17:687–707.

Curtin, P. 1970 *Two Jamaicas: The Role of Ideas in a Tropical Colony, 1830–1865*. New York: Atheneum.

Dante. 1965 [1899] *Paradiso*. The Temple Classics. London: J.M. Dent and Sons.

Dayton, D. 1980 The theological roots of Pentecostalism. *Pneuma*, Spring, pp. 3–21.

Eisner, G. 1960 *Jamaica 1830–1930: A Study in Economic Growth*. Manchester: Manchester University Press.

Gee, D. 1949 *The Pentecostal movement* (second edition). London: Elim Publishing Co. Ltd.

Geertz, Clifford. 1973 Religion as a cultural system. In: *The Interpretation of Cultures*. New York: Basic Books, pp. 87–125.

Gill, L. 1990 "Like a veil to cover them": women and the Pentecostal movement in La Paz. *American Ethnologist* 17:708–21.

Glazier, S., ed. 1980 *Perspectives on Pentecostalism: case studies from the Caribbean and Latin America*. Washington, DC: University Press of America.

Gordon, S. 1963 *A Century of West Indian education*. London: Longman Group Ltd.

Hart, K. 1989 *The Trespass of the Sign: Deconstruction, Theology and Philosophy*. Cambridge and New York: Cambridge University Press.

Higman, B. 1983. Domestic service in Jamaica since 1750. In *Trade Government and Society in Caribbean History. Essays presented to Douglas Hall*. London and Trinidad: Heinemann, pp. 117–38.

Hogg, D. 1964 *Jamaica Religions: A Study in Variations*. Unpublished PhD dissertation. Yale University.

Hollenweger, W. 1972 *The Pentecostals* (trans. R.A. Wilson). London: SCM Press Ltd.

Hopkin, J. 1978 Music in the Pentecostal church. *Jamaica Journal* 42:22–40.

Jayawardena, C. 1967–68 Ideology and conflict in lower class communities. *Comparative Studies in Society and History* 10:423–46.

Kapferer, B. 1979a Mind, self and other in demonic illness. *American Ethnologist* 6:110–33.

Kapferer, B. 1979b Emotion and Healing in Sinhalese Healing Rites. *Social Analysis* 1:153–76.

LaRuffa, A. 1969 Culture change and Pentecostalism in Puerto Rico. *Social and Economic Studies* 18:273–81.

LaRuffa, A. 1971 *San Cipriano: Life in a Puerto Rican Community*. New York: Gordon and Breach.

Lobdell, R. 1988 Women in the Jamaican labour force, 1881–1921. *Social and Economic Studies* 37:203–40.

Long, J. 1973 *Balm Jamaica Folk Medicine*. PhD dissertation. Department of Anthropology. University of North Carolina.

Manning, F. 1980 Pentecostalism: Christianity and reputation. In: *Perspectives in Pentecostalism* (ed., S. Glazier). Washington, DC: University Press of America, pp. 177–88.

Mbiti, J. 1969 *African Religions and Philosophy*. London: Heinemann

McKay, C. 1953 *Selected Poems of Claude McKay*. San Diego, London, New York: Harvest/HBJ Book.

Miller, E. 1990 *Jamaican Society and High Schooling*. Kingston: Institute of Social and Economic Research.

Mintz S. 1960 *Worker in the Cane*. New Haven: Yale University Press.

Moore, J. 1953 *The Religion of Jamaican Negroes: A Study of Afro-American Acculturation*. Unpublished PhD dissertation. Northwestern University.

Ricoeur, P. 1986 *Lectures on Ideology and Utopia* (ed., C.H. Taylor). New York: Columbia University Press.

Simpson, G. 1956 Jamaican revivalist cults. *Social and Economic Studies* 5:321–403.

Simpson, G. 1978 *Black Religions in the New World*. New York: Columbia University Press.

Sobo, L. 1993 *One Blood: The Jamaican Body*. Albany: State University of New York Press.

Stone, C. 1991. Rethinking development: the role of the state in third world development. In: *Rethinking Development* (ed., J. Wedderburn). Kingston: Consortium Graduate School of Social Science, pp. 87–100.

Stone, J. 1977 *The Church of God of Prophecy: history and polity*. Cleveland, TN: White Winged Publishing House.

Turner, V. 1967 *The Forest of Symbols*. Ithaca: Cornell University Press.

Walcott, D. 1974 The muse of history. In: *Is Massa Day Dead?* (ed., O. Coombs). New York: Anchor Press, Doubleday, pp. 1–12.

Weber, M. 1958 *The Protestant Ethic and the Spirit of Capitalism* (trans. T. Parsons). New York: Scribner's.

Wedenoja, W. 1978 *Religion and Adaptation in Rural Jamaica.* Unpublished PhD dissertation. University of California, San Diego.

Wedenoja, W. 1980 Modernization and the Pentecostal movement. In: *Perspectives on Pentecostalism* (ed., S. Glazier). Washington, DC: University Press of America, pp. 27–48.

Wilson, P. 1973 *Crab Antics: A Social Anthropology of English-Speaking Negro Societies in the Caribbean.* New Haven: Yale University Press.

10: ON THE "RIGHT PATH": INTERPOLATING RELIGION IN TRINIDAD

Aisha Khan

Introduction

While few cultural universals exist, belief systems concerned with inexplicable or unexpected events and involving ritual, supernatural beings or forces, cosmology, and myth seem to be characteristic of all peoples. When most of us talk about "religion," we tend to think of it as self-evident, a basic organizing principle that forms part of what makes us the culture-bearing animals that we are. Anthropologists have long been giving expert testimony on the cultural bases of behavior. Working within Western intellectual traditions, most twentieth century anthropologists have viewed religion as "a distinctive space of human practice and belief which cannot be reduced to any other" (Asad 1993:27). Approaching religion in this way implies that it has a fundamental identity and existence above and beyond specific contexts or processes, and that it is not necessarily interdependent with other dimensions of culture — such as political, economic, and so on (Ibid.:50). Contending that religion has an "autonomous essence," as an abstract *category of analysis*, encourages us to define it as "transhistorical and transcultural" (Ibid.:28) — that is, as a given that is recognizable across time and space. As one scholar recently stated it,

> Anthropologists of religion, at the very least, need to agree on what they are seeking. Once they find it they can begin to leave all definitions behind. (Stewart 1997:217)

The suggestion above, however, presumes that specific common denominators exist. Although anthropologists assume that we all recognize phenomena that are "obviously" *religious*, Talal Asad argues that a universal definition of religion is not possible because the social and cultural dimensions that religion encompasses are produced under particular conditions, and because definitions of religion are themselves historically specific to the ways in which they are conveyed (Asad 1993:29; cf. Spiro 1971; Harrison 1990). Religion is, instead, linked to social life in ways that necessarily shape its very identity and thus its usefulness as an abstract category of analysis (Asad 1993:53).[1]

When religious phenomena are approached in terms of bounded sets of beliefs and practices that precisely represent certain delimited groups of practitioners and with characteristics and parameters predetermined, we are not required to ask, "when is religion 'religion'?," or, "what makes it so?" In other words, reflection on the *constructedness* of religion as an interpretive category — what constitutes it at a certain moment in time and place — has been the exception rather than the rule. Yet the relationship between a category and the ethnographic realities it encompasses is critical to the way we come to understand the world. For labels and classifications of all kinds can overdetermine ethnographic reality, "explaining" phenomena in advance rather than elucidating them in process.

This is not at all to suggest something so dismissive as that there is no such thing as religion. Clearly the world abounds with examples of the supernatural, cosmological, ritual, and mythic. It is, however, to suggest that "religion" as an abstract category of analysis is as subject to historical and cultural invention (construction) as other such classifications — like race, ethnicity, sexuality, or gender — are currently understood to be.[2] Hence, our objective should not be merely to ask how local peoples play out familiar, somehow basic categories of experience, but how these categories, as analytical tools, might be re-visioned according to context-specific imperatives.

In this chapter I consider ideas about the configuration of the supernatural and superstition, and their relationship to religious interpretation in the Republic of Trinidad and Tobago.[3] I give particular ethnographic attention to *obeah* and *maljo*, which are in this Caribbean setting important mysterious forces. Framed in part by Asad's invitation to unpack "religion" as a reified construct, my approach is to *interpolate* religion in Trinidadian society; that is, borrowing from the dictionary definition, to insert between other things or to change by introducing new material.[4] I do this with particular focus on Indo-

Trinidadians, Trinidadians of South Asian descent ("East Indians"), whose arrival in the Caribbean followed the emancipation of enslaved Africans. In unpacking Indo-Trinidadian interpretations of religious phenomena — that is, local determinations of what can be categorized as "religion," and why — we must seek themes and patterns that emanate from the confluence of various sociocultural and historical processes; we must try dissolving familiar categorical boundaries (that delimit particular kinds of experience), thereby allowing the interpolation of diverse, and perhaps unconventional elements. Constructing interpretive categories (like religion), and allocating certain phenomena as belonging inside or outside of them, does not reflect universally recognizable realities. What appears universal is usually a matter of hegemony — where certain ways of thinking about the world are taken for granted as somehow natural and based in supposed objective fact.

Between 1838 and 1917 almost half a million people were recruited from India as indentured laborers to work the Caribbean sugar plantations in Guyana and Trinidad. During the 160 years of their settlement and incorporation into wider society, Indo-Caribbeans have undergone profound social and cultural transformations. In a population that was initially not uniform, these transformations gradually intensified social distinctions, with communities becoming more greatly stratified by class and varied in religious affiliation. Opportunities to move away from the plantation, coupled with a trend toward upward social mobility and conversion to Presbyterianism (beginning in 1868) and modifications over time to both Hinduism and Islam resulted in the contemporary profile of Indo-Trinidadians found in all sectors and walks of life in Trinidad. Thus, the elderly, whose autobiographies lie in the estate, and their formally educated, often upwardly mobile generations of descendants may comprise within one household representatives from a number of (lowest to highest) class positions, degrees of formal education, religious affiliations (Christian and non-Christian), and political loyalties. A not uncommon consequence of all this is the play of competing perspectives and interests within and among these communities, expressed through various idioms — of which religion is one.

However, these transformations also have been realized within a context of hegemonic ideas and practices of British colonial and Afro-Trinidadian postcolonial society, where Anglo-Christian "moral orders" (cf. Austin-Broos 1994) of the middle and upper classes have significantly shaped local values and expectations. In contending with Afro-Trinidadians, their nearest economic and political competitors, Indo-Trinidadians seek to be equal participants in local society without sacrificing their distinctiveness. My aim in this chapter is to offer suggestions toward understanding both the category "religion," as well as the phenomena it encompasses within a contemporary community of Indo-Trinidadians. Although increasingly put to the test in other regions of the world, these questions remain an underdeveloped area of inquiry with regard to religions in the Caribbean.

Roots and Historical Transformations

Colonized by the Spanish at the turn of the 16th century, Trinidad became imbued with the tenets of Catholicism. In this early period, native Amerindian worldviews undoubtedly had some bearing on the way Spanish Catholic religious doctrine was interpreted locally. Catholicism was reinforced, beginning in the late 1700s, by the emigration of French Caribbean planters and their slaves to Trinidad, who were responding to Spain's invitation to bolster its authority through a strengthened Catholic presence; doubtless Catholicism was also buttressed by later Portuguese and Irish settlers. Protestantism was brought with the British who had annexed Trinidad by 1802, and it exercises a profound cultural and social influence today. Other forms of Christianity, such as Greek Orthodox, came with early 20th century Syrian-Lebanese and Palestinian merchant traders (Lowenthal 1972:208). Enslaved and indentured Africans added to this religious matrix indigenous beliefs and, to a lesser extent, those of Islam, while Indian and Chinese laborers who arrived in the mid-19th century brought Asian cosmologies, notably Hinduism and a South Asian form of Islam (Khan 1995a; Samaroo 1996).

By any standard Trinidad and Tobago constitutes a complex arena of religious traditions, where the so-called "world religions" of Christianity, Hinduism, and Islam have interacted with indigenous African (and likely Amerindian) beliefs and practices. Moreover, each body of thought has its internal distinctions, and localized interpretations which derive from differences in social class, locality (region), and cultural histories. For example, just as there are many versions of

Christianity in Trinidad, Hinduism and Islam also have "orthodox," "folk," or "reform" perspectives, deriving from the subcontinent as well as from local influences. Thus, for example, while Sanatan Dharm and (Hanafi) Sunni may characterize the predominant perspective among Trinidadian Hindus and Muslims, respectively, Arya Samaj ideology has influenced the expression of Hinduism, as Ahmadiyya interpretations have for Islam.[5]

Intricate processes of creation and re-creation characterize religion in Trinidad, which observers have characterized as religious "syncretism." Describing these processes has often been the goal in the study of Caribbean religions, rather than being a point of departure, or step along the way. Contemporary Trinidadians have inherited a concept of "religion" typical of Western traditions, thanks in part to the historical domination of Christianity. Hence, it is not that Trinidadians lack this category as an organizing principle of experience; rather, it is profoundly shaped by diverse local perspectives such that it often says as much (if not more) about other dimensions of experience than what exterior views might assume to be religious. When exploring religion in Trinidad, at least three local criteria for establishing meaning are germane: distinguishing the mundane ("rational") from the fantastic, the faith-driven from superstition, the authorized or ecclesiastical from the subversive, and the moments where these distinctions are unclear. Moreover, we need to consider, rather than assume, when and why qualifying as "religion" is locally important to begin with.

In the Caribbean, the study of religions has not had a prolific or particularly varied tradition of research relative to studies of religion in other parts of the world or, for that matter, to other research foci in the Caribbean. Emphasis here has been directed largely to practices that are syncretisms of African indigenous and European Christian belief systems, and to variations of Christianity among peoples of African descent. Although attention is directed to syncretic processes, the religions involved are often treated (implicitly or otherwise) as initially discrete units that work in tandem, rather than as multi-dimensional and overlapping arenas of beliefs and practices that are mutually constitutive in different ways, depending on context. Much more recently, forms of Hinduism and Islam have come of interest to researchers. Especially, I think, in discussions of Indo-Caribbean peoples, an implicit model is often accepted as a given. Religious beliefs and practices tend to be treated as self-contained wholes that represent an ethnic group in its process of acculturation. Even when the articulation of ethnicity and religion among Indo-Caribbeans is addressed, the tendency has been to treat these as a priori entities and process is understood largely in terms of the effect that a changed social context has had on anticipated cultural practices.

If a theme prevails in the spectrum of this work, it is that religious beliefs and practices have been sought out among communities as examples of living continuities between "Old" (African, East Indian) and "New" (Caribbean, American), which have served as arenas of resistance to slavery and the forces of colonial ideology, and thus are a key means by which identities are re-created or sustained. Anthropologists and others have striven to demonstrate the vibrant re-creations and syncretisms that constitute religious traditions in the Americas. Early leads such as Smith (1976), as well as more recent work, focus on power and ideology as critical dimensions of any analysis of religion. At the same time, we have not sufficiently explored our typical use of "religion" itself as a self-evident and contained system that precisely and uniformly delimits (and predicts) specific communities, i.e.,what constitutes "religion" in this part of the world.

The "Right Path"

Among all communities in Trinidad, a concern with the interpretation of religious beliefs and practices is ubiquitous and forms a fundamental basis of Trinidadian perceptions of social reality, or worldview. Another crucial dimension of this worldview is that most Trinidadians believe they should somehow strive to conform to local conventional standards of propriety and fair play or at least develop elaborate rationalizations for why they do not. These ideal goals are commonly glossed as "living good with people." A central template, or idiom, in "living good with people" is ecclesiastical: scriptural, spiritual, and ritual guidelines that will help lead one along a path — the "right path," as many Indo-Trinidadians expressed it — of proper social interaction and reward in the afterlife. Specific religions are not at issue here, since the prevailing view is that ultimately "is all one God, anyhow." Among Indo-Trinidadians, Christianity, Hinduism, and Islam are encompassed by the broad principles of the "right path." These principles obviously assume the characteristics emphasized by their respective religions but they include temperance, fidelity, attention to carrying out ritual in the proper (authorized) ways, worshiping on a regular basis, sexual propriety, giving assistance including charity, possessing good intentions, conducting oneself ethically, not being "racial" (racist), working hard, all of which fall under the broad prescription for "living good with people," one shared by other, non-Indo Trinidadians. Of course these are ideals, and, like everywhere else, most people find difficulty living up to them. As attentive as anthropologists are to the disjunctures between ideal and real, the point here is not the extent to which people actually realize these goals. Rather, of interest here are the moral principles of the "right path" as a guide to defining and interpreting religious phenomena and, in turn, as a lens through which to view the larger (social, political, economic) concerns that inform "religion" and make it locally meaningful in various ways.

Through its moral principles the "right path" is more than a code for morality and behavior. It also acts as an implicit critique of hegemonic Afro-Trinidadian culture. Complicating these currents is the influence exercised by Afro-Trinidadians, who have been dominant in both the operation of the state apparatus and in re-defining the cultural configuration of the nation.[6] The post-independence inheritors of political power, a middle class intelligentsia of Afro-Trinidadians (along with some like-minded Indo-Trinidadian colleagues) developed a political culture where party mobilization was energized largely along racial lines, state patronage favored Afro-Trinidadian constituencies (significantly the middle class), and nationalist rhetoric that grew out of a concerted challenge to metropolitan devaluation of things Afro-Caribbean. Left out of the picture, Indo-Trinidadians have relied on strengthening group boundaries that secure them as a viable and legitimate community.

With a history of having to define themselves as distinct from and yet equal to their Afro-Trinidadian countrymen, Indo-Trinidadians find ways to navigate between the equally problematic choices of assimilation and acceptance, and absorption and marginalization. Converted Indo-Trinidadian Presbyterians formed a new middle class of educated elites, distinct from those arising from first or second generation business ventures not necessarily predicated on literacy.

Access to formal education, teacher-training, and school administration introduced Presbyterian Indo-Trinidadians to higher incomes, higher status, and first-hand knowledge of Anglo-Christian culture. In spite of this particular form of assimilation that Indo-Trinidadian Presbyterians have enjoyed, they, too, enjoin a rhetoric of the "right path" in defining authorized religious practice (as conveyed by the Presbyterian Church), and in safeguarding against being culturally engulfed by hegemonic values they see as not emanating from their own history and experience.

Although things may change under the influence of the current Indo-Trinidadian Prime Minister, for approximately a century and a half Indo-Trinidadians have attempted to strengthen their presence as a group in part by posing cultural contrasts (which get translated into ethnic boundaries) between themselves and Afro-Trinidadians. Among these contrasts, the concept of morality plays a significant role in signaling ostensibly contradictory world-views. Indo-Trinidadians see themselves, in contrast to Afro-Trinidadians, as predisposed to hard work, committed to what might be called family values, sexually restrained, and inclined to safeguard the future. The "right path" works to contest or subvert, even if obliquely, the pervasive atmosphere of Afro-Trinidadian culture. Importantly, Afro-Trinidadian hegemony is perceived by Indo-Trinidadian Hindus and Muslims as containing the values and prerogatives of a colonially constituted Christianity. The "right path," then, distinguishes the correct ("religious") means of asserting cultural identity for the necessary end of group success. Related to this, the "right path" also begs the question of the relationship between means and ends. That is, if religious goals are the same, can practices, beliefs, and behaviors diverge, or perhaps even contradict each other? How far can they deviate and still be equally defined as "religion"?

Taking Shape on Trinidadian Ground

Since their arrival in the 19th century, Indo-Trinidadians have grappled with the challenge of recreating themselves in an alien and often hostile environment — as all diaspora peoples in the Americas have done before and since. Reconstructing identity rests in part on resistance, the creative rejection of that which oppresses. For Indo-Caribbean (and Afro-Caribbean) peoples this has involved asserting and embellishing such highly charged cultural forms as religious belief and practice.[7] Religion as a site of resistance and reinvention is a slippery one because it is infinitely subject to varied and contradictory discourses, notably including competition among authorized and marginalized interpretations within a given religious tradition. Also involved are challenges as to what constitutes "religion" in the first place, and what significance these will then hold. In their culture of diaspora, Indo-Trinidadians represent various forms of Christianity, Hinduism, and Islam, and must in some way reconcile these attenuated and sometimes reinvented religious forms with a number of imposing influences. Key among these are the dominant, authorized representations espoused by orthodox clergy and canonical texts (such as the Bible, the Quran, and, to some extent, the Ramayana and the Bhagavad Gita); the multiple perspectives of local religious leadership, of late increasingly trained overseas (primarily in India and Pakistan); by educators and missionaries from abroad; and by race/class hierarchies fostered by (post-independence) Afro-Trinidadian hegemony.

Indo-Trinidadian ethnic identity, then, has formed through several vectors. One is the nature of post-independence political culture sketched above. Another is the pre-independence labor market segmentation, where sugar estate employment physically and socially marginalized them.[8] A third is the class distinctions that were gradually coalescing as independent entrepreneurship flourished, wage employment diversified, and formal education began to become more available. Dramatic upward class mobility was catalyzed by the economic boom of 1973–1982, along with the struggle to maintain it throughout the recession that followed. Finally, certain cultural forms, particularly religious, proved rich arenas of re-creation as resistance expressed through rejection of dominant values, yet also in the form of accommodation to those values.[9]

Muslim and Hindu Indo-Trinidadians secretly held prayer meetings and devotional rituals on sugar estates in defiance of European colonial administrators and settlers. They held commemorative festivals, such as Hosay (Muharram) that were suffused with oblique, and sometimes direct, challenges to the legal authorities that acted to circumscribe their lives. The most dramatic form of defiance would be in insisting on gathering en masse for these festivals, massive crowds always posing a threat to authority. Other, equally effective means of resistance were in the traditions that were maintained and re-created as reminders of an honorable past and as markers of group distinctiveness. These included, significantly, religious rituals, art forms such as songs and dances, dramas (*lilas*) in which ancient epic adventures and other cultural narratives were learned and re-learned — all in the attempt to keep alive a sense of discrete identity as well as affording solace and enrichment under oppressive conditions. Although involving to some degree all sectors of the population, historically these practices predominated among the poor and working-class Indo-Trinidadian Hindu and Muslim segments of the population engaging in diverse forms of cultural resistance.

Rituals, festivals, and other performances are common still among Indo-Trinidadians. It could be argued that today their character lies more in asserting ethnic group identity *within* the dominant discourse of Trinidadian political culture than in being peripheral to it, thereby changing the nature of resistance. Villagers and townspeople alike are keen to replicate the fundamentals of traditional practices, consulting religious verse and cultural experts at home and abroad, as well as the texts they write. But the shift from sugar estate to civil service and entrepreneurship as the defining sites of group identity, the change from British to Afro-Trinidadian political and cultural hegemony, the rise of post-independence racially based party politics, and Trinidad's place in the global economy and the international division of labor all work to foster expressions of cultural resistance that have new referents. These, in turn, change the medium if not the message. Despite accommodations to changing circumstances, rituals, festivals, and other performances remain potent arenas of identity construction.

In Trinidad religion suffuses state, civil society, and daily life. For example, irrespective of ethnicity, gender, region, or class, religious affiliation among Trinidadians is always assumed. Belonging to an arcane or unrecognized religion is less remarkable to Trinidadians than not belonging to any. Except perhaps among certain intellectual or political circles, there is no extensively developed discourse on atheism that I am aware of and emotional and philosophical commitment to God/s is a requisite for a worthy character and a successful life. However, within this broad, commonsensical understanding lie various paths (as well as degrees) of realization. Although most people assume implicitly that their own religious affiliation is the best choice, there also exists a public discourse of equality, where the adage, "is all one God, anyhow" becomes a rhetorical device that conveys tolerance and harmony — two important symbols of national definition in this self-consciously multicultural society. Moreover, Trinidadians recognize that religious belief and practice occur in broader historical and cultural contexts, and through the negotiation of social relations; hence, both worship and devotion are perceived as being subject to human frailty as well as good will. Some expressions of worship and devotion, then, are understood to be attributable to particular vested interests and linked to larger agendas, and are therefore contested. As such, they can be understood as *ideological* (Comaroff and Comaroff 1991). They may include, for example, a local Indo-Trinidadian Muslim organization's critiques of the works or operation of another, if these are perceived as being more in service of state patronage rather than the goals of Islamic theology — interpretations that are not, of course, uniform. These expressions usually will also include any suggestion of denominational superiority and inferiority, such as when Indo-Trinidadian Hindus take issue with North American evangelical denunciations of polytheism and "idol worship" — messages they can access on local television or during international proselytizing visits to the island.

In the context of everyday life, Indo-Trinidadians view certain phenomena as reflecting the beneficial forces of good/God(s), largely shaped by the canons of authorized religion — i.e., Hinduism, Islam, and Christianity. These phenomena are thereby positively glossed as being "religious." Here "religious" is comfortably linked with the spiritual, the divinely empowered. Other phenomena, what I call ethereal agents, are in a contested or ambiguous relationship to the realm of the "religious," are therefore suspect, and can be thus uncomfortably associated with illegitimate or dangerous manifestations of mystery and wonder. These agents (and the events associated with them) can be viewed as ideological, insofar as they are highly debated areas of discussion that reflect the often discordant interests of particular constituencies. While the prevailing view in Trinidad is consistent with the general idea that "religion" is transhistorical and transcultural, use of this category to identify and debate various

social and cultural phenomena speak to the way diverse local interests *construct* "religion" out of a complex mix of issues that include
class tensions, ethnic group conflict, and distinct cultural histories.
Religious phenomena constitute an idiom through which to debate
and express other than religious issues; and it is in terms of those
issues, as much as its apparently internal variations, that "religion"
comes to have multiple meanings (see, for example, Khan 1995b; cf.
Purpura 1997).

Ambiguous Distinctions

In its broadest interpretive work, the category religion in Trinidad is
informed by ambiguous distinctions between mundane/fantastic,
faith/superstition, and authorized/subversive. These locally recognized differentiations, while indefinite and shifting, are subsumed by
a broader (yet as ambiguous) distinction between natural and supernatural. The natural world is the world of the mundane, the everyday, the tangible — one that defines the normal. Included herein
might be such things as jobs and wage scales, suffrage and party
politics, kinship ties, styles of cuisine, and formal education. The
supernatural world contains phenomena that are beyond the limits
of this-worldly constraints while remaining integrally a part of them,
the extraordinary, the unexpected, or the otherwise inexplicable. Cuisine styles, for example, are not "supernatural" per se, but food is a
key vector in accomplishing goals through supernatural means. Or,
one's occupation as bank manager may be understood to entail ordinary work while at the same time whispers might suggest that the
position was secured through supernatural means. Somewhat less
equivocal, local legend recognizes a spirit, called a *soucouyant*, who
sucks blood and can lure people into dangerous situations.[10] Soucouyants are also blamed for bruises people find on themselves when
they cannot remember the injury that produced the bruise. (A more
precise description I was not able to elicit.) Not being neatly cleaved,
however, the natural and supernatural typically beg the question of
classification; even ritual itself is a routinized, sometimes daily activity, yet it has crucial other-worldly aspects.

Supernatural phenomena can be both claimed and contested as legitimate dimensions of "religion." This calls into question the determination of how "religion," as an interpretive category, is used to organize the world, how phenomena or events become identified as "religious," and what a given determination then signifies. Rather than being mutually exclusive, then, these spheres are context-specific and fluid linkages of various dimensions of power. Indeed, as I implied above, I use the dichotomy natural/supernatural advisedly since this generally "ethnocentric judgement" posits a "real" (natural) universe based in Western, "scientific" empiricism that is distinct from the allegedly "unreal" (super-natural) (Klass 1991:25).[11]

Morton Klass (1995) offers an interesting case in point, taken from his pioneering work in 1950s Chaguanas — historically an important sugar producing region of central Trinidad. During harvest time Indo-Trinidadian rice farmers attempt to ensure good future crops by commemorating the spirit of the original owner of the field — the *di* — by sacrificing a cockerel and sprinkling its blood on the ground and on a plate of flowers, biscuits, and cigarettes. To the farmers, the di is as real and as important to agricultural success as is the landlord who collects the rent which the farmers must pay to occupy the land. Yet since many landlords are absentee and farmers do not necessarily meet them in person, both di and landlord can be equally mysterious as well (1995:30).[12] For these Indo-Trinidadians, "both actions (propitiation and payment) are fully natural ones" (1995:29).

Although my distinction between natural and supernatural is appropriate here because these concepts are also referents in Trinidadian religious discourse, their unqualified use presupposes that any given individual will experience religious phenomena according to the dictates of this dichotomy. Thus, even when the duality natural/supernatural applies, it may be an unconventional distinction or a problematic one acquiring a different local knowledge and significance than otherwise anticipated. The world of the supernatural itself, therefore, is one in which the category religion is an indeterminate one, where it gets locally reified in different ways depending on the issues or interests involved, and where faith and conviction are, to a significant degree, realized contingently and idiosyncratically. The supernatural, then, encompasses both what is sacred — spiritual, ecclesiastical, recognizably legitimately linked to authorized religious discourse — basically, involving God(s) and text(s), and what is suspect — events, agents, or practices that may involve powerful forces not deriving from sacred sources and therefore straying from authorized religious discourse into the broad realm of what is locally known as "superstition."

Dubious Convictions? Superstition

In Trinidad, as in many other places, superstition refers to beliefs and practices that fall outside the dominant ideology that determines what "correct" ideas and practices should be; calling something superstitious is a gate-keeping concept, a way of reinforcing mainstream values. Yet the concept of superstition is not limited to distinguishing the rational from irrational, "true" religious knowledge from "false." While decrying ignorance it betrays fear, as well. Superstition mediates legitimate and illegitimate, but the potency, the potential danger of illicit or marginalized beliefs and practices are not necessarily in doubt, as we will see with regard to various ethereal agents below. This in turn reflects concern over the proper definition and interpretation of beliefs and practices as religion. Power is at issue here: not merely the authorizing power of canonical forces, but the power legitimated by beliefs and practices that are authorized by virtue of their being determined "religion." Superstition confers disapprobation and possible censure, as is evident, for example, in Trinidad's Festival of Sipari Mai.

An annual devotional event held on Holy Thursday and Good Friday in Siparia (southern Trinidad), this syncretic festival is associated with blessings and boons granted through a small black statue variously conceived as La Divina Pastora (the Virgin Mary) and Kali (a Hindu goddess).[13] Bridging authorized Catholic and Hindu discourse and the at times suspect mysteries of inexplicable forces, Indo-Trinidadian festival participants often feel torn between their own desire to attend and the opinions of those who see the veneration of Sipari Mai as in conflict with "orthodox" Hinduism. As one pandit (Hindu priest) was quoted, "the Hindus who go to worship the Catholic saint do so out of superstition" (*Trinidad Express* 4/1/88). This religious leader's most pronounced fear is losing Indo-Trinidadians to Christian conversion, particularly with regard to the evangelical Protestant proselytization that has been a presence to be reckoned with in the Caribbean since the mid-1970s. He also frowns upon devotion that involves slippage between the borders of sacred and suspect.

The degree of this censure varies. A person may face disapproving clergy, whose influence over village communities has been profound, or the relatively minor discomfort of personal embarrassment. For example, one afternoon, on my usual rounds of visiting my neighbors and other villagers, I stopped by the home of Leela, one of my "older head" friends.[14] In local Indo-Trinidadian parlance an "older head" is an elderly man or woman, but age here connotes wisdom and experience and is thus an implicit term of respect in referring to those who have reached the stage of having grown children. Leela was not formally educated, and, like most people of her generation in this part of Trinidad, had spent a lifetime laboring in the cane fields and, with her husband (long since deceased), raising several children. Also present that day was one of her daughters-in-law, Frannie, a young woman whose work was "staying home minding children" in this patrilocal household. As we sat talking in the hammocks strung between pillars (found in most Indo-Trinidadian open air first floors), Leela pointed to a mark she had on her thigh. She asked us what we thought it was.[15] Frannie identified it as a bruise, but Leela countered that it must be from a soucouyant; "soucouyant suck me," she affirmed.

As ethereal agents whose personae belong to the supernatural world, yet manifested in "natural" ways, invoking soucouyants usually connotes superstition. This connection, paradoxically, ousts them from the domain of "religion," and thus denies their existence, yet affirms their existence by recognizing their potential danger or harm. Rejection and affirmation of a particular interpretation or belief are often simultaneous in an individual's assessment, one perspective not necessarily ever entirely being replaced by its opposite. The superstitiousness of this "spirit" and its designation as lying outside the category "religion" — while remaining something to be reckoned with, speaks to the material and ideological transformations that different generations, and hence social classes, of Indo-Trinidadians have experienced.

Leela was born in the sugar estate barracks and had lived as a rural proletarian all her life. As a formally educated, somewhat more prosperous person growing up in a world two generations removed, Frannie's obvious unease about Leela's matter-of-fact acceptance of something suspect was telling. There have been massive changes in material conditions between the early 1900s, the time of Leela's birth, and the 1960s when Frannie was born. Moreover, the protracted influence of Christianity, along with the leverage of variously emphasized tenets espoused by local village pandits and imams,[16] has over time encouraged employing the category "religion" to interpret supernatural phenomena in increasingly exclusive ways. Superstition guards the valid from the invalid, but not strictly analogously to, say, the notion of heresy. Rather, it usually takes a more mild form among Indo-Trinidadians, essentially being a commentary on the ways they see their own historical progression from "traditional" to "modern," from "backward" to "enlightened." Because it is in this way contingent — that is, subject to community experience — the emblem of "religion" arises out of specific contexts that consciously deem it such, rather than being a bracketed set of phenomena that, as it were, travel. What is shared (for specific historical and cultural reasons) among populations of practitioners and observers alike, clearly, is the idea of what "religion" *ought* to be, as well as some recurrent patterns of what a given "religion," properly speaking, *is*. Certainly study of any diaspora must investigate shared ideas and recurrent patterns, for they are critical components of what diasporas entail. To assume compartmentalized domains of experience is to risk missing creativity, interconnections, and surprise.

Dichotomies classify phenomena. But the divisions are not necessarily definite or consistent, unlike, for example, the West's manichaen dualism between good and evil. Multiple interpretations can hinder neat classifications of phenomena as belonging to the mundane/profane, the sacred, or the suspect. Uniform or mutually exclusive meanings and explanations are thereby discouraged; the existence of alternative explanations encourage pondering how to classify and decipher potentially mysterious phenomena, as seen in the following case. My friend Nyla's eldest brother died and, after the cremation, I sat with Nyla at her home (along with several others), partly to comfort her and partly to show respect for the deceased. Nyla recounted a story to me that might have been inspired by the general atmosphere of the evening, contemplative and charged with particular awareness of the passage from this- to other-world. Late one evening in what had been the recent past, she was driving home from the weekly lecture given to surrounding communities by a visiting educator from India. Along the highway she saw, "an old Negro [Afro-Trinidadian] lady walking through the cane." When she later told this to some of her friends, they suggested she had seen, "some sort of evil spirit or jumbie [ghost]." Nyla was clearly divided as to which explanation she believed to be true. The more I pressed her to clarify her feelings, the more she seemed eager to interpret the vision in natural, this-worldly terms, as an actual person wandering about — "maybe somebody['s] senile grandmother." As her experience became more stark through verbalizing it, Nyla became self-conscious and reluctant to seem "backward" and "superstitious." The irresolution as to *how* to think something *properly* is an ever-present issue.

Although they are both a part of the world of supernatural phenomena, the relationship between *spirits* (suspect) and *spiritual* (sacred) is ongoing and fraught. When inquiring into particular religions, we need, therefore, to dismantle the diverse components glossed as "religion" and to seek the "kinds of affirmation, of meaning, [that] must be identified with practice in order for it to qualify as religion." Most people I interacted with in my field site express some ambivalence about the variety of explanations possible for perplexing phenomena. These lie between (1) authorized (acceptable or safe) solutions located either in the natural world of science and modernity or in the supernatural world's sacrality, and (2) marginalized or unauthorized (furtive or dangerous) solutions, belonging to another dimension of the supernatural world. The former is what people know they ought to believe and the latter is what they often discount with difficulty.

Dubious Convictions? Maljo and Obeah

Other examples of supernatural phenomena that I will consider here are *maljo* (*najar* in Hindi) and *obeah*. Both are theoretically the concern of all Trinidadians, regardless of religious, ethnic/racial, gender, or class identities. Maljo is the evil eye, a vector of spite, the punishment that is unintentionally transmitted by one's conscious envy or subliminal resentment of another's good fortune, large or small. A person can inadvertently *invite* maljo by showing (off) too freely the possession of something special. One can inadvertently *impart* maljo to others according to what allegedly lies behind one's gaze; that is, the feelings that are conveyed through scrutiny. Obeah refers to magical practices using mysterious (usually referred to in terms of supernatural) powers. Its association with the contested dimensions of the supernatural renders it illegitimate, as similar to soucouyants. Through the work of obeah, one can be affected both physically and/or psychologically/emotionally: respectively, that is, one can become ill or one's will can be conquered.

Resonant among Indo-Trinidadians, these two powerful forces have an uneasy relationship with authorized religion, since they can be seen as lying outside "religion" through incongruence with orthodoxy, yet they employ acceptable or legitimate means of interpretation and remediation. Hence, both carry the stigma of "superstition" while at the same time command the persuasiveness of forces that are alleged to work. Making a judgement — misconception versus a permissible component of the religious universe — is usually more a concern among middle-class and elite (including Presbyterian) Indo-Trinidadians. They are generally more formally educated, have a relatively privileged standard of living, as well as a correspondingly greater self-consciousness about contrasts between being modern and being traditional, being backward and being progressive. Their awareness has clear consequences for claims on the state in the name of equal participation and patronage, justified as these claims are by cultural and social congruence with Euro/Afro-Western worldviews. I believe that "grass-roots" people are often not as invested in conforming to particular authorized versions of religious ideologies. They tend to rely on whatever works: a person I met at the Sipari Mai Festival shrugged, "it's like going to one doctor. If he can't fix you up, you must go to a next one."

We cannot view maljo and obeah as distinctly belonging inside or outside a concept of religion. We must consider them in terms of how Trinidadian supernatural and natural worlds articulate and how supernatural phenomena are classified as part of "the right path" or as problematically deviant. If something is experienced, is it real in material terms or in mystical ones?; if the latter, is it a permissible or desirable encounter? In other words, describing the characteristics of maljo and obeah as part of the religious complex in Trinidad is a necessary project both for Trinidadians and for the external observer. But doing so should not take precedence over exploring the moral quandaries that people face. For this moral component reveals how the category religion is being socially constructed and thus what larger issues are involved. Again, if we think of religion in terms of an idiom, we can understand how religious phenomena are never for their own sake.

A significant part of what is highly charged in this social context is the occurrence of misfortune. Misfortune can be seen as being more or less of two different orders of distress, which have to do with both degree of suffering and extent of repercussions. Obeah often results in grave or profound consequences. Usually less weighty or threatening incidents, such as nausea, headache, vomiting, or anxiety come from maljo. Vulnerability here is, as far as I know, only physical/physiological. A possible indication of the difference in the order of magnitude of these two is their "cure." On the one hand, for maljo, one usually seeks out someone who can *jharray*; that is, who knows recitations from sacred texts (Quran, Gita) and who then silently repeats these over the afflicted person. Not synonymous with praying for someone, to jharray is to take away, to nullify the agent(s) of distress. Etymologically, this term may derive from the verb "*jharna.*" According to *Standard Illustrated Dictionary of the Hindi Language* (1977), jharna means "to brush, to sweep, to clean, to remove, to snatch away by force, to repeat spells for exorcising." When someone "gets jharrayed," it involves scripture; among Hindus and Muslims it may involve two or three straws from a broom, blowing onto the afflicted, or having them drink water; among Hindus alone it may involve implements such as peacock feathers. Anyone who knows the appropriate scriptures may jharray someone else; at least two people told me individuals can jharray themselves if acquainted with the texts. For more serious cases, however, a religious specialist, such as a pandit, imam, or older head will be sought.

Probably because maljo is a recognized phenomenon among all ethnic groups in Trinidad, to "get jharrayed" is a practice that benefits everyone. One afternoon, as I interviewed an imam by his mosque, an Afro-Trinidadian woman walked over to us, carrying an infant and holding a toddler by the hand. She asked if she were "in the right place" for someone "who does jharray." The imam casually directed her next door. When more is involved than scripture (which is decidedly sacred), however, the boundaries between sacred and suspect blur. One Indo-Trinidadian Muslim friend, Rashida, recounted a story from her childhood:

> When I was little I was drinking paynous [cow's first milk after the calf is born; a thick, yellow, sticky substance]...My mother boiled *so much* a man give her. And I *waited* for that. As the thing come down [was swallowed], I vomit, vomit everything out, and fever. How you explain the fever? Okay, I could get upset from eating too much. But sick, sick, diahrrea. And two days later my mother called an old man. He took three broomsticks and they were the same length. He kept jharraying and I saw, this is no joke, the sticks getting shorter and shorter. And by the time he was finished, I was good again.

In her story she refers to desire (she "waited" so eagerly), greed (she drank "so much"), and their unhappy consequences (vomiting, fever, diahrrea). Proof of their alleviation came not solely from faith in scripture, which is not visible, but from the mysterious diminishing of pieces of straw. The decrease in the length of sticks and straws was recurrently cited by friends and informants as they spoke to me of the efficacy of jharraying. Yet this proof is not congruent with the sacred, which need not be manifested visibly in order to be credited as a catalyst. A further example of this conundrum is illustrated in another friend's explanation. Parveen told me:

> Maljo...An imam could tell if it's maljo right away. They could see it on you. They could tell by your eyes, eyebrows, and eyelash. Maljo is some evil thing that you have to fight to get out. It could kill you. Everybody could get maljo. But everybody could not *give* it. Maljo could give you diahrrea, belly aches, vomiting, so upset. From small we know not to be eating anything in public, especially things like cake..., any food you *buy* [i.e., a special treat]. People could see you, people who hungry. And you don't know what could come out of that.

If maljo can kill, I asked, why do people bother with obeah? Her answer was that although not everybody is a bearer of maljo, anybody "could get some obeah down on your head. That's a sure thing.

That's why in hospitals people always carry [take along] a imam or a pandit. Something could follow you or be on you."

For obeah, the consequences are always dire. One must go to a "seer man" or religious specialist (often reported to be a pandit, rarely an imam, and never, to my knowledge, a priest or minister) who have access to esoteric knowledge and who can control the malevolent forces, conjuring or nullifying. These forces, which seem ubiquitous in their being constantly experienced by and discussed among my friends and informants, particularly the grass-roots and older heads, are an ever-present challenge to "living good with people." They are also a continual challenge to authorized religious belief and practice, and, as such, push the boundaries of "religion" as an interpretive category. The gravity of not "living good with people" sometimes makes for interpretations of causes that elide the scriptural and what some might call "superstition." This can result in grey areas that people must navigate, as they attempt to ascertain how to think about things properly, how to meet the criteria of "religion." For example, *djinns*, spirits that can assume animal or human form and exercise supernatural influence over people, are discussed in the Quran and are a legitimate part of Islamic theology. They can, as well, be associated with a larger matrix of supernatural forces. Sajida, a devout Muslim, said:

> Me personally, I believe in it. There are good and bad djins. What I know is hearsay, I never get involved in this djin affairs, thank God. But some people might tend to want to lead a good life, doing the right thing and being religious,...through this they're prospering. Other people might be jealous of that person, so they get into this act of putting a djin on you...They would put this djin to destroy what you have, to make you crazy...I believe, and Hindus believe in this thing [too]. All religions believe in this, but they'll call them different names, like obeah. But what is obeah, really?

Serious but less frightening consequences of obeah, and not to my knowledge associated with the work of djins, is marital infidelity, which is quite common, and the stress and conflicts that accompany it. For example, twenty-five years after the fact, an acquaintance recalled vividly "a family" [relative] who went "in 1964" to a seer man to ascertain the cause of troubles with next door neighbors.

The seer man revealed that the "comess" (conflict, trouble, confusion) this man was experiencing was linked to cuckoldry (perhaps
his own; this part of the story was left vague), explaining that the
neighbors "had worked obeah" on him and his family, "put[ting]
graveyard dirt and many other things in a buried heap" under the
outside stairs. I asked why no obeah was, in turn, worked on those
neighbors and was informed solemnly, "that is evil, God would
punish." In another case of infidelity I was told, a photograph of the
husband was taken by his wife to a pandit, who pronounced that the
"other woman used obeah, or something." The pandit added that he
could not undo it, as he "had not the powers." What he meant here
was not that he was ineffectual or insufficiently knowledgeable, but
that he did not involve himself with those particular kinds of (suspect) forces. The friend telling me this story assured me that she
doesn't "believe in it [obeah] but people say it happen." Her comment illustrates the different levels of meaning that obeah carries, at
least for many persons concerned with being pious. To *practice* obeah
is to engage, more or less, in evil. To *believe* in it seems a logical
assessment of empirical reality: obeah has the power of efficacy (it
causes intended things to happen); it can be offset by the stronger
(sacred) power of God/s; few admit to "working it" but most
"know" that it has been done.

Toward Conclusions

The necessary presence of the sacred (the positive, the constructive),
in supernatural discourse derives from at least two factors. As I
stated earlier, the entire fabric of Trinidadian society is imbued with
the importance of religion, with the Almighty/deities, prayer, ritual,
and faith. A second factor is that some disjunctures and fissures in
social relations are seen to reflect, in part, social inequalities that have
given rise to differences in position and prestige. Getting maljo from
eating a piece of cake in front of those who do not have any and
therefore may be envious, or a day-long headache caused by someone's admiration of your new piece of clothing, are not the most
forceful critiques of class differences. However, as meaningful events

in daily life they are examples of the myriad ways in which hierarchical distinctions within the community are managed. Furthermore, an error allegedly caused on the job due to envy, or the collapse of a new addition to a home before construction is complete because surreptitious actions invited calamity, may well be oblique critiques of social inequality. These usually are explained or rationalized in a way that should not further cause disjunctures and fissures. Class-based or "racial" social critique are therefore considered to be in the realm of "politics" and thus usually too highly charged to be directly addressed. Moreover, the interpretation of inequality is complicated because people may value and believe the ideology of achieved status and an "open" system while simultaneously resenting visible evidence of differences in achievement. A neutral and hence more effective means of explanation or justification is to employ ethereal agents. These agents or forces, whose precise agency remains unspecified as far as I know, inhere in the literal and figurative atmosphere of the community.

The quality of the spiritual, which includes people's basic ideas about their place in the world, is both defined and made compelling through broader mechanisms (sometimes symbolically glossed as the "right path") and motivations often a consequence of the pressures of cultural hegemony and cultural resistance.

Significant ideological tension inheres in the proximity of the sacred and the suspect within the supernatural world. Deciding what is sacred or, indeed, if degrees of sacrality within the religious universe are possible, contributes significantly to determining what is appropriately religious, what is merely and regrettably superstition, and thus what will prevail as the terms of religious discourse are debated and as the meaning of advancing along the "right path" is reinforced.

As what can lead away from the "right path," superstition, maljo, and obeah not only beg the question of what religion is, but also point to the array of issues and perceptions that go into determining what religion is good for. Obeah and maljo go beyond their conventional "religious" boundaries to reference, straightforwardly or roundabout, a wider arena of relationships (generational, class, ethnic), whereby religious beliefs and practices and other dimensions of everyday life mutually define each other rather than where a predetermined, unified whole — a religion — is played out in particular sites.

Power is always an integral dimension of religion. One way is through the distinction made, at least in the Western tradition, between the material and the mystical, the kind of relationship natural and supernatural forces are perceived to have with each other. Another way is through the debates about which interpretation of a given religion is correct, legitimate, or superior. A third way power is an integral dimension of religion is evident through disputation about what kinds of forces (natural, supernatural) can be determined religious at all, which in turn has implications for the way we understand social and cultural phenomena. For imagining a priori that certain forces, events, and beliefs are firmly rooted in the category of "religion" actually reflects assumptions about the character of religious phenomena as these are constructed out of power relations. At work is an "authorization process by which 'religion' is created" (Asad 1993:36–37).

More instructive is to think in terms of composition rather than in terms of character, to think of "religion" as a set of processes which include spiritual and supernatural ideas that suffuse human interaction, but also as particular expressions of power relations that involve certain meanings associated with specific practices that are variously interpreted as "religion" — for locally determined reasons. This allows us to approach "religion" as contingent — intimately and always linked to specific expressions of power and ideology. In a recent article, the biologist Richard Lewontin (1997) comments on the tension between modern and mystical explanations in contemporary Western societies. Locating this relationship within the history of conflict between "elite culture" and "popular culture" (1997:31), he astutely points out that it is not the truth that makes us free, it is possessing the power to discover the truth (1997:32). To put it another way congruent with this chapter, rather than remaining an essentialized and reified analytical category, religion can be viewed as, most basically, certain socially compelling combinations of worldviews, beliefs, moral values, and consciousness that work together according to particular cultural histories, social contexts, and vested interests. As Asad underscores, the force of these compelling combinations is distributed differently, has more than one impetus, and reflects diverse actors, social institutions, and bases of legitimate (authorized) knowledge (Asad 1993:29).

Interpolating religion, as I have suggested, requires us to unpack our categorical premises, where an otherwise reified construct might cloud the ways religious phenomena are defined and interpreted, and thus obscure their relationship with other domains of experience. Whether or not certain phenomena belong to the realm of the religious, these phenomena become registers of other domains of experience — notably the contests of power in which communities engage. This perspective enables us to pursue such questions as: what are the specific component dimensions that inform religion? How do certain ideas, highly charged by relations of power, become legitimated or decried; what is the basis of their acceptance as "religion"? When are socially compelling modes of thought "religion," when are they not "religion," and what significance does this distinction have for the way we understand the cultural histories and local experience among Caribbean peoples? In this way we may avoid overlooking (1) the character of the interface between natural and supernatural, (2) the new and perhaps idiosyncratic meanings that authorized religious doctrines take on in local contexts, and therefore the particular challenges these doctrines contend with, and (3) the unanticipated sources or interpretations that may point to more compelling explanations. The "right path," examined through the lens of interpolated religion, signals a complex underpinning of ethnic group identity, class stratification, generational perspectives, and cultural politics that are not contained within nor can be fully explained by universal or autonomous models of religion, in the Caribbean or elsewhere.

Endnotes

I am grateful to Allyson Purpura for her consistently invaluable suggestions. I also wish to thank Gerald Creed, John Pulis, and the volume's anonymous reviewers for their comments. Field research was supported by grants from Fulbright, the Sigma Xi Society, and the Wenner-Gren Foundation for Anthropological Research.

1. van der Veer (1996) suggests that while religious authority reflects local contentions, religion is not "simply a black box in which everything can be put according to the interests of the principal actors in a political arena. Religion is not an infinitely plastic resource for pursuing political ends" (1996:132). While I agree with van der Veer that religion is not "infinitely plastic," my premise here is that it is more protean, receptive, and mercurial than he might allow.

2. There are various kinds of social constructionist approaches in the ethnographic study of religion. See, among other examples, Scott (1994), Fernandez Olmos and Paravisini-Gebert, eds. (1997), Bowen (1993), and Christian (1989).

3. The fieldwork on which this chapter is based was conducted in Trinidad from 1987 to 1989, and again in 1992, 1995, 1996, and 1997. Quotations from the informants cited here occurred within this time frame and location. While I did not engage in fieldwork in Tobago, my discussion is relevant to both islands.

4. *American Heritage Dictionary of the English Language*, 1973, William Morris, ed., p. 685.

5. Arya Samaj and Ahmadiyya are reformist movements arising in 19th century India that called for fundamental changes in doctrine or practice of Hinduism and Islam, respectively.

6. In 1995 an Indo-Trinidadian Prime Minister, Basdeo Panday, was elected for the first time in Trinidad's history. His party, the United National Congress (UNC), is openly aligned with Indo-Trinidadian concerns, though not to the exclusion of Afro-Trinidadian interests. This election notwithstanding, the post-independence history of Trinidad and Tobago has been one where political and national culture have primarily represented Afro-Trinidadians. See, for example, Stuempfle 1995; Ryan 1972.

7. Interestingly, it is not clear if this is the case for the thousands of Chinese immigrants who in the 19th century traveled to such destinations as Trinidad, Cuba, and Guyana to work as indentured and free labor. Not enough work has been done on the cultural histories of this diaspora, and although we know that certain traditions were kept alive, the historical role of religious belief and practice among Chinese immigrants is less familiar than among Indo-Caribbean and Afro-Caribbean peoples.

8. Their indenture experience is commonly described as "isolating" them from the wider society. I would argue, however, that margin-

ality and isolation are two different things, and that Indo-Trinidadians were discouraged in their mainstream participation but never completely separated from it.

9. Indo-Trinidadian ethnic group identity is also presently reinforced by the recent expansion of the market for Indo-Caribbean music (especially "chutney"), a form of popular media increasingly interregional and international in its scope.

10. In his Caribbean travel memoir, John Vandercook gives one version of soucouyants, who "are most to be dreaded. A Soucouyan [sic] takes off his skin between midnight and the dawn and hiding it under a mortar, flies off as a ball of fire, and enters rooms through keyholes or under doors to suck fresh blood from the heart of a sleeping victim.... Certain very old women with red eyes are Soucouyans" (1938:275–76).

11. In trying to reconstruct "emic" and "etic" levels of analysis, Stewart (1997) suggests that, "[p]erhaps we can accept 'natural versus supernatural' as an etic fact that may then be construed in numerous different ways at the emic level of cultural subjectivity" (1997:217). But this still presupposes that there is a shared conceptualization of "religion"/religious phenomena, and/or that the etic construct will be the frame that directs discussion and analysis.

12. See also Karen McCarthy Brown's (1991) *Mama Lola: A Vodou Priestess in Brooklyn*, for a particularly successful ethnographic example of the way natural and supernatural domains (relationships among mortal devotees and Vodou spirits) can be distinguished without being separated.

13. Tothill (1939:238–39) refers to other "Black Virgins" in Trinidad. Historically and present day, however, La Divina Pastora of Siparia is most important.

14. This name is a pseudonym, as are all other names except those of public figures.

15. I should note that most of the people quoted here are women, as indicated by their (pseudo-) names. This should be seen as a consequence of my having far greater contact with women than men throughout my field work, rather than being an indication that these issues are of less relevance to men.

16. Hindu and Muslim religious leaders, respectively.

References

Asad, Talal 1993 *Genealogies of Religion*. Baltimore: Johns Hopkins University Press.

Austin-Broos, Diane 1994 Redefining the moral order: interpretations of Christianity in postemancipation Jamaica. In: *The Meaning of Freedom: Economics, Politics, and Culture After Slavery* (eds., F. McGlynn and S. Drescher). Pittsburgh: University of Pittsburgh Press, pp. 221–242.

Bowen, John 1993 *Muslims Through Discourse*. Princeton: Princeton University Press.

Christian, William 1989 *Person and God in a Spanish Village*. Princeton: Princeton University Press.

Comaroff, Jean and Comaroff, John 1991 *Of Revelation and Revolution: Christianity, Colonialism, and Consciousness in South Africa*, Vol. 1. Chicago: University of Chicago Press.

Fernandez Olmos, M. and Paravisini-Gebert, L., eds. 1997 *Sacred Possessions: Vodou, Santeria, Obeah, and the Caribbean*. New Brunswick, NJ: Rutgers University Press.

Harrison, Peter 1990 *"Religion" and the Religions in the English Enlightenment*. Cambridge: Cambridge University Press.

Khan, Aisha 1995a Homeland, motherland: authenticity, legitimacy, and ideologies of place among Muslims in Trinidad. In: *Nation and Migration: The Politics of Space in the South Asian Diaspora* (ed., P. van der Veer). Philadelphia: University of Pennsylvania Press, pp. 93–131.

Khan, Aisha 1995b *Purity, Piety, and Power: Culture and Identity among Muslims and Hindus in Trinidad*. PhD dissertation, City University of New York.

Klass, Morton 1995 *Ordered Universes: Approaches to the Anthropology of Religion*. Boulder, CO: Westview Press.

Lewontin, Richard 1997 [January 9] Billions and billions of demons. *New York Review of Books* 44:28–32.

Lowenthal, David 1972 *West Indian Societies*. New York: Oxford University Press.

McCarthy Brown, Karen 1991 *Mama Lola: A Vodou Priestess in Brooklyn*. Berkeley: University of California Press.

Purpura, Allyson 1997 *Knowledge and Agency: The Social Relations of Islamic Expertise in Zanzibar Town*. PhD dissertation, City University of New York.

Ryan, Selwyn 1972 *Race and Nationalism in Trinidad and Tobago*. Toronto: Toronto University Press.

Samaroo, Brinsley 1996 Early African and East Indian Muslims in Trinidad and Tobago. In: *Across the Dark Waters: Ethnicity and Indian Identity in the Caribbean* (eds., D. Dabydeen and B. Samaroo) London: Macmillan, pp. 201–212.

Scott, David 1994 *Formations of Ritual*. Minneapolis: University of Minnesota Press.

Smith, Raymond T. 1976 Religion in the formation of West Indian society: Guyana and Jamaica. In: *The African Diaspora* (eds., M. Kilson and R. Rotberg) Cambridge: Harvard University Press, pp. 312–341.

Spiro, Melford 1971 Religion: problems of definition and explanation. In: *Anthropological Approaches to the Study of Religion* (ed., M. Banton) ASA Monograph no. 3. London: Tavistock, pp. 85–126.

Stewart, Charles 1997 [Review of the book *Ordered Universes*]. *American Ethnologist* 24:217–218.

Stuempfle, Stephen 1995 *The Steelband Movement*. Philadelphia: University of Pennsylvania Press.

Tothill, Vincent 1939 *Doctor's Office*. London and Glasgow: Blackie and Sons Limited.

Vandercook, John W. 1938 *Caribbee Cruise*. New York: Reynal & Hitchcock.

van der Veer, Peter 1996 Authenticity and authority in Surinamese Hindu ritual. In: *Across the Dark Waters: Ethnicity and Indian Identity in the Caribbean* (eds., D. Dabydeen and B. Samaroo). London: Macmillan, pp. 131–146.

11: THE NOISE OF ASTONISHMENT: SPIRITUAL BAPTIST MUSIC IN CONTEXT

Stephen D. Glazier

Introduction: The Context of Musical Innovation

> It was my trumpet; and I knew the keys. If I were afraid
> to blow it, whom could I expect to do it for me? So I made
> a heaven of noise which is characteristic of my voice and
> an ingredient of West Indian behavior. The result was an
> impression of authority
>
> George Lamming, *The Pleasures of Exile*

As Lamming (1960:62–63) so astutely points out, noise can be bitter;
noise can be sweet; noise may appear chaotic, but — at the same time
— can be manipulated to bring about an impression of authority. To
be fully understood, Spiritual Baptist music — like every aspect of
West Indian culture — must be examined both as characteristic of the
West Indian voice and a rich and vital ingredient of West Indian
behavior.

The Spiritual Baptists are an international religious movement
with congregations in the West Indies, Venezuela, Toronto (Canada),
Los Angeles, and New York City. Membership is predominantly
working class African-Americans, but the faith has attracted a sizeable number of East Indians, Chinese, and Whites. All of the above
ethnic groups have had a profound impact on Spiritual Baptist music.
In "The Caribbean as a Musical Region" (1988), Kenneth Bilby characterized Spiritual Baptist music as a product of large scale nineteenth
century Protestant missionary activity, but also noted that Spiritual
Baptist music is not — as is sometimes stated — simply a matter of
Protestant hymns being sung to an "African beat."

A major complicating factor is that most nineteenth century Spiritual Baptists could not read music, and melodies had to be improvised or borrowed from selected bits and pieces of music that participants had heard elsewhere. This opened the way for rampant innovation and improvisation. Sources of innovation included: European-based churches (such as Catholics, the London Baptists, and Presbyterians), other religious traditions (such as Rada and Shango), and immigrant groups (such as the East Indians, Syrians, Portuguese, French Creoles, and Chinese).

A difficulty with competing claims concerning the "origins" of Spiritual Baptist music is much the same as Manuel, Bilby and Largey (1995:157) encountered in their search for the "sources" of Jamaican popular music. It is virtually impossible to prove or disprove competing claims since all presume a simple, linear path of development from a single source. Such is never the case. Caribbean music has evolved in a considerably more disorderly manner and has always been more stylistically heterogeneous and complex than such a view would suggest. It is not the case that competing claims concerning the alleged "origins" of Spiritual Baptist music are necessarily invalid, but that *all* origins could be said to have some validity.

This paper attempts to isolate bits and pieces from diverse musical traditions (Asian, African, and European) embedded within the Spiritual Baptist musical repertoire, with attention to the creation of a distinctive and constantly changing musical form which has influenced and continues to influence other Caribbean musical forms such as Trinidadian calypso and *Soca*.

Membership in the Spiritual Baptist church has been remarkably stable. Over the past twenty years membership in Trinidad has grown from about ten thousand in 1976 to twelve thousand. The largest membership increase has been among churches in the United States and Canada. For example, St. Peter's Spiritual Baptist Church in Brooklyn claims to have over 2,000 members and is said to be the largest single Spiritual Baptist congregation in the world. There are also a number of large Canadian churches; for example, Mt. Zion Spiritual Baptist Church outside Toronto claims to have over twelve hundred members. Actual membership in these churches is difficult to substantiate.

Most studies of Spiritual Baptist music have focused on churches in Trinidad. A number of field recordings have been made of religious services in Venezuela, St. Vincent, Guyana, and New York City, but these are in private collections. Few field recordings from other places have been archived nor are they available commercially. For this reason, this essay concentrates on the island of Trinidad. Much of what can be said of Spiritual Baptist music in Trinidad also holds for Spiritual Baptist music in the United States, South America, and Canada but holds to a lesser degree for music in Grenada, St. Vincent, and Tobago where churches are much more conservative and make fewer provisions for musical innovation. My field recordings of Spiritual Baptist music from St. Vincent in the 1980s are almost identical to recordings made in Trinidad by George Eaton Simpson thirty years earlier.

The Origins of Spiritual Baptist Music

As noted previously, Kenneth Bilby in his "The Caribbean as a Musical Region" (1988), characterized Spiritual Baptist music as a product of large-scale Protestant missionizing in the Anglophone Caribbean during the mid-nineteenth century. He correctly pointed out that such large-scale missionary activity took place relatively late when compared to French and Spanish islands such as Haiti and Cuba, and that missionization gave rise to a large number of independent African-Protestant sects in the British West Indies; notably: Revival Zion, Convince, and *pocomania* (*pukkumina*) in Jamaica, the Tieheads of Barbados, the Jordanites of Guyana, and the Spiritual Baptists in Trinidad, Grenada, and St. Vincent.

Spiritual Baptist music, Bilby argues, blends Protestant devotional songs and polyrhythmic clapping, banging of pews, and forceful stomping (sometimes called "adoption" or "hocketing") to create a unique musical form which has influenced and continues to influence other Caribbean music. For example, calypsonian David Rudder grew up in the Belmont section of Port of Spain and was thrice-baptized (Anglican, Spiritual Baptist, and Roman Catholic) as well as attending *Orisha* ceremonies (Rudder, 1990; see Houk, 1995). In 1986, Rudder won the Calypso Monarch Competition with two songs "The Hammer" (with its obvious Baptist and *Orisha* lyrics) and "Bahia Gyal" (which features Spiritual Baptist "adoption," "hocketing," and "trumpeting" and even mentions the Spiritual Baptists by name). The

Spiritual Baptists were also the focus of calypsonian Austin Lyons' (a.k.a. *Blue Boy's*) winning "Soca Baptist" (1980), but while Lyons's treatment of the faith was clearly derisive ("What to them suppose to be spiritual, to me, it was just like bacchanal"), David Rudder's "Bahia Gyal" cites the Baptists as the embodiment of a Pan-African spirit, emphasizing similarities between Baptist trumpeting and Brazilian *Somba* rhythms.

Kevin Birth (1994:173) reports that the single most popular calypso of the 1991 Carnival season — which followed an unsuccessful coup attempt led by Imam Yasin Abu Bakr and the Jamaat al-Muslimeen organization — was "Get Something and Wave" which prominently featured Mother Muriel, a fictional leader in the Spiritual Baptist church. The calypso's hook line "ding-a-ling-a-ling" was associated with Mother Muriel's bell and, by implication, with all Spiritual Baptist bells and visions obtained in the mourning room (Glazier, 1985:141–156).

Despite the absence of a trained clergy, theological seminaries, an established church hierarchy, and formal written creeds, Spiritual Baptist theology is remarkably uniform and exhibits many of the traits associated with worldwide, highly organized religious movements. This uniformity is all the more remarkable since Spiritual Baptist theology is not the privileged domain of a religious elite, but is carried out publicly within the context of religious ceremonies. Spiritual Baptist theology is embedded in Spiritual Baptist ritual. It is formulated in the midst of worship; in sermons, dance, prayer, and — most notably — in music.

Like ritual everywhere, Spiritual Baptist ritual formulates problems and fashions solutions to those problems. In the words of Sherry B. Ortner (1978:9), "the reshaping of consciousness or experience that takes place in ritual is by definition a reorganization of the *relationship* between the subject and what may be for convenience be called reality which ... emerges from a certain experience of self." Spiritual Baptist ritual and music simultaneously transform the participant's sense of self; his/her relationship with co-religionists; his/her relationship to the larger society; and his/her relationship with the spirits.

Music has been one of the most persistent forces for the perpetuation and transmission of African American and Afro-Caribbean culture (Courlander, 1963:35–79; Behague, 1994; Floyd, 1993). Malm (1983) suggested that over ninety percent of Spiritual Baptist ceremonies are taken up by music — most of it singing. This is a conservative estimate since it fails to take into account the considerable overlap of sermons, rituals, and music. My observations (Glazier, 1980, 1991) indicate that there is seldom a period in Spiritual Baptist ritual when no one is singing and/or clapping. Sometimes music is in the background — as when the paramount leader presents his sermon — but it is always there.

Spiritual Baptist Aesthetics

While segments of Baptist music might initially appear to be derived mainly from nineteenth century Protestantism and African rhythms, Baptist ceremonies need to be analyzed in their own terms. They follow their own rules and aesthetic principles which only the initiated can fully appreciate. It is only after nearly twenty years of fieldwork that I am able to guess correctly whether I have attended a "sweet" (aesthetically pleasing) service or a "reverent" (dull, less pleasing) service. Since so much aesthetic appreciation ultimately relates to the social context, one really has to "be there" in order to make an assessment. So-called "sweet" services have many of the attributes of George Lamming's (1960:62) observations of "noise." The "noise" of a sweet service gives expression to life's problems and enables one to better cope with them. Since it is impossible to judge Spiritual Baptist music outside worship, there is need to pay constant attention to the social dimensions of musical performances. Sociologically and politically, individual Baptists successfully utilize music in order to validate their own spiritual authority and their respective positions within the church hierarchy.

Baptist attitudes toward music and musical performance might best be described as pragmatic. Music is said to have many uses. It can dispel unwanted spirits, set a mood, and mark ritual phases (Williams, 1985:63–64). For example, "Lead Us Heavenly Father Lead Us" is common in processionals, "Nearer My God to Thee" is commonly sung while placing "bands" over the eyes of a "pilgrim," and "When the Saints Go Marching In" usually signifies a return from baptism. Different churches might use different hymns at different times, but once a hymn has been established it tends to be used regularly over a period of many years. While music serves to demonstrate and document patterns of authority within a church (Glazier, 1991), it also serves to "guide" candidates for baptism, offer supplication, and invoke the presence of the Holy Spirit. There is considerable disagreement within churches as to how and when a particular hymn should be sung. Most hymns can be sung in a variety of ways (e.g., slow or fast; allowing or not allowing for improvisations). Inasmuch as hymns are regarded as "tools," certain hymns are selected because they are thought to work better than other hymns in a particular context. Aesthetics is a secondary consideration.

Sometimes hymns provide veiled messages to congregants. Other times, messages are more blatant. Williams (1985:109) cites an example of a pilgrim who had a reputation for moving from church to church. His spiritual mother admonished him by raising up the hymn "I Was a Wandering Sheep."

Williams (1985:55) follows Herskovits (1939), Simpson (1961), and Glazier (1980) by classifying Spiritual Baptist music into four basic categories: 1) hymns, 2) "Sankeys" 3) trumpeting, and 4) intoned prayers. Hymns, Williams contends, are mostly taken from the Anglican *Book of Common Prayer*. Although the melodies of such hymns are often the same as those sung by Anglicans, the style of performance almost always differs among Baptists. Sankeys are hymns found in the books compiled by I.D. Sankey (1874). In the performance of Sankeys, there is much rhythmic accompaniment provided by hands and feet. Trumpets are short musical phrases which may or may not have texts. These may be introduced during a prayer, or to induce altered states of consciousness. Intoned payers may include hymns, Sankeys, and trumpets and may assume the form of a chant.

There is much variation in the actual performance of Spiritual Baptist music, but Williams's description remains by-and-large useful. According to Williams (1985:58–61), hymns are performed in a simple meter 2/2, 3/2, 4/4. Songs begin on one of the notes of the I (tonic triad) and end on the tonic. Antiphony is evident together with little ornamentation, and rendition of texts is mostly melismatic. Sankeys are performed in 4/4 meter with stress on the first and third beats. Harmony is sporadic. Trumpets are performed in 4/4 meter. Harmony is not evident, but voices perform different parts with constant repetition in a call–response pattern. There is much improvisation and each performance is dependent on the creativity and virtuosity of the members present. No trumpet performance is ever exactly the same, but there are notable regularities which have yet to be adequately explored. In my research, for example, I have isolated four distinct trumpet tones which correspond to different sequences of worship as well as regional differences. An important characteristic of trumpeting is the production of inhaled and exhaled notes to induce hyperventilation. Intoned prayers are performed slowly with little evidence of set tempo/meter. A major characteristic are call/response, overlapping repetition of words, and harmony based on the I and V chords. Intoned prayers start with the supplicant's hymn and end with recitation of the Apostle's Creed or a selected psalm. Psalm 23 is the most common.

Spiritual Baptist services do not simply consist of eighteenth and nineteenth century Protestant hymns being sung to an "African beat." Little of eighteenth century hymnology as characterized by Arnold (1991) can be identified in contemporary Spiritual Baptist music, and while nineteenth century hymns are more recognizable, they too have undergone considerable modification. Surprisingly few National Baptist hymns from the United States (Spencer, 1992:74–97) have been identified in Trinidadian services. British hymns are more prominent, although many of these hymns came to Trinidad indirectly. Select hymns by Issac Watts enjoyed considerable favor among slaves in South Carolina (Dargan, 1995:29–73) as well as among their ancestors who settled Trinidad's "company villages" in the early nineteenth century (McDaniel, 1994:119–143).

Melville and Frances Herskovits (1947) were among the first to note that opening Baptist hymns are subdued, and give forth a "heavy, doleful, dragging effect" which gradually give way to more lively hymns and intense rhythmic clapping.[1] The late Walter Pitts (1993:103) articulated this dynamic in terms of competing African-American aesthetic principles which he labelled "worship" and "service." Both aesthetic principles, he contended, were felt to be necessary components of religious ceremonies and both "worship" and "service" are highly valued in West Indian religions.

Pitts's distinction between "worship" and "service" closely parallels Peter J. Wilson's (1969:70–84) dichotomization of West Indian value-structures centering on "respectability" and "reputation" and also roughly corresponds to Karl Reisman's (1970) linguistic opposition of English standards of "decorum" and Creole argument or "noise" and Martha Ellen Davis's (1994) arguments concerning Caribbean "bi-musicality."

Wilson, however, concluded that in most cases the desire for "reputation" ultimately succumbs and is replaced by a desire for "respectability" (see Abrahams, 1979:448–453), while Reisman (1970:141) concluded that Creole noise is usually the dominant form. "Noise," for Reisman, provides an authentic expression of the West Indian spirit. He emphasizes that Caribbean people "take great joy in making noise." Reisman's assertions do not necessarily contradict Pitts's observations. Among Pitts's major contributions to the study of Caribbean and African-American ritual is his astute recognition that "worship" and "service" are both highly valued, but at different times and different places during ceremonies.

As noted previously, many Spiritual Baptist hymns would scarcely be recognizable to the American and British missionaries who originally brought these hymns to the Caribbean. The hymnals available to Baptists (primarily published by Sankey) provided only the lyrics. This was of minor consequence to converts since most nineteenth century Spiritual Baptists could not read music. Melodies had to be improvised — and as was common in African American religious traditions throughout the Caribbean and North America — were borrowed from selected bits and pieces of music that the Baptists had heard elsewhere. Moreover, the lyrics too had to be improvised since many early Baptists were also illiterate. Even today, the average member of a Spiritual Baptist congregation does not make use of a hymnal. Hymns are learned by repetition in much the same way members learns to follow the general order of worship and to interpret cues used during ritual performances.

Despite the prevalence of innovation and a stated lack of concern for preserving Anglican and American missionary hymns intact, Spiritual Baptists sometimes managed to preserve a high degree of fidelity to the original hymns. In 1984 — while sharing a field recording of Spiritual Baptist music with an intern at the Old Sturbridge Village Museum in Massachusetts — we uncovered several *stanzas* of an Anglican hymn which probably had not been sung for over 150 years. After consulting a mid-nineteenth century hymnal, we found the Spiritual Baptist rendition of this hymn to be "authentic" in all respects. A visit to the Newberry Library in 1985 uncovered additional evidence for "lost hymns" that are commonly sung during Baptist services. Thus, Spiritual Baptist music may provide an unanticipated treasure trove of lost musical forms: American, British, and (perhaps) African as well.

"Battles of the Spirit"

The way in which Baptist services are structured allows each participant to act as his/her own conductor, chorus member, and innovator. In theory, any member — under the influence of the Holy Spirit — could "raise up" any hymn at any time. But hymns are far from random. In fact, Spiritual Baptist services are extremely regular. While each church has a paramount leader who often owns the church building outright and is ultimately responsible for all aspects of worship, there is a great deal of turn-taking and leadership shifts constantly throughout the two-to-three hour service. Baptists state that they value full participation by all congregants, and that any attempt to direct an entire service would detract rather than enhance a paramount leader's authority and reputation. Nevertheless, such "battles of the spirit" do occur; especially among senior leaders and within established churches (Glazier, 1991). After service is well underway, it is permissible — but not desirable — for individual participants to attempt to "spontaneously" lead the congregation in a particular hymn. Often, two or more church members will lead different hymns at the same time. This is precisely the case in an unusually chaotic cut entitled "A Shout" on my album (Glazier, 1980) in which six different hymns begin simultaneously. Whichever hymn predominates is believed to reflect the will of God the Holy Spirit; and thus, the individual who initiated that hymn is thought to be closer and more "in tune" with God's will. It is common for dissident church members to try lead the congregation astray from a paramount leader's hymn choice. This is taken as a challenge to that leader's authority within his own church. A series of successful challenges could indicate a paramount leader's weakening position and could result in the selection of a new pastor. Hymn selection, therefore, is serious in its consequences and provides a means of pitting one's spiritual powers against the spiritual powers of one's co-religionists. Such "battles" are evident in other Trinidadian musical performances (e.g., calypso and *soca* — see Elder, 1964 and Warner, 1982).

Music is never evaluated alone. As noted, it is strongly embedded within the context of religious ceremony. Members do not distinguish the religious from the aesthetic, and see music as central to all religious expression. It is of interest that Spiritual Baptists evaluate Presbyterian, Pentecostal, and Catholic services by many of the same standards as they judge their own services.

Spiritual Baptist music is performative. Hymns have power in and of themselves. In making my album "Spiritual Baptist Music from Trinidad" (1980), a common rationale that Baptist leaders gave for allowing me to record their services is that when others hear the music they are likely to be converted to the Baptist faith. On the other hand, many also recognized that it was unlikely for anyone to be converted without fully participating in service. It is therefore possible but not probable that one could be converted on the basis of music alone.

Like much African-American music, there is no rigid division of audience into active performers and passive listeners. There is need to focus on what Kevin Birth (1994:175) has termed "the agency of participants." Performers and audience "become one" in the production of a unique musical event. Baptists hope that each member has at least a brief opportunity to perform and that each member takes time to listen to others' performances. If a service is to be deemed a success, everyone must have participated (including guests and the visiting anthropologist). It is not simply a matter of virtuosity, but total involvement by all members that makes for a "sweet" (outstanding) ceremony. The quality of interaction between participants is a major concern and is often discussed for several weeks following a service.

It is of great interest that despite differences in musical ability, Baptists do not openly criticize one another's singing; for example, several members of the Curepe church are tone deaf, but I have yet to hear disparaging remarks concerning their singing. This is out of character for the Baptists who criticize one another's performances in most other areas of church life: sermons. selection of scripture readings, performance of rituals, and so on. Baptist leaders, of course, are acutely aware that some members sing off key, but, in the words of one leader, "God speaks in many voices. Some voices are sweet and some are bitter." I have observed that Baptists deal with "bitter" voices by attempting to drown them out.

Although Spiritual Baptists focus on collectivity and cooperation, there is an equally strong emphasis on individual performance. Like jazz, one notes considerable turn-taking, and each member in succession tries to "stand out" from the crowd. As in other Caribbean musical forms (most notably calypso), flamboyant innovation and technical virtuosity are greatly admired, and while innovation and technical skill are not the only measures of a "good" performance, these are nonetheless highly regarded (Warner, 1982).

Richard Alan Waterman (1952:209) points out that since both the musical traditions of Africa and Europe emphasize the same basic concepts of scale and harmony, it was inevitable that European hymns would be seized upon by Africans and remodeled into their own musical forms. Waterman makes special note of overlapping call-and-response patterns in which a leader sings phrases which alternate with phrases sung by a chorus (see also Floyd, 1995:43, 62–63). This pattern is common throughout the world; but in African and Caribbean music, "the chorus phrase regularly commences while the soloist is still singing and the leader begins his phrase before the chorus is finished" (Waterman, 1952:214). Such overlapping patterns are an especially striking characteristic of Spiritual Baptist music, and are most notable during opening hymns and intoned prayers.

Spiritual Baptist music appears eclectic because Spiritual Baptist participants are often simultaneously involved in a number of musical traditions. Of the ten musical forms of sacred music outlined by Jon Michael Spencer (1990), seven of them — spirituals, the blues, the ring shout, the tongue song, holiness-pentecostal music, gospel music, and the chanted sermon — can be identified within Spiritual Baptist worship services. There is also ample evidence for what Kenneth Bilby has termed "polymusicality." Some prominent Baptists are themselves accomplished professional musicians; most notably, drummers who perform frequently at *Orisha* feasts and/or are members of steel orchestras. Two prominent Belmont Baptists are part of the Hilton Hotel's Friday night "folkloric" show. One

Spiritual Baptist church in Tunapuna includes among its members: two local calypsonians, members of a local *reggae* band, a jazz trio, and a concert violinist who has performed in Canada and the United States. The impact of popular music can never be overestimated. Music — *all kinds* of music — is everywhere in Trinidad, blaring from houses, cars, taxis, buses, stores, sidewalk vendors, and boom boxes in infinite variety. Whether from India, Jamaica, Brazil, or the United States, if it is a hit somewhere it can probably be heard in Trinidad and Tobago. Much popular music makes its way into Spiritual Baptist music, and in turn, Spiritual Baptist music has made its way into Caribbean musical consciousness.

In 1976 — long after Frankie Vallee and the Four Seasons were off the Billboard charts in the United States but were experiencing something of a revival in Trinidad — an unusually somber rendition of "I Heard the Voice of Jesus Say" was countered from the back of the church by a falsetto version of "I'll Be A Big Man in Town" and "Dawn, Go Away I'm No Good for You." {The use of falsetto voice is common in African tribal music, Waterman, 1952: 215.} I did not catch this until mixing my album in the studio several years later. Similarly, I have since identified bits and pieces from the music of Johnny Cash, the Beatles, Michael Jackson's "Thriller" album, Sammy Davis, Jr.'s rendition of "Mr. Bojangles," and Elton John. Manuel, Bilby and Largey (1995:143–182) carefully document the acknowledged and unacknowledged impact of Jamaican Convince music on *raggamuffin* and dancehall styles in Jamaican popular music.

There is less social and political commentary in Spiritual Baptist music than other Trinidadian musical forms such as calypso. Criticism that does make its way into musical forms is veiled following typical Caribbean patterns of indirection (Reisman, 1970). This may be because style and performance take precedence over content. It may also be because other outlets are readily available. Spiritual Baptists frequently denounce one another in public prayers and from the pulpit. Also, words are seldom a focus for innovation. Lyrics tend to be standardized. There is considerable repetition. Baptists are much more likely to change the rhythm, tone, or melody than to tamper with the lyrics. The Word is highly respected within Protestant traditions. While illiterate Baptist leaders may have jumbled lyrics in the nineteenth century, they are extremely scrupulous in following printed lyrics today (This is especially true for "opening hymns").

Rhythms of the Saints

Ideally, musical instruments (aside from the human voice) should not be part of Spiritual Baptist worship. Exceptions abound. I noted that a number of suburban churches (St. Joseph, Tunapuna, and Daberdie) featured electronic organ music just prior to service, but in most cases the organ was physically removed from the church prior to opening hymns and the arrival of the paramount leader. Baptist leaders are emphatic that drums are forbidden in Spiritual Baptist churches. However, I have noted trumpets, rhythm sticks, and chac-chacs (maracas) being incorporated into service, but such inclusions were always a matter of controversy. Spiritual Baptist music, it is contended, should be performed *a capella*. All churches have several hand bells, which are believed to be the "Voice of God." Bell ringing calls the service to order; indicates transitions in services; provides a mechanism to concentrate or diffuse spiritual power; or simply serves as a way to get congregants' attention.

In the absence of drums, other ritual objects have been modified to take their place.[2] Shepherd's crooks can be rhythmically struck on the concrete or wooden floor to considerable effect. Such crooks are often selected for their tonal qualities. Benches in Spiritual Baptist churches are of varying woods, heights, widths, and lengths. These, too, can produce dramatically different tones which roughly correspond to the tonal drumming in Shango ceremonies (Waterman, 1943, 1952; Simpson, 1961). Stuempfle (1995:37) points out how experimentation with common objects played a major role in the early development of Steelband. Indeed, boundaries separating Shango drumming, Steelband, and other forms of popular music are not rigid. As noted previously, a number of Spiritual Baptist participants are also professional Shango drummers. Some carryover is to be expected.

As John Blacking (1973:89) concludes in *How Musical Is Man?*, music is a synthesis of cognitive processes which are "present in culture and in the human body; the forms it takes, and the effects it has on people are generated by the social experiences of human bodies in different cultural environments." Spiritual Baptist music features the body itself as the ultimate musical instrument (see Cooper, 1995). Renu Juneja underscores the privileged position Spiritual Baptists assign to the body as primary negotiator between subjective experience and the sociocultural context by which "the body receives the spirit and through it the spirit flows into the world" (Juneja, 1993:216).

Spiritual Baptist music is believed to be pleasing to both humans and the spirits. It is understood primarily as an offering to God (or the gods) and secondarily as an offering to one's fellow Baptists. At the same time, music can be intensely political. It affords a way of working out theological differences as well as solidifying one's position in the church hierarchy. It is a test which, over time, reveals whether one is "in tune" or "out of tune" with the Holy Spirit.

Endnotes

Earlier versions of this paper were presented at the 1995 annual meeting of the American Anthropological Association in Washington, DC, and the 1996 Conference on Caribbean Culture in honor of Professor Rex Nettleford at the University of the West Indies, Mona, Jamaica. I thank John Pulis, Richard Price, Maureen Warner-Lewis, Barry Chevannes, and John Szwed for their helpful comments on earlier drafts. Research on this project was facilitated by my appointment as a Research Fellow at Yale Divinity School/ Institute of Sacred Music during the Fall 1996 term.

1. Samuel A. Floyd Jr. (1993:1) and Jon Michael Spencer (1996:2–3) have identified a number of traits in African-derived music that are also prominent in Spiritual Baptist music. Most notable among these are: an emphasis on competitive values that keep performers on their mettle; the complete intertwining of music and movement; call-and-response devices, polyrhythms, hums, moans, and grunts. Both scholars underscore the significance of the Ring Shout in the perpetuation of African musical traditions in the New World; especially in the reinterpretation of spirituals. Floyd (1995:43) contends that "it was the ring and in the ring that the spiritual had its most dramatic use, with the ring's manifestations depending on local customs" (see also Spencer, 1996:12–13).

2. As Stephen Stuempfle (1995:23–31) has aptly pointed out, creative improvisation with percussion instruments is a common characteristic of Trinidadian music. The use of a variety of bamboo and metal percussion instruments occurs in both Africa and other parts of the Caribbean (see also Cowley, 1996).

Discography

Cult Music of Trinidad. Recorded in Trinidad by George Eaton Simpson. Washington, DC: Smithsonian/Folkways. Folkways Ethnic 4478, 1961.

Charlies Roots — The Hammer. Kingston, Jamaica: Dynamic Sounds Recording Co., 1987.

Jesus Going to Prepare a Mansion for Me. St. Teresa S. B. Church. In: *An Island Carnival: Music of the West Indies.* Recorded and edited by Krister Malm (1969–71). Nonesuch Explorer Series 72091, 1983.

Soca Baptist Sung By Blue Boy (A. Lyons). Bridgetown, Barbados: Romney's Disco 45 RPM, 1979.

Spiritual Baptist Music from Trinidad. Recorded in Trinidad by Stephen D. Glazier. Washington, DC: Smithsonian/Folkways. Ethnic Folkways 4234, 1980

References

Abrahams, R.D. 1979 Reputation and respectability: a review of Peter J. Wilson's concept. *Revista/Review Interamericana* 9:448–453.

Arnold, R. 1991 *English Hymns of the Eighteenth Century.* New York: Peter Lang.

Behague, G.H. 1994 *Music and Black Ethnicity: The Caribbean and South America.* New Brunswick, NJ: Transaction Publishers.

Bilby, K. 1988 The Caribbean as a musical area. In: *Caribbean Contours* (eds., S. and S. Price). Baltimore, MD: The Johns Hopkins University Press, pp. 191–218.

Birth, K. 1994 Bakrnal: Coup, carnival and calypso in Trinidad. *Ethnology* 33:165–77.

Blacking, J. 1973 *How Musical Is Man?* Seattle: University of Washington Press.

Campbell, W. 1994 "Sing to the Lord a new song": reflections on the role of music in worship. *Caribbean Journal of Religious Studies* 15:34–37.

Cooper, C. 1995 *Noises in the Blood: Orality, Gender, and the "Vulgar" Body of Jamaican Popular Culture*. Durham, NC: Duke University Press.

Courlander, H. 1963 *Negro Folk Music, USA*. New York: Columbia University Press.

Cowley, J. 1996 *Carnival, Canboulay and Calypso: Traditions in the Making*. New York: Cambridge University Press.

Davis, M.E. 1994 "Bi-musicality" in the configuration of the Caribbean. *Black Music Research Journal* 14:145–161.

Dargan, W.T. 1995 Congregational singing traditions in South Carolina. *Black Music Research Journal* 15:29–73.

Elder, J.D. 1964 Color, music and conflict: a study of aggression in Trinidad with reference to the role of traditional music. *Ethnomusicology* 8:128–136.

Floyd, S.A. Jr. 1993 On integrative inquiry: toward a common scholarship. *CBMR* 6:1–17.

Floyd, S.A. Jr. 1995 *The Power of Black Music: Interpreting Its History from Africa to the United States*. New York: Oxford University Press.

Glazier, S.D. 1985 Mourning in the Afro-Baptist tradition. *Southern Quarterly* 23:141–156.

Glazier, S.D. 1991 *Marching' the Pilgrims Home: A Study of the Spiritual Baptists of Trinidad* (revised paperback edition). Salem, WI: Sheffield Publishing Co.

Herskovits, M.J. and Herskovits, F.S. 1947 *Trinidad Village*. New York: Alfred A. Knopf.

Houk, J.T. 1995 *Spirits, Blood, and Drums: The Orisha Religion in Trinidad*. Philadelphia: Temple University Press.

Juneja, R. 1993 Spirited bodies in Earl Lovelace's *The Wine of Astonishment*. In: *Reading the Social Body* (eds., C.B. Burroughs and J.D. Ehrenreich). Iowa City: University of Iowa Press, pp. 202–217.

Manuel, P., with K. Bilby and M. Largey 1995 *Caribbean Currents: Caribbean Music from Rumba to Reggae*. Philadelphia: Temple University Press.

McDaniel, L. 1994 Memory spirituals of the ex-slave American soldiers in Trinidad's "company villages." *Black Music Research Journal* 14:119–143.

Lamming, G. 1960 *The Pleasures of Exile*. London: Michael Joseph.

Ortner, S.B. 1978 *Sherpas Through Their Rituals*. New York: Cambridge University Press.

Pitts, W.F. Jr. 1993 *Old Ship of Zion: The Afro-Baptist Ritual in the African Diaspora*. New York: Oxford University Press.

Reisman, K. 1970 Cultural and linguistic ambiguity in a West Indian village. In: *Afro-American Anthropology: Contemporary Perspectives* (eds., N.E. Whitten and J.F. Szwed). New York: Free Press, pp. 129–142.

Rudder, D. 1990 *Kaiso, Calypso Music: David Rudder in Conversation with John LaRose*. London: New Beacon Press.

Sankey, I.D. 1874 *Sacred Songs and Solos with Standard Hymns*. London: Marshall, Morgan, Scott.

Southern, E. 1990 *African-American Tradition in Song, Sermon, Tale, and Dance, 1600s to 1920: An Annotated Bibliography of Literature, Collections and Artwork*. Compiled by E. Southern and J. Wright. Westport, CT: Greenwood Press.

Spencer, J.M. 1990 *Protest and Praise: Sacred Music of Black Religion*. Minneapolis: Fortress Press.

Spencer, J.M. 1992 *Black Hymnody*. Knoxville: University of Tennessee Press.

Spencer, J.M. 1996 *Re-searching Black Music*. Knoxville: University of Tennessee Press.

Starks, G.L. Jr. 1991 Singin 'bout a good time. In: *Sea Island Roots: African Presence in the Carolinas and Georgia* (eds., M. A. Twining and K. Baird). Trenton. NJ: Africa World Press, pp. 95–101.

Stokes, M. 1994 *Ethnicity, Identity, and Music: The Musical Construction of Place*. Oxford: Berg.

Stuempfle, S. 1995 *The Steelband Movement: The Forging of a National Art in Trinidad and Tobago*. Philadelphia: University of Pennsylvania Press.

Warner, K.O. 1982 *Kaiso!: The Trinidad Calypso, A Study of the Calypso as Oral Literature.* Washington, DC: Three Continents Press.

Waterman, R.A. 1943 *African Patterns in Trinidad Negro Music.* PhD dissertation, Northwestern University. Based on the Herskovitses' 1939 collection.

Waterman, R.A. 1952 African Influence on the music of the Americas. In: *Acculturation in the Americas* (ed., S. Tax). Chicago: International Congress of the Americanists.

Watts, I. 1836/1707 *The Psalms, Hymns and Spiritual Songs.* Boston: Crocker and Brewster.

Williams, M.R. 1985 *"Songs from Valley to Mountain": Music and Ritual Among the Spiritual Baptists ('Shouters') of Trinidad.* Master's thesis, Folklore Department, Indiana University.

Wilson, P.J. 1969 Reputation and respectability: a suggestion for Caribbean ethnography. *Man* 4:70–84.

12: CHAOS, COMPROMISE, AND TRANSFORMATION IN THE ORISHA RELIGION IN TRINIDAD

James Houk, Ph.D.

Introduction

The Orisha religion in Trinidad is one of a family of African-derived forms of worship in the New World that, like Santería, Umbanda, and Vodoun, could be loosely referred to as "Afro-Catholic" but is actually more complex than that term might suggest. Today Orisha is comprised of religious beliefs, practices, and paraphernalia drawn from not only West African and Catholic, but also Protestant, Hindu, and Kabbalistic traditions (Houk, 1995). These various elements are not necessarily syncretized per se, but are, rather, part of a somewhat amorphous complex of activities centered upon the Orisha religion. The common thread that binds together these various activities is the worshipers themselves. It is not uncommon for the same worshipers to attend Orisha feasts, Spiritual Baptist Sunday services, and Kabbalah banquets.

The eclecticism of Orisha could be attributed to a number of factors and influences perhaps the most obvious being the multicultural and pluralistic nature of Trinidadian society. In regard to more specific factors, however, the mourning ritual is without a doubt the most important mechanism of change in the Orisha religion. Unlike rituals that are generally associated with traditional religions, this rite is not static, repetitive, and conservative. No one, including the ranking functionaries, can predict just exactly what will happen during mourning, and each mourning event has the potential to radically alter the liturgy, symbolism, beliefs, and even the hierarchy of the religion.

There are, no doubt, any number of analytical schemes that one might use to address this interesting phenomenon but perhaps none would be as appropriate and incisive as one based on Victor Turner's

(1969) notion of *communitas. Communitas*, at least as this term is used by Turner, refers to the nature of the relations that obtain between fellow worshipers and between them as a group and society as a whole while undergoing a ritual of some sort, particularly during that period generally referred to as "liminal." This state is characterized by categorical ambiguity, equality, sacredness, the absence of status and so on. According to Turner, *communitas* need not be confined only to ritual but can also be manifested in the more mundane, everyday affairs of society. Given the fact that the mourning ritual is such an important source of change in the Orisha belief system, it is this aspect of the Turnerian notion of *communitas* which makes it germane to a discussion of Orisha. In fact, it is these very changes that serve to drive the structural dynamic of the religion since a number of mechanisms and processes have arisen to counter the gradual expansion and increasing eclecticism of Orisha.

Fieldwork and Methodology

I spent the better part of three summers and one full year researching the Orisha religion in Trinidad. During this time I conducted interviews (both structured and unstructured) with elders, shrine heads, and rank and file worshipers, mapped the distribution of shrines (I personally visited over a hundred), and catalogued various components of about forty shrines including their age, the particular orisha enshrined there, the absence or presence of religious traditions other than Orisha, and their physical layout. I also attended several feasts, often visiting as many as four in one week.

Since orisha worshipers have borrowed prodigiously from the other religious traditions present on the island, it was important that I become familiar with them as well. I attended Hindu weddings and general worship services, the Sunday services and other rituals of the Spiritual Baptist church, and Kabbalah banquets.

During much of my year long stay in Trinidad, I had the good fortune to live in an Orisha shrine (that also housed a Spiritual Baptist church) with an Orisha priest and Spiritual Baptist Leader, Aldwin Scott, and his wife, Mother Joan. ("Leader" and "Mother" are terms used to identify the ranking male and female at a particular

Spiritual Baptist church.) This gave me an opportunity to witness as well as participate in virtually all the activities associated with maintaining an Orisha shrine as well as a Spiritual Baptist church.

In May of 1989, I was baptized in the Spiritual Baptist church. A week later I was initiated into the Orisha religion during a three day ritual involving fasting, isolation, and instruction. My head was ritually washed and incised at that time and I now enjoy all the rights and privileges of an Orisha worshiper. During my time in Trinidad, I also became quite proficient at playing one of the three drums that are beat during Orisha ceremonies and was eventually allowed to beat the drums during the annual feasts.

My relationship with my contacts, then, was not that of the detached and passive observer. I grew quite close to the people I worked with and correspond with many of them to this day. It should be noted, however, that I never embraced the basic tenets and beliefs of the Orisha religion a fact that no doubt allowed me to maintain a degree of objectivity necessary to conduct research that was as free from personal bias as anyone can be. In other words, I had no interest in proselytizing for the Orisha religion or sharing the details of my personal relationship with the orisha as many worshipers would. I am, however, cognizant of the fact that religion is a slippery subject that cannot be understood using only empirical and quantitative methods. Thus, it is certainly not my intention to gloss over the ineffable and existential aspects of religion. The basic methodology that guided my research of the Orisha religion reflects these sentiments including as it does, for example, demographical analyses as well as extensive unstructured interviews with worshipers. Ironclad scientism, in my mind, should always be tempered with postmodernistic relativism, especially when one is dealing with human behavior.

Historical Development of the Orisha Religion

The Orisha religion presumably began about 150 years ago as a transplanted form of primarily Yoruba worship with strains of Congolese, Ewe-Fon, and no doubt other forms of African worship present as well. The African slave-based plantation society was not present in Trinidad until near the end of the eighteenth century. While it is probable that African religious worship of some form began to appear on the island at that time, it is my guess that the Orisha religion did not become a cultural force until later. I base this opinion on the fact that demographically the Yoruba were basically nonexistent on the island until sometime in the 1830s (Trotman, 1976). Also, given the fact that complete emancipation occurred in 1838, I choose to date the beginning of the Orisha religion at around 1840.

Sometime during the latter half of the nineteenth century, Catholicism, present in Trinidad since the Spanish established the first church in 1592, began to greatly influence the beliefs and practices of Orisha adherents. Exactly why this happened is a matter of some dispute. Some (for example, Bastide, 1972) argue that the Africans used Catholicism and its symbolism and paraphernalia as a facade for their own worship. Others (Herskovits and Herskovits, 1964; Trotman, 1976) contend that Africans voluntarily incorporated certain Catholic elements into their worship. It is also possible, as this writer argues (Houk, 1995), that both theories are probably correct to some extent and that the exigencies of surviving in a socially hostile environment determined when one process was more likely to occur than the other. Be that as it may, given the very early occurrence of Yoruba/Catholic syncretism, the relationship between these two components tends to be much more intimate than that obtaining between Yoruba and the other components noted above. Catholicism, however, while certainly prevalent in Orisha worship today, is no longer an active component in the belief system, and, in fact, shows signs of disappearing in some shrines around the island. The fact that Catholicism is being neglected or even actively purged from the Orisha religion has a lot to do with the particular aspects of Catholicism that was embraced historically. Much of Church dogma, for example, papal infallibility, Mariological doctrines, transubstantiation, and so on, was never embraced by orisha worshipers. Rather it is the saints and the doctrines and beliefs associated with them that have been important in the Orisha religion.

Around 1915 or so, the highly Protestant Spiritual Baptist religion made its appearance in Trinidad (Glazier, 1991; Houk, 1995) and, given the fact that adherents of both Orisha and the Spiritual Baptist church were drawn from the same ethnic group and socioeconomic class, it is not surprising that an exchange of beliefs and practices between the two religions occurred. The fact that worshipers of a polytheistic African traditional religion have borrowed certain beliefs and rituals from a predominately Christian Protestant faith, a practice somewhat unusual among African-derived religions in the New World, can be attributed to the fact that the demographic characteristics of worshipers of both religions are virtually coincident. The legacy of this exchange (which, by the way, has been reciprocal) in the Orisha religion includes singing and praying in a Spiritual Baptist mode during Orisha *ebo* (an annual four-day ceremony in honor of the *orisha* or gods), the presence of Spiritual Baptist Churches in Orisha compounds, and the mourning ceremony (discussed below). A large majority of Orisha adherents are Spiritual Baptists as well.

Around 1950 or so (as best I can tell) Orisha worshipers began to borrow extensively from the sizeable Hindu community in Trinidad. It is difficult to say exactly why this occurred but it should be noted that the incorporation of Hindu beliefs and practices in the Orisha religion has been accompanied by the influx of East Indians into the worship practices of the Orisha religion where they occasionally account for approximately ten percent of those present (Houk, 1993). Today it is not unusual to find Hindu shrines and paraphernalia in an Orisha compound. Some worshipers even recognize correspondences between certain *orisha* and Hindu gods not unlike the syncretism involving *orisha* and Catholic saints that is so salient in African-derived religions in the New World, Orisha included.

Finally, about 1970, Orisha adherents began to involve themselves in Kabbalah worship. The Kabbalah is an esoteric corpus of mystical and theological writings that utilizes a unique and complex symbolic and mathematical hermeneutic to apply various theosophical and theurgical principles in an attempt to actively interact with spiritual powers. According to some scholars (see, for example, Schaya, 1971 and Sheinkin, 1986), the Kabbalah is the esoteric counterpart to recorded Jewish and Christian knowledge that has been passed down secretively since the time of Moses.

The Kabbalah was apparently brought to Trinidad by the Spanish, French, or possibly the English. This is only an educated guess since, as far as I know, no substantiative documentation exists. Given, however, the fact that the Kabbalah, at least in its modern form, appeared in Spain and France in the twelfth century and had spread to England by the seventeenth century, it is probable that the colonizing Europeans were the source for Kabbalah in Trinidad.

The term "Kabbalah" used in a general sense refers to a complex system of teachings and activities regarding cosmography and the relationship between humankind and spiritual forces and powers. In Trinidad, however, the Kabbalah is a functional activity that is practiced to bring about a desired end. Trinidadian Kabbalah is highly theurgical as "entities," as they refer to them, are conjured and consulted for a variety of reasons. (The entities manifest themselves upon mediums specifically designated for this purpose.) Kabbalah worship and its structures and paraphernalia are carefully segregated from the more distinctly Orisha structures and paraphernalia in the compound. There is virtually no indication that Kabbalah/Orisha syncretism has occurred at this time, although I would guess that such a development is, to some extent, inevitable given the increasing prevalence of Kabbalah worship in Orisha circles. In a survey of fifty-one Orisha shrines (Houk, 1995), for example, I found that sixteen or thirty-one percent contained at least a special structure for Kabbalah worship or a Kabbalah flag or shrine.

The inclusion of the Kabbalah in the complex of religious beliefs and activities that comprise Orisha can, I feel, be attributed to the fact that prestige is conferred upon those ranking functionaries that have the ability to practice and work with a wide range of religious traditions. Also, those shrine heads and elders who incorporate Kabbalistic practices into their religious system are able to take advantage of a much larger pantheon that includes not only the orisha and saints, but Kabbalistic entities as well. This is important as those individuals who do "spirit work" in Trinidad can be called upon to offer a variety of services, even those that would be considered "negative"; in fact, I was told that only the entities would do work of this type.

A typical shrine, then, will include not only the three primary structures of Orisha worship, the *palais* (where most dancing and singing for the *orisha* is done), the *chapelle* (a sanctuary housing Orisha religious implements), and the *perogun* (an open-air structure containing small shrines for important *orisha*), but, as was noted above, Spiritual Baptist, Hindu, and Kabbalah structures, shrines, and implements as well. It is not uncommon for the shrine head to direct both Orisha rites and ceremonies and Spiritual Baptist services and rituals. He or she may also serve as a Kabbalah medium. What we are dealing with here is not a religion in the strict sense of the term, but rather a complex of diverse religious activities embraced and practiced by a common group of worshipers.

Not surprisingly, the Orisha religion and the complex of worship activities of which it is part, are characterized by various mechanisms that are conducive to rapid change. Among these are included the following: 1) a high degree of cultural pride among African Trinidadians defined by a tendency to embrace cosmopolitanism and celebrate the multi-cultural heritage of the island; 2) the loosely organized and highly decentralized structure of the religion; 3) the fact that status and prestige are conferred upon those shrine heads and other ranking functionaries who successfully incorporate the beliefs and practices of many different traditions into their worship practices; 4) a so-called one-to-many form of religious knowledge transmission from one generation to the next; and 5) the "mourning" ritual. The last of these, the mourning ritual, is, in my mind, perhaps the most important mechanism of change in the Orisha religion.

Mourning

The mourning ritual lasts anywhere from three days to a week and sometimes longer. During this time the "pilgrims" undergo a series of spiritual travels; Africa, India, China, and the United States are often mentioned (Glazier, 1991; Houk, 1995; Simpson, 1966). The pilgrim will typically encounter various spirits who offer instruction, counseling, or advice on different spiritual topics. It is not uncommon for the pilgrim to receive orders to build a shrine for the *orisha*, to offer an animal at a nearby feast, or to sponsor prayers. Finally, on occasion a pilgrim will be awarded a higher status role or position in the religion. The mourning pilgrim publicly announces the details of his or her experiences during services held at the conclusion of the three to seven day period.

The group as a whole has virtually no direct control over the mourning pilgrim and their testimonies. There are ranking functionaries who "guide" and "point" the pilgrim and they can influence the experiences and travels of the pilgrim up to a point. But, in the end, the group must assume that the pilgrim will give an honest and truthful account of their experiences. There are certain officers of the Spiritual Baptist hierarchy who are entrusted with maintaining the integrity of the mourning ritual. One way they accomplish this is to question the pilgrim if it is thought that particular details of the pilgrim's travels are dubious or if the pilgrim claims a higher position in the church without what appears to be justification to do so. It cannot be denied, however, that the experience as a whole is a subjective one based as it is on the experiences, attitudes, and sentiments of individuals. In other words, in spite of their best efforts to "police" and monitor the mourning ritual, the fact that no one other than the pilgrim was privy to certain knowledge and experiences makes it extremely difficult for the officers and other ranking functionaries to prevent the pilgrim from embellishing or even exaggerating the details of his or her travels. It is not hard to understand why the mourning ritual is such a potent mechanism of change in the Orisha religion.

All mourners, regardless of their current status or position, must go through the same ordeals. The heads of the pilgrims are wrapped and they are laid down on the earth, usually inside a special mourning room in a Spiritual Baptist church or inside the *chapelle* in an Orisha compound. The mourner is allowed little more than tea, crackers, or rice depending on how long they plan to be "on the ground." Only the Spiritual Baptist Leader or Mother and the "nurses" are allowed to interact with the mourners. The mourners' feet are bare and they are simply dressed.

The rank and file worshiper, the Orisha priest, the Spiritual Baptist Leader, and even the neophyte are all sequestered together while mourning and subjected to the same ritual process; all are treated similarly regardless of their status or prestige in the religion. Their experiences do, however, differ significantly in one respect: those who have mourned before will, during their travels, experience their religion at a richer and more sophisticated level. Orisha worshipers believe that the spirits will not impart to an individual knowledge that he or she does not have the intelligence or experience to deal with.

Turnerian *Communitas*

Many of those characteristics associated with liminality as identified by Victor Turner in *The Ritual Process: Structure and Anti-Structure*

(1969) are present in the mourning ritual including homogeneity, equality, anonymity, absence of status, uniform clothing, disregard for personal appearance, lack of wealth distinction, sacredness, silence, acceptance of pain and suffering, and, of course, *communitas*. Turner uses the term *"communitas"* to stand in contradistinction to "structure" where both terms represent the most general types of social relationships:

> It is as though there are here two major "models" for human interrelatedness, juxtaposed and alternating. The first [structure] is of society as a structured, differentiated, and often hierarchical system of politico-legal-economic conditions with many types of evaluation, separating men in terms of "more" or "less." The second [*communitas*], which emerges recognizably in the liminal period, is of society as an unstructured or rudimentarily structured and relatively undifferentiated *comitatus*, community, or even communion of equal individuals who submit together to the general authority of the ritual elders. (1969, 96)

The undifferentiated and unstructured aspects of *communitas* are generally characterized by a sort of anarchy which, in the case of the mourning ritual, is manifested in the apparent lack of control the group has over the knowledge and events encountered during the spiritual travels. This leads to the eventual incorporation of certain beliefs and practices into the Orisha religion that, in the absence of mourning, probably would not be part of the belief system. Some shrine heads or other ranking functionaries who practice the Kabbalah, for example, a practice generally considered to be diabolical and spiritually polluting by Trinidadians, but, nevertheless, powerful and efficacious, have confided to me that they probably would not do so if it were not for the fact that they were so instructed while mourning. Also, many experienced worshipers have told me that mourning is perhaps the most important source of the Hinduism that is now so prevalent in the Orisha religion.

It is also true that the colors of flags for particular *orisha* and other details will be given to mourners. The result is that not one *orisha* is associated with a standard flag color; in fact, some *orisha* may be represented by flags of as many as five or six color combinations. This example is merely one of many that could be given to illustrate the lack of uniformity in the religion, much of which can certainly be attributed to mourning.

Discussion and Analysis

Orisha has survived for approximately 150 years and is currently
flourishing with over 150 shrines on the island, many of them recently
constructed. But the current belief system continues to accrue beliefs,
practices, and paraphernalia of other religions. A few adherents have
even added Islam, Buddhism, and Rosicrucianism to the mix. Clearly,
any viable form of religious worship cannot continue to expand
ideologically without undergoing some diminution of comprehensi-
bility on the part of the worshipers. And, in fact, we do find normal-
izing influences in the Orisha religion that act to counterbalance or at
least temper the tendency towards eclecticism and decentralization
(Houk, 1995, 1996).

While Orisha shrines tend to be concentrated in the northwest
region of the island, they can be found virtually everywhere. Since
each shrine holds an annual feast or *ebo*, there is a general movement
among most worshipers from one shrine to another throughout most
of the year. This has the effect of bringing worshipers from different
parts of the island together to compare notes, so to speak, and to
critique one another's worship practices. While the spectrum of acceptable worship practices is certainly broad, one can occasionally
move even beyond the polar extremes. Group pressure will then be
brought to bear on the "heretical" practice and the individual in
question will be encouraged to change his or her practice to conform
to the dictates of group ideology, however loosely that may be defined and conceptualized. Some worshipers do not, however, so suc-
cumb and will continue their heretical practices. Such obstinacy
serves to slowly broaden the range of acceptable practices. In the end,
however, the feast circuit of travelling worshipers does at least act to
temper further expansion of the religious system.

Another mechanism that has acted to counter eclecticism and
syncretism is the recent tendency towards the Africanization of the
religion (Henry, 1983; Houk, 1993, 1995). Ten years ago, only a handful of the 150 or so shrines on the island exhibited this tendency but
today many more do. These Africanized shrines will generally contain few if any Catholic, Spiritual Baptist, and Hindu symbols and
paraphernalia. I did not mention the Kabbalah since this practice is
strictly segregated from Orisha worship anyway. So, for example,
even the highly Africanized shrines might contain specific areas set

aside for the Kabbalah. In the interest of clarifying a potentially confusing notion, I should mention that the term Africanization is used here to denote those shrines and practices that are perceived by the worshipers as being African. In most cases, the term is in fact an accurate one since Orisha worship in Trinidad and southern Nigeria overlap considerably in regard to ritual procedure, beliefs, and lexicon (Houk, 1995; Simpson, 1962).

Finally, the third mechanism working against further expansion of the system are the recent attempts to organize the religion on an island-wide basis. The most prominent organization at this time is the Opa Orisha (Shango) of Trinidad and Tobago. This group has been recognized by the government and regularly sends representatives to state functions. At this time approximately twenty-five percent or so of the island's shrines are affiliated with the organization. The Opa Orisha (Shango) is attempting to regularize worship by encouraging a standard liturgy and shrine layout; they have also attempted to organize the feast season to prevent the occurrence of more than one or, perhaps, two feasts on the same dates; and the group is also recommending various conservation strategies to prevent relatively rare animals, such as the morocoy (a large land turtle), from becoming extinct on the island as a result of continuous blood sacrifices.

There is, however, a certain amount of resistance to the group's attempt to consolidate the religion. The Orisha religion has a long history of independent and decentralized shrines which, of course, allows a considerable amount of freedom among worshipers. Many adherents have simply accepted the fact that the religion is a dynamic one and, in fact, many even celebrate the multicultural belief system of the Orisha religion.

Clearly, some Orisha worshipers do not view the continual assimilation of the selected traits of other religious traditions as a corruptive process, but many do. As I have commented elsewhere (Houk, 1995), Orisha adherents are perhaps experiencing the sort of existential angst that Jean-Paul Sartre associates with the rejection of God and religion, but this case represents a curious inversion of that condition characterized by the fact that their God has so many faces. In other words, it seems as though "too much" religion, at least from the point of view of the individual worshiper, is conceptually and psychologically equivalent to atheism.

So, there is an interesting sociocultural dynamic at work here. There are mechanisms and processes that are acting to expand the belief system allowing and perhaps encouraging the incorporation of religious traits from other traditions. As I mentioned earlier, even whole belief systems, for example Hinduism and the Kabbalah, have been incorporated into the worship complex during the last forty to fifty years. On the other hand, there are other mechanisms and processes at work that are acting to counter or temper the tendency towards expansion of the belief system.

The mourning ritual plays a significant role in this dynamic process. Much of the information and knowledge gained during mourning, however novel or, put another way, heretical or heterodox, eventually becomes part of the complex of beliefs and practices centered around the Orisha religion. It is in this sense that I use the phrase "the normalization of *communitas*." The subversion of standard social roles that occurs during mourning allows even the neophyte and rank and file worshiper to influence the religion along idiosyncratic lines since everyone's experiences are equally important. From the worshipers' perspective, it is through mourning that the spirits make their contribution to the religion by communicating their wishes, instructions, and admonitions to worshipers. Looked at in this way, the *communitas* of mourning revitalizes the structure of the belief system. In *The Ritual Process*, Turner speaks similarly of the purging and purification effect *communitas* has on structure.

Now, according to Turner, the general sociocultural process is a dialectic one involving a dynamic interplay between *communitas* and structure. Turner explains that in order for structure to remain meaningful it must be reinvigorated from time to time by an infusion of *communitas*. It is during *communitas*, after all, that mythology is legitimized, the strong become weak, the weak strong, and traditional status categories are reinforced by contrasting them with the potential anarchy and statuslessness of liminality.

In *The Ritual Process*, Turner implies that this dialectic might be either static or teleological. The former case would apply primarily to the role of ritual in traditional societies; in this case the *communitas* of ritual simply serves as a legitimizing contrast to everyday structure which remains basically unchanged through time. Structure and *communitas* follow and reinforce one another, yet everyday life remains basically unchanged as ritual serves primarily to periodically highlight and accentuate the basic notions and values that serve to define social structure.

In the case I have described as teleological, however, certain aspects of ritual, particularly those associated with liminality, fundamentally influence everyday life. No sooner does *communitas* become manifest in non-ritualistic contexts than it begins to undergo an attenuation of idealistic purity. For example, new social or religious movements organized around principles that are generally identified with *communitas* gradually become more and more structured as the everyday demands of property ownership and other contingencies of everyday life have to be dealt with. Turner's (1969) example of the dispute involving the Spiritual vs. the Conventual Franciscans is perhaps a perfect illustration of this case.

In regard to the mourning ritual and the Orisha belief system, however, neither the static nor teleological model applies exclusively. The static model, whereby ritual and *communitas* periodically revitalize a structure that resists change through time, does not apply here in a strict sense since the structure, very loosely defined in this case, of the Orisha belief system is constantly changing. The established or traditional standards upon which worship is based are very broadly conceived; such "standards" that do exist are constantly being created and reworked. The teleological model is relevant here but only up to a point since those aspects of *communitas* that become manifest in everyday life almost immediately become assimilated into the acceptable range of beliefs and practices and undergo little if any change.

Structure, used here in a more conceptual than tangible sense, is understood to mean accepted group standards that guide worship and organization. In regard to the Orisha religion, it is a bit misleading to speak of structure because the various shrines and adherents share only the most general worship practices. Many shrines on the island are highly decentralized and the worship practices associated with them do not follow any particular liturgical or ritual standards.

Those centrifugal forces and mechanisms at work in the Orisha belief system fueled by the mourning ritual and the normalization of *communitas*, have worked together to create an increasingly eclectic religion. This process has been aided and encouraged by those worshipers who embrace a generally existential and egocentric notion of religion, i.e., they view religion as a pliable and mutable system of ideas and practices that should be amenable to the dictates of subjectivity.

On the other hand, there are those worshipers who value the legitimacy afforded by the standardization of beliefs and practices. They are quite willing to give up the "luxury" of heterodoxy in exchange for a religious system that transcends the individual but does, nevertheless, serve to legitimize the beliefs and activities of the group as a whole (Houk, 1996).

Turner's notion that *communitas* periodically revitalizes structure is, as we have seen, certainly a viable notion. But, what happens when this process becomes disruptive? What happens when structure itself or, in regard to the case being discussed here, even the potential for structure is threatened by the chaos and novelty of *communitas*? At least in regard to the Orisha religion in Trinidad, the answer is simple: various mechanisms are put in place that act to temper and counter the effects of novelty and change brought on by the normalization of *communitas*. In the process, however, a rift has opened in the community of Orisha worshipers consisting of those who favor decentralized and autonomous shrines and those who favor standardization and organization of shrines under one common banner. This has been accompanied by a corresponding polarization of sentiments splitting those who favor a flexible and mutable belief system that caters to existential concerns and those who wish to establish a rigid and monolithic system to serve as a sort of storehouse of culture and society defining values and mores.

Communitas certainly revitalizes structure; *communitas* certainly purges and purifies structure. In the Orisha religion, however, structure traditionally has been lacking and the development of the belief system has been characterized, not by the interplay of *communitas* and structure, but rather by the normalization of *communitas*. It is this very process that has only recently produced attempts on the part of some worshipers to standardize the religion.

Conclusion

I am, of course, implying here that *communitas* begets structure, at least in the case of the Orisha religion in Trinidad. Since, however, *"communitas"* and "structure," like "good" and "evil," are semantic partners that are defined in terms of and in contrast to one another, it seems paradoxical to speak of *communitas* in the virtual absence of structure. But, it is at this point that the egocentric and existential aspect of religion becomes important. That this component is a significant one in the Orisha religion is confirmed by the fact that before structure came to the Orisha religion in the form of standardization and group organization, there existed at least a broad set of worship practices, albeit characterized by diversity and heterodoxy, that served as the binary counterpart to *communitas*. In the end, then, the normalization of *communitas* in the Orisha religion served to transform and redefine what little structure existed.

It is my guess that given enough time a symbiotic relationship will obtain between *communitas* and structure in the Orisha religion, i.e., the tendency toward standardization and group organization will persist but sources of novelty and heterodoxy like the mourning ritual will continue to enrich the religion as Orisha worshipers continue in their quest to create a belief system that appeals to a variety of sentiments.

Endnote

This paper is a revised version of a paper presented during the 94th Annual Meeting of the American Anthropological Association in Washington, DC, November 15–19, in the session "Caribbean Religions: Culture, Consciousness, Community at Home and Abroad." I would like to take this opportunity to thank John Pulis for his efforts in organizing and chairing the session. I would also like to thank our discussants John Szwed and Richard Price.

References

Bastide, Roger 1972 *African Civilizations in the New World* (trans. Peter Green). New York: Harper & Row.

Glazier, Stephen D. 1991 *Marchin' the Pilgrims Home: A Study of the Spiritual Baptists of Trinidad.* Salem, WI: Sheffield.

Henry, Frances 1983 Religion and ideology in Trinidad: The resurgence of the Shango religion. *Caribbean Quarterly* 29(3–4):63–69.

Herskovits, Melville J. and Herskovits, Frances S. 1964 *Trinidad Village*. New York: Octagon Books.

Houk, James T. 1993 Afro-Trinidadian identity and the Africanization of the Orisha religion. In: *Trinidad Ethnicity* (ed., Kevin A. Yelvington). London: Macmillan, pp. 161–179.

Houk, James T. 1995 *Spirits, Blood, and Drums: The Orisha Religion in Trinidad*. Philadelphia: Temple University Press.

Houk, James T. 1996 Anthropological theory, traditional belief systems, and public vs. private ideologies. *Journal for the Scientific Study of Religion* 35(4):442–447.

Schaya, Leo 1971 *The Universal Meaning of the Kabbalah*. Trans. Nancy Pearson. London: Allen & Unwin.

Sheinkin, David 1986 *Path of the Kabbalah*. New York: Paragon House.

Simpson, George E. 1962 The Shango cult in Nigeria and in Trinidad. *American Anthropologist* 64(6):1204–1219.

Simpson, George E. 1966 Baptismal, "Mourning," and "Building" ceremonies of the Shouters in Trinidad. *Journal of American Folklore* 19(314):537–550.

Trotman, David V. 1976 The Yoruba and Orisha worship in Trinidad and British Guinea: 1838–1870. *African Studies Review* 19(2):1–17.

Turner, Victor 1969 *The Ritual Process: Structure and Anti-Structure*. Chicago: Aldine Publishing Co.

13: NEITHER HERE NOR THERE: THE PLACE OF "COMMUNITY" IN THE JAMAICAN RELIGIOUS IMAGINATION

Kenneth Bilby

Introduction

Nearly two decades ago I had one of my first encounters with a practitioner of the Jamaican religion known as Convince or Bongo. At the center of this religion is the experience of possession by ghosts or spirits who identify themselves as "Bongo men" or "Africans."[1] One such spirit had just seized the body of the devotee sitting before me. The medium's cloth headwrap covered his eyes completely, giving the impression that he was no longer dependent on the vision through which physical objects are located in literal space. The possessing spirit, a talkative fellow who called himself Silence-Man, expounded on what he called his "nation." "We are Africans," he said. "We fly from Africa go to United States, go to England, go to North Pole, and go to the moon."

A few weeks later, another practitioner of this religion sang me a Convince song that put me in mind of what the first medium had told me. The words of this song were as follows:

doh doh, Bongo man
doh doh, yaya, doh doh
me da libi ya, but Bongo no mek no home[2]

Freely translated, the last line might be rendered in English as, "although I'm living here, the African makes no home."

Although these two men lived about fifteen miles apart and had never met or even heard of each other, as co-religionists they belonged to a "community" of sorts; they conceived of themselves as "Africans" or "Bongo men" belonging to a single "Convince nation" (to cite yet another expression gleaned from a Convince song).

I was beginning to realize that the spirits of this "nation" were neither here nor there; they were everywhere — in America, England, on the North Pole, and even the moon — and yet nowhere, without a home.[3] There was something about this "traditional" religion, described by Donald Hogg (1964: 262) more than three decades ago as one of the most "Africanoid" religions in Jamaica, that seemed distinctly "modern."

As Benedict Anderson (1983: 15) has argued, "all communities larger than primordial villages of face-to-face contact (and perhaps even these) are imagined." Anderson's explication of why the political phenomenon known as the *nation* must be considered an "imagined community" holds true for other kinds of large collectivities such as "religious communities" as well. According to Anderson, the nation, like other such "communities," "is *imagined* because the members of even the smallest nation will never know most of their fellow-members, meet them, or even hear of them, yet in the minds of each lives the image of their communion" (ibid). Any notion of place coinciding with such an imagined community — for instance, a national territory — can exist for individual members only in the imagination, for such a "place" could never be physically visited, known, or experienced in its entirety by any single person.

Imagine, if you will, the social landscape confronting a typical immigrant to a Caribbean plantation society such as that of Jamaica during the era of slavery. Torn from the local community into which he was born, not to mention any larger political or religious groupings with which he has come to identify, the newly arrived African finds himself in an entirely unprecedented state of social suspension. As overwhelming as the experience of enslavement is, this is compounded by the need to re-create oneself as a social being.

A good deal of theorizing has been done about the processes through which new creole societies and cultures were created in the Caribbean as a result of this need.[4] For the purposes of this paper, suffice it to say that in a colony such as Jamaica, once the indigenous population had been destroyed, new communities, whether of a face-to-face or more extensive kind, had to be formed through a process of near total reinvention. Except possibly among the tiny minority of European colonists, the new setting would have been devoid of preexisting units of social structure — even of the most basic familial kind — to which some sense of primary community would normally attach. These, like other aspects of social and cultural life, had to be created anew. The resulting cultural syntheses, combining materials and ideas of varying provenance, played a fundamental role in the building of communities where none had existed before. The point to be stressed here is that these historical conditions are not entirely unrelated to certain features of rural Jamaican society observable in the more recent past, or even today.

In Jamaica, as elsewhere, religion has often provided the symbolic means for the creation and expansion of imagined communities. But in Jamaica, with its lack of broadly shared institutions and its history of cultural creolization, the process of imagining such communities appears to have been a particularly open, adaptive, and variable one. As a result, the island today is home to a range of co-existing indigenous religions, all of which play a role in mediating understandings of the relationship between group identity and place, but which vary in the degree to which the identities they mediate are bound to specifiable local geographies or actual face-to-face communities. Three such religions are Kumina, Convince, and Rastafari.

Kumina: The Expansion of an Imagined Community

The neatest and simplest fit between cosmological space, territorial place, and community identity in Jamaica is perhaps displayed by the eastern Maroon communities, where the traditional Kromanti religion, closed to non-Maroons and now in a state of decline, is concerned almost exclusively with communication between living Maroons and the spirits of their remembered ancestors, who have traditionally been buried on Maroon lands within fairly clearly demarcated boundaries.[5] Next would be the similarly family-oriented ancestral religions found in certain non-Maroon areas, one of which is Kumina.

Kumina provides a good example of the variable ways in which the relationship between identity and place can be mediated within a single religious framework, since this religion accommodates both close-knit, co-residential communities of worshippers and, at the same time, a more broadly conceived and geographically dispersed "community" of co-religionists. Among the core practitioners of Kumina living in St. Thomas parish — those descended from the

Central African contract laborers who introduced the primary elements of the Kumina tradition to Jamaica in the 19th century —
Kumina worship is largely a face-to-face religion.[6] In this part of the
island, past generations of Kumina devotees often lived close together, on or near estate properties, and later, in marked sections or
"districts" within larger villages or communities, typically given the
name "Bongo Town." Nearly every major settlement in central and
eastern St. Thomas had its own Bongo Town, and every Bongo Town
had its own cult of possessing ancestors, whose names and relationships to living residents were known to most local worshipers.[7]

There was, and continues to be, much visiting between Kumina
practitioners of different St. Thomas communities, and many individuals maintain personal ties with others living a good distance
away. Ceremonies often draw participants from several different
parts of the parish. The anthropologist Joseph Moore noticed the high
degree of mobility among Kumina participants more than forty years
ago. "There is no center of great activity, nor is this a backwoods
affair," he remarked. "Ceremonies are fairly evenly distributed
throughout the area under study" (Moore 1953: 114). To get some idea
of the scope of ceremonial life in this part of the island, Moore kept
track of the itinerary of one drummer over an eight-month period in
1950, listing the locations of the more than sixty Kumina dances this
man attended between January and August. The ceremonies tabulated by Moore took place in more than forty different villages and
districts, spanning virtually the entire parish of St. Thomas, from
Rocky Point on the eastern coastal plain to Cedar Valley in the western highlands (approximately twenty miles apart as the crow flies,
and many more than that over land) (Moore 1953: 117–119).[8] This
extraordinary amount of visiting required careful planning. "For
many of the dances," writes Moore, "arrangements are made for
trucks to pick up parties throughout the territory [and] often, as many
as five or six trucks are used for a given ceremony. It is not unusual
to visit one Cumina, paying one's respects until two in the morning,
then traveling to a second Cumina in order to be there at five in the
morning when the sacrifice of the goat and the dance of the queen of
the Cumina are conducted" (Moore 1953: 119).[9]

Since St. Thomas covers a considerable land area and has a sizeable
population — though only one of fourteen parishes in Jamaica, it is
larger than most of the smaller island nations of the Caribbean — it

is impossible, despite frequent inter-ceremonial visiting, for all Kumina practitioners to know one another.[10] Nonetheless, all Kumina devotees in this part of the island consider themselves members of a single "nation," which they call the "Bongo nation." They see themselves as united through their shared religion, which is the primary locus of their identity as "Africans."

Nor is Kumina limited to St. Thomas; it can be found as far west as St. Mary and Clarendon parishes, spanning nearly the entire eastern half of the island. The farther one gets from its core in St. Thomas, however, particularly in urban areas, the more detached the "Bongo" identity associated with it becomes from specific, named ancestors and the lands on which they are buried.

Despite limited contact between them in recent years, Kumina practitioners in St. Thomas and other parts of the island, such as Portland, St. Mary, St. Catherine, Clarendon, St. Andrew, and Kingston, consider themselves "Africans" — which is to say, members of a unitary "Bongo nation." The objective cultural differences that now characterize regional variants of the tradition do not conceal the many remaining similarities, and representatives of all branches of the Kumina religion are quick to recognize and respond to these similarities.[11] Cultural overlap continues to provide a powerful basis for co-identification whenever far-flung members of the "Bongo nation" travel outside their own parishes and happen to encounter local variants of Kumina practice somewhat different from their own.

Clearly, Kumina has proven adaptable to a wide variety of contexts. Thanks to the non-exclusive, incorporative ideology of this religion, its membership has never been limited by its historical association with a highly specific local geography. The flexible fit between physical place, genealogical space, and definitions of group identity that have characterized Kumina since its inception have led it in some areas to lose its links to the founding ancestors whose spirits continue to be known by name and to possess devotees in St. Thomas Kumina strongholds such as Seaforth, Leith Hall, and Port Morant; but this flexibility has also allowed the boundaries (or potential boundaries) of the "Bongo nation" to spread well beyond the highly localized "Bongo Towns" of St. Thomas to which the Kumina religion appears to have once been confined.[12] Indeed, over the last century Kumina has been able to spread across virtually the entire eastern half of the island, carried by an increasingly mobile population. This capacity for adaptation may be seen as a legacy of the historical process of creolization from which this religion emerged.[13]

Convince Spirits: Workers on the Move

Of the older indigenous Jamaican religions, the one most striking for its disengagement of identity from place is Convince, also known as Bongo, or Flenke — the religion we briefly glimpsed at the beginning of this essay. Convince, like Kumina, appears to be limited to the eastern half of the island. Like Kumina practitioners, Convince devotees identify themselves as "Bongo" or "African" people who belong to a single "nation"; although they distinguish this nation from the one that practices Kumina (as well as the entirely separate "nation" to which Maroons claim to belong), there is evidence that from the beginning Convince has incorporated influences from Kumina, and to a lesser extent, from the Maroon Kromanti religion (Hogg 1960; Bilby 1981: 81–88).[14]

My research with a number of Convince mediums leads me to believe that the original appearance of what is today known as Convince can be pinpointed to a relatively small area in the northwestern portion of what is today Portland parish, and that it probably dates back to the mid- or late 19th century. In this limited geographic area, and neighboring parts of St. Mary, present-day Convince practitioners, though they are scattered, loosely knit, and seldom linked by close ties of kinship, nonetheless speak of specific local cemeteries where famous Convince mediums of the distant past lie buried. I have not found this to be the case among those who practice Convince elsewhere in the island. Furthermore, a number of well-known Convince spirits that possess mediums over a wide area extending to eastern Portland and St. Thomas — for instance, Cotton Tree Massa, Dover (Road) Massa, Frederick McCleary, and the most famous of all Convince spirits, John Walbert (or Walsbert) — are still identified by some of their mediums with specific communities in western Portland, where they are believed to have once lived.

A preeminent characteristic of Convince is its lack of centralization and its extremely fluid organization. Regularity and structure, inasmuch as they exist in Convince, emerge only in the context of ceremonies held by individual Convince men, who decide when and where to call a meeting. There are no established authorities, no churches or temples, no immovable sacred sites to which the faithful are bound.[15] To cite Hogg once again,

> like their spirits, Bongo Men do not recognize authorities or establish permanent, cohesive groups among themselves. Indeed, the cult has very little formal organization at all. Independent Bongo Men live scattered about the countryside, each presiding over his own ceremonies. Thus, while a given member is in effect a cult leader at his own meetings, he becomes a follower when he attends the ceremonies of others. (Hogg 1960: 7)

My own observations support those of Hogg: Convince workers and their spirits alike refuse to be tied down. Eschewing "permanent, cohesive groups," they opt for independence and mobility. They are perpetually on the go, prepared to migrate as the occasion demands. They do so, however, with the expectation that sooner or later they will encounter other practitioners who, as "independent Bongo men" like themselves, have become "scattered about the countryside."

If mobility is a fact of life for Convince workers, it is even more so for their spirits. Wherever it is practiced, Convince is, quite literally, a "fly by night" affair, and though some of the spirits who visit the living routinely announce the names of the rural districts in which they once lived, the idea of staying put in any one place appears to be foreign to them. Zinging across the hills and coastal plains, darting through the air from one medium to the next, they cover vast distances and appear to be in non-stop motion.[16] Earlier writers such as Joseph Moore and Donald Hogg noted that most Convince men have several spirits who often possess them in rapid succession, and I was able to confirm this; none of the mediums with whom I am acquainted has fewer than five spirits, and some have more than ten; another medium I heard about was reputed to have more than fifty. This profusion of spirits serves an imagined community of mediums and clients whose expanse is far too great to be handled by smaller numbers of spirits, no matter how powerful. On one typical occasion, I was greeted by an impatient possessing spirit named Hunter-Man who told me through his medium that he had to leave immediately, for he had been called to a big Convince meeting in Westmoreland parish on the far side of the island (where, incidentally, Convince as such is not normally practiced); he informed me that another spirit named Old Kito would take his place in a moment; Old Kito, who was also pressed for time, simply wanted to convey the message that yet another very busy spirit, Cotton Tree Jonjo, wanted to talk with me and would be arriving close on his heels.

Although at least some of the specific villages and districts named by possessing Convince spirits appear on Jamaican maps, and some mediums are familiar with some of the locations mentioned by their spirits, no Convince worker has firsthand knowledge of the entire landscape over which his spirits roam, and some have never visited any of these places. The imaginary maps that spirits draw when they arrive on their mediums and identify themselves are full of place names that have legendary significance, as sites where famous or powerful Convince men once held sway. Places such as Buff Bay in Portland or Hampton Court in St. Thomas, for instance, are known for having once been centers of Convince activity. There are powerful spirits, such as Hampton Court Massa and Dover Road Massa, whose very names evoke the places with which they were most closely associated when they practiced Convince as living men. And arriving spirits frequently announce their presence with situating statements such as, "I am Bongo man Fredrick McCleary from Black Hill, Portland" or "Bongo man Aaron Lowe from Swift River come fi tek body."[17] These customary citations of places help to foster the image of a dispersed community of individualistic spirits who, though grounded to some extent in local history, range freely over an unseen and potentially unlimited expanse of land — the uncharted and largely unknown (though very "real") territory of the "Convince nation."

At times this landscape veers off into what might be called a more purely mythic realm. One spirit, named Missa Binaman, used to tell me he was not from Jamaica at all, but rather, from "Guinea Country" (which he alternately referred to as "Bongo Country" or "Bongos place").[18] And one Convince medium, who lived deep in the eastern Blue Mountains, far from most of his fellow practitioners, insisted that *all* his spirits come from the "Guinea Coast" — which, he said, is the same as "dead country" (i.e. the country of the dead). After all, he explained, Convince spirits are "Africans," and their mediums, as

"Bongo" people, belong to a single "nation." This "Guinea Coast" of Convince cosmology closely parallels the "Guinea" (*Ginê*) of Haitian Voodoo/*Vodou*. According to Métraux (1972: 91), "the *loa* [gods], or at any rate the most important ones, live in Guinea. This name has for long been without real geographical meaning, for Guinea is a sort of Valhalla, not situated anywhere. The *loa* leave it when they are called to the earth."[19]

As earlier mentioned, both Kumina and Convince practitioners refer to themselves as "Bongo" people, or "Africans." But unlike more knowledgeable Kumina specialists, who say *their* "nation" can be further divided into what they call "tribes," such as Kongo, Muyanji, and Mumbaka, Convince men recognize only a more generalized "African" identity, and their spirits apparently never claim more specific "tribal" affiliations.[20] Just as the spirits of Convince are less rooted in the earth — where the graves of ancestors are located — than are Kumina spirits, so are they less concerned with familial relationships or ancestral ties connecting the living to ethnically specific pasts.

"All Creole People": Community as a Constantly Emerging Potential

A closer look will reveal that the religious ideology of Convince in some ways actually replicates the processual logic of creolization. This historical process of cultural reconfiguration and community-building is still clearly referenced by certain elements of ritual performance that seem to be common to Convince wherever it is practiced. The concept of "creoleness" itself, for example, would appear to be symbolically encoded in the marked speech of possession: whenever Bongo spirits possess their mediums, they typically address the living people around them with the formulaic expressions "creole massa," "Jamaica creole," or "creole people." Donald Hogg (1960: 13) noted this in passing more than thirty years ago, writing that "each [spirit] has his own uniform, and the Bongo Man must be re-dressed whenever one spirit leaves and another possesses him. Clothed to his satisfaction, the ghost shouts 'Good morning to all creole people,' recites a Christian prayer, and then begins to dance and sing."

One Convince man with whom I worked explained the significance of this expression as follows:

> These men [i.e. Convince mediums] are creole Bongos, but those other
> men [i.e. the spirits that possess them] are salt-water Bongos. Those
> men you hear me calling — [spirits like] Cotton Tree Massa, New
> Hungry, Richmond Diver — they were born in Africa, they know the
> true, deep language. You see, when they talk that language, they have
> to teach it to us [i.e. the creole people], because we only hear them
> talking but we don't understand.[21]

In other words, the "creole Bongo" people, the present generation of
Convince workers, are no longer divided by the various African
languages once spoken by their ethnically diverse "salt-water Bongo"
forebears; today they all share the contemporary English-related creole of Jamaica as their native language. And yet, as this passage also
makes clear, the same African-born "salt-water Bongo" spirits (themselves no strangers to creolization) teach their devotees a unique
"Convince language" that forms an important component of the
distinctive "Bongo" identity underpinning Convince practitioners'
newfound sense of community (or, as they express it, "nation"-hood).
Though putatively "African" (and though it has indeed borrowed a
handful of African-derived words from Kumina and Maroon
Kromanti), this possession language is in fact an entirely new creole
argot with a largely English-derived vocabulary, much of which has
been thoroughly transformed through innovative word play.[22] Similarly, most Convince songs, though characterized by devotees as
"Bongo" or "African" songs, represent unique combinations of musical and textual features derived from various European, African,
and Jamaican sources. In these respects and others, Convince is a
typically creole cultural synthesis; and the above-mentioned Convince tropes referencing "creoleness" — expressions such as "Jamaica
creole," "creole massa," and "creole people" — might be seen as
symbolic allusions to the historical process through which this new
culture came into being.

But the term "creole," in the Convince context, also has other,
deeper implications. Particularly interesting is the way it is employed
by Convince workers and their spirits to denote an all-inclusive
imagined community no longer divided by distinctions based on

place of origin, or for that matter, place of any kind. As another Convince medium told me:

> When [the spirit] says "creole people," it means the "family" that is present. It doesn't have to be one family, but, I mean, those in the congregation. When he says, "goodbye to all Jamaican creole people," that simply means goodbye to all who are at that spot for that period of time.[23]

Thus, the community of "creole people" conceptualized by this medium — glossed as a "family" or "congregation" — is an ad hoc and emergent one; it has no fixed place, but rather, exists as a potential that can be realized anytime and anywhere.[24]

It is not difficult to imagine the value such a fluid conceptualization of community would have had for displaced Africans of past centuries, who at first shared little more than a common living space, the predicament of enslavement, and the need to build a livable creole society.[25] Nor would this image of community as an unfolding potentiality have lost its utility in later years when the emancipated — the "creole people" or "Jamaica creoles" of the 19th century — strove to build new lives on the ashes of the plantation system, or when future generations were forced by economic necessity to migrate and to adapt to new social surroundings. The building of community in such contexts has always involved a kind of ongoing creolization.

As I later learned, the breadth and inclusiveness of the imagined community implied by the term "creole" in Convince is limited only by the imagination of the individual invoking it.[26] I once heard the spirit John Walbert, for instance, while possessing a medium in St. Thomas, tell his audience:

> I as a Bongo man agree to converse with creole people. Not even Jamaica creole people — all creole people from the whole world.... All who are creole people, we come to [them] as friends. We Bongo men are great to all Jamaica people, and to all people in the world.[27]

It was not until several years later, in western Portland, that I was told by another Convince man that in the distant past, both whites and East Indians used to dance Convince along with the Africans.

And in 1995, for the first time, I heard Convince practitioners assert that there are Americans today who "jump the same Convince in Chicago."[28] That same evening I saw a Convince medium from this group become possessed in rapid succession by three North American spirits — a loud-talking Chicagoan named Roy Clark (who demanded whiskey rather than the usual rum), an apparently Hispanic-American woman who calls herself Senarita (i.e. Señorita), and another ghost from the United States named Julie Parlor. It has taken some time, but the imagined community embraced by Convince seems finally to be penetrating international borders and making new leaps across boundaries of race, ethnicity and gender.[29]

New Communities of the Displaced: Bongo Brethren in Babylon

The one indigenous Jamaican religion that has truly gone international is of course Rastafari. In some ways, Rastafari might be seen as a logical extension of trends already observable in Convince. Like Convince men past and present, those Jamaicans among whom Rastafari first took root came from the ranks of the dispossessed, displaced, and despised — those at the very bottom of the Jamaican social hierarchy. Descendants of African slaves in an ex-plantation society, the majority of early Rastafari started out as landless and small-holding peasants, most possessing little more than their own labor. For most of these rural Jamaicans, there were few alternatives to the lives of crushing poverty into which they had been born. For many, the answer was migration.

Migration has always been fundamental to the Rastafarian experience (Chevannes 1994: 51–63). The earliest Rastafari, those who became followers of Leonard Howell in St. Thomas parish during the 1930s, were primarily transient agricultural laborers and menial workers from various rural areas struggling to get by in coastal centers of sugar and banana production such as Duckenfield and Port Morant. Before long, they were joined by their urban counterparts — migrants to the city of Kingston who found themselves living in similarly precarious situations and began gravitating toward a number of independent prophets of Rastafari in and around the capital.

As rural–urban migration skyrocketed, squatters' settlements sprang up overnight, and West Kingston shanty towns teeming with the displaced — chaotic, de facto "communities" such as Back-o-Wall and the Dungle — grew into hotbeds of Rasta consciousness. "It was under such conditions," writes Chevannes (1994: 16–17), "that Rasta-fari became a hospice for the uprooted and derelict masses cast off by society and left to the mercy of the elements."

Wherever Rastas assembled and strove to create new lives for themselves, this shared experience of uprooting and relocation constituted a fundamental given. Whether in the Maroon-like rural commune headed by Leonard Howell at Pinnacle during the 1940s, the semi-urban settlements pieced together by squatters in various parts of West Kingston during the 1950s, or the "camps" established by younger brethren at Wareika Hill ("Warrior's Hill") and Back-o-Wall ("Egypt") in the early 1960s (Homiak 1995), Rastas were continually faced with the necessity of building a community where none had existed before. Atomized, drawn from different parts of the island, and brought together by chance crossings of migratory paths, these early brethren (and sistren), like their African ancestors, were forced to re-create themselves as social beings from the shreds of their individual pasts. Of course, all Jamaicans (barring some members of the elite) by this time possessed a broadly shared creole culture, and this would serve the displaced as the initial basis on which to build a viable sense of community. But this was not enough. In imagining their new communities, the Rastas countered their oppression by inventing new forms of culture and new ideological weapons — the language of I-tesvar, the drumming of Nyabinghi, the dreadlocks covenant, the "Higes knots" ("natural" attire), and the philosophy of I-tal livity ("natural" living) (Homiak 1995) — that were as "creole" (and in their own way, as "African") as any before them (Warner-Lewis 1993).

These new spiritual communities, like those imagined by Convince men and other displaced fellow travelers throughout Jamaican history, were supported by ideologies that were not only oppositional, but just as importantly, open, adaptable, and inclusive.[30] Partly because of these qualities — which may be seen as an important component of Rastafari's creole inheritance — a new religion that might otherwise have remained bound to a series of scattered, localized enclaves of face-to-face worshipers has long since been able to break free from its original breeding grounds and to blossom into a unified (though amorphous) movement and imagined community that continues to expand into new territories.

Given their common genesis in displacement, migration, and creolization (not to mention their overlapping historical ties to the larger Afro-Jamaican religious tradition), it is not surprising that Convince and Rastafari, as different as they are, present a number of striking parallels. Some of these are of special interest to this discussion. Like Convince, for example, Rastafari has long been noted for its lack of centralized authority, its high degree of individualism, and its loose-knit, highly flexible ideology.[31] And like the spirits of Convince, Rastas, who see themselves as exiles in Babylon, have no "home" — at least on this side of the ocean. Whereas Convince has been moving away from localized cults of ancestral ghosts tied to community burial grounds, in favor of an ideology emphasizing unattached spirits with no fixed dwelling, Rastafari has abolished the ancestral spirits altogether, cutting all ties with the dead, including deceased relatives whose burial sites might otherwise bind Rastas to specific parcels of land (Owens 1976: 136–139; Chevannes 1994: 203–204). In Rastafari ideology (if not always in practice), this process of disengagement with a local world of spirits is nearly complete, the focus of worship having shifted to a singular supreme divinity, Selassie I, and the ancestral homeland of Africa/Ethiopia. For many Rastas, this sacred continent, much like the "Guinea Country" of Convince mediums, or the *Ginê* of Haitian worshipers, is more a "state of mind" than an actual expanse of land; to borrow the words of Métraux (1972: 90), it is "not situated anywhere." As with Convince, the imagined community united in worship of Rastafari is open-ended, and equally impossible to pin down to any precisely specifiable physical place.

Conclusion: History and Modernity

In their malleable conceptions of community and place, Rastas, like their counterparts in Convince, partake of a Caribbean "modernity" that predates by centuries the onset of that condition in most other parts of the world. No one has done more to remind us of this special Caribbean heritage than Sidney Mintz. "Because of the lengthy connection between Caribbean societies and the West," he writes, "and the immigration (much of it forced) of people from other world areas into the Caribbean, this is a region in which older social forms broke down at an early time, and important redefinitions of the self, of the bonds of kinship, and of the many-stranded relationships of the individual to the group were established" (Mintz 1989: xvi). Some three decades ago, Mintz pointed out the relevance of this centuries-long Caribbean experience of displacement and reinvention to the rapidly changing world at large:

> it can be contended that many other societies, only recently propelled in a "western" direction, are likely to take on more and more similarity to the Caribbean mold, at least in certain sectors of their social systems. Whereas Europe and the United States have been able to develop a heavily individualistic emphasis in social relations, they have done so from the vantage-point of long-established forms of group integration. It is perhaps of some interest, then, that those aspects of modern western society regarded as most depersonalizing and "anti-human" — the view of persons as things and as numbers, interchangeable, expendable, and faceless — have a very lengthy history in the Caribbean area, and developed there in the context of very imperfect transfers of European social institutions. (Mintz 1971 [1966]: 41–42)

In his recent exploration of "popular music, postmodernism and the poetics of place," George Lipsitz (1994) echoes Mintz's insights, replacing the latter's Caribbean focus with a broader "diasporic" sweep, and adding a politically engaged "cultural studies" spin of his own. "The solutions to what seem like our newest problems," writes Lipsitz from a nineties perspective, "may well be found in communities that have been struggling with them for centuries. The most 'modern' people in the world that is emerging may be those from nations that have been considered 'backward'" (Lipsitz 1994: 19). Elsewhere, Lipsitz makes clear just what "communities" and "nations" he has in mind here, and why he thinks their experience has a special significance for a world in which globalization is rendering notions of identity and place ever more problematic:

The populations best prepared for cultural conflict and political contestation in a globalized world economy may well be the diasporic
communities of displaced Africans, Asians, and Latin Americans created by the machinations of world capitalism over the centuries. These
populations, long accustomed to code switching, syncretism, and hybridity may prove far more important for what they *possess* in cultural
terms than for what they appear to *lack* in the political lexicon of the
nation state. (Lipsitz 1994: 31)

Although Lipsitz is concerned specifically with the role of contemporary popular music in the construction of new "communities" and
identities on a global scale, the kinds of cultural processes to which
he alludes, as we have seen, have been occurring for centuries in
what has often been styled the "crucible" of the Caribbean — in
music as in other spheres (Bilby 1990). Indeed, it is no accident that
in his book Lipsitz places special emphasis on the distinctively Caribbean phenomenon of Rastafari, returning again and again to the
local and transnational linkages between peoples made possible by
the global spread of Rasta themes and symbols via reggae music (pp.
15, 31, 97–114, 127–128).[32] As he recognizes, this Afro-Caribbean religion, born of the same creolizing process that produced Kumina,
Revival, and other indigenous forms of religious expression in Jamaica, is deeply rooted in a specific history of economic, cultural,
and political struggle; but what particularly interests Lipsitz is the
way it has also proven — partly owing to its Caribbean creole origins
— remarkably adaptable when placed in other contexts.[33] Today, as
a result, Rastafari is neither here nor there; it is everywhere, taking
the form of both a local (as well as diasporic) community of Jamaican
worshipers and a world religion with no known boundaries (Yawney
1993).[34] As Barry Chevannes (1994: 278) so succinctly put it, "internationalization has brought Rastafari to a new stage." And so the
brethren and sistren, once confined to a local Babylonian prison, are
now world citizens. But as they continue to scatter across the globe,
in both the spirit and the flesh, the still-unrepatriated masses of
Rastafari, wherever they are, remain — like the growing legions of
migrants and travelers around the world — "only visitors here"
(Yawney 1997).

Because of its preoccupation with a mythic past, Rastafari, like
Convince, has sometimes been portrayed as a "nativistic" religion;

yet, it could easily be argued that there is no religion on earth more "modern" than this one. As we approach the millennium, it is perhaps fitting that the imagined community continually being reinvented by Rastafari brethren and sistren finds itself increasingly represented in that quintessential placeless realm called cyberspace. These days, Rastafarians dispersed half-way across the globe (and of all hues and ethnicities) can, and often do, fire off intercontinental e-mail reasonings with a speed rivaling that of Convince spirits as they race across the Jamaican skies. And it may be but a matter of time before Jamaican Bongo men, not to mention Convince-jumping Chicagoans, discover the internet as well.

Limitations of space require me to bring this essay to a close here. Perhaps the discussion can be continued on an appropriate listserv. But that's neither here nor there. In the meantime, those who doubt what I have said about the growing Rastafarian presence in cyberspace are invited to pay a visit to the "Virtual Niahbingi" on the World Wide Web at http://www.nation.org/.

Endnotes

An earlier version of this paper was presented at the 1995 Annual Meeting of the American Anthropological Association in Washington, DC, as part of a session entitled "Caribbean Religions: Culture, Consciousness, Community at Home and Abroad." The session was organized by John W. Pulis. John Szwed and Richard Price acted as discussants.

1. All information in this paper that is not credited to other authors is derived from my own research with Convince and Kumina devotees. This began in 1978, while I was conducting a study of social ties between ritual specialists in the Windward Maroon communities and the surrounding area (see Bilby 1979, 1981), and has continued over the years since. Although my research focused on Maroons, I also spent a considerable amount of time working with Kumina and Convince practitioners. See Bilby and Fu-Kiau (1983).

2. From a tape recording made in Port Antonio, Portland, on June 5, 1978. All quotations of Convince practitioners in this paper are identified only by location and date of recording, since under current

Jamaican law Convince workers are subject to prosecution for practicing "obeah" (a concept that remains legally ill-defined, but nonetheless has been used by Jamaican law enforcement officials at their
whim to cover a wide range of spiritual, magical, and medicinal
practices).

3. It is interesting to compare the boundless realm through which the
   spirits of Convince are able to travel with the similarly vast spiritual
   landscape over which adepts among the Converted of St. Vincent
   roam. According to Wallace Zane (in this volume), "places to which
   the Converted regularly travel are a spiritual version (or the spiritual
   aspect) of Zion, Africa, China, India, Jerusalem, Bethlehem, Canaan,
   the Valley of Jehosaphat, the Desert, the Jungle, as well as various
   places on top of and under the sea, and a large number of other cities,
   countries, and islands."

4. See, for instance, Mintz and Price (1992), from which several of the
   points that follow have been distilled.

5. A detailed description of the Maroon Kromanti religion, based on
   ethnographic fieldwork, may be found in Bilby (1981). For an examination of the role of this religion in Jamaican Maroon ethnogenesis
   (an historical example of community-building), see Bilby (1996).

6. The best source to date on the history of Kumina is Schuler (1980),
   which uses a combination of archival sources and oral traditions to
   establish beyond doubt that the Kumina religion is derived primarily
   from traditions introduced to Jamaica by "voluntary" African laborers who arrived after emancipation in 1834.

7. This depiction of settlement patterns among the Central African
   immigrants who introduced Kumina to Jamaica is based on my
   reading of Schuler (1980), my interviews with a large number of St.
   Thomas Kumina practitioners, and my own observations of residen-
   tial patterns in those communities where Kumina remains strongest.

8. When I worked in St. Thomas in 1978, I found that inter-ceremonial
   visiting was still a very important factor in Kumina, much as it had
   been in Moore's day. See Bilby and Fu-Kiau (1983).

9. The spelling of Kumina has varied. When Moore was writing (in the
   1950s), it was often spelled "Cumina." Today, the generally accepted
   spelling is "Kumina."

10. The land area of St. Thomas is 780 square kilometers (300 square
    miles); in 1982, according to the official census, the population of the
    parish was 76,347 (Senior 1983: 157).

11. For a discussion of some of the cultural differences characterizing Kumina as practiced in St. Thomas, St. Mary, St. Catherine, and Clarendon, see Ryman (1984: 121–124).

12. It is not difficult to find parallels elsewhere in the Caribbean. See, for instance, the recent discussion by James Houk (1995: 169–179) of the Orisha religion in Trinidad as an "open system."

13. It is worth adding that there exist yet other variations on Kumina, some of which are even farther removed from the original St. Thomas tradition than the regional offshoots of the religion mentioned above. For discussions of some of these other versions, ranging from the original (pre-Nyabinghi) Kumina-based form of Rastafari practiced by the followers of the Rasta prophet Leonard Howell to choreographed renditions of Kumina ritual by "official" state-sponsored performing troupes, see Bilby and Leib (1985), Nettleford (1985: 145–148), Manuel et al (1995: 159–164), and McPherson (1995).

14. The ubiquitous occurrence of the word "nation" in native terminology to denote the imagined communities embodied in Jamaican religions such as Kromanti, Kumina, Convince, and Rastafari corresponds, interestingly enough, to Anderson's (1983) privileging of what he calls the "nation" (defined as a political unit) as the paradigmatic imagined community. The work of Edward Kamau Brathwaite (1984) on "nation language" in the Caribbean also resonates with Anderson's focus on the concept of "nationhood." See also John Homiak's chapter on the expanding boundaries of the Rastafari "nation" in this volume.

15. Compare this aspect of Convince with what Zane (in this volume) has to say about the flexibility of notions of sacred space among Spiritual Baptists (including the Vincentian Converted): "In a way, all of Spiritual Baptist locality is provisional ... it is the presence of the Converted who make the site sacred ... they carry the sacredness with them. The site is far less important than the fact that the Converted are there."

16. One finds a similar emphasis on mobility in the spirit worlds imagined by a number of other African-Caribbean religions. In St. Vincent, for instance, according to Zane (in this volume), "the emphasis of the Converted is always on travel [of a spiritual rather than physical kind] ... they are always going somewhere."

17. Convince spirits usually refer to the act and state of possession as "tek body" (i.e. to take the medium's body), rather than *myal* (as in Kumina and the Maroon Kromanti religion).

18. Hogg (1960: 4–6) was told that "the strongest Bongo ghosts come from Africa, which is supposedly the birthplace and heart of Convince. Others derive from ancient Jamaican slaves who presumably represented its early local branches."

19. This portrayal of the realm called "Guinea" by Haitian worshipers is seconded by Lowenthal (1978: 393) and other writers since.

20. For more on the specific "tribal" affiliations still claimed by Kumina practitioners in St. Thomas, see Moore (1953: 123) and Bilby and Fu-Kiau (1983: 9–12).

21. From a tape recording of an interview, Bryans Bay, Portland, October 7, 1978.

22. This Convince "language" forms part of a broader pattern of linguistic inventiveness in Jamaica. See Pulis (1993), Pollard (1994), and Homiak (1995).

23. From a tape recorded interview, Whitehall, St. Thomas, July 23, 1978.

24. That the community of spirits and worshipers actualized and embodied through Convince possession (and associated rites) is conceptualized by practitioners as a placeless, timeless potentiality is apparent from a number of other statements I recorded on tape, such as the following remark made by a Convince devotee I interviewed in 1995: "It doesn't really matter where you go, you know, or when. It just is when the spirit dem ready to ride the Convince, at that time. They must ride [possess] you anywhere. Anywhere. It doesn't matter where. Anywhere." (From a tape recording of an interview, Albany, St. Mary, March 4, 1995.)

25. In an insightful discussion of the concept of "yard" (a term which is used by Jamaicans, both literally and metaphorically, to mean "home"), Werner Zips (1991) makes a number of points that overlap with my argument here. Tracing the Jamaican "yard" concept to the period of slavery, he argues that it originally applied to the public "meeting places" between slave huts or barracks, which functioned as important sites of cultural construction and reproduction. Like the trope of "creole people" in Convince, this broader concept of "yard," Zips argues, "reflects symbolically the collective memory [of] the development of new communicative forms of expression" — the development of such new forms having been part and parcel of the process of constructing new (i.e. creolized) communities and cultural identities in Jamaica. The flexibility of this concept of "yard" (which

combines connotations of "home" and "meeting place" in a single term) is such that it can be employed as an expression of cultural identity divorced from literal space, as when used in contexts or locations outside of Jamaica that have been remade and / or redefined by immigrants as "Jamaican."

26. The Jamaican concept of "yard" — which, like the Convince term "creole people," references aspects of the historical processes of creolization and community-building — carries a similar potential for inclusiveness, as Zips (1991: 77) makes clear when he points out that "the term Yardie can even be applied to people who are not of Jamaican descent, but know [how] to participate in the Jamaican codes of communication."

27. From a tape recording made during an episode of possession, White-hall, St. Thomas, July 23, 1978. The spirit's comments in this passage were conditioned by the fact that a foreigner (myself) was present, as well as a visiting Jamaican who was unfamiliar with the Convince tradition.

28. It should be pointed out that such references to Chicago in Convince are not fortuitous. Because Chicago is home to DeLaurence, the publisher of a number of much sought-after esoteric manuals and "Science" (magic) books, this North American city has long been seen by many Jamaicans as a mythic center of spiritual power (see Hogg 1961, Elkins 1986).

29. Although at least one well-known Convince worker of the distant past, known as Mother Flenke, was a woman, Convince mediums and spirits today are overwhelmingly male, which is why I repeatedly use the term Bongo *man*, without further qualification, in this paper. For more on this question, see Hogg (1964: 437).

30. As Yawney (1976: 231) and many others have pointed out, "despite their unequivocal rejection of entire classes of people on ideological grounds, the Brethren always make exceptions for any individual who comes among them with a sincere intent." Following biblical scripture, they see their imagined community as encompassing "remnants of all nations" (ibid).

31. In a thoughtful discussion, Yawney (1993) elaborates on one important aspect of this ideological flexibility when she attributes the globalization of Rastafari to a kind of built-in "symbolic ambiguity." This tendency toward symbolic ambiguity is shared, to a greater or lesser degree, by all Afro-Jamaican religions, including Convince, and may be viewed, at least in part, as a correlate of creolization.

32. Beginning in the mid-1970s, the influence of Rastafari began to be felt around the world, owing largely to Jamaican migration toward metropolitan centers and the growth of an international market for reggae music (Bilby 1983); more recently, a number of other factors have also become significant in the spread of the movement, such as sophisticated transnational networking by Rasta elders and the dissemination of audiovisual materials (Yawney 1993; Homiak 1994; Homiak 1997).

33. One such context is London, where, among West Indian immigrant groups and others who participate in carnival celebrations, certain elements of Rastafarian ideology function as "articulating principles for the formation of primary neighborhood groups" based on "communal relationships and cultural forms supported by cultural imperatives" (Cohen 1993: 36, 83). For more on the adaptability of Rastafari, see Carole Yawney (1993: 161; 164).

34. For a recent examination of the spread of Rastafari across the globe, see Savishinsky (1994).

References

Anderson, B. 1983 *Imagined Communities: Reflections on the Origin and Spread of Nationalism*. London: Verso.

Bilby, K.M. 1979 *Partisan Spirits: Ritual Interaction and Maroon Identity in Eastern Jamaica*. Unpublished M.A. thesis, Wesleyan University, Middletown, CT.

Bilby, K.M. 1981 The Kromanti dance of the Windward Maroons of Jamaica. *Nieuwe West-Indische Gids* 55(1/2):52–101.

Bilby, K.M. 1983 Black thoughts from the Caribbean: I-deology at home and abroad. *New West Indian Guide* 57(3/4):201–213.

Bilby, K.M. 1990 Puentes composicionales en un mundo insular: vínculos espontáneos en la tradición musical Caribeña. *Del Caribe* 6(16/17):112–119.

Bilby, K.M. 1996 Ethnogenesis in the Guianas and Jamaica: two Maroon cases. In: *Culture, Power, and History: Ethnogenesis in the Americas, 1492–1992* (ed., J.D. Hill). Iowa City: University of Iowa Press.

Bilby, K.M. and Fu-Kiau kia Bunseki 1983 *Kumina: A Kongo-Based Tradition in the New World*. Brussels: Centre d'Etude et de Documentation Africaines.

Bilby, K.M. and Leib, E. 1985 Kumina, the Howellite church and the emergence of Rastafarian traditional music in Jamaica. *Jamaica Journal* 19(3):22–28.

Brathwaite, E.K. 1984 *History of the Voice: The Development of Nation Language in Anglophone Caribbean Poetry*. London: New Beacon Books.

Chevannes, B. 1994 *Rastafari: Roots and Ideology*. Syracuse, NY: Syracuse University Press.

Cohen, A. 1993 *Masquerade Politics*. Berkeley: University of California Press.

Elkins, W.F. 1986 William Lauron DeLaurence and Jamaican folk religion. *Folklore* 97:215–218.

Hogg, D. 1960 *The Convince Cult in Jamaica*. Yale University Publications in Anthropology 58.

Hogg, D. 1961 Magic and "science" in Jamaica. *Caribbean Studies* 1(2):1–5.

Hogg, D. 1964 *Jamaican Religions: A Study in Variations*. Unpublished PhD dissertation, Yale University, New Haven, CT.

Homiak, J.P. 1994 From yard to nation: Rastafari and the politics of eldership at home and abroad. In: *Ay BoBo: African-Caribbean Religions* Part 3: *Rastafari* (ed., M. Kremser). Vienna: WUV-Universitätsverlag.

Homiak, J.P. 1995 Dub history: soundings on Rastafari livity and language. In *Rastafari and Other African-Caribbean World Views* (ed., B. Chevannes). London: Macmillan.

Homiak, J.P. 1997 From soundscapes to mediaspaces: mapping the boundaries of the Rastafari nation. In this volume.

Houk, J.T. 1995 *Spirits, Blood, and Drums: The Orisha Religion in Trinidad*. Philadelphia: Temple University Press.

Lipsitz, G. 1994 *Dangerous Crossroads: Popular Music, Postmodernism and the Poetics of Place*. London: Verso.

Lowenthal, I.P. 1978 Ritual performance and religious experience: a service for the gods in southern Haiti. *Journal of Anthropological Research* 34:392–414.

Manuel, P.; Bilby, K.M.; and Largey, M. 1995 *Caribbean Currents: Caribbean Music from Rumba to Reggae*. Philadelphia: Temple University Press.

McPherson, E.S.P. 1995 *Kulungu: Traditional Rastafari Kumina Songs, Prayers and Reasoning of the Howellites, the First Rastafari Community* (set of four compact discs, and accompanying pamphlets). Brooklyn, NY: Black International Iyahbinghi Press.

Métraux, A. 1972 *Voodoo in Haiti* (second edition). New York: Schocken.

Mintz, S.W. 1971 The Caribbean as a socio-cultural area. In: *Peoples and Cultures of the Caribbean* (ed., M.M. Horowitz). Garden City, NY: Natural History Press.

Mintz, S.W. 1989 *Caribbean Transformations* (New Morningside edition). New York: Columbia University Press.

Mintz, S.W. and Price, R. 1992 *The Birth of African-American Culture*. Boston: Beacon Press.

Moore, J.G. 1953 *Religion of Jamaican Negroes: A Study of Afro-Jamaican Acculturation*. Unpublished PhD dissertation, Northwestern University, Evanston, IL.

Nettleford, R. 1985 *Dance Jamaica*. New York: Grove Press.

Owens, J. 1976 *Dread: The Rastafarians of Jamaica*. Kingston: Sangster.

Pollard, V. 1994 *Dread Talk: The Language of Rastafari*. Kingston: Canoe Press.

Pulis, J.W. 1993 "Up-full sound": language, identity, and the world-view of Rastafari. *Ethnic Groups* 10:285–300.

Ryman, C. 1984 Kumina — stability and change. *ACIJ Research Review* (Kingston) 1:81–128.

Savishinsky, N. 1994 Transnational popular culture and the global spread of the Jamaican Rastafarian movement. *New West Indian Guide* 68(3/4):259–281.

Schuler, M. 1980 *"Alas, Alas, Kongo": A Social History of Indentured African Immigration into Jamaica, 1841–1865*. Baltimore: Johns Hopkins University Press.

Senior, O. 1983 *A–Z of Jamaican Heritage*. Kingston: Heinemann and The Gleaner Company.

Warner-Lewis, M. 1993 African continuities in the Rastafari belief system. *Caribbean Quarterly* 39(3/4):108–122.

Yawney, C. 1976 Remnants of all nations: Rastafarian attitudes to race and nationality. In: *Ethnicity in the Americas* (ed., F. Henry). The Hague: Mouton.

Yawney, C. 1993 Rasta mek a trod: symbolic ambiguity in a globalizing religion. In: *Alternative Cultures in the Caribbean* (eds., T. Bremer and U. Fleischmann). Frankfurt: Vevuert.

Yawney, C. 1997 Only visitors here: representing Rastafari into the 21st century. In this volume.

Zane, W.W. 1997 Spiritual baptists in New York City: a view from the Vincentian converted. In this volume.

Zips, W. 1991 "Yard": Ort der Begegnung: zur Flexibilität des jamaikanischen Zuhause-Konzeptes. *Mitteilungen der Anthropologischen Gesellschaft in Wien* 121:77–84.

14: BETWEEN THE LIVING AND THE DEAD: THE APOTHEOSIS OF RASTAFARI HEROES[1]

Barry Chevannes

Introduction

The funeral of popular Rastafari reggae singer Garnet Silk, who was burnt to death at his home in December 1994, was conducted by the Ethiopian Orthodox Church, and I recalled that the funerals of reggae superstars Bob Marley and Peter Tosh were also conducted by the same institution. It thus struck me that the Ethiopian Orthodox Church had become a sort of vehicle or instrument for negotiating the passage of heroic Rastafari from the land of the living through to the land of the dead, where they take their place alongside such natural heroes as Sam Sharpe as ancestral spirits of the nation; becoming deities, in fact. Left to very orthodox Rastafari teachings alone, there would have been no rite of final passage for any of these superstars. However, through the ethical content of their music and their identification with Africa/Ethiopia and nationalist defense of black people, they earned a local reputation as prophets. Silk was being hailed as the next Marley, following the decade-long dominance of dance-hall music in Jamaica, which had turned from the conscious lyrics of Marley to the bawdy trend begun by Yellow Man. That they should be accorded a fitting rite of passage was a cultural imperative of the Jamaican people, who having idolized them in life as prophets, must now enshrine them in death as ancestors. How this cultural imperative was accomplished, in light of the heroes' own publicly known declared adherence to Rastafari, a belief system that denies any ritual place to death, is the subject of this chapter. As background I first describe Jamaican mortuary practices, relate them to relevant aspects of the Jamaican worldview, and introduce the Ethiopian Orthodox Church (EOC).

Mortuary Practices in Jamaica

Considering that the mortuary practices of the Jamaican folk are the most important of their life-cycle rituals, if one were to judge by the complexity of the process of disposing of the dead, the extensive ritual symbolism involved and the amount of material resources consumed, it is surprising that so very little is written directly on the subject.[2]

Among Jamaicans, the process of burying the dead is marked by rites of separation and containment, rites of transition and rites of veneration and respect. These are very much in keeping with the tripartite schema of Van Gennep (1965) — separation, liminality and rebirth — but under the influence of modernization certain aspects have been collapsed.

Separation and Containment

In the Jamaican worldview the spiritual order is a source of person-alized and non-personalized power. Personalized powers include God, lesser deities and ancestral spirits, while non-personalized power is a quality not unlike raw electricity — dangerous to those who do not know how to harness it, but a source of great prestige and power to those who do. Death as a gateway to the spiritual world exposes the living to the dangers of unregulated spiritual power. Until it is regulated through the mortuary ritual processes and the deceased is transformed into an ancestral spirit, ritual separation of the dead from the living and containment of the deceased's power become paramount. The rites of separation and containment involve four aspects:

1. **The expression of grief.** In most societies, "crying is the best-described type of emotional behavior of be-reaved persons" (Rosenblatt 1976:15). In Jamaica, as also among the Igbos,[3] the bereaved, especially the women, are expected to bawl (wail) and collapse. The greater the depth of feeling for the deceased, the more intense the bawling is expected to be. However, excessive grief may be interpreted as hypocritical, while

repressed grief evokes concern for the psychological health of the bereaved. From the functional point of view, then, bereaved grieving among Jamaicans is a social act requiring the support of friends and neighbors to console the inconsolable, to empathize, to treat as though sick. Kinfolk and very close friends initiate procedures to contain the spirit of the departed. These involve covering the mirrors and emptying all containers of water,[4] placing an open Bible on the bed and keeping a bottle of white rum and a saucer of salt in the house. The house is then arranged to receive visitors, the house and yard are cleaned, valuables are put away and certain rooms put off-limits, and the house and yard prepared for the more formal aspects.

2. **The set-up**. Up to the early 1950s, when George Eaton Simpson carried out his path-breaking research in Jamaica (Simpson 1956), a set-up was held every night until the funeral, which would have taken place within three days of death. The "corpse was laid out in the house — with a saucer of salt placed on the body" (Besson and Chevannes 1996:219), while grieving relatives, friends and neighbors of the deceased or of the deceased's family visited the deadyard, and kept company with the bereaved, singing hymns and playing games. As Besson and Chevannes note, the nightly set-up has faded, and the emphasis is now on a set-up on the night before the funeral. This is called the *nine night*, or, in rural Trelawny, the *singing night*.

3. **Personal rituals of containment** of the power of the departed are observed by visitors to the deadyard: exiting through the gate without looking back, making a counterclockwise revolution once outside the gate, and on the day of burial carrying the corpse feet-first.

4. **The nine night**. In the past this final act of separation and containment followed nine days after death, and would have been preceded by the burial, which, be-

fore the advent of refrigeration, took place within two
or three days after death. Nowadays, the period between death and burial takes between ten and fourteen days, on average. As a result of this change, the
nine night ceremony now takes place on the night
before burial. As soon as the visitors reach a critical
mass, they gather around a small table in the yard, on
which are placed a glass of water, a saucer of salt and,
sometimes, pieces of lime, a bottle of white rum and
a second saucer with brown sugar. The water, white
rum, salt and lime are sacred objects for appeasement
of the spirit, while the sugar is said to keep the voice
from getting hoarse. Following a scripture reading
and short prayer, the "bookman" tracks each hymn,
line by line. Nine night singing is distinguished from
that of other religious ceremonies by its lugubrious
and mournful movement. This goes on the whole
night, interspersed with Revival choruses and special
nine night songs of a joking nature.

Liminality

At the same time, the nine night ceremony expresses the liminal or
transitional nature of the deceased at this stage of the process. Though
dead, the deceased is still as it were in the world of the living. Together
with several other acts, the nine night marks the final moments before
the stage of regeneration. In the turning-out ceremony at a nine night
(Chevannes 1996:16), after scripture reading, prayer and asperging
with water, the mourners process, the last one marching backwards,
facing the spirit, to the nearest crossroad or intersection, where, after
they march around it three times, a glass of water is smashed and the
dead admonished not to return. Back at the house, the room in which
the person slept is then swept and the furniture rearranged. Singing
continues until the singers are exhausted and leave for home. Those
not joining in the singing sit and play games, the current favorite
being dominoes. A liberal flow of liquor and food is provided by the
bereaved, the family of the deceased.

The liminal aspects of the mortuary rites are best understood by the beliefs of Jamaicans likening dying and burial as a journey (Pigou 1987:25). Until that journey is complete, the deceased will not rest in peace. Observing proper rituals affects the transition. Among the practices at this stage are the public viewing of the body, which many Jamaicans consider a necessity, and which is always done in a church but sometimes at the graveside as well. It allows viewers the chance to comment on the condition of the deceased for this final stage. In some cases, the procession to the grave will pass a particular house, workplace or socializing spot such as a bar, with which the deceased was identified — a sort of march-past. At this stage the deceased is believed to have the power to derail the best of plans. In the *coffin-dance* phenomenon reported in deep rural St. Thomas (Tomlinson 1991), a clear continuity from the eighteenth century (Pigou 1987:24), the coffin bearers "dance," that is, make involuntary movements on the way to the grave, as the "coffin" dictates. This custom, according to Pigou (1987:24), "relates to the belief in the capacity of the spirit to have wishes and desires and to be able to communicate them. It also relates to the need to please the departed spirit and remove any cause for its acting maliciously towards the living."

Respect and Veneration

The funeral itself completes the journey but also enhances the payment of respect towards and veneration of the dead. Changes and improvements in technology and transportation seem to afford Jamaicans increased scope for veneration, making funerals large and very costly events. Funerals are often delayed for days, sometimes weeks, to facilitate the assembly of the lineage. Attendance is morally compelling. Expensive, often imported, caskets have replaced the community-built coffins of yesteryear, which used to cost very little or nothing. Committing of the body, or "churching," is also a necessity, requiring negotiations with the clergy if the deceased is a non-member. But it is unthinkable that a person could be buried without churching. It is also unthinkable to be buried without a eulogy. The eulogy is the occasion to say flattering things about the dead, often to the point of distorting truth, a much-abused practice that led the local Roman Catholic Church to ban eulogies altogether. The bigger the attendance, and the more lavish the outlay, the "nicer" the funeral is thought to be. In urban city communities in Kingston, funerals are occasions for making fashion statements. The dead are sometimes interred with articles reminiscent of their life.[5] The interment itself no longer takes place in an earthen grave, but in an expensively built vault, and grave diggers nowadays have to know how to tie steel and cast cement. With the innovation of the vault, the earlier practice of entombing the dead on the first anniversary of death, thus completing the rite of transition, no longer becomes necessary.

Many burials take place in the family plot, at least 30 percent by my estimate.[6] The family plot is a burial ground situated on family land. Family land, as we know (Besson 1987; Clarke 1953), is land bequeathed by an ancestor to all his or her descendants in perpetuity; it bestows on them rights of use, but not of disposal. It cannot (meaning it should not) be sold.[7] The burial spot is situated in close proximity to the house, where it is marked by sacred foliage like the croton and the dragon plant, and regularly bushed, whitewashed and tended. This custom is also very old, being reported as far back as the eighteenth century (Besson and Chevannes 1996:213). I agree with Jean Besson (1994) that family land is thus a symbolic expression of lineage solidarity, serving to unite the living with the ancestors and with those yet unborn.

When all this have been done, regardless of where the interment takes place, the departed is said to have been given a "good funeral." Good funerals are costly funerals, incurring debts. The costs have gone up, not just because of inflation, or big business, but because newer ways are being adopted to honor the dead. The logic is not to save money to spend on the living, but to pay the dead the respect due to them, within the limits of what the living can afford. As ancestors, they communicate with their descendants through dreams, and visit in the form of those large moths Jamaicans call "bats," which alight in dark crevices where they remain for hours, even days.

Underlying these mortuary rituals is a web of beliefs about the spiritual world and its relationship to the world of the living. I have already mentioned the concept of the spiritual as akin to electrical power. While this is not the place to enter into a discussion of the people's cosmology, mention must be made of another aspect of the spiritual order as a source of non-personalized power, namely the possibility for human beings to harness and manifest spiritual power and of becoming powers after death. Great and heroic men and women have while they lived managed to harness and manifest spiritual power. Marcus Garvey did so; that was why he could have done the things he is mythologized as having done — sealed prison doors, prophesied of things to come, imposed curses, rode the winds of storms (Chevannes 1988). Similar feats were attributed to Alexander Bedward, the Revival healer and leader, and to the founders of Rastafari (Chevannes 1994). Indeed, this worldview makes it quite intelligible that such men could possess divinity. Bedward was to his followers "the Lord and Master"; Howell and Claudius Henry were worshipped in song; to his followers, Claudius Henry was a member of the triune Godhead (Chevannes 1976), alongside Haile Selassie and Marcus Garvey; the Bobo Rastas regarded Prince Emmanuel in a similar light (Chevannes 1994); and even Bob Marley has joined the Godhead — this is the significance attached to his inheritance of His Majesty Emperor Haile Selassie's ring (see White 1983:214, 313–15; Lazel 1994:71). Such beliefs and practices are made possible by a worldview in which the relationship between the spiritual and temporal orders is in the direction of the temporal, making it possible and even necessary not only for human beings to harness and use spiritual power, but for spirits to incarnate themselves. I am of the opinion that what most Jamaicans at the time found objectionable about Haile Selassie as a kind of messiah was not that God could become man again, but that he was black and African. While it is true that the identification of the reincarnated Godhead is usually confined to members of a charismatic group (and this is not peculiarly Jamaican or African), beliefs about the reincarnation of the spirit of popular heroes like Marcus Garvey are more broadly based (Chevannes 1994).

Ethiopian Orthodox Church

Jamaican interest in the Ethiopian Orthodox Church probably dates to the time of Marcus Garvey, when his own African Orthodox Church saw fit to "develop relations with the Ethiopian and Russian Orthodox churches" (Gordon 1988). With the rise of Ethiopianism in the 1930s stimulated by the coronation of Ras Tafari as the new

Emperor of Ethiopia, Haile Selassie I, the country's invasion by Mussolini, and the organization of support across the African diaspora, interest was sustained by certain members of the Rastafari movement. According to Selassie-Dewar (1988), a group of Rastafari "began communication with and petition to the Patriarchate in Addis Ababa, Ethiopia for a branch of the Ethiopian Church to be established in Jamaica." Van Dijk (1993:190) pinpoints these petitions to "[as] early as 1954." But given the fact that Joseph Hibbert, one of the founders of the Rastafari in the 1930s, was among those pressing for the Church to come, it is quite likely that communication was earlier. Hibbert had founded the Ethiopian Coptic Church in the 1930s, instructing his followers with extracts "from the *Ethiopic Bible of St. Sosimas*, including the *Ethiopia Dascalia* [Apostolic Constitution]" (Smith et al. 1960:7). The eighth recommendation by the authors of the *Report on the Rastafari Movement in Kingston, Jamaica* that "The Ethiopian Orthodox Coptic Church should be invited to establish a branch in West Kingston" (Smith et al. 1960:38) could have derived from suggestions by Rastafari under Hibbert's influence.

These were not the only ones interested. As van Dijk (1993:191) argues, members of the Jamaican elite were hoping that the EOC would succeed where the Moral Rearmament Movement failed years before in undermining the Rastafari. The Minister of Education, Edwin Allen, took advantage of Haile Selassie's state visit in 1966 to suggest to the Ethiopian Ambassador "that it would be best for all concerned if a branch of the Ethiopian Orthodox Church could be established in Jamaica" (Mandefro c. 1971:17).

Thus, when finally the church was established in May 1970 by Archimandrite Abba Laike Mariam Mandefro, the Archbishop of the Western Hemisphere, it received support from both local Rastafari and from the establishment, each side having its own motive. The Rastafari turned out in their hundreds to meet the Archbishop and his entourage and later to be baptized, and some to receive the sacrament of matrimony. At the same time, the Anglican and Roman Catholic churches became hosts to the baptismal and eucharistic ceremonies of the EOC, while its Building Fund Committee attracted the patronage of the Governor General and the membership of the heads of the Roman Catholic, Anglican, United and Moravian churches.

This contradiction was not lost on the Rastafari, a group that had consistently pilloried the established churches for their role in the suppression of black people in Africa and the diaspora and had nought but contempt for Catholicism because of the Pope's granting a blessing to Mussolini's troops as they were sent off to conquer Ethiopia. Before long many who had undergone baptism fell away. The popular reggae group The Ethiopians voiced what was the feeling of many Rastafari that *Nyah no wan'* baptism. The discovery that the Church did not revere Haile Selassie as God or baptize in his name proved stumbling blocks to many. One baptism ritual was actually abandoned when a number of Rastafari candidates "demanded that they be baptized in the name of Ras Tafari" (Mandefro c. 1971:31).

Nonetheless, the Church continued to grow. Within a year, after four visits by the Archimandrite, membership in the Church stood at two thousand (Mandefro c. 1971:26). The Rastafari who remained rationalized (and continue to rationalize) their status with the argument that "Selassie and Christ were one and the same" (van Dijk 1993:193). The facts that the Church bears the name *Ethiopian*, is one of the oldest, if not the oldest, in Christianity, and was the Emperor's church, make it an attractive institution to Jamaicans alienated from Western Christianity.

For its part, from the very beginning the EOC took a very sophisticated approach to the Rastafari. It named Joseph Hibbert a "Spiritual Organizer" (Mandefro c. 1971) and avoided making any outright demand that Rastafari renounce the divinity of Haile Selassie. From the very beginning Mandefro elaborated the policy of the Church. The occasion was an attack in the press by one Rev. J.E.C. Farrell, who accused the Church of supporting falsehood and hypocrisy by harboring the Rastafari, who "are already busy teaching that Haile Selassie is God" (Mandefro c. 1971:30). Farrell called on the Church to set out its "Biblical doctrine and principles" before asking Jamaicans to support its work. In a long letter to the editor of *The Daily Gleaner*, Mandefro (c. 1971:30–31) outlined the fundamental doctrines of the EOC that were shaped by the ecumenical councils between 325 and 431 C.E., and then defended the Church's embrace of the Rastafari.

> Does the name Rastafarian, appl[ied] to an individual or group, diminish that individual's or group's humanity or citizenship? For many years Rastafarians just existed; today they are seeking, with their own incentive, because of the Orthodox Church, to establish themselves as citizens of Jamaica, the world, black men and children of GOD.

The Rastafari, he argued, notwithstanding their name, are human beings searching for their place in the world. He went on to share his experience of them as "an honest, peace-loving, God-fearing and very creative people," who "by their membership in an ancient Christian Church obviously do not oppose Christianity." This last point is crucial. It takes the broadest interpretation possible of membership in the Church, namely that those who join are in some ways Christian or disposed to Christianity.

Rastafari Tenets

A central tenet of the orthodox Rastafari is that a life of righteousness empowers humankind to triumph over death. I use the word "orthodox" because, in recent years, there has been a significant, though by no means decisive, shift from the rigidity of this tenet (Chevannes 1994). In its orthodox form it holds that death has no power over the righteous-living Rasta; that death is proof that one had strayed from the *livity*, that is, from Rastafari ethical standards.

Although this belief is strange to most Jamaicans, it is not at all illogical, given the colonial contexts out of which Rastafari arose. Influenced by the Pan-African nationalism of Marcus Garvey, they held to the idea that the Emperor of Ethiopia was the Returned Messiah, and inherited a tradition of colonial and religious propaganda that emphasized hard work, docility and religious observance in this life, as the guarantee of divine reward in the next. This was the gist of the Baptist missionary Reverend William Knibb's exhortation to the Africans not to go on strike around Christmas 1831.[8] Knibb knew from the general attitudes of the colonial ruling class that any message linking the condition of blacks with divine displeasure would make it impossible for him to work freely, if not bring about the expulsion of the Baptists. As it turned out, the Baptists were persecuted anyway, though in fact they neither knew of the plans nor were involved. The 1831–32 "Baptist War" was entirely the work of the slaves. Thirty-four years later, however, the Governor exonerated the majority of the Baptist ministers from having any part in the [Morant Bay] rebellion and praised them for their support for the authorities, their teaching of loyalty and industry to the people, and their endorsement of the "Queen's Advice," a royal dispatch ... that promised the people that their lot could only improve by self-help and hard and consistent work for wages. (Stewart 1992:159)

In the face of popular unrest over racism and economic hardship, the general attitude of the institutional churches became one, says Stewart (1992:183), that sought "to tranquilize the blacks" through more religious instruction. The churches remained acutely sensitive to the charges of being political, should they champion the material causes of the people, right into the twentieth century.

> Rejecting this approach to life that divorces the purposes of religion from social and economic realities, the Rastafari substituted another kind of doctrine that sought to align the struggle in this life with rewards in this life. Such a discourse called for a profound sense of faith in the possibility of life eternal being in fact real, rather than metaphorical.

The Rastafari Dilemma

This was the cultural and religious tradition rejected by the Rastafari. I do not know whether, as I have argued elsewhere concerning the innovation of the dreadlocks (Chevannes 1995b), this was an act of young radicals in the 1950s, but none of the foundation members I interviewed made any reference to a funeral. This does not mean none was practiced, but it is difficult to see the early Rastas placing any significance on burials. The two central tenets sowed from the beginning were that Ras Tafari was the living God, and that redemption by means of repatriation was to be realized in the present life. Acknowledging the Black Messiah was the basis for realizing the hoped-for redemption throughout the 1930s, and an ideological and sometimes violent struggle was waged around the identification of and allegiance to Haile Selassie as the King of Kings of the African race. Their hopes pinned on a living person, the focus of the Rastafari was on the present. It stands to reason that in this context Rastafari would have clashed with all religions that placed redemption beyond death, and this would hold true both for the institutionalized church as well as the traditional folk religion, including Revivalism.

Following the end of slavery, the colonial churches no longer condemned the social order as contrary to the will of God, and instead shifted blame for the status quo on to the individual. But Revivalism also, having failed to influence a change in the status quo, as Myal and the Native Baptist Movement[9] had tried to do between the 1760 Taki rebellion and the 1832 Sam Sharpe rebellion, positioned redemption as a state beyond death. This was the meaning of Bedward's so-called ascension to heaven in 1921 (Beckwith 1969 [1929]:170–71). Bedward was perhaps the greatest Revival preacher/healer ever, with a following reaching Jamaican migrants in Central America. His call in 1895 for the "black wall" to rise up and crush the "white wall" that surrounded and was oppressing it had failed (Chevannes 1971). With the colonial state positioned to crush him, Bedward decided "to bring the world to an end" (Beckwith 1969 [1929]:169). Thus both traditions, the colonial and the traditional, were rejected by the Rastafari as pie-in-the-sky-when-you-die. In place of them the Rastafari affirmed the triumph over death as a this-worldly possibility, made so by a life of righteousness. There was no need then for the development of any mortuary rituals.

How, then, did the Rastafari deal with the reality of death? What happened when a member died? The only case I came across was that of founder Robert Hinds, who my informants tell me was buried in the May Pen cemetery with only his sister in attendance. I had interpreted this piece of information as an example of how the mighty had fallen, of how one of the largest Rastafari organizations had dissolved into nothing by splintering. But another interpretation could be that Hinds's death was taken by his members as deserved. Former members accused him of immorality and of compromising Rastafari by getting mixed up in politics. Along this line of reasoning, the physically dead would have to be buried by the spiritually dead, that is, by their non-Rastafari kin.

The death in 1981 of Robert Nesta Marley marked the first time that Rastafari was publicly confronted with the necessity of a funeral. The reported death of the Emperor a few years before had, it seemed, posed the issue of death squarely. But at the time, and even up to the present, many brethren stoutly rejected the report. Marley's song, *Jah Live*, was a direct response. If man cannot die, how can God? But his own death carried the issue further, raising the problem of disposal of his remains.

Why was this a problem? Bob Marley was no ordinary Rastaman. Had he been ordinary, his relatives would have arranged a quiet funeral with a church, in keeping with popular tradition. He had been a hero to hundreds of thousands of Jamaicans long before his international reputation. Through his artistry and personal appearances, he spread the central messages of Rastafari far more than all other artists put together, becoming prophet, Rasta prophet, to millions of people the world over, and pointing the way to Rastafari. Through his influence, continental Africans, Australasians, Japanese, Europeans and Americans came to respect Rastafari, some of them adopting its tenets, others adopting its *livity*, many more its critique of Babylon, and still more its most visible symbol, the dreadlocks. By what logic, then, could the death of such a prophet be a sign of his own sinfulness and unrighteousness? And even if Rastafari orthodoxy concerning death had prevailed, Bob's relationship with the people demanded that he be given a rite of passage befitting his status in life. This is where the Ethiopian Orthodox Church came in, and traditional practices of ancestor veneration asserted themselves.

By virtue of having conferred on Marley one of the highest national honors, the Order of Merit, in the month preceding his death, the Jamaican Government accorded him an official funeral. However, it was conducted by the EOC. It was rumored that Marley had undergone a deathbed conversion to the Church, rejecting the Twelve Tribes, and that was why Skill Cole, his close friend and a Twelve Tribes member, so it was said, chose to read his own passage of scripture at the official funeral service instead of the one chosen by the Church. The fact is that neither Twelve Tribes nor any other Rasta group had instituted rituals for the dead.

Frank van Dijk (1993) treats the arrival of the EOC in Jamaica as an attempt at co-optation by the State. While, as I have already mentioned, there is evidence to support this, the role played by the Church in Bob's funeral and the funerals of Peter Tosh and Garnet Silk sheds more light on the Church's relation to Jamaican society. The EOC, by virtue of its own origins and the sensitivity of

its representatives, is positioned as the only institution able to perform the mediating role between Rastafari orthodoxy and Jamaican
traditions of ancestor veneration, which begin with a normal burial.
By contrast, the other churches in Jamaica have an unenviable past as
part of the colonial apparatus, effecting with a misinterpreted Bible,
so goes Rastafari critique, what the state does with the gun. Rastafari
criticism of society has always been framed in terms of "Church and
State." Moreover, Rastas say, the churches suppress the true identity
of God and Jesus, especially the latter, whom the churches identify as
a white man. It is thus difficult to imagine any Christian Church with
this history and theology being acceptable to the Rastafari to perform
a Rasta funeral. But what is particularly striking is the ecumenism of
the officials of the Ethiopian Church towards the Rastafari. At Bob's
funeral, the Archbishop referred to him as "a prophet" and noted that
"[a]s a Rastafarian, Marley had brought dignity to that movement."

At Garnet Silk's funeral, which I attended on December 22, 1994,
Kes Gabre Egziabher, the Church's Administrator and celebrant, had
the following to say:

> Some will not recognize the works of great men until their death. There
> are some people that are living in our society today [who] do not
> realize the Godly works of Garnet Silk. Some might say, "Oh! he is just
> a Rasta man, calling upon Haile Selassie's name, saying He is God."
> But suffice me to refer from a speech on religion from His Imperial
> Majesty, Haile Selassie I. And I quote: "To make our will obedient to
> good influences and to avoid evil is to show the greater Wisdom." In
> order to follow this aim one must be guided by religion.... Since nobody
> can interfere in the realm of God we should tolerate and live side by
> side with those of other faiths. In mystic traditions of the different
> religions we have a remarkable unity of Spirit. Whatever religion they
> profess they are spiritual kinsmen. While different religions in their
> historic forms bind us to limited groups and militate against the devel-
> opment of loyalty to the world community, the mystics have already
> stood for the fellowship of humanity, in harmony with the Spirit of the
> Mystics gone by.
> No one should question the faith of others, no human being can judge
> the ways of God.
> ... Surely, we can say today, Garnet Silk was not without God. In his
> songs it bears a religious message to the Godly and the ungodly.
> He and many others, like Bob Marley, Peter Tosh, have fulfilled the
> prophecy as the Psalmist put it: The Lord gave the word: Great was the

Company of those that published it.

We give thanks to God for the works of Bob Marley, because he was able to bring a consciousness of God to the people. Thus we say he was like a prophet unto us. Garnet Silk too is a contemporary prophet. His words are religious, spiritual and Godly centered. His message in his music has changed the lives of many.

We have to give thanks for this renewal in the music.... We should also give thanks to those who change the gun culture by calling upon the name Selassie or God in their music.[10]

In this excerpt from his sermon, Kes Egziabher addresses the concern of the narrow-minded that because a person professes Haile Selassie as God such a person cannot be godly. He does so by appealing first to the authority of none other than His Majesty himself, to the effect that one shows greater wisdom by submitting to any influence that draws us from evil to good. Greater than what, we may ask? Greater, Kes Egziabher implies, than the narrow adherence to the rules of one's religion. For, he goes on to point out from history, different religions have produced great and holy men whose holiness and insights transcend group and denomination. This is why we should be tolerant of the religious beliefs of others. This is how Rastafari can produce prophets like Bob Marley, Peter Tosh and Garnet Silk. Thus, it does not matter that in calling upon God, they invoke the name of Haile Selassie. What matters is they have turned people away from evil by publishing His word.

This sermon was a theologically sophisticated exposition of Christian tolerance and defense of the Church's embrace of the Rastafari, in keeping with the policy set by Abba Laike Mandefro around the time of the Church's coming to Jamaica in 1970. The Church therefore had no difficulty, as some of the western denominations would certainly have had, in reconciling popular belief in Haile Selassie with the Church's orthodoxy and thus enabling popular traditions of respect and veneration to assert themselves in a context where, left to the Rastafari orthodoxy, they would never have taken place.

The funerals of all three Rasta prophets followed the same pattern. They were put to lie in state, Marley and Tosh, in the National Arena, where, as is the custom, their bodies were viewed. The bodies of Garnet Silk and that of his mother were cremated, and, although there was no lying in state, the urns were placed in full view hours

before the service began. The venue allowed tens of thousands of
people to pay their respects by attending the service, and many
travelled from afar.

However, it is in the burial, rather than the funeral, that the Jamaican folk traditions asserted themselves. All three were buried on
family land — Marley in Nine Mile in St. Ann, Tosh in Belmont in
Westmoreland, and Silk in Top Greenvale in Manchester. But while
their burial symbolically connects them to their family and transforms them into ancestors, the mausoleums constructed to enclose
their remains seem to transform the family land into shrines for
popular pilgrimage and veneration. This is most of all the case with
Marley.

To summarize, three prophetic voices were silenced, one by natural causes, one by murder and another by an accident. As public
Rastafari, all three proclaimed life rather than death. Their own
deaths posed the issue of reconciling popular veneration with the
stricture of orthodoxy. I suggest that this has been skillfully dealt
with by the role played by the Ethiopian Orthodox Church. The
Church has thus become an instrument through which Rastafari has
been able to in a public way adjust to the reality of death, while
retaining legitimacy as a force for change. By the reassertion of the
tradition of family land burial, the three Rastafari heroes in life have
become ancestral spirits in death.

Endnotes

1. The term *apotheosis* simply means deification, as any student of
   Greek mythology would immediately recognize. My use of it is in
   no way influenced by, nor intended to contribute to, the debate
   between Gananath Obeyesekere (1992) and Marshall Sahlins (1995).
   The word *deification* would have served just as well. In this chapter,
   apotheosis refers to the status certain great men attained in becoming
   the objects of popular veneration after their death.

2. Pigou (1987) pulls together centuries-old historical accounts of African burial customs in Jamaica. The only study of contemporary

practices I know of was one prepared by Marjorie Brown for the African-Caribbean Institute of Jamaica, which, unfortunately, has been reported lost for the last ten years. The presentation herein is based on my own attempt over several years at systematizing what I have known and experienced about Jamaican mortuary practices.

3. Basden (1996b:270), as quoted in Rosenblatt et al. (1996:13).

4. See Erna Brodber's novel, *Lousinana* (p. 91). The emptying of all water containers upon the death of a member of the household is also a common practice in St. Lucia.

5. I have come across cases of men buried with bottles of beer, rum and ganja to remind them of the friends with whom they shared while alive. Marley was buried with his guitar.

6. The data for this was collected from newspaper notices every Saturday and Sunday over a period of three months in early 1994. The *Daily Gleaner* and *The Sunday Gleaner* have a virtual monopoly on death notices, which are usually quite elaborate. They give the official as well as the familiar names and nicknames, identify the kin group by name and category if possible, and, of course, the place and time of the funeral and the interment. Thirty percent is a high proportion, given the use of church and public cemeteries in cities and rural townships.

7. While this is generally so, both Carnegie (1987) and Espeut (1990) have found cases where family land has been disposed of without feuding within the lineage.

8. See Chevannes (1971).

9. Myal was the name of the Jamaican folk religion when it first emerged in the middle of the eighteenth century as a unifying force among disparate African ethnic groups. See Schuler (1979). A few decades later, when the Baptist missionaries began proselytizing, African Myal absorbed Christian elements and so led to the Native Baptist Movement. In 1860, in the midst of a great revival among the Christian churches, Myal adopted the name Revival. For accounts of these historical developments, see Chevannes (1995a) and Wedenoja (1978).

10. I am grateful to Kes Egziabher for making a copy of his sermon available.

References

Basden, George Thomas 1966 [1938]. *Niger Ibos*. London: Cass.

Beckwith, Martha 1979 [1929]. *Black Roadways: A Study of Jamaican Folk Life*. New York: Negro Universities Press (University of North Carolina Press).

Besson, Jean 1987. Family land as a model for Martha Brae's new history: culture building in an Afro-Caribbean village. In: *Afro-Caribbean Villages in Historical Perspective* (ed., Charles V. Carnegie). African-Caribbean Institute of Jamaica Research Review No 2.

Besson, Jean 1994. Religion as resistance in Jamaican peasant life: the Baptist Church, revival worldview and Rastafari movement. In: *Rastafari and Other African-Caribbean Worldviews* (ed., Barry Chevannes) Houndmills and London: Macmillan.

Besson, Jean and Chevannes, Barry 1996. The continuity-creativity debate: the case of revival. *New West Indian Guide* 70(3–4):209–228.

Brodber, Erna 1994. *Louisiana*. London and Port of Spain: New Beacon.

Carnegie, Charles V. 1987. Is family land an institution? In: *Afro-Caribbean Villages in Historical Perspective* (ed., Charles V. Carnegie). African-Caribbean Institute of Jamaica Research Review No. 2.

Chevannes, Barry 1971. Revival and black struggle. *Savacou: Journal of the Caribbean Artists Movement*, No. 5.

Chevannes, Barry 1976. Repairer of the Breach: Reverend Claudius Henry and Jamaican Society. In: *Ethnicity in the Americas* (ed., Frances Henry). The Hague and Paris: Mouton.

Chevannes, Barry 1988. Garvey myths among the Jamaican people. In: *Garvey: His Work and Impact. Kingston: Institute of Social and Economic Research* (eds., Rupert Lewis and Patrick Bryan). University of the West Indies.

Chevannes, Barry 1994. *Rastafari: Roots and Ideology*. Syracuse: Syracuse University Press.

Chevannes, Barry 1995a. Introducing the native religions of Jamaica. In: *Rastafari and Other African-Caribbean Worldviews* (ed., Barry Chevannes). Houndmills and London: Macmillan.

Chevannes, Barry 1995b. The origin of the dreadlocks. In: *Rastafari and Other African-Caribbean Worldviews* (ed., Barry Chevannes). Houndmills and London: Macmillan.

Chevannes, Barry 1996. African-Caribbean approaches to the spiritual. In: *Theology in the Caribbean Today 2: The Spirit World*. Castries, St. Lucia: Archdiocesan Pastoral Centre.

Clarke, Edith 1953. Land tenure and the family in four communities in Jamaica. *Social and Economic Studies* 1(4):811–18.

Espeut, Peter 1990. *Land Reform and the Family Land Debate: Reflections on Jamaica*. Unpublished paper presented at a Symposium on Plantation Economy, Land Reform and Peasantry in a Historical Perspective: Jamaica 1838–1980, Kingston, 19 May.

Gordon, Ernle P. 1988. Garvey and black liberation theology. In: *Garvey: His Work and Impact* (eds., Rupert Lewis and Patrick Bryan). Mona, Jamaica: Institute of Social and Economic Research and Department of Extra-Mural Studies, University of the West Indies.

Hall, Douglas 1978 [1959]. *Free Jamaica, 1838–1865: An Economic History*. Aylesbury, England: Ginn and Company Limited (Yale University Press).

Lazel, Barry 1994. *Marley: 1945–1981*. London: Hamlyn.

Mandefro, Abba L.M. ca. 1971. *The Ethiopian Orthodox Tewahedo Church and Its Activities in the West*. New York: Ethiopian Orthodox Church.

Obeyesekere, Gananath 1992. *The Apotheosis of Captain Cook: European Mythmaking in the Pacific*. Princeton: Princeton University Press.

Pigou, Elizabeth 1987. A note on Afro-Jamaican beliefs and rituals. *Jamaica Journal* 20(2):23–26.

Rosenblatt, Paul C.; Walsh, R. Patricia; and Jackson, Douglas A. 1976. *Grief and Mourning in Cross-Cultural Perspective*. HRAF Press.

Sahlins, Marshall 1995. *How "Natives" Think: About Captain Cook, for Example*. London and Chicago: University of Chicago Press.

Selassie-Dewar, Amaha 1988. *Ethiopian Orthodox Church in Jamaica: Brief History*. Pamphlet.

Schuler, Monica 1979. Myalism and the African Religious Tradition in Jamaica. In: *Africa and the Caribbean: The Legacies of a Link* (eds., Margaret E. Crahan and Franklin Knight). Baltimore and London: Johns Hopkins University Press.

Simpson, George Eaton 1956. Jamaican revivalist cults. *Social and Economic Studies* 5(4).

Smith, M.G.; Augier, Roy; and Nettleford, Rex 1960. *Report on the Rastafari Movement in Kingston, Jamaica.* University College of the West Indies, Institute of Social and Economic Research.

Stewart, Robert J. 1992. *Religion and Society in Post-Emancipation Jamaica.* Knoxville: University of Tennessee Press.

Tomlinson, Richard 1988. *The Coffin Dance: A Study of Funeral Practices in Somerset and Neighbouring Districts in East Rural St. Andrew.* Unpublished. Caribbean Studies paper. Kingston, Jamaica: University of the West Indies, Mona.

van Dijk, Frank 1993. *Jahmaica: Rastafari and Jamaican Society, 1930–1990.* Utrecht: ISOR.

Van Gennep, A. 1965 [1908]. *The Rites of Passage.* London: Routledge and Kegan Paul.

Wedenoja, William 1978. *Religion and Adaptation in Rural Jamaica.* PhD dissertation, University of California.

White, Timothy 1983. *Catch a Fire: The Life of Bob Marley.* London: Elm Tree Books.

15: "CITING[SIGHTING]-UP": WORDS, SOUNDS, AND READING SCRIPTURE IN JAMAICA

John W. Pulis

"Bredren," declared a Rastafarian who lives in a hamlet in rural Jamaica, "first book dat! Yes I," he continued in response to a question concerning the way he read or "cited[sighted]-up" from the Revelation of John, "dey jumble-up da bee-ble (Bible), tek da first book an a mek it last, da man no see?" The fact of the matter was I had not seen and it took me a while before I understood how practitioners produced meaning from texts.[1]

Reading is one of those activities anthropologists include under the rubric of literacy and literacy practices. Like writing, it involves a text and it is generally defined as a social activity through which a reader or groups of readers make sense of symbols, be they inscribed in clay, chiseled in stone, or printed on paper. But reading is this and so much more. We do not read the autobiography of Sojourner Truth in the same way that we read Toni Morrison, nor do we hear the sounds of Kamau Brathwaite in the same way as we hear Maya Angelou or Derek Walcott. Whereas making sense of symbols would appear to be a universal activity, there are few people or societies that produce meaning in identical ways.

This chapter discusses a way of reading known to practitioners of Rastafari as "citing[sighting]-up." Expanding upon recent work in the ethnography of literacy (cf. Collins, 1995; Chartier, 1995; Boyarin, 1993; Szwed, 1981), it describes how local folk produce meaning from texts, explores a number of issues associated with reading as an interactive process, and suggests that "citing[sighting]-up" [hereafter citing-up] is a subversive activity in which Rastafarians subordinate the text, the printed word, and associated understanings of literacy to the spoken.[2] Like most social activities, citing-up is not practiced in a vacuum. This chapter opens with a discussion that places local

practice in a social, political, and interpretive context. From a discussion of context it proceeds to a situated account, a citing-up that
demonstrates how meaning is socially and lingusitically constructed.
And it concludes with an analysis that details how a local practitioner
has brought a tradition of resistance and struggle to bear in transforming the printed text into an orally recounted Bible or "living
testament" of African history and culture.[3]

Background: Texts, Contexts, and Pretexts

The Rastafarian Brethren are one of several folk religions practiced
in contemporary Jamaica.[4] They coalesced as a community of practitioners during the interwar decades when several early leaders
proclaimed the Ethiopian Emperor Haile Selassie to be a black Messiah, declared the Island of Jamaica to be a New World Babylon, and
referred to themselves as the "elect" and "chosen" spoken of in the
Old and New Testaments.[5] Their proclamations and declarations did
not go unheard. Expressed in a black vernacular known as "call and
response," the reaction to their calls led to arrests, incarcerations, and
an ongoing confrontation with the forces and relations of the colonial
and post-colonial state.[6]

   Their calls and proclamations achieved international acclaim
when they were carried around the world by musicians such as Bob
Marley, poets such as Mutabaruka, and a cadre of Elders in the 70s,
80s, and 90s.[7] No longer confined to Kingston, their distinctive iconography (red-gold-green), their unique way of speaking (known as
I-yaric or Dread Talk), and their sense of style and comportment
(dreadlocks) have been incorporated into post-colonial society, often
in contradiction to their origin and meaning. For example, the colors
of the covenant (red, a reference to a living hell; gold, to the riches
stolen from Africans; and green, for Zion or heaven on Earth) have
been used as logo on an array of alcohol-based "sankeys" or commercial tonics sold in Europe, the Caribbean, and North America.
The word-sound "I-rie" (meaning happy, joyful) is now the call-sign
of "I-rie FM," a Kingston radio station and it is not uncommon to
hear the sounds of I-yaric transmitted along with the "cool vibes" of

Bunny Wailer and Bob Marley. Once deemed vulgar and repugnant and associated with the "outcasts" of colonial society, dreadlocks have become synonomous with the vanguard of post-colonial art, fashion, and cultural identity.[8]

Whether practiced at home or abroad, there are few accounts that describe how practitioners produce meaning from texts.[9] What local folk refer to as citing-up is one of several oral or verbal activities that constitute what can best be described as the discursive practice of Rastafari.[10] By discursive practice I mean a set of interrelated social and linguistic activities associated with but by no means confined to Jamaica. Citing-up is similar to a speech event known as "reasoning" and a form of talk-singing known as "chanting" in that it is not a passive, contemplative, or solitary ritual performed in silence, but an aural and a multi-vocal event. It differs from both in that it mediates between and subordinates the text, the printed word, and associated understandings of literacy to the spoken, be it tabloid media such as newspapers or sacred and canonical texts such as the Revelation of John.[11]

Like the performances of musicians and poets, citing-up can not be discussed or described apart from the context. By context I mean what ethnographers of speaking (cf. Hymes, 1974; Tedlock, 1987; Bauman, 1990; Briggs, 1996) refer to as the speakers, the setting, and the larger social, economic, and political circumstances within which such performances occur.[12] Contextualization is critical to any account of local activities. First, citing-up is not practiced in churches but in a variety of settings and a discussion of speakers is necessary to situate practitioners in local communities of interpretation.[13] Second, the meaning produced by citing-up is not carried by the text nor are literary conventions such as voice, narration, and textuality bounded by the ink and pages of a book. Attention to the performative will shift the focus of description and analysis from the text (and a text-centered exegesis) to the relation between biblical texts, historical events, and everyday life.[14] Third, the Rastafarian Brethren are not a unitary movement and deployment of the terms brethren and movement has tended to mask a diversity of ideas, beliefs, and practices. In addition to adding the voices of local folk to that of their more renowned counterparts, providing a situated account of the tension between the spoken and the printed will help clarify how literacy and literacy practices have become implicated in change.[15] Fourth, ethnography is not a solipsist monologue between an abstract "other" and an equally abstract "self." Reproducing the dialogics of a citing-up will ground the discussion and analysis that follows in the interpretive efforts of the participants and point to ethnography as a site of production as well as shared endeavor.[16]

Speakers, Settings, Scenes

I had set in motion a project during the late-1970s whose goal was to explore the relation, broadly conceived, between the social production of "words" and an array of activities needed to sustain a "livity" or way of life in Jamaica. Previous field experiences indicated that long-term participation was necessary to move beyond functionist-type analyses and polar dichotomies such as oral/written. I opted to engage in a series of conversations or "reasonings" in the assumption that such activities were creative practices and that ongoing participation would reveal what scholars such as Williams (1977) and Gates (1986) refer to as "structures of feeling," domains of aesthetics, creativity, and experience.[17]

The name Bongo is a pseudonym for a Jamaican who, to borrow a phrase from everyday discourse, "turned dread" during the 1960s.[18] Bongo was not an "ancient" or an "elder," a member of the prewar generation. He was born in a rural community during the 1940s and was "pulled" to Kingston in the late-1950s. Bongo's use of the word "pulled" expressed the way he talked about and situated his life-history in postwar social, economic, and political trends. The community into which he was born had once been a Moravian mission-village carved from coffee estates during the early 19th-century. It underwent sweeping social, demographic, and ecological transformations due to the discovery of bauxite and the expansion of the industry that occurred during the postwar decades.[19]

Like many of his generation, Bongo traveled to Kingston seeking employment and he toiled in the construction trades as a postcolonial metropolis of high-rise offices, apartments, and shopping malls began to eclipse the old or colonial city downtown. He circulated through the network of yards and camps that crisscross the City and established a residence in once such yard where he became affiliated with a grouping or association of brethren known as the House of Nyabinghi.[20] He remained in Kingston until the late-1970s when what he referred to as the "tribalism" or politically sponsored violence of the time "pushed" him and several of his brethren back to the country.[21]

Bongo's entrance into the world of Rastafari was mediated in part by an "ancient" known as "daddy Rob." Rob and his life mate Gerte were members of the prewar generation. Known in the local community as a "Jah-folk," they were credited with "carrying the word" of Rastafari to the local area. Both had been members of a native-Baptist congregation in Kingston, both had under gone conversion experiences during the interwar decades, and both became avid supporters of Rastafari during the postwar decades.[22]

Although Bongo was not an elder, he was recognized by Rastafarians and nonRastafarians alike as a "rootsman" whose "countenance shined." The terms rootsman and countenance were expressions used by local folk to signify the comportment, the linking of character and personality with behavior and inter-personal relations. Bongo's countenance shined because his "words" or rhetoric did not contradict his "livity" or way of life. He refused to consume alcohol, animal protein, or commercially processed foods and he rejected the "sport," the social behavior practiced by men and women in the local rum bars. He produced most (but not all) of what he consumed on his "vineyard," a four acre farm that hugged the slope of his mountainous residence, and his "gates" or household was one in an informal network that connected the local backcountry to Kingston and points beyond. Like many but by no means all brethren, his gates were open to dread and nondread, African and European alike, and was noted for its lively debates or "reasonings."[23]

We met through a fortuitous set of circumstances. Although Rastafari first emerged in Kingston, I opted to explore the relation between discursive and nondiscursive formations from a rural rather than an urban point of view. Previous research led me to conclude that the country and the city were not as distinct as the literature suggested and I centered my project in a parish located about eighty miles from Kingston and Montego Bay.[24] The parish was undergoing a revitalization due to a resurgence of bauxite mining that followed the elections of 1980. Unable to locate housing near the parish market (a focal point of activity), I searched the adjacent communities and rented a house in a hamlet located a few miles away. Bongo's household was located within easy walking distance and our paths crossed late one afternoon. I was running along one of the foot paths that bisect what local folk call the "bush" (Bible in hand, trying to catch a bus in the village below) when I ran into Bongo approaching from the opposite direction. We stopped, exchanged greetings, and set in motion a conversation that continued until the present.[25]

As I noted above, the focus of my project centered around the relationship between discursive and nondiscurisve formations. While rural settings framed the scene, it was the importance of the Bible to local practice that constituted the interpretive context. Bongo's world, so to speak, was punctuated by two principal activities. He rose at dawn or "first light" and spent the morning hours weeding, planting, and reaping a meal from his vineyard while he devoted most afternoons to reading his Bible. One of his favorite expresssions was "a chapter a day keeps the devil away," and hardly a day passed when he and the folks with whom he reasoned did not gather at one yard or another to read or cite-up. Bongo frequently lamented that his Authorized or King James Bible ("Authorized by who?" was one of their favorite comments) was neither the "hardest," that is, the clearest in meaning, nor did it contain what they referred to as "crucial I-tations (meditations)," books and chapters about African culture and history.[26]

In addition to expressing the way discursive activities were incorporated into a livity, Bongo's lamentations opened a window on the importance of literacy, reading, and textual activities. Few texts in Jamaica are revered more than the Holy Bible. The ability to quote the book by chapter and verse has not lost its efficacy (socially, culturally, and politically) in an age of fax machines, satellite dishes, and the Internet. Discussions concerning ethics, morals, and biblical virtues permeate everyday discourse and, with the rise of "gun culture," it is not uncommon to read commentaries extolling Scripture in the tabloids. Rastafarians not only share this reverence with the larger society but they have reinvented themselves as the contemporary or "living" representatives of an oral and a critical tradition. The books and chapters that constitute the Bible are of central importance to Rastafari and they are considered by most practitioners to be an encyclopedic resource of African culture and history "buried" or "locked off" within the ink and pages of a book.

Whereas few Rastafarians are unfamilar with the Bible, Bongo's knowledge of Scripture and his ability to transform what he and others referred to as the "dead letters of print" into "livicial sounds" was recognized in both the City and the Country. Unlike those with whom he reasoned, Bongo was a beneficary of the postwar educational reforms and, although he never completed school, his ability to bring the social and political significance associated with literacy to a highly stylized, ritual-like invocation of his King James served to establish him as one of several "voices" in a local community of interpretation. When I asked why his King James was not the "hardest," he assembled a host citations (to "lost" books), footnotes (concerning "false" prophets), and references (to Africa, Ethiopia and Cush) to support his contention that books and chapters about Africa were "jumbled-up." When I asked what he meant by "jumbled-up," he turned to the New Testament and began to compare and contrast the differing accounts of the crucifixion as described by Matthew, Mark, and Luke. When I asked why he read out loud, he turned from the New Testament to the Old and recounted Eli's renunication of Hannah (1 Samuel 1, verse 12–15) for praying without speaking.[27]

As I mentioned earlier, citing-up is a discursive activity in which the printed word is subordinated to the spoken. The word itself is one of several verbal constructs known as "up-full" or "livical sounds" that express the agency or "word-sound-power" Rastafarians have invested in language. A detailed discussion of words and word-formation exceeds the scope of this chapter, but a few examples will help clarify how Rastafarians have transformed reading into a subversive activity.[28]

Language, for Rastafarians, is an arena, a site of struggle and transformation. Since English is considered the language of enslavement and captivity it was not deemed "heartical," capable of expressing black culture and consciousness. Upfull sounds were created by bringing the "word-sound-power," the tonal or sound-based semantics of Creole to bear on transforming English (spoken and printed) into a way of speaking known as I-yaric, I-ance, or Dread Talk. The acoustic or phonetic structure of English was interrogated, that is, sounded out loud, broken apart to expose contradictions between sound and sense, and reassembled into a vocabulary of spoken or livical sounds. For example, the /un/ sound in the word understand was replaced by the /o/ as in over to create the word-sound /overstand/ because the negative sound associated with /un/ implied one speaker was under and below and hence less competent, fluent, and literate than another. Similarly, the /con/ sound in the words consciousness and control was deleted because of its similarity to the Creole /kunni/ or con-man. It was replaced by the first person /I/ to create the word-sounds /I-trol/ and /I-sciousness/.[29]

Unlike the above, in which sounds were added and deleted, the similarity in sound in the homophones /cite/ and /sight/ led to the compounding and convergence of their meaning in the word-sound /cite[sight]-up/. In this case, the tension or antagonism between a spoken and printed literacy (understood here as that between cite as aurality or the sounding of words and sight as a reference to visualizing the scribal or printed word) signified a way of reading and a form of interpretation that compared, contrasted, and realigned textual citation with historical events and cultural constructs. This was not an either/or negotiation. Rather than simply delete sounds (replace one literacy for another), the tension between the two enabled local folk to contest normative or accepted interpretative frames as they subordinated the printed to the spoken. As we shall soon hear, the books and chapters that constituted the Bible were sounded out loud, interrogated for contradictions, and reassembled into an orally recounted Bible or "living testament."[30]

Citing-up framed the context of my interaction with Bongo. It became a means of communication through which we negotiated and constructed a shared world.[31] Rather than hostility or conflict, the dialectic was reflexive and in addition to opening a discursive space (in which I introduced questions) it generated a profusion of ideas. The following conversation, rendered here as reported speech, is one such example. It was produced early on and expresses issues that circulated through the local community, questions that I carried into the field, and ideas that were situationally invoked.[32] I have opted for the descriptor reported speech rather than narrative because the following is not a story that was told and retold within the local community but a transcript, albeit edited, of a conversation produced by Bongo and myself. I have inserted and appended contextual information, where needed, to situate this conversation in a ongoing series one built upon the other. Along with contextual information, I have hyphenated verbal constructs unique to Rastafari and have upper-cased words and sounds that were stressed in an attempt to reproduce and convey in a printed medium the tonal or sound-based semantics and the generative or interactive dynamics characterisitic of reasoning.[33]

Testimonies Written and Spoken[34]

"Drink mon," said Bongo as he handed me a tin can filled with water, "it rough ina Jam-roc [the island of Jamaica]. I trod [walk] up and down more times, I na do it more den once, da man no see?"

Like most households in central Jamaica, Bongo's "gates" were located well off the beaten path and access was limited to a single foot path that wound its back and forth up a forty-five degree slope. I sat under the shade of an old breadfruit tree catching my breadth, took a few gulps of water and was about to comment about the climb when the smell of something burning caught our attention.

"Ahee, furnace hot!" he yelled as he ran over to his cook house, a three by seven foot structure, closed on three sides, with an open fire or "barbecue" nested at waist-level in the far corner. The words "fi-re burn" came billowing out of the doorway along with clouds of smoke followed by Bongo flipping from hand to hand what appeared to be a loaf of bread.

"Da man taste sweet potato pudding?" he asked as he cut away burnt banana leaves with his cutlass, "it good mon, I-tal, I no use no-ting, jus potatoes from de vineyard [farm] ana sugar."[35]

"No, yes, sure, sure."

"Yes I," he continued, as we sat in the shade of a old breadfruit tree, "Jam-roc! Dis here de place Jah [Haile Selassie] revealed HIM-self [His Imperial Majesty] to I-n-I [the Rastafarian community]."

"You mean it's not all Babylon?"

"Babylon ... YES, Selassie-I reveal himself said way, ert [earth] run-nings, da man no see?"[36]

"No, no, I don't. In fact, it's odd that you ask, ah, bust that sound ..."

"What I tell da MAN, Selassie-I mystical! Jah reveal himself said way, dem try to kon-fuse-I, tell I HIM pass off [die]. I-n-I [the Rastafarian community] KNO dat na tru, cause him reveal himself tru da bless-ings..., da wind, rain."[37]

The topic of this exchange (a living Messiah) was an expansion upon a previous conversation in which we discussed what was at that time an issue of considerable debate and discussion among local practitioners: the death or disappearance of Selassie. Exploring the way practitioners incorporated historical events into the worldview of Rastafari was one of several problems that I carried into the field and the examples given (da rain, da wind, etc.) were offered as evidence for the existence of Selassie in contradiction to what the media (local and global) referred to as his death.

"How does the I know that's Jah?"

"Tell I, da man cite-up from de book?"

"Not really."

"Na really? A wah dat mean, YES or NO?"

"No, no, I never have, never have."

"Da man na go church?"

"No."

"How da man come to kno Christ ana dem tings?"

"I was always interested in religion, what makes people believe in different gods ..."

"... Da man a SCIENTIST," he interjected, "only one GOD, Jah Ras-Ta-Fari, Selassie-I, the first and last, Alpha and Omega. Jah create de ert, I-mon [man], an all de tings. Wha science do, dem na create LIFE, only DEAD-struction, only one god, wha church da man go?"[38]

"Ah ... well ... ah, Catholic ..."

"... BLOOD FIRE, Pope sent da man!" he interjected as he got up, walked over to his house and reached through a cloth covered window to retrieve an old Bible, "Da man na cite de book den, cause de Romans now, dem like de others. No sah! Only dem little priest use it, ana dey na cite it, dem jus hold it up der like so," he continued, smiling as he raised his arm, Bible in hand, and waved it back and forth mimicking a preacher in a pulpit, "Baptist an others cite it, de Roman part, de no use de prophets, dem heathens. Still," he added as an afterthought, "I-n-I a heathen, till I see Selassie."[39]

As we sat reasoning, an elderly woman (whom we shall know as Gerte) approached with a five gallon bucket balanced on the top of her head. Bongo "controlled" what was known locally as a "tank," a concrete-like catchment contructed from limestone, and he provided water for residents in the local area, Rastafarians and non-Rastafarians alike.[40]

"Yes I, Give thanks to see de sistren again." Bongo declared as Gerte approached.

"I come fer waa-ta dread, tank emp-ti!" she replied as she stopped, smiled, and turned her attention first to Bongo and then to me.

"Dis here JOHN," he said, reading her body movements, "Da mon from New York, him reason wit I."

"I see da man dis morning," she said.

"Oh ... [really, where?]."

"... Sister Gerte and brother Rob, I-dren," Bongo interjected and, as he turned from addressing me to Gerte, he added, "I-n-I tek da man to de gates, I tell da man, Selassie na partial."

"A tru, Jah na partial, dem people [me], na see tings said way," she added. "Wha da man seh?" she asked of me, "Da man know Selassie king?"

"Hum, well, I believe ..."

"Believe? Black people na believe, dey KNOW!" she replied sharply and turning to Bongo added, "Dread, tell da man about Mary?"

"I no hide no-ting," he replied shaking his head from side to side as Gerte disappeared around the corner, "dem sounds bust when dem ready."[41]

As I mentioned earlier, English is considered to be the language of captivity. Gerte's reaction to my answer had less to do with me and more with my choice of the word believe to describe what Rastafarians "know and feel." In the discourse of word-sound-power words like belief function as ideophones, cues or markers to a language that masks the signs and sounds of enslavement. According to this logic, such words have "buried" or submerged within them sounds (be/

lie/f) that negate their meaning, and the formation of such words was considered a form of politics intended to perpetuate "mental slavery," i.e., to deceive speakers into accepting the meaning associated with a word as natural.[42]

> "A wa da man seh," he asked, "da man wan check fer Jah?"
> "Sure, er, yes, only I know little about the Bible ..."
> "... Bee-ble, bradda John, bee-ble," he corrected, "I tell de man, Jah na partial. I-n-I mus cite-up more times, cause dem dat have eyes SEE, an dem dat have ears HEAR!"
> "Oh?"
> "Bredren, here I!" declared Bongo in a sharp, terse tone that tele-graphed a shift or change in dynamics, "dis here de FIRST book, Yes I," he continued as he walked his fingers through the pages of his Bible stopping at the Revelation of John, "dem mek it LAST, try ti kon-fuse-I, hide-up HIM words."
> "First book ...?"
> "... Dat wha I seh, first book!," he repeated loudly, "Yes I, dey jumble-up da bee-ble, tek da first book, ana make it last, da man no see?"

Similar to the meaning Rastafarians associate with words such as belief, changes in tonality were aspects of communcation freighted with meaning. Whereas contradictory sounds pressed a concern for the ideological, changes in resonance were cues that signalled a shift from the interactional dynamics characteristic of reasoning to that between readers and texts. Participating in local activities mandated learning to "hear" much in the same way performing artists and musicologists learned how body movements and musical rhythms are invested with significance. Along with indicating a break on Bongo's part, I gradually learned to "hear" such cues as "calls" on my part to shift from seeking answers to questions to that of explor-ing the relation between performance and reception.[43]

> "What I tell da man [about the image of Selassie], him na a little dream like duppi-spirit ting, him come as de Word, siin! [understand]," he explained as he read aloud from Chapter 1, verse 5: 'Blessed dem dat readeth ana dey dat hear da word [of this prophecy],' ana check der

so [verse 8], 'I AM ALPHA AND OMEGA, THE BEGINNING AND THE END,' Selassie dat!"[44]

"Ah, Bongo, it said ... [the testimony of Jesus]?"

"Dis I-dren, John, him a Rastaman, Yes I, Jah reveal HIM-self to said bredren, check der so [verse 10]: 'I was in the spirit, ana I man hear a voice, a trumpet.' Jah na some little dream-like duppi ting, HIM come as de WORD."

"What [does 'in the spirit' mean] ..."

"... Check der so (verse 12): '... and I mon turned to see who spake.' Dat mean to seh, reason, siin. Ana who da bredren see? 'Hair like WOOL, ana out of his mouth went a sharp two-edged sword.' Dem hard bradda! Him come was da word, na duppi spirit ting."

"Bongo, the book reads, ah ... says, 'I was in the spirit.' What does 'in the spirit' mean, then, if not a dream or vision?"[45]

"Bradda John, tell I, da man in school?"

"Yes."

"Siin! Tell I, how da bredren see sound?"

"What?"

"Da book na talk! I tell da man da system, da system jumble-up de book, da man mus penetrate da words to overstan dem! Yes I," he continued, responding to my question, "Vision now, said bredren have him vision, vision na a spirit-ting. Faawod, I-aya, see wha him a deal wit," he added, as he pushed on to verse 12: "'Ana I turned to see the voice dat spat wi me.' Wha I tell da man, how said I-dren see a voice? It WORDS I-aya! Jah na a spirit, Him a mon! Look der so, tree [three] times him say, 'him dat have ear, I tell da man, dem try to kon-fuse-I, da man no see?'"[46]

"Wha[t] ... "

"BEHOLD," he declared glossing my question as he read or cited from Chapter 3, verse 20: "'I stand at da door ana knock: if any man hear my voice and open the door, I will come in to him, and sup with him, and he with me.' Wha I tell de man, dem dat have ears HEAR! Dem day have eyes SEE! Da man no see?"[47]

"Ah ... "

"Faawod I-aya, da beast reveal demselves. I tell de man, de system take many forms."

"Yes."

"A who de eagle? De bear? De lion? Said ting, yet different, da man no see? All de beast said way, coming faawod [in time or history], dem mus bow before I, who open de seals? Na de beasts, dem na have paawa [power] of creation," he declared, adding, "who Jah reveal da seven seals to?"[48]

"The what ... ?"

"Check der so (7:1-12): 'Angel from de east, having de seal of de living God.' Dat Selassie, I-aya, and cite der: 'Till we have sealed the servants of our God in our foreheads, ana de one hundred and forty-four thousand.' Dat I mon, RASTAFARI."

"Bongo ... ?"

"Check dis," he added as he moved to Chapter 19 (verse 10): "'I am thy fellow-servant, ana he had a name no man knew.' Him no stranger to I, Selassie dat! 'Ana his name is de word of God, and on his vesture is King of Kings, and Lord of Lords, I am Alpha and Omega, the beginning and the end.' Dem hard bradda! 'And out of his mouth goeth a sharp sword.' All de nations now, dey bow to Selassie, de Pope, I-taly, England, cause dem know Jah da MOST HIGH, who else proclaim 'Lord of LORD, King of KINGS? Na Je-sus. Who else hear da word, black people. Da man mus see dat!'"

Reading Scripture: A Discussion

Anthropological field work is not a singular and monological but a shared and reflexive endeavor. Bongo's comments concerning "science" and "heathenism" expressed the way we negotiated relations of power and opened a discursive space. Power in this context had less to do with assymetrical social relations and more with what local practitioners have referred to as the "system." Similar to the negative connotations associated with belief, the word "system" has been used by Rastafarians to denote an ensemble of signs, symbols, and social relations associated with the enslavement of black folk. The above mentioned comments were not concerned with accusation or complicity but with ascertaining how different yet related systems of knowledge (academic or theoretical and folk or traditional) would affect our ability to "bust sounds," "reason," and take this encounter "to the heights." On the one hand, the ability to control or channel the dialogics of interaction is an aspect of performance that distinguished reasoning from ways of speaking among the non-Rastafarian community.[49] On the other hand, taking this encounter to the heights mandated exploring whose meanings got talked about. While Bongo and Gerte agreed on the hidden meaning in belief, they parted company over the importance of biblical figures such as Mary and Jesus Christ. The remainder of this chapter is concerned less with the dynamics of negotiation and more with discussing a number of issues associated with the production (and consumption) of meaning, contesting interpretations of divinity (a living Messiah vs. Jesus Christ), and oppositional claims to authenticity (knowledge vs. belief).[50]

As I suggested earlier, citing-up is a subversive activity in which practitioners subordinate the text, the printed word, and associated understandings of literacy to the spoken. We listened as Bongo withdrew passages from his Bible, transliterated them into the logic of Dread Talk, and discussed their importance to the worldview of Rastafari. Leaving aside for the moment issues concerning biblical verses, reading aloud was not some long-forgotten genre reconstituted by backcountry folk. As historians and literary critics have documented (cf. Coleman, 1997; Street, 1984; Chartier et al., 1990, 1995), reading or sounding texts out loud was a standard practice in societies where fluency in the culture of print was restricted, limited, or confined to a minority. Emphasis in the production of texts (such as the King James Bible) was placed on the poetics of sound and the intonational contours of the sentence as a discourse meant to be spoken.[51]

While Rastafarians revere the Bible as resource, the literacy traditionally invested in the printed word was not considered the equivalent of spoken or livical sound. As a way of reading, citing-up was an aural and a literary event keyed to the production (consumption and distribution) of "vibrations." What local folk meant by vibrations had to do with the tonal semantics, the relationship between word-sound-power. All words possess a contour, a distinctive sound pattern that when busted or sounded out loud produce a resonance or vibration that was "felt" or embodied internally, as it was "known" or heard externally. Like the relation between words and meaning outlined earlier, reading the Bible without speaking divorced the vibrations, the acoustics, theatrics and performance of livical sound from the power associated with Scripture. Rather than the signs and notations of alphabetic or print literacy, Bongo was reading sound and it was this phenonmenology of vibrations, sound/reading/aurality as a lived or "known and felt" experience, that was important. In addition to expressing literacy as a socially constituted experience, reading out loud negated the currency associated with the visual and electronic media in postcolonial society. Rather than a literacy carried by the printed text emphasis on the interactive, the vocal, face to face, and personally mediated dynamics of communication, was intended to subvert the currency associated with media that divorced or separated the medium from the message.[52]

Transforming the "dead letters" of print into a narrative of "livical sounds" entailed more than a word for word conversion of a written into a spoken medium. While citing-up can best be described as an aural event, neither the form (or sequential structure) nor the content (or thematic orientation) of the Authorized canon were accepted at face value. As an interpretive practice, citing-up is a critical engagement with the Bible as a artifact designed and crafted by human labor. Along with conveying the agency or power Rastafarians associate with sound, Bongo's comments concerning John ("him a Rastaman") expressed the way he "penetrated," that is, established a voice, identified protagonists, and appropriated or reclaimed the Bible as a black text.[53]

Establishing a voice, not just any voice, but a specifically black and a specifically Rastafarian voice, was all-important. As a way of speaking, Dread Talk departs from both Creole and English in its use of personal pronouns. The second person /him/, /she/, /we/, and /you/ of English and the /me/ characteristic of Creole were replaced by use of the singular /I/ as in /I-trol/ and the plural /I-n-I/. I-n-I is a multi-valent, context-senstive noun-phrase. When used to signify a plurality, the first person /I/ of Dread Talk replaced the second person /me/ of Creole and the plural /we/ of English and was used to signify a speech community known as I-and-I. These were not arbitrary speech conventions. Similar to the tension between cite and sight, the multiple meanings and usages provided Bongo with a point of view, a shifitng or double-voiced subject position. As scholars such as Smitherman (1977), Gates (1988), and Hill (1993) have commented, a shifting or double-voiced subject position is a rhetorical strategy frequently associated with self-representation. Bongo used the singular /I/ to indicate when he was speaking as an individual (as in "faawad I-aya, mus penetrate de vib") and the collective /I/ to "ground" or position his voice as one consonate with the narrative world of Rastafari (as in "him no stranger to I-n-I"). In the case of the former, singular usage placed control ("I-trol") over the production of vibrations within the domain of individuals while collective usage served to position his voice as one within a larger community of interpretation.[54]

Along with a voice, establishing a subject position enabled practitioners such as Bongo to identity protagonists, contest authorship, and reclaim ownership. The idea of an anonymous narrator was not accepted by Rastafarians. As Bongo stated, "how do we see a voice." Like the importance of Babylon and Ethiopia, allusions to African characteristics (such as "wool") and the use of reported speech ("I was walking along the road"), multiple voices ("I turned to see a voice"), and the positioning of stories within larger stories and events ("I was in the spirit") supported the tenet that the narrator was black, that the stories in the Bible were originally told by African folk, and that the printed text was an oral history "locked off," imprisoned within and dispersed throughout the ink and pages of a book.[55]

Bringing the spoken word to bear on "penetrating" or breaking apart the form and content of Authorized canon departs from reading by rote, the Bible as a magic or "conjure-book," and the recantation of a concordia of texted-based verses or "chant-phrases." There are few definitive texts in Rastafari and what local practitioners called a living testament referred to an official narrative of sorts and to individual testimony. Although the preceding is not an official story, it reveals much about the way practitoners produce meaning (created or "I-rated" knowledge) and construct a narrative or living testament of African history. The first chapter of Bongo's testament began not with the gospel according to Mark (and crucifixion or "passion narrative") or with the beginning according to Moses (and the creation Genesis), but with an apocalypse or revelation associated with a living African Messiah. The title of a living Messiah was not a hollow appellation arbitrarily associated with Haile Selassie. On the one hand, transforming the last book of the European and printed canon into the first chapter of an oral testimony expressed the way Bongo interpolated, that is, removed selected verses, reinscribed them with meaning (from "dis here time"), and wove them (biblical plots and historical events) into a living testament. As he and his cohort reasoned, it was not Jesus Christ, John the Baptist, or an Afro-Christian "duppy" who declared himself "Lords of Lords" and "King of Kings" in the Revelation of John but Haile Selassie. Whereas the tension between livical sounds and dead letters enabled local folk to break apart the text, the correspondence between cite and sight allowed them to reach beyond and outside the text and to link or "ground" their calls and proclamations to historical events. Rather than a second Christ or a new Adam, the product of a text-centered exegesis, the events that unfolded during the interwar decades, from the coronation of Haile Selassie to the global conflict that ensued, "manifested" the attributes practitioners associated with a living African Messiah "ina dis here time."[56]

On the other hand, this understanding of narrative as a spoken or living testament resonates closely with what Beverely (1993: Ch. 4) refers to as "testimonio" and what Gates (1987: 48–9), Smith (1994: 151), and Smitherman (1977: 87–8, 147–51) refer to as "testifying," a black discursive strategy in which text-like stories are told and retold in a variety of contexts. It is not warranted to suggest that Bongo's testimony, while not official and subject to local variations, closely approximates the way he was first introduced to Rastafari. As he mentioned somewhat reflexively, he too was a heathen until he first "saw" or understood the importance of Selassie not just to the worldview of Rastafari but for black history as well. Along with laying the foundations for a shared world, such comments tell us much about "structures of feeling," what local folk experience (know and feel) when they cite-up and how such structures of feeling (i.e., revealed knowledge, "him no stranger to I") are historically constituted (embodied) as the nuts and bolts of social change.[57]

As I stated earlier, not one but two generations of Rastafarians have come of age in Jamaica. Along with expressing the way ideas were situationally invoked, Gerte's comments (and Bongo's gloss) concerning Mary demonstrates the way multiple voices and divergent interpretations wrest and contend with each other. As representatives of a post and prewar generation, Bongo and Gerte agreed on the difference between belief and knowledge, but they parted ways over the relation between Christ and Selassie. This was more than a gendered or a male verses female reading but expressed the way literacy and literacy practices have become implicated in generational change and, like the tension between the spoken and the printed, competing voices opened a window on alternate and oppositional ways of knowing ("knowledge" vs. "belief") and contesting interpretations of divinity ("Jesus Christ" vs. "living African Messiah"). In addition to official dogma and creeds, Rastafarians also reject what anthropologists call the "architectronics," the ritual or sacralized space of churches, the stained glass, and the statues associated with Christian iconography. In their place they created their own imagery in the form of a living icons such as Jamaica as a Babylon, Rastafarians as the elect, and Selassie as a black Messiah. To Gerte (and other members of the prewar generation) Christ and Selassie were in some way interrelated in a lineage or genealogy of messiahs, while to Bongo (and members of the postcolonial generation) the image of Christ and his association with docility was considered to be an example of "mental slavery," the product of a colonial and colonized mentality. Bongo's elaboration on the difference between "dreams" and "visions" and "false prophets and living Messiahs" was an attempt to clarify and distinguish "belief" in Christ and the intervention of "duppi spirit tings" from a "knowledge" he and others associated (i.e., "know and feel") with a living Messiah. The words "duppy," "duppy business," and "duppy ting" were used to signify the multi-spirited world of Revival and a ritual practice based on glossalia or speaking in tongues and spiritual embodiment associated with a host Afro-Christian gods and spirits. Known as trance, ritual dissociation, or possession-trance, the personas and caricatures associated with saints and duppies were invested with power and were believed to control and manipulate the relationship between thought and behavior or mind and body.[58]

Belief in Christ and the intervention of duppies were superseded by what Bongo, and the cohort with whom he reasoned, referred to as a "knowledge" (a vocabulary of up-full sounds and a living testament) they linked or associated with Selassie. The events that unfolded during the interwar decades served to verify to a postwar, postcolonial generation that "knowledge," as opposed to "belief," was a product of human agency. Like the vibrations associated with sound, the power of this imagery negated the mimeticism, older or traditional Afro-Jamaican worldviews that have reworked images and icons associated with colonialism. While several local leaders (Alexander Bedward, Prince Emanuel) have laid claim to the title of

Christ, few have achieved the attributes associated with that text-based persona. Rather than a pantheon of spirits who reside in the sky and communicate in tongues, Selassie was considered a living Messiah whose activities were associated with Africa and Africans as makers of their own history.[59]

Suffice it to state that the worldview of Rastafari is not etched in stone. Each performance, from the music of Bob Marley to the livical sounds of backcountry folks, has added to and expanded upon an ever-changing living testament. Similar to the interwar years, the events that unfolded during the postwar decades, from the "disappearance" of Selassie to the "death" of Marley, were subjected to the open-ended dynamic between language and everyday life. As sketched earlier, Bongo became grounded in Kingston. He expanded upon his "groundation" by appending his experience as a member of the postwar generation and then transferred this "knowledge" to the countryside where he used it to support a "livity." While the advent of Selassie will forever remain a "crucial event," he and the cohort with whom he reasoned departed, somewhat, from the earlier generation in their understanding of repatriation. This is not to suggest that he or any other Rastafarian negated this critically important tenet. For Bongo and a number of others the movement or "trod" back to Africa began in Jamaica. In addition to expressing change in terms of contesting mentalities, the tension between dead letters and livical sounds enabled a postcolonial generation to transform belief into knowledge, the politics of marginalty into a landscape of informal economic activities they associated with a Zion or heaven on Earth.

It seems fitting to conclude by saying that citing-up framed a research agenda. On the one hand, there is evidence to suggest that contesting interpretations, conflicting claims, and oppositional voices have part of the religious landscape for quite some time. Documentation in the form of missionary accounts and memiors suggests that biblical verses such as Pslam 68 and Revelations 19 may have served as a grid or framework for social memory, plots and subplots in the mnemonics of an aural and oppositional narrative that was passed on from generation to generation.[60] On the other hand, subordinating the printed to the spoken, transposing the last book into the first, linking global events to local prophesy bears similarities to a form of interpretation known as biblicial figuralism. Biblical figuralism is a type/anti-type method wherein text-based people, places, and events are connected to their extra-textual counterparts. It differs from other methods in that text-based figures are complemented (but not superseded) in such as way that the first signifies the second and the second fulfills or encompasses the first. If the Revelation of John generated a dialogue in which we explored the attributes associated with a living African Messiah, then our reading of Genesis framed a second and equally important testimony concerning "I-and-I," a living Messiah and the elect or chosen coming "faawod in time."[61]

Endnotes

1. An earlier version of this chapter was presented at the 88th Annual Meetings of the American Anthropological Association in Washington, DC. The writer would to thank the Inter-America Foundation for a dissertation fellowship; Fulbright-Hays for a post-doctoral American Republics Research Fellowship; Rex Nettleford, Dept. of Extramural Studies, and Barry Higman, Dept. of History of University of the West Indies, Mona, for their assistance while in Jamaica; Phil Curtin and the members of an NEH Seminar on Plantation Societies; Richard Blot and John Szwed for their comments; and last but not least the "rootsmen" of St. Elizabeth and Manchester without whose assistance and cooperation this chapter could not have produced. A fuller presentation can be found in *Gates To Zion: Voices, Texts, and the Narrative World of Rastafari* (New York: Gordon & Breach, forthcoming).

2. See Collins (1995), Boyarin (1993), Iser (1979), and Ingarden (1977) reading as a social constituted and constituted activity. By discursive practice I mean, following Sherzer (1987), Bauman (1992), & Briggs (1996), a set of interrelated social and linguistic activities. As Certeau (1984) and Chartier (1995) have commented, studies of literacy have tended to equate readers as victims and the reader-text interface as a passive rather than as an active process. By subordinate I mean, following Hoggart (1957), Certeau (1984) and Radway (1994), an interactive process in which readers appropriate what they want from texts.

3. By narrative I mean, following Tedlock (1987), Finnegan (1992), and Beverley (1993), a text, a testimony or a text-like work (oral or written) that was circulated within a given speech community. By social contruction of textuality I mean, following Hanks (1989), the various ways texts are connected, linked, or related to a social and cultural world. For similar understanding of narrative as a oral or "living testament" see the published accounts of Rastafarians such as Ras-j-teste, *The Living Testaments of Rasta-for-I* (Kingston: Tennyson Smith, 1980), and Honor Ford Smith, *Lionhart Gal* (Toronto: Women's Press, 1986) for gender, women, and oral testimony.

4. I prefer the term folk religion over the terms cult and sect because the former expresses religion as a lived experience. Of the 145 denominations tabulated by the World Council of Churches (Barrett 1982: 214), only Revival, Revival Zion, Pocomania, Cumina, Convince, and Rastafari are folk religions in the sense that they are unique to Jamaica.

5. See Hobsbawm (1983), Sollars (1989), Anderson (1982), and Radway (1994) "invented tradition," "community of practitioners," and "interpretive community."

6. Alexander Bedward was a native-Baptist preacher who organized a congregation near the University of the West Indies. He baptized his followers in the Mona river and amassed a following of thousands and received Island-wide acclaim when he and his followers paraded through Kingston foretelling the earthquake of 1907. He was labelled a subversive for comments concerning a "black and white wall" and, along with Marcus Garvey, was under continual surveillance by the Jamaica Constabulary. He declared himself to be Jesus Christ and announced that he would ascend to heaven and return to a new world order. It needs to be stated that while Bedward has been depicted as a "lunatic" the Jamaican Native Baptist Free Church was a legally registered and bonafide religious organization. See Beckwith (1927) for an interview prior to his "ascent"; Williams (1932, 1934) for an account of his prophesies; Pierson (1969) for a history of the Native-Baptist Free Church; and Lewis (1987a&b) for the relationship between Bedward, Garvey, and pan-Africanism.

7. See Reckord (1977), Lieb (1983), Waters (1985) and Bibly and Lieb (1986), for music and politics; see Yawney (1985) and Homiak (1994) for a discussion of elders, globalization, and the international activities.

8. See Brodber & Greene (1981) for rude boys and dreads and the impact of Rastafari on the formation of a postcolonial identity. In the elections of April 1993, there were no references to Rastafari, a clear indication that their ascendency had waned.

9. See Nettleford (1971), Campbell (1987), and Chevannes (1994) for Rastafari as an ideology of resistance. As Yawney has recently argued (this volume), there has been relatively little new descriptive material on Rastafari nor has there been any attempt to place local practice within theoretical debate concerning postcolonial or transnational studies. The importance of the Bible and the way dominant theoretical discourses such as millennialism, revitalization, and resistance have intervened in theory and practice is the case in point. Lawrence Breiner's, "The English Bible in Jamaican Rastafari," *Journal of Religious Thought* 16(4), 2–12, Joseph Owen's, *Dread* (Kingston: Sangsters, 1976); and Peter Clark's, *Black Paradise* (London: 1987) are, to the best of the writer's knowledge, the only published works that address this issue.

10. What local practitioners refer to as reasoning is a highly stylized communcative event that is practiced wherever Rastafarians gather. It is analogous to language and speech as verbal art and performance throughout the Caribbean, black America, and Africa. Chanting can be characterized as a form of talk-singing, a ritual performed to the accompaniment of drums, in which Rastafarians have "lined out," taken hymns, songs, and biblical themes and linked them to specific rhythms or percussive sounds. Like reasoning, it has analogues in the use of sacral music in black tradition throughout the Americas. Citing[sighting]-up is similar in that it is a multi-vocal activity that includes a text in a fashion somewhat similar to the use of drums in chanting. It has analogues in the performed word, the "old time preaching" and "chanted sermon" as practiced by black preachers in Jamaica and North America. Though all three are multi-vocal, chanting is monological in that the folk involved produce a unitary voice, while reasoning and citing-up are dialogical in that there are a multiplicity of voices, contesting subject positions, and conflicting interpretations of meaning. See Bilby & Lieb (1986: 24, 27n.7) for chanting and for an excellent example of the way different meanings can be attached to identical cultural forms. See Homiak (1995) for multivocality and Pulis (1993) for reasoning as a dialogical process and the way meaning is inscribed to sound. See Heath (1982), Davis (1985), and Raboteau (1995) for "old time preaching," "chanted-sermons," and the "performed Word" in black religious tradition.

11. Citing-up, while similar and often performed along with chanting in annual, semi-annual, and informal gatherings known as a "bingis," is a multi-vocal textual activity in which Rastafarians mediate between and subordinate the printed word to the spoken. By mediate I mean, following Williams (1977: 95–106) and Smith (1994: 123–4), an ongoing and open-ended process of oscillation or moving back and forth between the spoken and the scriptural as distinct yet interrelated codifications and the imposition of aural understandings over scriptural or text-based understandings of literacy and textuality. For a similar understanding of orality, literacy, and reading as a cultural construction see Wolfgang Iser, *The Act of Reading* (Baltimore: Johns Hopkins Press, 1977), Jonathan Boyarin (ed.), *The Ethnography of Reading* (Berkley: University of California Press, 1992), Shirley Heath, *Way with Words* (London: Cambridge University Press, 1983), and Brian Street, *Literacy in Theory and Practice* (London: Cambridge University Press, 1983).

12. For a discussion of performance, poetics, and the importance of context to oral and verbal traditions see Bauman and Briggs (1990) and Tedlock and Mannheim (1995).

13. Rather than a unified organization as current usage of the term movement implies, what has been referred to as the Rastafarian Brethren is a loose aggregation of practitioners, some of whom have formed official and semiofficial organizations (known as the "House of Nyabinghi," "Bobo Shanti," "Twelve Tribes of Israel") that disagree and much as they agree on basic ideas and practices.

14. As in most oral traditions, meaning is socially and lingusitically and not textualy bounded. If, as Iser (1977), Ingarden (1973), and Thompkins (1980) suggest, reading is an interactive engagement, then meaning is both social and culturaly, i.e., inter- and extra-textually, contructed. The social construction of textuality (how practitioners produced meaning, "I-rated knowledge," and how that meaning was internally and externally connected) is a multi-layered and dialogical process between readers and texts. See Boyarin (1992) for a similar understanding; see Radway (1984), Certeau (1984), and Chartier (1995) for reading as an interactive process; and see Williams (1977), Hanks (1989), and Beverly (1993) for textuality as a socialy constituted and constituting experience.

15. Since the 1930s, two generations of Rastafarians have matured: "ancients" and "elders" and a second generation that matured during the postcolonial decades. If the 1970s witnessed the popularization

of Rastafari, then the 80s began an era of fragmentation and dispersal to North America and Europe as well as Africa. How literacy became implicated in processes of change (social, political, and generational) within and between Rastafari and the larger society is a much neglected topic.

16. Discussions and debates concerning postmodernism are too numerous to list. See Sperber (1982), Clifford and Marcus (1986), and Marcus and Fischer (1986) for discussion of ethnography as a site of production and a form of cultural knowledge. See Roseberry & Polier, "Tristes Tropes: Postmodern Anthropologist Encounter the Other and Discover Themselves," *Economy and Society*, Vol. 18 (1982), and Beals, "Reflections on Ethnography in Morocco," *Critique of Anthropology*, Vol. 15 (1995) for critiques of postmodernism; see B. Tedlock,"From Participant Observation to the Observation of Participation," *Journal of Anthropological Research*, Vol. 47 (1991) and D. Tedlock, "Questions Concerning Dialogical Anthropology," *Journal of Anthropological Research*, Vol. 43 (1989) for both an historic overview and a survey of issues, trends, and debate in dialogical anthropology. As D. Tedlock has commented (1989: 326–7) critical approaches to to ethnograghy have long genealogy. See also Stanley Diamond, "The Politics of Field Work," In *In Search of The Primitive* (New Jersey: Transaction Books, 1974) and Bob Scholte, "Toward a Reflexive and Critical Anthropology," in D. Hymes (ed.), *Reinventing Anthropology* (New York: Random House, 1969) for early and in many ways still relevant calls for a critical ethnography. See also Frederic Jameson, "Regarding Postmodernism," *Social Text*, Vol. 17 (1987); John Beverley, *Against Literature* (Minneaplois: U. of Minnesota Press, 1993); Raymond Williams, *Marxism and Literature* (New York: Oxford, 1977), especially p. 192–98 for a similar understandings of "authors," "enactive interpretation," "text-works," and critiques of postmodernism.

17. Research began with preliminary work in New York (1976), Africa (1977), and the West Indies (Jamaica, Barbados, Trinidad, 1978). It was during these early sojourns that the importance of Bible and a tension or antagonism between the spoken and printed word became evident. A site in Jamaica was established in 1979 and I returned in 1981 to initiate a long term field project. Follow-up research was conducted in 85, 86, and 87 and I returned in 92 to set in motion a second and related project (1992–93). By social production of words I mean a string of interrelated questions concerning epistemology and metaphysics: how readers identified with biblical protagonists, constructed a biblical identity, and contested normative or tradi-

tional understandings of subjectivity, i.e., masculinity and femininty. By a "livity" or way of life I mean a string of questions concerning political economy: how and in what ways local folk produced sustenance, what forms of labor were employed, how exchange and use-value were determined, and what commodities were deemed "I-tal." Similarly, while chanting, reasoning, and citing-up are interrelated, reconstructing a culture history of these practices and which were targeted for reinterpretation lay at the center of my project. Historical research had less to with a search for origins and more with the way cultural forms both express and are implicated in historical processes. For example, research to date suggests that each may have a separate and distinct culture history and that citing-up (as related yet distinct from normative understandings of reading) may have coalesced as a practice in the late 18th-century with the arrival of black preachers from North America.

18. The appellation Bongo expresses this person's affilation with the House of Nyabinghi, their emphasis on names and metaphors that denote and depict "thunder and lightening," and his way of life as a "rootsman." See Chevannes (1994: 156, 231–9) and Homiak (1995: 132) for names, naming, and the House of Nyabinghi. The term nyabinghi and its meaning of "death to the white oppressors" has come to be associated with Rastafari in Jamaica. It needs to be restated that Jamaican usage was predated by African usage, and the term nyabinghi was first deployed in Uganda during the late 20s where it was associated with anti-colonial nationalism. How such discursive formations were deployed in Africa, when and by what means of communication (tabloids, radio, newsreels, word of mouth) they were transported to Jamaica, and how they became implicated in local affairs remains to be documented.

19. The Moravian Brethren were the first protestant missionaries to proselytize in Jamaica. They began their mission in 1754 and over the course of a century established a series of mission-villages and black townships throughout what is known as the "South-Coast" of the Island. Bongo grandparents and great-grandparents (but not his parents) had been slaves.

20. Grounded, grounding and groundation refer to learning as both a means of introduction and a mode of response to the word-sound-power of Rastafari. Yards, camps, and houses, and their rural analogues gates and vineyards, are local terms that refer to the ritual space, the social, political, and historical landscapes where Rastafarian culture is practiced. In a series of earlier conversations Bongo

described how he first heard the chanting from an area known then as Abacka or Back-o-Wall, one of several enclaves that formed to the south and west of the Coronation Market. He was not unfamiliar with Rastafari having encountered several members of the prewar generation in Manchester. It was during the late-60s that he and several of his agemates established a camp in the north of the City and it was during the early-70s that this camp acquired the prefix international when, in addition to constituting a northern circuit (in a community of practitioners that spoke I-yaric), it became one of several points of entry in an Island-wide network that vended "I-tal," commodities produced in the country and consumed in the city. See Brodber (1975), Brodber & Greene (1981), and Beckford & Whitter (1980) for a background history of "yards;" see Chevannes (1994: Ch.4) and especially Homiak (1995: 160–9) for "houses," "camps," and Rastafari in Kingston.

21. Tribalism was the term used in everyday discourse to describe the violence associated with political culture in postwar Jamaica. In addition to tribalism, Bongo's move was precipitated by "control" of a "vineyard," a small farm located near a regional meeting place for gatherings known as "bingis."

22. Robb and Gerte were members of the prewar generation. Rob was originally from Manchester and Gerte was from Spanish Town. They met in Kingston, became members of Bedward's Native Baptist Free Church, and followers of Leonard Howell during the 30s. They abandoned Howell (and Pinnacle, "Sligo-Back") during the late-40s and traveled to Manchester when Rob inherited a small plot of land in what had once been a Moravian village. Rob worked as a day laborer and passed away in 1983 and Gerte toiled as a domestic and passed away in 1986. Their household was one of several that constituted a local network of culture and communication.

23. Countenance is a term used by local folk to refer to the persona or sense of subjectivity projected by dreads. Bongo's "countenance shined," meaning he was recognized by dreads and non-dreads alike as a Rastafarian whose words or rhetoric did not contradict his works or behavior. Unlike some Rastafarians who cite-up to the accompaniment of drums, Bongo looked upon the use of animal skin as contagion, the intrusion of death and destruction into an event celebrating life. The popularization that occurred during the 70s had both positive and negative consequences and led, on the one hand, to the appreciation of many Rastafarian ideas and, on the other, to their appropriation and reinterpretation by the non-

Rastafarian community. A discussion of Bongo's day to day routine exceeds the scope of this chapter but his livity as a rootsman was a reaction to what the Rastafarian community understood as a subversion or transgression of basic tenets. His rejection of alcohol and animal protein erected a set boundaries and situated him within a community of I-n-I, a network of inter-connected gates, camps, and houses whose intention was to reestablish a covenant with the Most High. Bongo's vineyard was a nodal point in a series of inter-connected households (I-n[and]-I) and social relations (I-nity) that crisscrossed the Island, and it was possible to travel from one end of the island to the other via such local households. He produced a livity from four very marginal acres by providing commodities to camps and yards in Kingston as well as to a local camp near Porus.

24. Manchester is one of 14 parishes in Jamaica. Located on a highland plateau, it was not a sugar-producing parish and it was created by a consortium of coffee planters in 1814 to become a center in the coffee and cattle trade. It became known as a "blessed parish" during the post-Emancipation years because once large coffee/cattle estates were broken up to become the holdings for an emerging class of small farmers. Several of brethren whom I encountered in Kingston "hailed" from Manchester and, having accompanied said brethren to a camp near Porus, I opted to center my project in the parish concluding that such a focus would provide balance and a rural counterpoint to studies that had focused on Kingston.

25. When we reconstructed our social genealogies, it turned out that we both had frequented a camp in southwest Kingston and we were both acquainted with many of the brethren who reasoned there.

26. Little attention has been devoted to reading, textual iconography, or how textual activities have been incorporated into a way of life. In their rejection of official religion, Rastafarians also reject the architectronics or ritual space of churches, chapels, and the "idolatry," the use of stained glass, pictorial art, and statues such as the cruixificon of Christ that consititute Christian iconography and in their place they have invented their own religous imagery. By religious imagery I mean the creation and use of icons such as a black and a living Messiah, a New World Babylon, and Rastafarians as the "elect" or "chosen." Although they share some of this imagery with religious practice in North America, there meaning differs. See Moses (1993: 184) and Smith (1992: 158) for North America.

27. When I pushed Bongo he pointed out that there were citations to books that were omitted from his Bible. In 2 Esdras 14: 37–48, for

example, some 90 books are recounted of which only 24 were "made public." Similarly, diffused throughout Isaiah, Jeremiah, and Ezekiel were references to Ethiopia, Zion, and blackness which were cited[sighted] as confirmations that the Bible was the oral history of African peoples "locked off" in print. Bongo's use of the term "Maccabbee Bible" was a reference to the pseudographical and deutrocanonical texts excluded from the standard King James. The book of Maccabbe was of especial importance because it was read as a test of faith and an expansion of "knowledge" as revealed to the seventh generation of Africans exiled in Jamaica. Such texts were considered subversive literature and were banned in Jamaica until 1976. See May & Metzger (1977 II: 157) for pseudo-graphical and deutro-canonical books. For a similar understanding of the Bible as a secret or hidden history of black folk see Yosef Ben-Jochanan, *The Black Man's Religion* (New York: Alekebu-Ian Books, 1974) and *Black Man of the Nile* (New York: Alkebu-Ian Books, 1972); James Rhoades, *Black Characters and References of The Holy Bible* (New York: private printing, 1980); Joseph Williams, *Hebrewisms in Jamaica and West Africa* (New York: Dial Press, 1930); Howard Brotz, *Black Jews In Harlem* (New York: Schocken Books, 1970); and St. Claire Drake's *Black Folk Here and There* (Los Angeles: U. of California Press, 1987).

28. It is beyond the scope of this chapter to discuss Creole languages. For Creole language studies and Jamaican Creole see Cassidy (1982[1961]), Cassidy & Le Page (1967), Hymes (1985[1971]), Roberts (1988), Romaine (1988), and Holm (1988); for language as resistance see Devonish (1986), Jah Bones (1988), Alleyne (1988), and, especially, Brathwaite (1974).

29. While the various changes are suggestive of phonological rules (aphesis, syncope, apocope) unique to Atlantic Creoles in which syllables are omitted from the beginning, the middle, and end in Creole word formation (see Holm 1988, Vol. I, 108–9), Rastafarians bring the tonal semantics or "word-sound-power" of Creole to bear on transforming Jamaica Talk and English into "up-full sounds." For a similar understandings of the relationship between sound and sense see Walter Ong, *The Presence of the Word* (New Haven: Yale U. Press, 1967), Peter Roberts, *West Indians and Their Language* (London: Cambridge U. Press, 1988), Geneva Smitherman, *Talkin'and Testifyin'* (Detroit: Wayne State University Press, 1977), and John W. Pulis, "Upfull Sounds: Language, Identity, and the World-View of Rastafari," *Ethnic Groups*, Vol. 10 (1993), 185–200.

30. Like many of the up-full sounds that constitute the vocabulary of Dread Talk, the term living testament is polysemous and conveys multiple meanings and messages. On the one hand, it was used by Bongo to denote a narrative discourse that was circulated within and between certain sectors and networks in the speech community of Rastafari. On the other hand, he used it to describe and signify his living testament or testimony as an account that was related to but yet departed from that what may be considered, for heuristic purposes only, to be an official worldview. Bongo's understanding of a living testament resonates closely with what Gates (1987: 48–9), Smith (1994: 151), and Smitherman (1992[1977]: 87–8, 147–51, especially 150–1) refer to as "testfyin," a black discursive strategy in which text-like stories are told and retold in a variety of contexts. How and in what way Bongo testified, i.e., picked up, expanded upon, or otherwise changed these text-like narratives constituted the nuts and bolts of field work. For an excellent analysis and overview of "testimonio," first-person narratives, and text-like works as a genre and cultural form see Beverley (1993: 69–87).

31. Research experience in New York, Africa, and in Jamaica indicated that long term participation was necessary to move beyond existing scholarship, open windows on heretofore under-represented domains, and, as in black culture in North America, discover aspects of creative expression through discourse. See Carolyn Cooper, *Noises in the Blood* (Durham, NC: Duke U. Press, 1995), Geneva Smitherman, *Talkin and Testifin* (Detroit: Wayne State U. Press, 1979), and Elizabeth Tonkin, *Narrating Our Past* (New York: Cambridge, 1995) for the relation between the spoken and printed word in African and African-American oral traditions.

32. Our interactions progressed from learning "up-full sounds" and "busting" or speaking I-yaric to participating in daily activities or "works." The following is presented here as a transcript of a social and lingusitic interaction. I have opted for the descriptor of reported speech because although the aforementioned contains elements that were part of a orally recounted narrative it was neither a verbatim transcription as such nor does it constitute a text that was circulated through the speech community of Rastafari. Offering any such dialogue as a text representative of what has become a gobal phenomenon runs the risk of reification. On the one hand, no single ethnographer can speak for the scope and breadth of Rastafari. The movement is far to diverse for the compass of any single ethnographer and such an approach obscures ethnography as a site of production and reduces reflexive practices to monological events. The focus of

my project was on local rather than global practice: how literacy acquired new and threatening meanings and how practitioners interpolated themselves into and transformed texts such as the Bible. On the other hand, Bongo was not a composite "other" formed from collective encounters and the aforementioned is not a collage cut and pasted from selected lingusitic exchanges. Reported speech preserves the enactive, co-authored, and double-voiced charactertisic of discursive activities. The following is presented as a transcript of a dialogue, a conversation, a text-like "work" produced by Bongo and myself that contains examples of reasoning, citing[sighting]-up, and the tonal semantics or word-sound-power, and it functions here as both a transcript and as a reference or text-work for the discussion that follows. See Jane Hill & Judith Irvine, "Introduction," in *Responsibility and Evidence in Oral Discourse* (New York: Cambridge University Press, 1993), for reported speech; and Tedlock (1989: 329–330); Hanks (1989: 97–8); Beverley (1993: 73); Williams (1977: 192–98); and Smith (1994: 133–4), for "authors," "enactive interpretations," and "text-works."

33. There are few transcriptions of the discursive activities practiced by Rastafari. I have followed the orthographic guides outlined by Cassidy in *Jamaica Talk* (1982) for pronunciation and the guidelines suggested by Dennis Tedlock, *The Spoken Word and the Work of Interpretation* (Philadelphia: University of Pennsylvania Press, 1983), Elizabeth Fine, *The Folklore Text: From Performance to Print* (Bloomington: Indiana U. Press, 1984), and Paul Atkinson, *The Ethnographic Imagination: Textual Constructions of Reality* (London: Routledge, 1990) for transcribing oral into printed dialogue. All such guides are relative to context.

34. This conversation was recorded on March 16, 1982.

35. I-tal is formed by deleting the /v/ and the /na/ from the words vital and natural and appending the pronoun /I/. While it has been associated with the natural, organic, or vital quality of non-processed foods, it was used to signify a processes of commodification whereby determinations of needs, wants, and desires are reified, assumed to be natural and organic. There was little natural in the labor Bongo expended to produce the ingredients of sweet potato pudding but they were absolutely vital or I-tal to his "livity" because they removed him and his labor-power from the networks that vended processed or commerical foods.

36. "Ert" or earth runnings refer to the everyday activities that characterize life in Jamaica. The worldview of Rastafari does not recognize

the hierarchical realms of heaven, earth, and hell. There are no realms of existence above or below the earth synonomous with Christianity. While the words hell and Babylon are multivalent and often used interchangeably, they are associated with the exile, captivity and living hell endured by African peoples in the New World and it is the runnings or labor power of human or earthly agents that constitute the landscape of Rastafari and not a supernatural realm inhabited by invisible gods or spirits.

37. My query here was an attempt to probe and understand how natural events wind, rain, etc. were used by practitioners to verify the existence of Selassie in light of the events that unfolded during the 1970s. How events such as the death of Selassie affected ways of knowing was a major issue and this question was one in a string concerning epistemology: how Rastafarians know, the various ways of knowing or producing knowledge, and the use of alternate understandings or theories of knowledge. It was relatively straightforward, so to speak, to argue that Selassie was a living Messiah because the object and the subject could be substantiated by an event that unfolded in a external world. Direct verification as a basis of argument became problematic when the object/events are no longer extant. This issue, one of argument and verification concerning Selassie, constituted a topic of debate within both the immediate and the larger speech community of Rastafari. Resolution of the problem led to the diaspora to North America that gained momentum in the 1980s.

38. As used by Bongo, science signified Western or secular theories that proposed the study of and belief in non-human causation. It was less the linking or association of science with materialism that Rastafarians such as Bongo found objectionable and more the disassociation of human agency and social relations from cause and affect. Study, belief, and science were placed in oppostion to a local "knowledge" informed by everyday experience.

39. Although a discussion and comparison are beyond the scope of this chapter, Bongo's parody of body movements was set in oppostion to the fire and brimstone of "old time preaching" and the control of literacy, reading, and the "performed word" by the first generation of Rastafari.

40. Rob and Gerte were "ancients," members of the prewar generation of Rastafarians, and were not "elders" in the sense described by Yawney, Homiak, or Chevannes.

41. Bongo disagreed with many of their interpretations. The issue of Mary and Christ was one such point on contention. Rob and Gerte adhered to the tenet that Christ preceeded Selassie in a genealogy of Messiahs. Bongo disgreed and maintained that Christ and the events discussed in the New Testament were a fabrication (fostered by the Romans, the Pope, and the Catholic Church). As he stated, Selassie "trod ert frum I-ration" (the beginning). These points of argumentation express the hermeneutics, the ongoing and open-ended relationship between language and generational change within and between Rastafari and Jamaican society.

42. The word "intoxication" is another example of how English words function as ideophones. If the root "toxic" meant poison then why consume a product (alcohol) and participate in an activity ("sport") that produces death. For ideophones see Fortune (1962), Courtenay (1976), and Samarin (1967,1970); for cues and markers/signs and notations see Erkkila (1995), Williams (1977), Coward & Ellis (1977), and Silverman & Torode (1980); for the relationship between language, thought, and ideology see Volosinov (1986[1926]), Woolard (1985), Hill (1985), and Friedrich (1989).

43. See Smitherman (1977:104–7) for the importance of call–response to black modes of discourse. What Bongo experienced or thought occurred to him when he read was as important to my way of understanding as any other aspect.

44. Bongo's gloss and erasure of Jesus was consistent with his affilation in a community of interpretation that considered Jesus as a fabrication, a textual icon created by false prophets. While there are parallels here with what Certeau (1984) refers to as "poaching," the term evokes medieval images of European folk, and a folklore, based on theft from royalty. Bringing the power of word-sound to bear on penetrating the printed released or "unlocked" the voice of Africans from imprisonment within the pages and bindings, the jumbled-up books and chapters of the Bible. The operative phrase "locked off" meant the submersion or captivity of the spoken within the printed. While the Bible was an encyclopedic resource, cultural knowledge was locked off to black folk.

45. Bongo's comments concerning "dreams," "visions," and "duppies" were another point of contention with the prewar generation. Bongo associated dreams with "duppies" or spirits, speaking in "tongues," and the "pocoism" or possession-trance characteristic of Revival. In a series of reasonings, Gerte conveyed to the writer what can best be

described as a conversion experience in which she described how her spirit left her body and was taken or escorted by another spirit on a journey during which she saw or visited Zion or Africa. When she turned to see who the spirit was, she saw the face or image of Selassie.

46. In addition to distinguishing his understanding of reading and literacy from mine, Bongo's comments concerning "John," "voices," and "sounds" expressed the way he identified protagonists.

47. This issue (awareness, perception, and the biblical dramas and historical events associated with revelation or revealed knowledge) was one in a group of questions concerning metaphysics. Bongo's emphasis on revelation or intuitive knowledge fell back on a rethinking of the senses, e.g., "wha I tell dan man, mus use de ear to see." It not only opened a window on the use of resemblance/regularity as a form of argument but led him to draw, reflexively, upon and position his own life-history as an example of conversion, e.g, "still, I-n-I a heathen till I see Selassie."

48. These were likened to the United States, the Soviet Union, and Great Britain. As I commented earlier, reasoning and citing-up were creative activities that generated a host of ideas. The significance of these was not discussed during this encounter.

49. The idea of retribution was an important point. Although Old Testament and biblical, the idea of revenge, an "eye for an eye," a "tooth for a tooth," was not a major component of the moral economy of Rastafari. Yes, Bongo and all Rastafarians want to end an enforced exile but they do not seek to do so by exchanging and reproducing one form of violence for another. Rather than an "eye for an eye," the operative phrase in this respect was "one love." This term and its relation to a moral economy, breaking a cycle of revenge/exchange (if A does to B, then B must do to A) was part of a reconstituted biblical identity in which notion of an "elect" or "chosen" seeks not to impersonate or duplicate but to depart or break with a moral economy based on an eye for an eye. It was the importance of this relationship and its possible association with tribalism, political culture, and shifting or changing ideas concerning repatriation that I was interested in exploring. See Kerrigan (1995) for a review of revenge and its relationship to violence, exchange, and a moral economy. For a similar understanding of linguistic or dialogical banter as "contrapuntal argument" in the West Indies see Reisman (1989[1974]).

50. By social production I mean our interaction as well as the way Bongo performed, explained, and discussed the way he cited-up. While we were co-authors, it was the importance of this relationship, a rethinking of context and recontextualization, as applied both to the worldview of Rastafari and our encounter, that I was interested in exploring.

51. Literary historians have documented fundamental shifts in reading practices from reading out loud to reading silently, from reading in groups to reading alone, and from close reading or "reading between the lines" to scanning a number of texts. The acquisition of literacy was not a lineal evolution or transition from one form to another. While reading aloud has been associated with working-class literacy, it must be recalled that poetry readings were common place events in the history of European reading practices. See Saenger (1990: 142–3) for differences between phonetic and comprehension literacy; Chartier (1995) for shifts in reading practices, and see Marrotti (1995) for aesthetics, aurality, and textuality as interactive in Western literacy practices.

52. As alluded earlier, reading silently was equated with intoxication and was associated with 1 Samuel 1, verse 12–15 where Eli rebukes Hannah for reading without parting her lips. In most of the organized or institutionalized religions, silent reading was associated with communion or communication with God. Since Rastafari explicitly rejects the idea of a divinity that resides outside or above, such communication was considered as another example of "duppi business." By vibrations, Bongo referred to or meant aurality, the tonal semantics, the word-sound-power, contained or associated with the spoken word. It was this all-important phenomenological dimension that was separated by electronic and visual media. It must also be stated that this phenonmenology or reading sound as a "known and felt" experience was enhanced but can by no means be reduced to the consumption of cannabis.

53. Transliteration, emplotment and narrative sequencing are strategies that are by no means confined to text-based practices. By identify with I mean how Bongo constructed protagonists, saw through the eyes of biblical actors; by voice I mean a point of view, presence, and speaking postion; by interpolate I mean how Bongo inserted himself into the text and constructed a "one-reality," an inter/extra-textual world; and by narrative sequencing I mean the way biblical verses or "chant[cant]-phrases," i.e., text-based plots and sub-plots were

removed from texts, reinscribed with meaning, and woven into a living testament of African culture and history. See Smitherman, Chapter 5, "Black Modes of Discourse," in *Talkin*; Cooper, Chapter 7, "Chanting Down Babylon," in *Noises in the Blood*; Gates, Chapter 4, "The Trope of the Talking Book," in *The Signifying Monkey*; H. Adlai Murdach, "Displacing Marginality: Cultural Identity and Creole Resistance," *Research in African Literatures*, Vol. 25 (1994); Tejumola Olaniyan, "Agones: The Constitution of a Practice," in *Scars of Conquest/Masks of Resistance* (New York: Oxford University Press, 1995); and especially Betsy Erkkila, "Ethnicity, Literary Theory, and the Grounds of Resistance," *American Quarterly*, Vol. 47 (1995), 572–75, for point of view, double-voicing, and historical identities in black discourse.

54. This polysemic dimension and its relation to voice, subject position, and shifts or movement between first and third person narrative is glossed in Pollard (1994). Bongo's use of I-n-I as a shifting and double-voiced (first and third person) strategy must be set in the context of the Caribbean. As Brathwaite has noted (1984), the British West Indies produced two distinct but interrelated narrative traditions: one codified in the printed accounts of colonial historians, missionaries, and travellers, and a second in a spoken or oral tradition. While they were committed to alternate and oppositional means of communication, they shared a mutual context (setting, plot and discourse).

55. While scholars have commented upon the importance of the Bible and have noted the repertoire of biblical phrases articulated by Rastafari (cf. Owens, 1976), we know very little concerning textual iconography or how Rastafarians bring rhetorical and interpretive conventions to bear in creating a narrative or living testament. In addition to expressing cues and markers, these were literay constructions intended to antagonize, to resist accepted or normative readings, and enabled Bongo to hold a number of contradictory subject positions simultaneously. See Tonkin (1994: 32–33), Williams (1977: 164–72), and Smitherman (1977: 146–7) for cues and markers/signs and notations in black oral history. Along with "dis here time" and "coming forward," Bongo used the phrase "just so" to indicate a shift in temporality from past to present.

56. As May & Metzger (1976) have commented the Revelation of John belongs, or more properly speaks, to the Books of Daniel and Jeremiah. Bongo's choice of passages, Revelations 19 as opposed to Revalations 10:9–10 (where an angel give John a book to eat), had to

do with textual iconography, the way Rastafarians create images ("I-rate") by linking textual with living or everyday people, places, and events. See Loughlin (1995) for an interesting discussion of how Revalations 10:9–10 (eating the text) became associated with the Eucharist and Christian understandings of transubstantiation.

57. This distinction can also be understood as gendered reading. For example, when I read or cited-up with Gerte she turned not to the Book of Revelation but to the Gospel of Matthew and told me how it was Mary and no one else who came to the assistance of Christ.

58. The term duppy or dupe is West African in origin and refers to a cultural tradition of multiple souls. A dupe was considered the spiritual force inside the body of a person and what was referred to as a "shadow" was considered or associated with external expression. While there are doctrinal distinctions between them, Revival et al. share a mutual belief in Jesus Christ, a pantheon of saints, spirits or duppies, and reliance on possession and possession-trance. The multiple soul concept constitutes Afro-Jamaican cultural construction of social being. Each individual is born with a unique character (duppy-soul) and an accompanying personality (shadow-spirit) associated with socially defined understandings of good and bad. When a person dies the duppy travels to an other worldly realm while the shadow is believed or though to remain or lurk behind. In a series of rituals, the shadow is dispatched below the earth insuring that it will not be used by an obeahman. For West African word usage see Bascom (1969), Field (1939,1960), and Rattray (1927); for Afro-Jamaican word meaning see Cassidy & Le Page (1967) and Cassidy (1961); for Revival, Pocomania, and obeah see Beckwith (1929), Williams (1934, Simpson (1956), Moore (1954,1965), Moore & Simpson (1957/8), Hogg (1967), Barrett (1976), and Moorish (1982).

59. Eclipsed rather than replaced is the operative word. While Bongo likened the seven seals to ears and eyes, inverting or reversing normative or accepted patterns, i.e., using ears or sound to see better, enabled Rastafarians to contest and negate cultural constructs. For a similar understanding of ethno-theories concerning the senses, perception, awareness, and constructions of consciousness see Howe et al. (1991), Jackson (1989), Classen (1990), and Stoller (1989). These were linked by Bongo to a foundation-structure mediation and were placed in opposition to the embodiments/constructions offered by Revival. Ritual performances were social activities that expressed and reproduced a form of "knowledge" associated with the relationship between thought and activity. For example, "getting in the

spirit," the culturally learned and socially performed embodiment of a god, duppy, or spirit, was enacted by drumming, dancing, and hyperventilation in a variety of "workings;" that is, exhalation and/or inhalation known as "trumps," "groaning," "laborings," or "shouts." The importance of this concept to folk culture and Rastafari cannot be overstated. Individuals perform or enact the personas they embody; some are threatening, others are friendly, some speak in unintelligible tongues, while others engaged in dialogue. Both Moore (1954: 59–60) and Hogg (1967: 262–65) described "Bongomen" who recognized Christian deities, but who only enacted the caricature of powerful obeahmen and maroons.

60. See Phillppo (1843: 270–271) and Waddell (1863: 35–36) for debates between concerning reading by rote, contesting interpetations of divitinty, and for the difference between European and Afro-Jamaican biblical interpretation; see also the unpublished diary of G. Planta, *The Diary of a Moravian Missionary, 1760–1772* (Moravians Archives of Jamaica, no date, no pages numbers, entry of 3 April 1762) for what may be the first use of "chant-phrases" by black folk in Jamaica.

61. See Hans Frei, *The Eclipse of Biblical Narrative* (New London: Yale U. Press, 1974), Northrop Frye *The Great Code* (New York: Harcourt & Brace, 1982), Henry Louis Gates, *The Signifying Monkey* (New York & London: Oxford, 1988) and Theophlius Smith, *Conjuring Culture* (New York: Oxford, 1992) for biblical typology and modes of figuration.

References

Abrahams, R. 1983 *The Man of Words in the West Indies*. Baltimore: Johns Hopkins.

Allen, Lillian 1982 *Rhythm An' Hardtimes*. Toronto: Domestic Bliss Publishers.

Alleyne, Mervyn 1988 *Roots of Jamaican Culture*. London: Pluto Press.

Anderson, B. 1983 *Imagined Communities*. London: Verso.

Austin, Diane 1987 Pentecostals and Rastafarians: cultural, political, and gender relations of two religious movements. *Social and Economic Studies* 36(4):1–39.

Bailey, Beryl L. 1966 *Jamaican Creole Syntax*. Cambridge: University Press.

Barrett, David, ed. 1982 *The World Christian Encyclopedia*. Nairobi: Oxford University Press.

Barrett, Leonard 1977 *The Rastafarians*. Boston: Beacon Press.

Bauman, Richard 1977 *Verbal Art as Performance*. Rowley: Newbury House.

Bauman, Richard, ed. 1992 *Folklore, Cultural Performances, and Popular Entertaiments*. New York: Oxford University Press.

Bauman, Richard and Briggs, C.L. 1990 Poetics and performance as critical perspectives on language and social life. *Annual Review of Anthropology* 19:59–88.

Bauman, Richard and Sherzer, J., ed. 1989 *Explorations in the Ethnography of Speaking*. Cambridge: Cambridge University Press.

Beckford, G. and Whitter, M. 1980 *Small Garden ... Bitter Weed; The Political-Economy of Struggle and Change in Jamaica*. Morant Bay: Maroon Publishing House.

Beckwith, Martha 1969 *Black Roadways; A Study of Jamaican Folk Life*. New York: Negro Universities Press.

Bell, Bernard 1987 *The Afro-American Novel and Its Tradition*. Amherst: University of Massachusette Press.

Beverly, John 1993 *Against Literature*. Minneapolis: University of Minnesota Press.

Bilby, Kenneth 1983 Black Thoughts from the Caribbean: I-deology at Home and Abroad. *New West Indian Guide* 57(3/4):201–14.

Bilby, Kenneth 1985 The Half Still Untold: Recent literature on Reggae and Rastafari. *New West Indian Guide* 59(3/4):211–17.

Boyarin, J., ed. 1992 *The Ethnography of Reading*. Berkeley: University of California Press.

Brathwaite, Edward Kamau 1984 *History of the Voice*. Port of Spain: New Beacon Books.

Brathwaite, Edward Kamau 1986 *Roots*. Havana: Casa de las Americas.

Breiner, Lawrence 1986 The English Bible in Jamaican Rastarianism. *Journal of Religious Thought* 16(4):2–12.

Brodber, Erna 1975 *A Study of Yards in Kingston*. Kingston: Institute of Social and Economic Rresearch.

Brodber, E. and Green, J.E. 1981 *Reggae and Cultural Identity in Jamaica*. Kingston: Institute of Social and Economic Research.

Burke, Peter and Porter, Roy 1982 *The Social History of Language*. Cambridge: Cambridge University Press.

Cassidy, Frederic 1982 *Jamaica Talk; Three Hundred Years of the English Language in Jamaica*. London: Macmillan Caribbean.

Chartier, Roger 1995 *Forms and Meanings*. Philadelphia: University of Pennsylvania Press.

Chartier, Roger, ed. 1989 *The Culture of Print*. Princeton: Princeton University Press.

Chevannes, E. Barrington 1994 *Rastafari: Roots and Ideology*. Syracuse: Syracuse University.

Chevannes, E. Barrington 1995 *Rastafari and Other Afro-Caribbean Worldviews*. The Hague: Institute of Social Research.

Collins, Christopher 1991 *Reading the Written Image*. Philadelphia: University of Pennsylvania Press.

Collins, James 1995 Literacy and literacies. *Annual Review of Anthropology* 24:75–93.

Cooper, Carolyn 1995 *Noises in the Blood*. Durham: Duke University Press.

Courtenay, K. 1976 Ideophones defined as a phonological class. *Studies in African Linguistics* 6(Suppl):13–26.

Davis, Gerald 1985 *I Got the Word in Me and Can Sing It, You Know It*. Philadelphia: University of Pennsylvania Press.

de Certeau, Michel 1984 *The Practice of Everyday Life*. Berkeley: University of California Press.

Diamond, Stanley 1974 *In Search of the Primitive*. New York: The Free Press.

Erkkila, Betsy 1995 Ethnicity, literary theory, and the grounds of resistance. *American Quarterly* 47:563–94

Finnegan, Ruth 1992 *Oral Tradition and Verbal Arts*. London: Routledge.

Frye, Northrop 1982 *The Great Code*. New York: Harcourt, Brace, and Jovanovich.

Gates, Henry Louis Jr. 1988 *The Signifying Monkey*. New York: Oxford University Press.

Goody, Jack. 1987 *The Interface Between the Written and the Oral*. London: Cambridge University Press.

Gray, Obika 1991 *Radicalism and Social Change in Jamaica*. Knoxville: University of Tennessee Press.

Hanks, W.F. 1988 Texts and textuality. *Annual Review of Anthropology* 18:95–127.

Heath, Shirley 1983 *Ways with Words*. New York: Cambridge University Press.

Hill, Robert 1981 Dread history: Leonard P. Howell and millenarian visions in early Rastafari religion in Jamaica. *Epoche* 9:30–71.

Hobsbawm, E. and Ranger, T. 1987 *The Invention of Tradition*. Cambridge: Cambridge Press.

Holm, John 1988 *Creole Studies*, Vol. 1. London: Cambridge University Press.

Homiak, John 1994 From yard to nation. In: *Ay Bobo: African-Caribbean Religion* (ed., Manfred Kremser). Wein, Austria: WUV.

Homiak, John 1995 Dub history. In: *Rastafari and Other Afro-Caribbean World Views* (ed., Barry Chevannes). The Hague: Insitutute for Social Research, pp. 127–80.

Hymes, Dell 1969 *Reinventing Anthropology*. New York: Vintage Books.

Hymes, Dell 1974 *Foundation in Sociolinguistics*. Philadelphia: University of Pennsylvania Press.

Iser, Wolfgang 1978 *The Act of Reading*. Baltimore: Johns Hopkins Press.

Ingarden, R. 1973 *The Literary Work of Art*. Evanston: Northwestern University Press.

Jackson, Michael 1980 Rastafarianism. *Theology* 83:26–34.

Jan van Dijk, Frank 1988 Twelve Tribes of Israel. *New West Indian Guide* 62:1–25.

Jauss, H.R. 1982 *Toward an Aesthetic of Reception*. Minneapolis: University of Minnesota Press.

Kerrigan, John 1995 *Revenge Tragedy*. Oxford: Clarnedon Press.

Loughlin, Gerard 1995 *Telling God's Story: Bible, Church History, and Theology*. Cambridge: Cambridge University Press.

Marotti, Arthur 1995 *Manuscript, Print, and the English Renaissance Lyric*. Ithaca: Cornell University Press.

May, Herbert G. and Metzger, B.M. eds. 1977 *The New Oxford Annotated Bible with the Apocrypha.* New York: Oxford University Press.

McConnell, Frank, ed. 1986 *The Bible and the Narrative Tradition.* New York: Oxford University Press.

Miller, Marian 1993 The Rastafarian in Jamaican Political culture: the marginalization of a change agent. *Western Journal of Black Studies* 17(2):112–17.

Moorish, Ivor 1982 *Obeah, Christ, and Rastaman: Jamaica and Its Religion.* Cambridge: James Clarke & Sons.

Moses, Wilson Jeremiah 1993 *Black Messiahs and Uncle Toms.* University Park: Pennsylvania State University Press.

Nettleford, Rex 1970 *Mirror Mirror.* Kingston: William Collins.

Nettleford, Rex 1979 *Caribbean Cultural Identity.* Los Angeles: University of California.

Ong, Walter 1967 *The Presence of the Word.* New Haven: Yale University Press.

Owens, Joseph 1976 *Dread: The Rastafarians of Jamaica.* Kingston: Sangster.

Phillippo, James 1843 *Jamaica: Its Past and Present State.* London: Dawsons.

Pollard, Velma 1994 *Dread Talk.* Mona: Canoe Press.

Post, Ken 1970 The Bible as ideology: Ethiopianism in Jamaica, 1930–38. In: *African Perspectives* (eds., C. Allen and R W. Johnson). London: Cambridge University Press, pp. 185–210.

Post, Ken 1978 *Arise Ye Starvelings.* The Hague: Martinus Nijhoff.

Post, Ken 1981 *Strike the Iron I & II.* Atlantic Highlands, NJ: Humanties

Pulis, John W. 1993 Up-full sounds: language, identity, and the worldview of Rastafari. *Ethnic Groups* 10:285–300.

Pulis, John W. *Gates to Zion: Voices, Texts, and Narrative World of Rastafari.* New York: Gordon & Breach (forthcoming).

Raboteau, Albert 1995 *A Fire in the Bones.* Boston: Beacon Press.

Radway, Janice 1994 *Reading the Romance.* Chapel Hill: University of North Carolina Press.

Ras-j-Tesfa 1980 *The Living Testaments of Rasta-for-I*. Kingston: Tennnyson Smith.

Reckord, Verena 1977 Rastafari music; an introductory study. *Jamaica Journal* 11(1/2):6–8.

Reckord, Verena 1982 Reggae, Rastafarianism, a cultural identity. *Jamaica Journal* 46:70–9.

Reisman, Karl 1989 Contrapuntal conversattions in an Antiguan village. In: *Explorations in the Ethnography of Speaking* (eds., Richard Baumann and J. Sherzer). Cambridge: Cambridge University Press, pp. 110–124.

Saenger, Paul 1989 Books of hours. In *The Culture of Print* (ed., Roger Chariter). Princeton: Princeton University Press, pp. 141–73.

Samarin, William 1967 Determining the meaning of ideophones. *Journal of African Linguistics* 4(2):35–41.

Samarin, William 1970 Inventory and choice in expressive language. *Word* 26:153–69

Savishinsky, Neil 1994 The Baye Faal of Senegambia: muslim Rastas in the promised land? *Africa* 64(2):212–19.

Schechner, Richard and Appel, Willa 1990 *By Means of Performannce*. Cambridge: Cambridge University Press.

Schuler, Monica 1980 *Alas, Alas, Kongo*. Baltimore: Johns Hopkins.

Seaga, Edward 1969 Revival cults in Jamaica. *Jamaica Journal* 3(2):3–14.

Semaj, Leachim 1980 Rastafari: from religion to social theory. *Caribbean Quarterly* 26(4):22–31.

Simpson, George Eaton 1978 *Black Religions in the New World*. New York: Columbia U. Press.

Smith, M.G., et al. 1976 *The Rastafari Movement in Kingston*. Kingston: I.S.E.R.

Smith, Theophus 1994 *Conjuring Culture*. New York: Oxford University Press.

Smitherman, Geneva 1977 *Talkin and Testifyin*. Detroit: Wayne State University Press.

Stewart, Robert 1992 *Religion and Society in Post-Emancipation Jamaica*. Knoxville: University of Tennessee Press.

Szwed, John F. 1981 The ethnography of literacy. In *Writing: The Nature, Development, and Teaching of Communication* (ed., M. F. Whiteman). Hillsdale, NJ: Erlbaum, pp. 13–23.

Tafari, I. Jabulani 1980 The Rastafari: successors of Marcus Garvey. *Caribbean Quarterly* 26(4):1–11.

Tanna, Laura 1983 Anansi: Jamaica's trickster hero. *Jamaica Journal* 16(2):20–30.

Tanna, Laura 1987 *Jamaican Folk Tales and Oral Histories*. Kingston: Institute of Jamaica.

Taylor, Patrick 1989 *The Narrative of Liberation: Perspectives of Afro-Caribbean Literature, Popular Culture, and Politics*. Ithaca: Cornell University Press.

Tedlock, Barbara 1991 From participant observation to the observation of participation, *Journal of Anthropological Research* 47:69–83

Tedlock, Dennis 1983 *The Spoken Word and the Work of Interpretation*. Philadelphia: University of Pennsylvania Press.

Tedlock, Dennis 1989 Questions concerning dialogical anthropology, *Journal of Anthropological Research* 43:325–44.

Tedlock, Dennis 1992 Ethnopoetics. In *Folklore, Cultural, Performances, and Popular Entertaiments* (ed., Richard Bauman). New York: Oxford University Press, pp. 81–86

Tedlock, Dennis and Mannheim, Bruce, eds. 1995 *The Dialogic Emergence of Culture*. Urbana and Chicago: University of Chicago Press.

Tilton, Jeff Todd 1988 *Powerhouse for God*. Austin: University of Texas Press.

Thompson, Paul 1988 *Voices of the Past*. New York: Oxford.

Tonkin, E. 1995 *Narrating Our Pasts*. Cambridge: Cambridge University Press.

Tonkin, E., McDonald, M. and Chapman, M. 1989 *History and Ethnicity*. London: Routledge.

Volosinov, V.N. 1973 *Marxism and Language*. Cambridge: Harvard University Press.

Waddell, H.M. 1863 *Twenty-Nine Years in the West Indies and Central America*. London: T. Nelson & Son.

Wallace, Anthony F.C. 1956 Revitalization movements. *American Anthropologist* 58:264–81.

Williams, Raymond 1977 *Marxism and Literature*. Oxford: Oxford University.

Wilson, Bryan 1973 *Magic and the Millennium*. New York: Harper & Row.

Yawney, Carole 1995 *Representing Rastafari in the 21st Century*. Paper presented at the 94th Annual Meeting of the American Anthropological Association, Washington, DC.

AFTERWORD / ECHOES

Richard Price

That this collection stresses the Anglophone Caribbean and that our models for understanding the development of Caribbean religions derive from historical linguistics provides ample excuse to begin with a poetic fragment by Tobago-born Marlene Nourbese Philip (1989:55–59):

English
is my mother tongue.
A mother tongue is not
not a foreign lan lan lang
language
l/anguish
  anguish
—a foreign anguish.

English is
my father tongue.
A father tongue is
a foreign language,
therefore English is
a foreign language
not a mother tongue.

What is my mother
tongue
my mammy tongue
my mummy tongue
my momsy tongue
my modder tongue
my ma tongue?

I have no mother
tongue
no mother to tongue
no tongue to mother
to mother
tongue
me

Edict 1

*Every owner of slaves
shall, wherever possible,
ensure that his slaves
belong to as many ethno-
linguistic groups as
possible. If they can-
not speak to each other,
they cannot then foment
rebellion and revolution.*

I must therefore be tongue
dumb
dumb-tongued
dub-tongued
damn dumb
tongue

but I have
a dumb tongue
tongue dumb
father tongue
and english is
my mother tongue
is
my father tongue
is a foreign lan lan lang
language
l/anguish
anguish
a foreign anguish
is english—
another tongue
my mother
  mammy
  mummy
  moder
  mater
  macer
  moder
tongue
mothertongue

tongue mother
tongue me
mothertongue me
mother me
touch me
with the tongue of your
lan lan lang
language
l/anguish
  anguish
english
is a foreign anguish

> ### Edict 2
>
> *Every slave caught speak-*
> *ing his native language*
> *shall be severely pun-*
> *ished. Where necessary,*
> *removal of the tongue is*
> *recommended. The of-*
> *fending organ, when re-*
> *moved, should be hung*
> *on high in a central place,*
> *so that all may see and*
> *tremble.*

Around the time I began teaching, the available syntheses on the "religions" of the diaspora were books like Angelina Pollak-Eltz's *Afro-Amerikaanse godsdiensten en culten* (1970) or George Eaton

Simpson's *Religious Cults of the Caribbean* (1970), neo-Herskovitsian attempts to summarize what anthropologists thought they knew. Despite the best of intentions, they managed to make it all sound pretty dull.

Now, we have a new generation of Caribbeanists, closer to Caribbean realities, sharing an imaginative and multi-sited research agenda, and filled with fresh enthusiasms. Although, as Aisha Khan makes clear in her contribution, the quintessentially Western category of "religion" remains a central part of the analytical problem, the chapters in this collection nonetheless signal how very far we've come. It's not just Nyabinghi brethren righteously reasoning on the Internet or Orisha worshipers sacrificing to Hindu gods. It's also that the "traditions," "heritages," and "authenticities" we once so carefully sought are now being reexamined in all their movement, migration, change, and instability. Before our very eyes, we are witnessing the unfolding of creolization processes that we formerly were only able to imagine as part of what must have happened during the earliest days of colonization. And we are seeing the remarkable cultural creations of Caribbean peoples continuing to develop and expand almost explosively — in the islands, in the metropoles, and in all the "non-places" of this fin de siècle. What we are witnessing is nothing less than "continuous creolization," the ongoing invention and reinvention of unique Atlantic worlds.

Writing in this volume of the situation of Rastas at mid-twentieth century, Bilby stresses that they "were continuously faced with the necessity of building a community where none had existed before. Atomized ... [they] were forced to re-create themselves as social beings from the shreds of their individual pasts" (p. 316). And he argues persuasively that the Jamaican Convince he knows first-hand actually encodes allusions to the historical processes through which that new religion came into being (pp. 312–313). I have made similar arguments in terms of very early religious creolization among the Saramaka Maroons of Suriname, and since the processes involved now appear to be quite general, a brief revisit may be relevant.

Our entrée is a description of the goings-on within a tiny band of maroons, many of them African-born, at the end of the seventeenth century, soon after their successful rebellion and escape.

During their stay at Matjau Creek (while fomenting new rebellions among slaves they had known when in whitefolks' captivity, and conducting periodic raids on vulnerable plantations), Lanu, Ayako, Seei, and the other Matjau-people were engaged in the everyday process of building new lives in the unfamiliar forests — forging anew everything from horticultural techniques to religious practice, building on their diverse African memories as well as their New World experience with both transplanted Europeans and local Amerindians. As they prepared their fields for planting, they encountered local forest and snake spirits who they had to learn, by trial and error, to befriend and pacify; a Watambii mother of twins inadvertently discovered, via a monkey, the complex rituals that would forever thereafter be a necessary accompaniment to the birth of Saramaka twins; and newly-found gods of war joined those remembered from across the waters in protecting and spurring on Saramaka raiders when they attacked plantations for guns, pots, and axes, as well as to liberate their brothers and, particularly, sisters still in bondage. (Price 1990:18)

What are the more general processes? First, the "trial and error" by which early Saramakas learned to identify, befriend, and pacify local forest and snake spirits involved a tightly interwoven complex of pan sub-Saharan African ideas and practices regarding illness, divination, and causality. A misfortune (an illness or other affliction) automatically signalled the need for divination which in turn revealed a cause — often, a previously unknown local deity (previously unknown since these people had never before lived in this particular environment). The *idea* that local deities could cause illness when they were not respected (e.g., by having a field cut too close to their abode in a large tree or boulder) was widespread in rural West and Central Africa. But the identity of the deities, their specific definitions, varied widely.

Here, the process of communal divination, with people from a diversity of African origins asking questions (through a spirit medium or other divinatory agent) of a god or ancestor, in order to evoke a detailed picture of the personality, whims, and foibles of a particular new type of local deity, permitted the codification by the nascent community of new, African-American religious institutions — classes of gods such as *apukus* (forest spirits) or *vodus* (boa constrictor dieties) or *wintis* (saltwater gods), each of which has a complex and distinctive cult including shrines, drum/dance/song plays, languages, and priests and priestesses. And the establishment of a new kind of ancestor shrine generations later, during the 1840s, by a similar kind of communal divination, shows how *ongoing* religious change in Saramaka is similarly produced and sanctioned (Price 1983:5–6).

It is worth noting that while twentieth-century Saramakas recounting their early years in the forest envision a discovery process (an unfolding series of divine revelations that occurred in the course of solving the practical problems of daily life), we might say, rather, that these particular spirits were being created or invented to fit into a generalized religious model that would have been familiar to most members of the various African ethnic groups present.

The "Watambii mother of twins" provides a somewhat different kind of example of Saramaka conceptualizations of this culture-building process. Here, the metaphor is not divination but a kind of divine intervention. Nevertheless, it represents a precise Saramaka way of speaking about the process of legitimizing a newly created institution nearly two centuries ago. The story, as told to me in 1978 by my Saramaka friend Peléki runs as follows:

> Ma Zoé was an early Watambíi[-clan] runaway. Once in the forest, she gave birth to twins. One day she went to her garden, leaving the infants in a nearby open shed. But when she returned for them, she saw a large monkey sitting right next to them. So she hid to watch what would happen. She was afraid that if she startled the animal, it might grab the children and carry them into the trees. She was beside herself and didn't know what to do. So she just kept watch. She saw that the monkey had amassed a large pile of selected leaves. It was breaking them into pieces. Then it put them into an earthenware pot and placed it on the fire. When the leaves had boiled a while, it removed them and poured the leaves into a calabash. With this it washed the child. Exactly the way a mother washes a child! Then it shook the water off the child and put it down. Then it did the same with the other child. Finally, it took the calabash of leaf water and gave some to each child to drink. The woman saw all this. Then, when it was finished, the monkey set out on the path. It didn't take the twins with it! And the mother came running to her children. She examined the leaves — which ones it had given them to drink, which had been used for washing. And those are the very leaves that remain with us today for the great Watambíi twin *óbia*. (Price 1983:60–61)

Today, this Watambii cult services all twins born in Saramaka, involving their parents and siblings in a complex of rituals that draws on ideas and practices from a variety of West and Central African societies (including the widespread African association of twins with monkeys). In my view, Peléki, who is himself a twin and therefore a frequent witness to the Watambíi rites, is describing — through this metaphorical historical fragment — a particularly pure example of the process of inter-African syncretism. Sidney Mintz and I, several years before I heard Peléki's story (and thinking as much, I would guess, of early Haiti [Saint-Domingue], where an elaborated African-American twin cult has been much written about, as we were of Suriname) imagined the more general culture-building process as follows:

> We may speculate, for example, that one of the earliest slaves on a particular plantation in a new colony gives birth to twins (or becomes insane, commits suicide, or has any one of a number of experiences which would have required *some* kind of highly specialized ritual attention in almost any society in West or Central Africa). It is clear to all that *something* must be done, but our hypothetical mother of twins has no special expertise herself, nor does anyone of her own ethnic background on that plantation. However, another woman, one of whose relatives may have been a priestess of a twin cult in another group, takes charge of the situation, performing the rites as best she can remember them. By dint of this experience, then, this woman becomes *the* local specialist in twin births. In caring ritually for their parents, in performing the special rites necessary should they sicken or die, and so on, she may eventually transmit her specialized knowledge (which may well be a fairly radical selection and elaboration of what her relative's cult had been) to other slaves, who thereupon carry this knowledge, and the attached statuses and roles, forward in time. (Mintz & Price 1992:46)

As for the "newly-found gods of war [who] joined those remembered from across the waters in protecting and spurring on Saramaka raiders," inter-African syncretism again dominated the culture-building process. Each of the great war *óbias* known to me (many of which are discussed somewhere in *First-Time* or *Alabi's World*), including those with names that point to a particular African people or place such as Komantí (from Cormantin), are radical blends of several

African traditions, forged in processes very similar to that of the Watambii twin cult.[1]

In a recent article, historical linguist John McWhorter pushes back to the Old World the starting point for the creation of all the Atlantic English-based creoles — it happened, he tells us, during the 1630s at Cormantin, among the "castle slaves" on the Gold Coast (1997:59–102). The papers in this book now make clear that in terms of "religion," the creolization process that began back there has never stopped. Characteristically, W.E.B. DuBois — despite the limitations of his Victorian-era anthropological concepts — understood that this central culture-building project was there from the outset: "This [Negro] church was not at first by any means Christian nor definitely organized; rather it was *an adaptation and mingling of heathen rites among the members of each plantation*" (1989:160, my italics). And my own Saramaka materials help flesh out DuBois's insights for the early period of colonization.

But the present volume takes us well beyond these initial, primarily inter-African syncretisms. We see the eighteenth-century arrival in the Caribbean not only of new shiploads of Africans, often from societies not yet represented in their new communities, but of a variety of European missionaries, whose teachings slaves selectively built into their own developing understandings. We see the new waves of missionaries, now often from North America, who arrived in the early nineteenth century, and who were followed after Emancipation by hordes of contract laborers from every corner of the world — the Congo, India, Indonesia — who brought their own radically different cultural contributions to the changing mix, which was forever creolizing and indigenizing, often for purposes of continued resistance. And then the incessant traveling, linked to labor migrations, of late nineteenth- and early twentieth-century Anglophone Caribbean folk, in constant motion from Jamaica to Panama to New York, London, and beyond. And, as the pace of communication picks up — first with jet planes and then TV, now the Internet, world music, and all the rest — we are confronted with postcolonial creolization in all its blooming diversity — Trinidadians, Vincentians, Guyanese, and Jamaicans renegotiating what it means to be a Spiritual Baptist among the Lubavitchers in Brooklyn, Maori Rastamen and Saramaka Bahia's forging new identities out of fragments originating half way around the world. At home abroad, abroad at home, and so often on the move, Caribbean peoples continue to create and recreate — in specific cultural styles — incessantly.

In "Names," Walcott proclaims, and then asks:

> I began with no memory,
> I began with no future,
> but I looked for that moment
> when the mind was halved by a horizon....
>
> Have we melted into a mirror,
> leaving our souls behind?
> The goldsmith from Benares,
> the stonecutter from Canton,
> the bronzesmith from Benin.

The papers in this book suggest an optimistic answer. Souls wander, and may even travel back and forth between the islands and Benares or Canton or Benin. The diverse men and women who found themselves in the Caribbean succeeded against all odds in forging communities and cultures, quite fully remaking themselves and their world. Today, their descendants continue the process. And we are all the richer for it.

Endnotes

These remarks were prepared in my role as discussant for the panel organized by John Pulis at the 1995 annual meeting of the American Anthropological Association and have been lightly modified for publication.

1. I am less concerned with championing the metaphors of creolization or syncretism (as opposed, say, to hybridization or any other current descriptor of mixing or blending) than I am in insisting, with the contributors to this volume, that we must focus on historical processes. Each such metaphor contains its own particular "thinginess," and each also carries its particular connotational baggage. As Michael Taussig has suggested, "syncretism" (as it's been traditionally

employed) often lacks specific reference to power relations, and he prefers, for example, to talk of the "folding of the underworld of the conquering society into the culture of the conquered not as an organic synthesis or 'syncretism' of the three great streams of New World history — African, Christian, and [Amer-]Indian — but as a chamber of mirrors reflecting each stream's perception of the other" (1987:218).

References

DuBois, W.E.B. 1989 *The Souls of Black Folk*. New York: Penguin. [original 1903].

McWhorter, John 1997 It happened at Cormantin: locating the origin of the Atlantic English-based creoles. *Journal of Pidgin and Creole Languages* 12:59–102.

Mintz, Sidney W. and Price, Richard 1992 [original 1976] *The Birth of African-American Culture*. Boston: Beacon Press.

Philip, Marlene Norbese 1989 Discourse on the logic of language. In: *She Tries Her Tongue, Her Silence Softly Breaks* (ed., Marlene Norbese Philip). Charlottetown, Prince Edward Island: Ragweed Press, pp. 55–59.

Pollak-Eltz, Angelina 1970 *Afro-Amerikaanse godsdiensten en culten*. Roermond, Netherlands: J.J. Romen & Zonen.

Price, Richard 1983 *First-Time: The Historical Vision of an Afro-Amercan People*. Baltimore: Johns Hopkins University Press.

Price, Richard 1990. *Alabi's World*. Baltimore: Johns Hopkins University Press.

Simpson, George Eaton 1978. *Religious Cults of the Caribbean: Trinidad, Jamaica, and Haiti*. Río Piedras, PR: Institute of Caribbean Studies, University of Puerto Rico

Taussig, Michael 1987. *Shamanism, Colonialism, and the Wild Man: A Study in Terror and Healing*. Chicago: University of Chicago Press.

Walcott, Derek 1976. Names. In: Derek Walcott, *Collected Poems, 1948–1984*. New York: Farrar, Straus and Giroux, 1986, pp. 305–308.

INDEX

Abolition, 19, 20, 22

Adventists, 215

Africa, 17–18, 75, 173, 357

Africanization, 17–18

African National Congress, 173

Afro-Creole, 13, 22

Afro-Catholic, 295

Afro-Christianity, 23

Afro-Jamaican, 324

Afro-Trinidadian, 207, 249

Agency, 2

Amerindians, *see* Caribs and Tainos

Ancestors, 311, 318

Angelou, Maya, 357

Anglican Church, 13, 21

Anglophone, 3, 10n6, 13

Antigua, 13

Anti-slavery, 20

Arawak, *see* Tainos

Arrivants, 7, 67

Asad, Talal, 7, 247

Asia, 7, 248–249

Atheism, 247

Austin-Broos, Diane, 5, 215

Back-a-Wall, 95

Baker, Moses, 23, 31n7, 379n10

Bantu, 17

Baptism, 129

Baptist Missionary Society, 19–21

Baptists, 16, 19, 284

Barbados, 13, 14

Barbuda, 13

Belize, 14

Berbice, 14

Bible, 8, 236, 357, 358, 362

Biblical
poetics, 217, 22, 227, 236
typology, 377, 394n61

Bilby, Kenneth, 6, 39, 311

Binghi, 97–99

Black, 67, 361

Black loyalists, 31n8

Blasphemy, 189

Bogle, Paul, 24

Bongo (as pseudonym), 360, 382n18

Bongo-man, 6, 311, 317

Bongo-Poro, 88–89

Bongo-Town, 314

Brathwaite, Edward Kamau, 2, 13, 357

British Guiana, 13

British Honduras, 13

Brooklyn, 45, 46, 125, 138

Bustamante, Alexander, 4

Call & Response, 1, 358

Calypso, 2

Cape Town, South Africa, 173

Caribs, 14, 15

Carnival
Brooklyn, 46, 51, 52
Trinidad, 189

Chants, 143, 359

Christianity
  black, 23–25
  European, 19–23

Church Missionary Society, 19

Church of England, 13, 15, 18,
  19, 36

Church of God in Christ, 37

Citing[sighting]-up, 8, 357, 364,
  379n11, 386n30

Columbus, Christopher, 13

Communitas, 296

Congo, 26

Congregationalists, 26

Consecration, 135

Contestation, 97, 160, 167, 193

Contextualization, 359,
  380n11&12

Converted, 126

Convince, 6, 311, 316

Coromantee (Kromante), 26

Creole, 7, 72, 311, 319
  slaves, 28, 29
  language, 1, 19, 330n22

Creolization, 5, 9, 18, 10n8,
  312–313, 320, 409

Cuba, 3, 52

Cudjoe, 27

Cultural studies, 8, 11n9

Culture, 4, 72, 94

Danish Virgin Island, 14

Deconstruct, 8

Deification, 4, 327, 354n1

Deities (*see also* Spirits), 4, 14, 15,
  25–26

Demerara, 14

Dialogics, 360, 381n16, 366

Dialogue, 93, 366–370

Diaspora, 1, 67, 159

Dichotomies, 8, 262

Discursive practice, 359, 379n14

Displacement, 1

Diviniation, 406

Dominica, 14

Doption, 136

Double-voice, 372

Drake, St. Clair, iii

Dread talk, 372, 392n54

Duppies, 374, 393n58

East Indian, 250

Elders, 97, 163, 360, 380n15

Encounter, 7, 67

Ethnicity, 7, 47, 69, 81, 255

Ethnography, 6

Evangelicalism, 8, 13, 14, 15,
  16, 19

Exodus, 1

Exorcism, 215

Garvey, Marcus, 343

Gates (as yard), 361

Glazier, Steve, 5, 277

Glossalia (*see also* Tongues), 215

Globalization, 155

Goevia, Elsa, 19

Greater Antilles, 16

Great Revival, 37

Green, Garth, 189

Grenada, 14

Guides
  orisha, 301
Guyana, 14

Haiti, 7, 26
Hasidic, 7, 45
Healing, 223
Hegemony, 2
Herskovits, Melville J., ii, 2
Hinduism, 33, 34
History, 6
Hispanola, 15
Holiness, 221–222
Holy Spirit, 14, 215
Homiak, John, 5, 87
Houk, James, 5, 295

Iconography, 374, 392n56
Indeterminacy, 6, 312
India (South Asia), 249
Indo-Trinidadians, 7, 247–248
I-n-I, 372, 394n54
Islam, 250

Jamaica, 1, 14, 15, 97, 311, 357
Jews (*see* Hasidic), 13, 35
Jaharray, 265

Kabbalah, 296
Khan, Aisha, 7, 247
Knibb, William, 15, 17, 23
Koramantin (*see* Coromantee),
  26, 329n14, 409
Kumina, 313

Language, i, iii, iv, 330n22, 363
  semantic broadening, 5
  homophones, 364
Lewis, George, 379n10
Liele, George, 23, 379n10
Liminality, 340
Literacy, 8, 357
Livical sounds, 363, 372
Living testament, 8, 186, 358, 364,
  386n30
London Missionary Society, 21–23

Magic, 7, 215
Maljo, 248, 263
Marley, Bob, 1, 2, 357
Maroons, 7, 25, 27, 68, 313, 405
McKay, Claude, 234
Meaning, 6, 357
Mediascape, 87
Methodists, 15–16
Migrants, 7, 68
Minority, 67
Mintz, Sidney, 2
Modernization, 2
Montserrat, 14
Morant Bay, 24
Moravians, 16, 360, 382n19
Mourning ritual, 14, 129, 301
MOVE, 172–173
Multicultural, 74
Multisite ethnography, 154,
  159, 168
Music, 112, 277
Muslims, 8, 26, 247
Myal, 24, 353n9

Narrative, 8, 202, 372

Nation, 202, 312

Nation language, 13, 329n14, 405

Native-Baptists, 27, 28

New York City, 2, 7, 125

Nevis, 14, 24–25

Noahites, 24

Noise, 277

Nommo, 2, 9n4

Nyahbinghi, 97, 327, 359

Obeah, 24, 248, 263

Obias, 408

Oral

    performance, 186, 277, 358, 38n14

    vs. spoken, 357

Orisha, 128, 132, 279, 295

    shrines, 295

Pagan, 75

Penetration, 372–373

Pentecostalism, 215

Performance, 186, 359, 380n12

Pietism, 13–14

Pilgrim's Journey, 138, 147n1, 301

Planno, Mortimer, 154

Pointing, 130, 301

Pointing mother, 130

Polysemy, 372, 392n54

Possession, 125, 311

Postcolonial, 8, 160

    theory, 11n11

Postmodern, 8, 160

Price, Richard, 2, 403

Protestant Christianity, 4–5, 13, 29

Puerto Rico, 14

Pukkumina, 127, 143, 364

Pulis, John, 357

Race, 160

Rastafari, 2, 39, 87, 153, 327, 337, 346

Reading, 8, 357

    out loud, 371

    and resistance, 357, 377n2

    as subversion, 363, 384n27, 380n11

Reasoning, 93–94, 359, 366–370

Religion, 1, 67, 247

Reputation, 215

Revelation of John, 357, 373

Revival, 26, 215

    Zion, 15

Right path, 7, 247, 252

Saints, 225, 277, 281

Schuler, Monica, 26

Scripture, 8, 357, 362

Secularization, 21

Shakers, 125

Shango, 131, 295

Sharpe, Sam, 24, 337

Sher, Phil, 45

Simpson, George, 39, 405

Sighting, *see* Citing[sighting]-up

Site, 87

Spirits, 14, 24–25, 267, 285

Spiritual Baptists, 138, 277, 297

Sound, 357

Soundscapes, 87

South Africa, 173
Syncretism, 4, 18, 409
Szwed, John, i

Taino, 14
Testifying, 374, 391n53
Testimonio, 374
Text, 8, 265, 357, 358
Textuality, 378n3
Tongues (*see* Glossalia), 220
Trindiad & Tobago, 14, 191, 247, 295, 279
Turner, Victor, 302

Umbanda, 295

Van Wetering, Ineke, 7, 67
Vibrations, 371, 391n52

Video/videography, 110
Voice, 110, 359, 372
Vodun, 295

Walcott, Derek, 9, 227, 357
Winti, 68
Women, 166, 225
Words, 357
Word–Sound–Power, 90, 186, 363, 364, 385n28
Worldview, 18, 73, 234

Yawney, Carole, 6, 153, 185

Zane, Wally, 5, 125
Zemis, 14
Zion, 127, 360

Other titles in the Library of Anthropology

RITUAL, MYTH, AND THE MODERNIST TEXT
The Influence of Jane Ellen Harrison on Joyce, Eliot, and Woolf
Martha C. Carpentier

SOMEONE TO LEND A HELPING HAND
Women Growing Old in Rural America
Dena Shenk

RELIGION, DIASPORA, AND CULTURAL IDENTITY
A Reader in the Anglophone Caribbean
Edited by John W. Pulis

This book is part of a series. The publisher will accept continuation orders which may be cancelled at any time and which provide for automatic billing and shipping of each title in the series upon publication. Please write for details.